MAKE/BELIEVING THE WORLD(S)

Make/Believing the World(s)

Toward a Christian Ontological Pluralism

MARK S. MCLEOD-HARRISON

McGill-Queen's University Press

Montreal & Kingston · London · Ithaca

© McGill-Queen's University Press 2009
ISBN 978-0-7735-3593-0

Legal deposit fourth quarter 2009
Bibliothèque nationale du Québec

Printed in Canada on acid-free paper that is 100% ancient forest free
(100% post-consumer recycled), processed chlorine free

This book has been published with the help of a grant from George
Fox University.

McGill-Queen's University Press acknowledges the support
of the Canada Council for the Arts for our publishing program.
We also acknowledge the financial support of the Government of
Canada through the Book Publishing Industry Development Program
(BPIDP) for our publishing activities.

Library and Archives Canada Cataloguing in Publication

McLeod-Harrison, Mark S., 1956–
   Make/believing the world (s): toward a Christian ontological pluralism /
Mark S. McLeod-Harrison.

   Includes bibliographical references and index.
   ISBN 978-0-7735-3593-0

   1. Christianity and other religions. 2. Religious pluralism – Christianity.
   3. Humility – Religious aspects – Christianity. 4. Mysticism. I. Title.

BR127.M356 2009   261.2   C2009-903925-7

This book was typeset by Interscript in 10.5/13 Sabon.

Contents

Preface   ix

PART ONE MAKE/BELIEVING THE WORLD(S):
AN INTRODUCTION

1 An Overview with Terms and Definitions   3

PART TWO THREE ONTOLOGICAL PLURALISTS:
STRENGTHS AND SHORTCOMINGS

2 Hales's Philosophical Relativism   35

3 Lynch's Ontological Pluralism   51

4 Goodman's Irrealism   70

5 Irrealism, Nominalism, and Properties   95

6 Possibilities of the Actual   108

PART THREE HOW AND WHY TO BE
AN IRREALIST

7 An Argument for Irrealistic Pluralism   127

8 Idealism and Irrealism   145

9 Toward a Theory of Truth   155

10 Make/Believing What Is, and Other World Renderings   182

11 Saving Pluralism: Why Irrealism Needs God   200

PART FOUR TRADITIONAL CHRISTIANITY,
THEISTIC IRREALISM, AND PLURALISM

12 The Traditional Christian   223

13 Christianity, Realism, and Logic   234

14 The Divine, Its Furniture, and Virtual Absolutes   258

15 The Many Ways God Is   284

16 God and Objectivity   300

17 History, Humans, and God:
    Toward a Christian Irrealist View of God's
    Redemptive Work   322

18 Irrealism, Worlds, and Mystical Experience:
    God as the Final Framework   343

    Notes   355

    Bibliography   371

    Index   377

Preface

The pool he had just got out of was not the only pool. There were dozens of others – a pool every few yards as far as his eyes could reach. You could almost feel the trees drinking the water up with their roots.

This wood was very much alive. When he tried to describe it afterward Digory always said, "It was a *rich* place: as rich as plumcake."

* * *

"I've just had a really wonderful idea," said Digory. "What are all the other pools?"

"How do you mean?"

"Why, if we can get back to our own world by jumping into *this* pool, mightn't we get somewhere else by jumping into one of the others? Supposing there was a world at the bottom of every pool."

"But I thought we were already in your Uncle Andrew's Other World or Other Place or whatesver he called it. Didn't you say —."

"Oh bother Uncle Andrew," interrupted Digory. "I don't believe he knows anything about it. He never had the pluck to come here himself. He only talked of *one* Other World. But suppose there were dozens?"

"You mean, this wood might be only one of them?"

"No, I don't believe this wood is a world at all. I think it's just a sort of in-between place."

* * *

"The Wood between the Worlds," said Polly dreamily. "It sounds rather nice."

"Come on," said Digory. "Which pool shall we try?"

C.S. Lewis,
The Magician's Nephew, 32, 38, 39

Lewis's fantasy world Narnia is only one of many worlds Aslan creates. But Aslan doesn't create alone, and the worlds do not stand alone and apart from one another. The sons of Adam and the daughters of Eve are free to enter at least a good many of the alternative worlds, and they do enter at least two besides Earth, viz., Charn and Narnia itself. In at least one instance, something from our world, Earth, is planted in another world, Narnia, and from it grows a lamppost. The creative contributions of humans are recognized in Lewis's worlds, not only in what the children bring from Earth to Narnia but in their actions and decisions in Narnia. They change and shape the way Narnia is.

What I suggest in the following pages is that humans can and do enter many different worlds, or at least different ways the world is, from the perspective of various conceptual schemes. Nevertheless, like the Wood between the Worlds, there is common ground to all the worlds humans help to create. I argue that the common ground is the presence and creative activity of God, and I go on to argue that such a view is consonant with a traditional account of the Judeo-Christian story. In short, I present an irrealist, pluralist account of the world(s) but one deeply shaped by the Christian tradition.

I am unapologetic for the stance I take. A good many of my Christian colleagues (philosophers and others) are suspicious of pluralism – in many cases, for good reason. However, I believe the position developed here is the right way to think of the world, specifically from a Christian point of view. God made us creative, and that doesn't end with the ability to shape the world God delivers to us (that is, to create artifacts from ready-made material), but to shape the world itself (that is, to make the ontology of the world different in different conceptual schemes). None of this takes away, I believe, from the central teaching of the Scriptures that God created "the heaven and the earth."

There are many people to whom I owe gratitude in regard to this book, most of whom will perhaps disagree with what it says. But it

is out of such conflicts that new worlds arise. First, I'd like to thank
A.R. "Pete" Diamond who many years ago, when we were both ju-
nior faculty, encouraged me to think and write. He is a tremendous
teacher and scholar. I miss his regular presence in my life. He and I,
and a number of other colleagues, met regularly to discuss how to
think Christianly. It was a time of great intellectual ferment for me.
The roots of this book go back to those conversations. Pete was one
of the people from whom I learned the most in those days, and I
still admire his courage. He thought deeply and well about how to
be a Christian scholar.

William P. Alston led a seminar on realism and antirealism in the
summer of 1999. I learned a great deal from Bill and my other colleagues during those six weeks at Calvin College. I want to thank
the Pew Charitable Trust for funding that seminar and Calvin College for its commitment to Christian scholarship. Gratitude is also
due to Greg Gannsle for stimulating comments on my work and to
two anonymous reviewers for McGill-Queen's University Press for
helpful comments and suggestions on the draft of this work first
submitted to MQUP. I want to thank two of the best students I've
ever been privileged to teach, Brady Romtvedt and Sean Merrick.
They "coerced" me into teaching a joint independent study on realism and antirealism, so I "forced" them to read an ancestor of
this book. They were insightful and enthusiastic and I thank them
for their encouragement. Thanks to my colleague and friend Phil
Smith for a critical reading of chapters 8 and 9. I want to thank
Philosophia Christi for permission to reprint portions of "Rejoinder to Ganssle's 'Real Problems with Irrealism,'" "Epistemizing
the World: A Reply to Gregory Ganssle," and "Hales's Argument
for Philosophical Relativism." The first two appear in chapter 4, while
the last appears in chapter 2. Parts of chapter 13 first appeared in *Ars
Disputandi*, an online journal for philosophy of religion, www.
arsdisputandi.org. Finally, I want to thank the Provost's Office of
George Fox University for a generous subvention in support of the
publication of this work.

I would like to thank my two sons, Ian McLeod and Micah
McLeod-Harrison. They have put up with a father who thinks too
much about some things and not enough about others. To Ian I say,
"Well, you've grown up and you no longer dance God's dance in
my living room. But I love you now, just as I did when you were
Micah's age." And to Micah I'd like to say, "Dance on, little one,

dance on. You will grow up too fast for my liking." And to both of them I say, go make some worlds.

Finally, I'd like to thank my wife, Susan J. McLeod-Harrison, for helping me in my life. She has been a consistent, healing presence in everything from my writing to my becoming a better feminist. She continues to believe that I have something to say and that it is worth saying. I'm never sure of either of those things. But I am sure that I wouldn't be saying anything at all were it not for her and her love. My world has changed into our world over the last six years, and it is to her that this book is dedicated.

PART ONE

Make/Believing the World(s):
An Introduction

I

An Overview with Terms and Definitions

We make out, make love, make pies, make do, make off, make up, make haste, make war, make friends, make room, make fast, make peace, make sure, make known, make bold, make book, make eyes, make good, make hay, make like, make sail, make time, make tracks, make way, and make it. We make ready, make over, make faces, make merry, make fire, make trouble, make whoopee, make babies, and make public. We make the bed, make the team, make the train, and make the distance. We make decisions, make away with, make a quorum, make them do it, make up our minds, and make for the door. We make a good teacher, make a go of it, make a new president, make superintendent, make Oklahoma home, and make something of ourselves. We make the distance so many miles and we make something of someone's behaviour.

For all these makings, common sense says we can't make some things. We can't make a silk purse out of sow's ear, nor a horse to drink, even upon leading it to water. More definitively, we can't make either the sow or the horse. In the opposite direction, our makings are sometimes a sort of necessity, as when we must make do or must make a go of it. We are told, too, that making things up in doing science and in answering our parent's questions are bad. Yet making things up is absolutely necessary for fiction and childhood games. Finally, while we think we can make the world a better place we are reserved about thinking we can make the world.

I propose, with qualifications, that we do make the world, but not alone. God plays an essential role in world-making and God's creativity limits how we can construct the world. Just as human making in general is diverse and rich but has limits, so world-making is diverse and rich but has limits. A chair simply can't be made of jell-o, and when it comes to world-making, the limitations, although different, are no less stringent.

1 GOALS

My general goal is to explore the pervasive and fundamental sort of making I call "make/believing." "Make/believing" (not make believing – see below) is a semi-technical term for what is described more carefully as human noetic contributions to the way (or ways) things are. Specifically, my goal is to explore the role human noetic feats have in making the world by setting forth a positive account of an irrealism rooted in both humans and God. The proposed irrealism is pluralistic, not monistic. The world is many ways and these are not always compatible with each other. Furthermore, things made by human noetic feats are made relative to noetic frameworks rather than in virtue of them.[1] This distinction is analogous to building a house with materials at hand (relative to) vs creating, *ex nihilo*, that same house (in virtue of). But it is only analogous. For a human to build a house, materials must already be at hand. Likewise, for a human to build a world, materials must be at hand. The disanalogy is the nature of the material. In world-making, God provides what is a kind of noumena and humans shape it into various sorts of things. In house-building, the material already has shapes. In neither case, however, do humans create from nothing.

Philosophers have set out any number of pluralisms, irrealisms, and relativisms. I cannot hope to cover them all. Instead I pick three recent accounts, sketch and criticize them, and then build and defend a stronger irrealistic pluralism. Although I explore these three accounts at some length, my goal is not primarily exegetical but rather to take the best of these views, expand irrealism into a theistically based theory, and then show that these moves mesh well with traditional Christianity. The seven central theses of the essay are as follows.

1 Irrealism is the best view on the relationship between the world and noetic activity. Simply stated, irrealism claims that the world is how it is because human noetic feats make it so.
2 Ontological pluralism, while not entailed by irrealism, is the best way to handle certain problems generated by the argument for irrealism.
3 Ontological pluralism requires both a realist account of truth and a fairly rich actualism in modal theory.

4 Irrealism qua ontological pluralism requires that the very humans who exist in one ontological framework exist in each and every alternative framework.

5 Irrealism qua ontological pluralism requires the existence of God in each and every ontological framework.

6 Although God's core is not shaped by human noetic work, how God is in various conceptual schemes is shaped by human noetic work. God is therefore not entirely dependent upon human noetic work and is, so far forth, noetically real. However, God is embedded in God's conceptual scheme(s) and therefore does not escape noetic dependence. So although the pluralistic irrealism proposed is not total, it is nearly so.

7 The first six theses can be placed amid the claims of traditional Christianity without disturbing anything of importance to those claims, and doing so illumines some important ways of thinking about Christian theology.

Part 1 of the essay, the introductory chapter, provides an intuitive feel for my position, along with a general introduction to the theory and some important terms and distinctions. Part 2 presents three contemporary pluralist positions that provide grist for the mill generating my version of irrealism qua pluralism, as well as correctives toward a stronger irrealism. Part 3 develops and defends what I call theistic irrealism and its concomitant ontological pluralism. Finally, Part 4 explores how theistic irrealism works embedded in traditional Christianity.

In a very broad way the book's direction is foreshadowed by noting that, as a Christian, I believe God is the ultimate source of creation. The relationship of God to the world is described in the first few chapters of Genesis. Christians take this passage seriously as teaching that God is the ultimate source of what is.[2] Beside God's creation of the world, we also find here the Garden of Eden story. Christians take this story seriously as well.[3] God makes the Garden and likewise Eve and Adam. Adam and Eve disobey God and hence fall. But humans are portrayed as making things. For example, the humans make crops in an organized manner (it was a garden and not a wild area). After they make themselves sinners, they make leaf coverings for themselves. They make conversation and name the animals. In particular, they make livestock, and do so simply by naming them such.[4] Although Scripture is not philosophy, the implications of humans naming things are oft-times overlooked. Things, at least sometimes, apparently are what they are because of the naming. Humans in some ways make the world, and we do so, I submit, by naming or, more specifically, by using concepts.

However, and here I depart from many Christian thinkers, I think there can be and are many worlds; my philosophical position is pluralistic. So when I say there are many worlds, I'm saying that more than one true description holds of the way things are or that more than one accurate account of ontology obtains. Let me here tag my use of the term "world" as a quasi-literal one, providing more details below. For now, I'll say we make various worlds because God made humans creative and we are so quite powerfully. But we cannot be creative alone. God must be present in each world made. I call this ontological, pluralistic irrealism "theistic irrealism."

2 MAKE/BELIEVING: OR MAKING THINGS WITH CONCEPTS

We make things with concepts. Although words are attended by concepts, concepts are not limited to the linguistic. So our making a world is not limited to the concepts attending words but inclusive of pictorial, gestural, or other kinds of concepts. I call our making-of-worlds "make/believing." In our typical use of the term "make believe" we have in mind some sort of playful or joyful pretense attached to the conscious suspension of typical beliefs. Largely, make believing is something children do at play. We do not think of make belief as generating a reality. Children, we think, can leave their play and return to "the World" (that is, the real one) when called to dinner. While adults can engage in such play, generally speaking adults who confuse make belief with their "real" lives need professional therapy, be it psychological or philosophical. Reality is thought distinct from make belief.

Yet there are times when the so-called suspension of reality is not only acceptable but necessary; every play and movie we watch or novel we read depends on it. In contrast to a pejorative use of "make believe," where some critic might charge a philosophical or scientific theory with being "merely make belief," I press the term into use (with the modification of changing "make believe" to "make/believe") precisely because I argue that the distinction between reality and our beliefs (and other cognitive attitudes) about it is overdrawn. Our believings, along with many other noetic activities, contribute to the way things are because ultimately our believings and other cognitive attitudes grow organically out of the conceptual. Not the least of these contributions are creative work in the arts and our emotions. One important assumption I make is that education in our society (starting with elementary school) tends far too much to theory and its verbal approaches to reality. The result is the downplaying of artistic worlds and the emotions. The term "make/believing," bridging as it does child's play and our entering various artistic worlds, is thus useful for its pliability.[5] Make/believing as children is perhaps the most fundamental of all human creativity. I think it appropriate to appropriate the term for all kinds of human creativity: in philosophy, science, the arts, and human relationships, and in particular for the making of the many worlds in which we live.

Our believings, indeed the entire range of our noetic doings, often don't receive due credit. Having said that, I remind the reader that human noetic activity is not free of limits. Indeed, our make/believing the worlds we do is not arbitrary, I shall argue, but rooted ultimately in God as God is understood in the Christian tradition. Objectivity, and hence the limits of world-making, rest in God. When God is pleased with our world-making, we make God dance with pleasure.

3 MAKING (IRREAL) WORLDS: AN INTUITIVE INTRODUCTION

We say children make mud pies, carpenters make houses, and chefs make food, but children don't make dirt, nor carpenters wood, nor chefs cauliflower. So, at least, goes common sense. We make things out of the world but we can't make the world itself. We make theories and we make storylines; we don't make the things we make theories about – material objects, for example – and storylines are not made out of whole cloth. Fiction, no matter how wild, is rooted at least loosely in the world. We keep running, so to speak, into the world as we find it. Yet there are exceptions, for sometimes we do make the things we make theories about – artworks, computers, and theories themselves – and we can tell stories about story-making. But these things we've made – computers and artworks – in the end are made of the world or parts or aspects of it. We don't make "the real world." So goes, as Nelson Goodman says, our common nonsense.[6]

Consider a father and his young son one night at bath time. The father plops the bar of Ivory soap into the water. The son sees it floating by and says, "Look, Dad, a boat!" The father, not missing a beat, replies: "Yes, it's a great little boat, isn't it? See it sailing along!" Here an everyday object, a bar of soap, changes its ontological status before our very ears simply by a little conceptualizing done by a young boy and his playful father. Common sense tells us the floating object isn't really a boat but rather a bar of soap. Yet why should we settle on the object really being soap instead of a boat? Why not say it is really a collection of molecules arranged in a certain way, or atoms and the particles thereof, or really a toy or a potential carving or an illustration in this philosophy discussion? Which is it really? Why settle for one description over another?

Maybe these comments and questions make sense because I speak of an artifact and, after all, we know we can make artifacts a variety of ways. They are not, so far forth, part of the world we find. But what about natural objects like trees, for instance? Trees fall into a variety of camps, coniferous and deciduous, to start. I was taught as a boy that this distinction is roughly the one between evergreens and those losing their leaves in the cold. But of course, some coniferous trees lose their leaves in the winter (the Tamarack, for example). What about softwoods and hardwoods? The latter are good for stoking the fire on winter nights, the former less so, but some softwoods make great tables and so do many hardwoods. So what is this thing in front us, really? Is it a deciduous, a hardwood, a table-making tree, or a warmer night in January? Or again, is it certain molecules strung together one way rather than another, or positrons and electrons? What is it, really, and why think we can make a bar of soap but not a maple tree?

Common sense tells us we cannot make maple-sugar saplings but we can make babies. Both are natural and both, for that matter, are made of other natural things. But of course, just because we can make babies doesn't entail that we can make baby trees or cats or elephants. We can only make human babies. Again we might be told that we aren't really making a baby. We are having sexual intercourse and, once nature takes its course, it makes the baby.

But things aren't so simple here, for people can have sexual intercourse without making a baby by using contraception. So human will plays a role in making babies (at least sometimes) but it doesn't in making maple trees. Yet that isn't quite right either, for we can plan to make a maple-sugar sapling too, by getting the right seed, planting it in the right soil, adding water and light and some good organic compost. In that regard, making a baby (human or maple sapling) is somewhat like making a table. But still, making a baby requires nature to do its stuff whereas making a table involves just a decision to make one and following through. This is human artifactual stuff and not natural. Nothing is left up to nature. But that isn't so either, for if one is in the middle of the Sahara, no amount of willing can make nature co-operate and generate the trees to make the wood to make the table. Yet making a baby requires the right stuff (sperm, ovum, etc.) just as a table requires wood (or other material). The difference here is that we can plan to make a table and we cannot plan to make a baby, where by "plan" I don't mean just "decide" but "work out the details of" how the table will look, its materials, size, and so on. In the former case, we can plan to make a maple table rather than a metal table but we cannot plan to make a red-haired child rather than a dark-haired one. But of course, that is just a matter of time and technique, isn't it?

No common set of properties exists in virtue of which a game is a game. Nor does a common set of properties exist in virtue of which a making is a making. Both are Wittgensteinian family resemblances, the family of makings a sort of (uneven) continuum extendable in new ways in new circumstances. One entry point is the making of a bar of soap into a boat. Some sort of observation is made (the thing floats and moves; if one threw the bar of soap across the room, the boy in the illustration could have said it was a plane or a spaceship). The right concept is then introduced into the circumstance (in this case a boat as a thing that floats and moves) and perhaps the right relevant or historical properties (being a boat). We go from there all the way through making babies to making tables, to making art, to making plans, to making concepts, to making trees (and here I don't just mean planting a seed but rather conceptualizing a world with trees rather than not). In each case, we start with a "raw material" (a bar of soap; a free romantic evening with one's spouse; the idea for a table, building, or artwork; bits and pieces of other aspects of the world "at hand" or perhaps we'd best say "at mind"). We make a star, as Nelson Goodman says, just as we make a constellation: by putting its parts together and marking off its boundaries.[7] But we don't make stars exactly as we make bricks, for the latter we make with our hands, the former with our languages and symbol systems.

But we'll have neither a brick nor a star without concepts and some sort of raw material with which to work (the noumenal material God contributes).

The critic may suggest that I'm equivocating on the term "making" and that it actually has several different meanings. I hope to show this challenge to have less bite than bark. The concept of making something, whether a baby, a table, a story, a theory, or a world, begins at home in the everyday language we use to describe our lives. What we make of our lives, indeed, results from a long series of makings. To make is to create and to create is what humans do. To create is to act out of the freedom God gives us. John McDowell notes well that we humans are capable of spontaneity within the "logical space of reasons" and our capacity for the use of reason in belief, judgment, and the like makes us human. But McDowell places spontaneity completely within nature (though not within what he calls "bald naturalism") and at the same time wants to avoid "reenchanting nature."[8] I'm happy to say, in contrast, that our spontaneity – our adeptness at movement within the logical space of reasons – is, in fact, not completely natural, and that nature is, indeed, enchanted. Nature is enchanted by God as well as a sort of minimalist idealism.[9] My idealism is minimalist because the ways the world is depends not merely on the human mind but on God's mind. As such, it is not a full-blooded idealism claiming that if there were no humans there would be no world at all. There would be a world if there were no humans – what I'll later refer to as "God's world."

I argue that we can and do create many kinds of things with our concepts. Some worlds we make via linguistically expressible concepts. Some we make via concepts that are not linguistically connected. But all concepts are ultimately rooted in world views. A world view includes our beliefs, our emotional commitments, and our interests. Thus, insofar as we make our world views what they are, we make the ontologies with which we live. While I do not think anyone can simply make up a world view out of whole cloth, I believe we can do things to influence our world views. Those things are rooted in history.

4 HISTORY

My position is not committed to an extreme relativism simply by admitting that our world views make worlds. Indeed, I am quite against extreme relativisms, both among the intelligentsia and in popular culture. Whence the limits to relativism? One source is the history of one's world view. As Hilary Putnam puts it in describing Goodman on the new riddle of induction, "entrenchment depends on the frequency with which we have actually inductively projected a predicate in the past" but then he generalizes and writes, "whether Goodman is writing about art or induction, what he prizes is congruence with actual practice as it has developed in history."[10] I follow Goodman here, for we make worlds out of world views where the latter are not created *ex nihilo* any more than the former are. Furthermore, we do not live in just one world that is separate from the world(s) of others. Goodman says we cannot just make up worlds willy-nilly anymore than a carpenter can just throw some lumber together and make a chair. I would add that what once was a table could become a chair, and what was a world view-*cum*-world can become a different world view-*cum*-world with a plan and a lot of hard work. We work out of the historical circumstances in which we find ourselves, and radical departures are often wrong-headed or perhaps just not coherent. These historical limits are not arbitrary but rooted in lived experience and pragmatics.

Finally, history is linked to the way God interacts with the worlds we make. God thus enters the picture in a significant way, and our thinking about God, while not making God in a core way, is not separable from our personal relationship to God. Some branches of the Christian tradition emphasize the personal rather than the abstract. In the end, I believe God is fundamentally relational and not to be understood, primarily, in terms of the possession of a fixed set of abstract characteristics. Our thinking and conceptualizing about God has limits, if one is to remain a traditional Christian, but the role of abstract theorizing about God is less significant than the tradition itself sometimes admits. So while some statements are truly said of God, it is God as the ultimate ontological reality who is the source of objectivity. Hence God personally provides the limits on world-making rather than some set of fixed, unbending truths about God. Objectivity provides for truth, not truth for objectivity.

I propose that God is not only not left untouched by human contributions to the divine, but God is delighted with our contributions. Having made human creatures to create, God recognizes that our access to the One who created the world is both intimate in relationship and creative in intellectual understanding. As we make/

believe, living lives of creative fidelity, we come to see God in many ways, including seeing God in all God's mystery. This seeing is not a bland, passive receiving of information but an active understanding of the ways God is. We can make God dance by theorizing creatively not only about the worlds but about God as well.

Most of the remainder of this chapter introduces how I will use various terms. Terms such as realism, irrealism, nonrealism, antirealism, pluralism, and monism, are protean in their uses. I do not attempt to separate the stew but rather simply explain my usage.[11]

5 WORLDS

There are many worlds. The term "world" I use in a quasi-literal sense, eschewing, on the one hand, the claim that there are literally many completely distinct actual worlds made by human noetic activity and, on the other hand, that there is only one actual world with only one true description that we humans discover. While there is only one world (that is, we are in the only actual world there is), there are in this very world many different conceptual schemes and things are what they are relative to those schemes. The latter's incompatible ontologies are, I say, different worlds, the worlds in which we live. I take the term "world" to be elastic.[12]

So although there is only one world, there are many worlds. The first "world" of the last sentence is a technical sense of the term pressed into use to avoid certain problems parallel to the transworld identity problem found in possible world semantics. When I talk about the world in this sense I write it: World. The second "world" from the first sentence is a more relaxed sense of the term which, when lower-cased, I use as a moniker for the plural ways the World is, thus: world.[13] So, the World is made up of many worlds.

Thus "world" has a quasi-literal sense falling somewhere between literalness and metaphor. It is akin to the nearly frozen metaphor we use in saying "she lives in the world of the Calvinist" or "he lives in the world of the wage-labourer." But merely akin. I do not mean simply to pick out epistemological perspectives but differing ontologies. Furthermore, when I participate in one world as opposed to another, I am not barred from leaving one and moving to another. Indeed some worlds overlap in various ways; worlds are not incommensurable. However, I cannot move from one World to another World, supposing there could be more than one actual World.

Three more notes on terminology. First, when speaking of Nelson Goodman's position, I use the term "G-worlds" or "Goodmanian worlds." Goodman holds that there are many actual worlds that we make via concepts (and no singular one "underneath"). He uses the term "world" and so to distinguish his position from mine, I relabel his term "world" as "G-world." Second, when speaking of the noetic realist sense of the world I use the term "World" (or "the World") in quotation marks. On the noetic realist's understanding there is, typically, only one "World" and only one way that "World" is. So "the World" is also the World.[14] "The World" is the actual world which has a single true description and is not significantly contributed to by human noetic activity.

Finally, there are exceptions to my general pattern of word usage. When speaking of possible worlds, for example, I leave "world" in lower case for there is no easy or clear overlap between possible world talk and talk about worlds, G-worlds, the World, or "the World." I do not by this lapse intend to imply anything about the status of possible worlds vis-à-vis irrealism or realism. It is clear when I've shifted from the irrealistic to the modal because the term "possible" or "actual" always attends the latter. Another exception occurs when I talk about another philosopher's work and report, let's say, on something said about the empirical world. Again, I do not imply anything about this type of world vis-à-vis realism and irrealism by this lapse in usage. Such lapses should be clear because the term "world" is attended by the term "empirical" or some parallel term.

6 NOETICISM AND ONTOLOGICAL PLURALISM

Is it best to think of there being many actual and completely independent Worlds or one World with many worlds or alternative ontologies? I take the latter approach throughout, defending it at some length. But it is helpful briefly to introduce the issue here to clarify my understanding of pluralism. Let's say a monist is one who thinks human noetic contribution to the way the World is makes the World with a singular true description. Kant's position comes to mind. On the other hand, a pluralist thinks human noetic contribution to things makes them with a number of different, incompatible, but nevertheless true descriptions. Nelson Goodman and Michael Lynch are good examples. Furthermore, pluralism comes in at least two forms. A pluralist can hold to one actual World with many different but equally true descriptions or many actual Worlds, all of which have true descriptions. The former is found in Lynch, the latter in Goodman.

The many-Worlds pluralist denies a singular World underlying our various competing descriptions and also denies that those many Worlds would exist without noetic contributions from humans. Thus, "[t]here are ... many worlds if any."[15] Goodman is quite comfortable with talk of many Worlds. Lynch does not care for Goodman's many Worlds language.[16] He writes that "[i]n its most general form, pluralism is the idea that there can be more than one true story of the world; there can be incompatible, but equally acceptable, accounts of some subject matter."[17] More specifically, and more directly relevant to our purposes, Lynch writes that "[m]etaphysical pluralism is *pluralist* because it implies that true propositions and facts are relative to conceptual schemes or worldviews; it is *metaphysical* because the facts in question concern the nature of reality – facts about God, mind, and the universe [italics his]."[18] Who is right here, so far as pluralism is concerned, the many-Worlds or the singular-World pluralist? I argue below that the latter option wins the day. Put into the terms of this essay, the single-World pluralist can be said to hold that there is one World but many worlds.

What provides for ontological pluralism? Most pluralisms, insofar as they are provided an account, are rooted in some sort of noeticism, that is, a view in which the human mind contributes to the nature of reality. The mental contribution is thought of as something beyond humans merely thinking up ideas and implementing them into the World as we find it (as furniture designer/builders do). Call this "weak noeticism." It is, so far forth, not philosophically controversial. Whenever humans invent or build something, weak noeticism is in play, viz., a set of human ideas or concepts changes the things found in the World by adding artifacts or the ideas themselves.

By contrast, in strong noeticism, the worlds (including both the artifactual and the natural things therein) are made or shaped by us. So while there may be a World independent of human noetic schemes, no worlds (and their contents) exist independent of human noetic work. I remind the reader that worlds might be made relative to or in virtue of conceptual schemes. In "relative to" makings, humans may shape the (noumenal) stuff of the World but not create anything in the World *ex nihilo*. Furthermore, we can distinguish active vs passive makings. In the former, humans actively make the various ways the World is. In the latter, it simply turns out that the World is the various ways it is passively. These points are relevant to a distinction between a modest and a strong idealism. I'll return to the various sorts of idealism below. Here, let's simply note that whether noeticism eventuates in a modest or a strong idealism, something more than a weak noeticism is required.

Views leading to various idealisms are contentious. Let's group them under the title "strong noeticism." Further details on strong noeticism follow below (under the more specific heading "noetic irrealism") but for now, let's say that a strong noeticist believes that the World is dependent upon human noetic feats so that were there no human contribution to the (non-artifactual, non-idea) World, the World itself would be different than it is. The point is not trivial. It suggests that the World would lack something besides just human ideas and artifacts were there no humans. The boldest versions of strong noeticism eventuate in a strong idealism implying that were there no humans there would not only be no worlds but no World. I reject strong idealism for I claim that God, alongside humans, contributes to the ways the World is. But there are weaker notions, to which I'll return below.

Before that, it is worth noting that God's role in my view is not simply that of Alvin Plantinga's "theistic creative antirealism" where God creates "the World" via divine noetic activity, while humans do not, except via weak noeticism.[19] On Plantinga's view, God makes the World and humans discover it. On my view – theistic irrealism – God and humans jointly make worlds. Theistic irrealism generates a weak idealism. Although weaker than strong idealism, its claims are not paltry. For while I think there would be a World even *sans* humans, I do not think there would be any stars *sans* humans. Since God makes and sustains the World, there would be a World, even without humans. This purely "divine" World would have neither natural nor artifactual things in it where those are dependent upon creative human noetic work. The World exists in virtue of God's creative work but the ways the World is (the worlds) exist relative to human noetic work. The World, *sans* human noetic contribution, is a sort of noumenal World, a World bare of particular things or kinds of things.

One might wonder what relationship holds between my view and William Alston's "sensible metaphysical realism" where he suggests

that there are many things that are real, while other things are irreal
– that is, "up to humans." I cover this in more detail in chapter 13
but we can note that he provides a number of examples where humans can choose their nature: beliefs, propositions, and physical
objects (Whiteheadian vs Aristotelian).[20] Yet in Alston's proposal,
huge ranges of things are not dependent on human noetic contribution. Certainly God, humans, and a good deal of what we learn via
science are not. My position is more radically irrealist than Alston's
(and hence the descriptor "irrealism" rather than Alston's "realism"). I believe everything is irreal – whether humanly or divinely
so. More on this distinction below. So far as human noetic contributions go, there are fundamentally only three independent realities: the bare existence of the World, God, and humans themselves.
Unlike Alston, I think we do, in fact, make the stars and that vast
stretches of reality are not absolute. Even God and humans are significantly made the way they are by humans. God, of course, does
not depend at God's core upon human noetic work. Neither do humans depend on human noetic work for their core nature. Yet both
God and humans are noetically shaped by humans on my view, in
contrast to Alston. The role of God's noetic work, and secondarily
the role of human noetic work vis-à-vis the divine and the human
being, I explore in chapters 14 and 15. For now let's say that humans cannot make themselves *ex nihilo*, even though we do contribute to our own way of being-in-the-world. Furthermore,
although humans don't make God's divine core, humans do contribute to aspects of God's being as well.

7 REALISM AND ANTIREALISM

Ontological pluralism is rooted in a strong noeticism. My version is,
more particularly, rooted in "noetic irrealism." Unfortunately, it is far
from clear what the term "irrealism" refers to, or how realism and irrealism are related to truth. Indeed, all discussions of realism and irrealism are complicated by the great variety of ways in which the
terms "real," "irreal," "antireal," and their cognates are used. My task
in the next sections is to provide an overview of three types of re-
alism/irrealism and to suggest how they are related, at least in a
general manner.

    First a note on the terms "realism," "irrealism," and "antireal-
ism." I'm not sanguine about these terms. After all, it's not as if the

pluralist's worlds are fake for being nonreal or irreal. The worlds are actual ways things are; they are not merely possible (in the technical sense) nor are they insubstantial. The stone still hurts one's foot upon being kicked. The worlds are where we live and move and have our being. In the end, I'd prefer to use some other language. But I can think of no obviously good substitute. So I have chosen the following: I use Goodman's terms "irrealist" and "irrealism" rather than "nonrealist" and "nonrealism" or "antirealism" and "antirealist." The latter two groups of terms leave one with the impression that the worlds are somehow fake. "Nonrealism" sounds negative, as does its cousin "antirealism" – perhaps even pejorative (compare the older "realism/idealism" language; unfortunately, not all irrealists, nonrealists, and antirealists are idealists). These terms seem to deny the very being of the world. "Irrealism," in contrast, does not so obviously deny the being of the worlds but shifts their ground from an independent to a dependent status. The one exception to my usage is the first kind of realism/irrealism I consider, viz., existence realism/irrealism/nonrealism. Also, I occasionally use the term "antirealist," "radical antirealist," or even "radical postmodernist" to point toward the most radical of relativists among us. My use of these terms is simply shorthand for positions I believe, in the end, cannot be sustained as viable pluralisms.

8 EXISTENCE REALISM/NONREALISM

We can start with metaphysical versions of realism/nonrealism in which the existence of certain kinds of things (beings, relationships, properties, etc.) are acknowledged or rejected. Let's call these "existence realism/nonrealisms," for here "nonrealism" more accurately describes what I'm after than does "irrealism," the latter not being negative. Examples of existence realism/nonrealisms might deal with the existence of God, or moral acts, or quarks. In an existence realism/nonrealism, God or moral acts or quarks are either acknowledged (a realist position) or rejected (a nonrealist position).[21]

Existence realism/nonrealism emphasizes what there is and what there is not in the World (and the worlds) and can be considered from an entirely noetic and alethic realist framework. I'll return below in detail to these last two notions. For now, an alethic realist is one who holds that truth is nonepistemic, that is, that what makes a truth-value bearer true is the world (or the World) and not (generally, at least) the one holding the truth. A noetic realist is one who holds that the World is what it is independent, generally, of human noetic contributions. Given alethic and noetic realism, what exists, and what is truly described as existing, does not in general depend on human noetic contributions.[22]

Given alethic and noetic realism, an existence nonrealist about God is just an old-fashioned atheist. Such a person believes there is a "World" and that "the World" is describable truly only in a singular way, and that that singular, true description contains the true claim that God does not exist. Let's call such an existence nonrealist a "simple existence nonrealist." An existence nonrealist about God might be so under other circumstances as well. For example, he might be a noetic realist about physical objects but an emotivist about religious objects. Such a person denies the real existence of God beyond the existence of certain feelings or attitudes subjective to the theistic believer. This person may count as an existence nonrealist about God, but for somewhat special reasons. He may, indeed, continue to talk about God as if the divine were noetically real but deny that his language about the divine refers to anything independent of his feelings or attitudes. The final reference of his theistic language is a subjective human state. Such a theistic nonrealist is an atheist in one sense (denying the traditional independent God) but not in another sense (insofar as he associates God merely with a set of feelings or attitudes). God exists in one sense for this person, and hence he is not a theistic simple existence nonrealist (an old-fashioned atheist), but God does not exist in a noetically real sense and hence this believer, we might say, is an "existence irrealist" about God.

In a parallel but not identical way, a Berkeleyan subjective idealist is not a simple existence nonrealist about mountains but rather believes they should be understood in an atypical way, namely, as ideal. The Berkeleyan view of mountains is thus a sort of existence irrealism. The Berkeleyan does not say mountains do not exist, any more than the emotivist Christian would say God doesn't exist. They simply give alternative accounts of the relevant items.

An atheist (a God simple existence nonrealist) could be, and likely is, an existence realist about plenty of other things, such as tables, people, trees, and so forth. God does not exist, while tables, humans, and trees do. Someone who denies the existence of quarks might be a realist about furniture-size physical objects. But again, depending on the details, this person might be either a simple existence nonrealist about quarks or a quark irrealist, understanding quarks as entirely heuristic fictions.

The relationships among various existence realism/nonrealisms and noetic realism/irrealisms are complex. In some cases, the judgment as to whether something exists is made in the context of a noetic realism about other things. For the old-fashioned atheist, God simply fails to exist, where existence is understood in noetic realist terms. For the God irrealist, one's views on noetic realism can be mixed. One can be a noetic realist about some things (let's say material objects) but not about others (God or morals). Where these views tend to be strongly materialist or naturalist, they generally incline either toward a reductionist materialist model or toward a sort of verificationism in which morality or God is some sort of emotion or expression thereof. The kind of noetic irrealism found in these cases is not dependent upon conceptual schemes so much as on other aspects of our world view, such as emotional needs. God or morals are noncognitive on these verificationist views, while on reductionist models, "God" refers to nothing at all, whereas the thought of God is reducible simply to some brain state or other.

To further muddy the waters, note that if what exists is dependent on human conceptual schemes, where there are many conceptual schemes distinct in content, then what exists will vary scheme to scheme. Thus, God may exist according to some conceptual schemes and not according to others.[23] Pluralism understood in this way is inconsistent with any totalizing atheism. In the context of pluralism it is simply not clear how to go about showing that God does not exist, period. Perhaps if someone could show that a conceptual scheme simply can't be devised in which God exists then a totalizing atheism would make sense on pluralism. But doing that seems as difficult as, if not more difficult than, showing that God is an impossible being. So, given that God could exist in some scheme or other, how could one deny God's existence in some final, total way?

The scenario suggested by a totalizing atheism, in the context of a radical noetic irrealism, remains unclear in part because there would be, on atheism, literally no "God's eye point of view" from which to judge for or against God's existence. Couldn't there be a conceptual scheme according to which God exists? How would we know? Furthermore, God seems to be the kind of thing that, if God exists at all, must exist universally – that is, within every conceptual scheme. This is the intuition, I believe, found behind various ontological arguments for God's existence. But of course in ontological arguments typically the concern is God's existence in all possible worlds and therefore the actual world. The many actual Worlds of a rich Goodmanian type of ontological pluralism are not the main concern in the various versions of the ontological argument for God's existence. Regardless of these details, I suggest that God's existence cannot be considered without reference to the role of human noetic feats in the way (or ways) the World is.

9 NOETIC REALISM/IRREALISM

Most pluralisms are rooted in a noeticism wherein the worlds are dependent in some significant manner on the human mind. I call my version "noetic irrealism." It is easiest to approach an account of noetic irrealism via noetic realism. A noetic realist on the issue of what the mind contributes to the way things are might report that the World is the way it is independent of human noetic feats of any kind. Noetic feats include any (human) thinking about, conceptualizing, believing anything about, knowing that, emotional attachment toward, or taking any other kind of epistemic or cognitive attitude toward "the way things are." In contrast, noetic irrealism holds that (at least some of) these noetic feats do contribute to the way(s) the World is.

Some obvious and commonly accepted exceptions to any universal application of the claims of noetic realism exist. Even the most ardent noetic realist admits that human thoughts and emotions depend upon us noetically for their being. Thus, it would be strange for anyone to be a complete or global noetic realist. Also, certain social institutions, such as contracts, marriage, or corporations depend upon our noetic contributions, although perhaps less directly than in the case of thoughts themselves. Finally, in weak noeticism, the construction of new buildings, computers, or clothes depends in some way on our noetic activity.

Yet a clear sense exists (given noetic realism) in which, once a building is created, it is independent of noetic feats. This is a "common sense" intuition about things. There is a more opaque sense in which social institutions are independent of the human mind once created, for things such as marriage remain at least partly noetic, even once the "idea" is released into the World. Marriages, unlike buildings, depend on human interaction for their continued existence. Of course, ideas always depend upon the mind that is thinking them, so they are never real in the sense spelled out in our initial account of noetic realism. Thus noetic realism is never truly global. I simply set aside these counter-instances to noetic realism, assuming the reader recognizes that any realism about "the World" does not include human thought itself and probably not marriages, contracts, and the like either. We can think of noetic realism, thus, as nearly global noetic realism and the obvious exceptions as an innocuous sort of noetic irrealism. What does it take to have a significant sort of noetic irrealism?

Let's follow up on an observation made earlier, viz., noetic irrealism can either be narrowly compartmental or more universal. A narrow irrealism might hold that while religious or moral or aesthetic facts depend on human noetic feats, nothing else does. A broader noetic irrealism might say that most fields of discourse pick out irreal things whereas only the physical realm is noetically real. Can noetic irrealism be global so that *everything* depends on the noetic contributions of humans? Perhaps solipsism is such a view. But even in solipsism not everything is irreal, for I am real in a peculiar sort of way. On solipsism, my being is somehow different from the being of my noetic actions, the latter dependent logically, if not causally, on the former. But solipsism is not generally pluralistic. My world is my world and there are no others. But were we to push solipsism in a pluralist direction it seems that one's own being – even if it is purely mental – is different from the being of other things. It is one point to think a tree depends upon my noetic contribution, quite another to think that my own being is dependent upon my own conceptual contributions.[24] My own being, even if mental, seems related to me in a manner different from the being of things other than myself. Global noetic irrealism based strictly in human thought is at least odd, if not perhaps a sort of grand human arrogance. So what is noetic irrealism and how far can it extend? What role does the human thinker play? Whence the human's reality?

10 COGNIZING

Before I answer these questions (the general burden of the book but for which I give a brief overview in section 12), let me say something about the nature of human contributions to reality as I understand them. That is, I want to say something about the human feats – the cognizings – that make the worlds.

Noetic feats come in all sorts and to have a thought is not just to consider a linguistically expressible notion. Thoughts can and certainly do include ideas linguistically construed. "That ball is green" is clearly a thought. But the feeling of love is equally a thought, as is experiencing an abstract artwork. One shouldn't confuse the awareness of what is exemplified by a "purist" painting and the beliefs one might form about it. The experience of patterns, shapes, and colours is no less conceptual than the idea "what I'm looking at is regular, square, and purple." Both, I assume throughout, fall within the range of cognition. Given that, at least four kinds of cognitions exist, that is, four kinds of noetic feat: epistemizing, conceptualizing, emoting, and perceiving.

Epistemizing generally involves some sort of grasping, understanding, or ranking of truth-value bearers (propositions, statements, assertions, beliefs, acceptances, claims, sentences, and so forth) in regard to their being true or rationally acceptable. Epistemizing is not what makes truth-value bearers true, making alethic realism false. More on this in section 11. For now, note that epistemizing sets out to describe what there is without begging questions about what makes it be there.

In conceptualizing, in contrast, we do cognitive but not necessarily epistemizing work. For a person to conceptualize about a chair is for her to think about, apply concepts to, or otherwise engage in cognitive activities that do not epistemize. Such conceptualizing is typically explained in terms of the linguistic. To have the concept "chair" is to be able to apply the linguistic term "chair" in the proper manner. That we appeal to the linguistic is not to say that we always think with language. It is to say that for these sorts of concepts we use a linguistic symbol system; a linguistic symbol system is required for a linguistic conceptualizing to occur. To epistemize is to take something already conceptualized linguistically and do the additional work of grasping, understanding, or ranking propositions, beliefs, acceptances, claims, or sentences in regard to their being rationally acceptable or true. Conceptualizing itself – even linguistic conceptualizing – need not involve propositions or beliefs (etc.) but epistemizing does. One cannot epistemize the notion "chair" but one can epistemize the claim "the chair is leaning against the table." Some sort of conceptualizing is required for epistemizing but not the reverse. No epistemizing is required for conceptualizing. However, epistemizing a world typically depends more or less directly on the conceptualization of the things in that world.

Another sense of conceptualizing need not be linguistically focused. Some concepts are pictorial. Others are diagrammatic, gestural, or presentational. Consider when we experience a work of art or a tailor's sample or a mechanic holding up a certain nut and bolt combination to show her apprentice what he is to pick up at the parts shop. All involve the conceptual but not necessarily the linguistically expressible. Certainly some sort of mental activity is occurring, but not anything linguistic. Sometimes we also use the linguistic in these circumstances, but then we use a different sort of conceptualizing. So some symbols and symbol systems are not linguistic. But within nonlinguistic symbol systems, concepts are invented, reinvented, and pressed into a variety of uses, new and old (just as with the linguistic). Yet none of the nonlinguistic ones need the linguistic and sometimes cannot even be accounted for within the linguistic. Such conceptualizing may not, therefore, be related to the epistemic, at least in anything like the way one orders propositions in terms of truth or rational belief.

Emoting – the third type of cognizing – is harder to describe. Although I hold that emotings are cognitions, they are not easily capturable by language, if at all. Perhaps it is just another kind of nonlinguistic conceptualizing. We take on various attitudes and emotions toward people, objects, truth-value bearers, experiences, and other thoughts. So although these do not organize the world in terms of linguistic concepts, they do organize the world. They influence how we value things and ideas, order them, and act on them. Sometimes we can conceptualize emotings linguistically. We then can use them in forming truth-value bearers and epistemize the propositional results. Such linguistic descriptions, however, are mere reports about inner, subjective things to which no other human but the emoter has immediate access. The emoting itself is not reducible to reports about it, any more than a dance is reducible to an essay about it.

Finally, when we perceive we, once again, conceptualize but nonlinguistically. What we are aware of perceptually varies person to person and even within the experience of a single person. We shape what we experience. These are one and all aspects of cognizing.

Some noetic irrealists seem to be primarily concerned with epistemizing (for example, the Richard Rorty of *Philosophy and the*

Mirror of Nature[25]) or primarily concerned with linguistic conceptualizing (the Hilary Putnam of *Realism with a Human Face*[26]) and
others seem inclusivist in their approach, holding that all these
kinds of cognizings – including emoting and perceiving – make
worlds (Nelson Goodman in *Ways of Worldmaking*[27]). Others are
mainly emoting irrealists, but they tend to limit irrealism to certain
domains, such as religion, morality, and aesthetics. Traditionally,
compartmental emotivists cast their positions in terms of noncognitivism, claiming that such field-relative descriptions are nonfactual
or neither true nor false. While I think emotive contexts do not lend
themselves to true/false categories, I also think some emotive contexts are right and others wrong. Thus we need to give attention to
all cognitive contributions to the worlds.

I generally talk about epistemizing and conceptualizing, including
in the latter category not only linguistic conceptualizing but all the
various symbolic approaches (pictorial, gestural, etc.) as well as emoting and perceiving. I break into more specific language when relevant
for the context. Please do not, however, construe this shorthand as an
admission that concepts are only linguistically expressible.

Before leaving this section I want to note the importance of
concepts, so far as meaning goes, in everything we do. By "meaning" I have in mind roughly what John McDowell does when he
writes of meaning as we humans encounter and use it in the logical space of reasons (after Sellars) or the faculty of spontaneity
(after Kant). McDowell draws a contrast between spontaneity and
nature where the latter is understood as falling in the realm of law,
although he rejects "bald naturalism" in which nature is strictly
understood as the realm of law and through which spontaneity
and understanding are inexplicable. I'll return to McDowell's position in chapters 8 and 9. But it is helpful if we have some of his
terms in the background early on. A brief quotation suffices for
now. McDowell writes:

> Kant makes his remark about intuitions and concepts ["intuitions
> without concepts are blind"] in the course of representing empiri-
> cal knowledge as the result of a co-operation between receptivity
> and spontaneity, between sensibility and understanding. Now we
> should ask why it seems appropriate to describe the understanding,
> whose contribution to this co-operation is its command of con-
> cepts, in terms of spontaneity. A schematic but suggestive answer

is that the topography of the conceptual sphere is constituted by rational relations. The space of concepts is at least part of what Wilfred Sellars calls "the space of reasons." When Kant describes the understanding as a faculty of spontaneity, that reflects his view of the relations between reason and freedom: rational necessitation is not just compatible with freedom but constitutive of it. In a slogan, the space of reasons is the realm of freedom.[28]

Concepts are so intimately tied to understanding and hence to human freedom that to do without the conceptual is to do without humanness. To do without the conceptual, the vehicle through which meaning is enlivened, is to do without freedom, and to do without freedom is to undermine what it is and means to be human.

McDowell argues that since the rise of modern science, philosophers have been caught in what appears to be a dilemma. If we affirm the realm of meaning – that we live in the space of reasons and that the faculty of spontaneity is central to what makes us human – then we have to choose between a system of belief more-or-less independent of empirical input and which finds justification for its beliefs completely internally and the myth of the Given. The myth says that something in nature provides justification even though no concept attached to the Given rationally connects it to the faculty of spontaneity. McDowell proposes a third way. Briefly, he says that experience arrives passively in us but already shaped by concepts. This does not commit us to idealism, and in fact he proposes his model as a way to allow for the empirical world to impinge on us, causing "friction" in the realm of judgment, belief, and other activities of spontaneity.

I want to call attention to McDowell's claim that the concepts bound up with experience itself, while passively received, share much in common with those we use in making judgments and forming beliefs. Two quotations will suffice here. First, in speaking of how receptivity works, he writes,

The relevant conceptual capacities are drawn on *in* receptivity … It is not that they are exercised *on* an extra-conceptual deliverance of receptivity. We should understand what Kant calls "intuition" – experiential intake – not as a bare getting of an extra-conceptual content. In experience one takes in, for instance, *that things are thus and so.* That is the sort of thing that one can also, for instance, judge. [italics his][29]

Add the following remark:

The conceptual capacities that are passively drawn into play in experience belong to a network of capacities for active thought, a network that rationally governs comprehension-seeking responses to the impacts of the world on sensibility. And part of the point of the idea that the understanding is a faculty of spontaneity – that conceptual capacities are capacities whose exercise is in the domain of responsible freedom – is that the network, as an individual thinker finds it governing her thinking, is not sacrosanct. Active empirical thinking takes place under a standing obligation to reflect about the credentials of the putatively rational linkages that govern it. There must be a standing willingness to refashion concepts and conceptions if that is what reflection recommends. No doubt there is no serious prospect that we might need to reshape the concepts at the outermost edges of the system, the most immediately observational concepts, in response to pressures from inside the system. But that no-doubt unreal prospect brings out the point that matters for my present purpose. This is that although experience itself is not a good fit for the idea of spontaneity, even the most immediately observational concepts are partly constituted by their role in something that is indeed appropriately conceived in terms of spontaneity.[30]

Much could be discussed here, but at this juncture I simply enjoin the reader to see McDowell's comments as a framework for understanding the role of concepts in shaping the World, with a promissory note to return to these themes later.

11 ALETHIC REALISM/IRREALISM

A third category of realism/irrealisms is alethic, that is, relevant to truth. Leaving open what, in the final analysis, truth-value bearers are (propositions, beliefs, and so forth), an alethic realist affirms that a truth-value bearer is true when things are as the truth-value bearer says they are. William Alston suggests that in alethic realism the content of the truth-value bearer itself gives us everything we need to specify what it takes for the truth-value bearer to be true.[31]

In contrast, alethic irrealism minimally denies that a truth-value bearer gives us everything we need to specify what would make the truth-value bearer true. One wonders what else one might need, and thus a more complicated story has to be told by the alethic irrealist. Alston argues that the realist conception of truth seems to be what we have in mind when we say something is true. Thus who, we might wonder, would argue with it?

There are some, perhaps. Absolute idealists such as Bradley and pragmatists such as Dewey and James seem to have held views denying alethic realism. The former suggests that truth is a satisfying of the intellect or the ideal expression of the coherent universe, and the latter assert that truth is what we can assimilate or verify. Various postmodern thinkers appear to deny that truth is independent of culture or human thought. In analytic circles, some provide for epistemic accounts of truth. Under these views, for example, what is true is what the ideal scientific community will give us at the end of the grand global research project or what the ideal epistemic observer would say, or perhaps some sort of coherence among propositions or beliefs, etc. These are not clearly compatible with the realist conception of truth. As such, they are the best accounts available for alethic irrealisms.

A little more detail about alethic realism can help to show how other alethic theories might be irrealist. Michael Lynch writes:

> Minimally speaking, a proposition is true in the realist sense
> when things are as that proposition says they are. Some aspect
> of objective reality must simply be a certain way. If it is, then the
> proposition is true; if not, the proposition is false. The truth of
> the proposition hinges on the world alone, not on our thought
> about the world. In short, realism about truth minimally implies
> two commitments: (a) truth is an authentic property that some
> propositions have and others lack, and (b) the concept of truth is,
> in Putnam's words, "radically nonepistemic"; that is, whether a
> proposition is true (in most cases) does not depend on what I or
> anyone else believes or knows.[32]

I prefer not to narrow the field of possible truth-value bearers to just propositions, but with that proviso, Lynch's account captures what a minimalist alethic realism requires. While epistemic theories of truth such as Dewey's and James's fail to meet the second requirement for minimal alethic realism, deflationary accounts[33] fail to meet the first. Deflationary accounts of truth are thus irrealist, for they hold that the words "true" or "truth" pick out nothing in the World or at least nothing that has a nature. Thus, deflationary accounts claim that truth is not a property of anything. Consequently, they fail to meet Lynch's first requirement for minimal alethic realism.

In conclusion, please note this important caution. That noetic irrealisms appeal to epistemic or conceptualizing noetic feats when giving an account of what makes the World the way it is says nothing, so far forth, about what makes a truth-value bearer true. One can put alethic realism thus: "p" is true iff p. This construal of the concept "true" can be right, even if what makes p the way it is, is some conceptual or epistemic scheme or other. Noetic realism/irrealism is not the same as alethic realism/irrealism. Indeed, in *A Realist Conception of Truth*, Alston provides a solid case that alethic realism, in the minimal sense, can be compatible with both noetic realism and noetic irrealism. Lynch goes further and argues that minimal alethic realism is compatible with a quite rich ontological pluralism where conceptual schemes influence what objects there are.

12 NOETIC REALISM, NOETIC IRREALISM, AND TRUTH

Finally, we return to the questions, What is noetic irrealism and how far can it extend? I briefly describe a significant version of noetic irrealism by first describing noetic realism. A noetic realist believes that the way the natural realm (the nonartifactual realm) is, with the more or less obvious exceptions of mental entities such as ideas, is not dependent upon any human noetic feat – any cognizing. As well, human artifacts are real, once made, although it is supposed that the creation of artifacts depends on human noetic contributions in a way non-idea natural objects do not. In contrast, the noetic irrealist claims that both natural and artifactual aspects of the World are shaped by human cognizing. Working within the pluralist framework, the noetic irrealist denies that the worlds are what they are independent of how I (or we) think about them, cognize about them, believe about them, know about them, and so forth. The relationship between the worlds and our cognitive dealings with them is one of close intimacy. The relationship can include the worlds causing or influencing our thinking, believing, cognizing, etc., about them, but it is not at all limited in this unilateral way.

The reverse holds too, viz., our thinking, believing, cognizing, and so forth can have causal effects upon, and can influence in a variety of ways, the worlds. So, although there are noetic feats that "put us in touch with" the worlds, the worlds are not what they are independent of human noetic feats, whether those feats are conceptualizing, emoting, perceiving, or epistemizing feats. There is, thus, no singular way things are which we can simply describe and then compare with "the World" (that is, the noetically real World). This is the wrong way to think about knowledge and truth. Yet we don't lose a realistic theory of truth, even if noetic irrealism is the case.

Lynch writes that "[r]ealism about truth ... is the view that a proposition is true just when the world is as that proposition says it is."[34] Lynch presents the minimal account of realistic truth in terms of propositions, but this is not a necessity. According to Alston, Lynch's tutor in these matters, propositions are the best of the possibilities when trying to identify what it is, ultimately, that bears truth. There are some important details here, but they are details safely skipped over at present, for as Alston writes,

> my choice of truth-value bearers is completely neutral with respect to the view we adopt on the nature of propositions and of propositional content. In fact, I can be even more permissive than this. So far as I can see, the issues with which I will be dealing assume the same shape whatever we take the bearers of truth values to be, provided our choice is not untenable on other grounds. If it is defensible to take sentence tokens to be the primary bearers of truth value, then everything in the rest of the book could be restated in those terms.[35]

Lynch, too, settles on propositions as the best place to rest the realist account of truth. For the present, I want to remain open about this issue, returning to it in chapter 9.

Lynch defends the claim that a thoroughgoing metaphysical pluralism is compatible with realism about truth. I agree and use Lynch's work as a sounding board for my arguments. I also agree with Alston's claim that there is a variety of ways truth-value bearers can be understood, without damaging the realistic account of truth. Goodman too does not overtly deny a realistic account of truth. However, in order fully to affirm a realist account of truth, he has to give up certain aspects of his position, although nothing essential, by his own lights, to irrealism. Nevertheless, Goodman sees truth as less central than Lynch or most of the others writing on these matters. My third pluralistic model, Hales, can less clearly provide for an alethic realism.

A few words are in order about the relationship between noetic irrealism and both idealism and metaphysical realism. Metaphysical realism says, minimally, that "the World" is describable, truly, in only one way and that "the World" (with some obvious exceptions for the mental) is the way it is independent of the mind. Sometimes a third requirement is added: a correspondence theory of truth.[36] I forgo discussing either the first or the third aspect, concentrating on the claim that "the World" is independent of the mental. Idealism is typically thought to deny metaphysical realism insofar as it denies the second aspect, that "the World" is independent of the mind. Irrealism can certainly seem to entail idealism.

I noted the distinction between an "in virtue of" and a "relative to" dependence of a world (or the World) on a conceptual scheme. The former seems clearly to entail that there would be no World were there no human minds, for the World is caused, in some fairly strong sense, by human noetic feats. Such is a clear case of idealism – what I earlier called "strong idealism." The latter, however, only commits one to the view that the World is shaped by human noetic feats and it's therefore less likely to be accused of strong idealism, although it is a case of weak idealism. There could still be a World even if not shaped by noetic feats.

My talk of human noetic feats making the World the various ways it is suggests some sort of causal relationship between the conceptual scheme and the way the World is. What sort of cause is in play here? At first it sounds as if the cause is similar to God's action in *creatio ex nihilo*. But the observation doesn't bear up. When I make a table, I only cause the table to be in a secondary sense. It is not *ex nihilo* creation. Only God can do that. Here the notion of limits comes to the fore, limits on how worlds can be made to exist. One starts with the materials available and shapes them into things. So the question, "would there be stars if there were no humans?" is answered negatively without thereby admitting that there would be nothing at all if humans didn't exist. So the irrealism I'm proposing doesn't entail a strong idealism objected to by so many metaphysical realists.

But neither does it presume no causal connection between what is and the conceptual scheme supporting what is. Causes can shape and influence things without bringing them into being out of nothing.

God could be sustaining the World and the worlds while leaving ample room for human noetic shaping. Irrealism does not rule out some sort of mind-independent World. I mentioned that we can think of this World as a noumenal material out of which other things are shaped. Its being noumenal, however, does not entail that we know nothing of it or that it underlies everything that is. God, for example, who creates the contingent World, would not necessarily be a noumenal aspect of the World per se.

PART TWO

Three Ontological Pluralists:
Strengths and Shortcomings

2

Hale's Philosophical Relativism

Nelson Goodman says we build new world-versions, and hence new worlds, out of old ones. In this section, I attempt just that. My goal is to introduce, criticize, and expand three older worlds to provide building blocks for a new, improved one. In short, Steven Hales's relativism, Michael Lynch's pluralism, and Goodman's irrealism become the quarry for a joint excavation/reconstruction project. While my intentions are expository initially, I do not do exhaustive work. I present what is needed both in building blocks and in criticism to construct a framework for a theistically based pluralism.

I begin with Hales's philosophical relativism, turning then to Lynch's relativistic Kantianism in chapter 3, and finally Goodman's irrealism in chapter 4. The first two views are clearly stated, while the last has a certain kind of richness missing in the other two. Together they provide a sufficiently clear and rich set of building blocks. Chapters 5 and 6 criticize and expand the views found in Lynch and Goodman, while the criticism of Hales is found in the present chapter. A brief section at the end of this chapter presents what we learn, positive and negative, from Hales.

Steven Hales is a self-described, if unhappy, relativist about philosophical propositions, holding that true philosophical propositions are true only within a perspective.[1] So the beliefs of the Christian philosopher, the secular analytic philosopher, and the hallucinogenically induced beliefs of some Ecuadorean shamans, although conflicting, are all true. He also claims that philosophy has a foundational structure dependent on what he calls "rational intuition." Rational intuition is self-justifying and it is not any more or less likely to give us knowledge of philosophical propositions than either Christian revelation or the ritual use of hallucinogens. Thus, we must choose among nihilism, skepticism, and relativism. Hales opts for the last, since the others are, he believes, untenable. While there are a good many things to be learned from Hales's account of relativism, the argument he presents for it fails.

I THE LOGIC OF RELATIVISM

Hales limits his relativist logic, showing why global relativism is self-refuting while a more limited relativism need not be. To begin, he compares "everything is relative" to "everything is possible." This is important for although it is false that everything is possible, it is clearly true that everything true is possibly true. In parallel, while it is false that everything is relative, it is true that everything true is relatively true. Hales writes:

> Suppose that everything is possible. That is, for all Φ, $\Diamond\Phi$. Allow Φ to be "it is necessarily not true that everything is possible." Then the following turns out to be true: possibly, it is necessarily not true that everything is possible. A well-known theorem in modal system S5 tells us that whatever is possibly necessary is necessary. We can thereby conclude that it is necessarily not true that everything is possible. Thus, by reductio, it cannot be the case that everything is possible. So what should we do? Should we abandon all talk of modality, give up possibility and necessity, and purge ourselves of possible worlds? Of course not ... Yet everyone *is* prepared to affirm this thesis: everything true is possibly true [italics his]. (*Relativism*, 99, 100)

This last thesis does not entail that nothing is necessarily true. Possible truth is not mere possibility. Something's being possibly true doesn't rule out its being necessarily true. Furthermore, possible truth is not a "cheap" version of real or actual truth.

Hales introduces two operators, ◆ and ■. The former indexes sentences to perspectives so that ◆Φ is to be read: "it is relatively true (true in some perspective) that Φ." The latter operator is an "absolute" operator so that ■Φ is to be read: "it is absolutely true (true in all perspectives) that Φ." If we then accept the S5-like theorem that whatever is relatively absolute is absolute (for all Φ, ◆■$\Phi \Rightarrow$■Φ) (he calls this P) and we take "it is absolutely not true that everything is relative" as a substitution instance of Φ, we derive the conclusion that it is absolutely not true that everything is relative. Thus global relativism is self-refuting.

Hales's argument rests heavily on the truth of P and he presents a good case for it. Global relativists say relativism is merely relatively true, that is, true in some perspectives and not true in others. But how would this work? Hales first considers that relativism is not true in some perspectives. In that perspective absolutism (not relativism) is true. Absolutism claims that some proposition has the same truth-value in all perspectives. Call this situation p. In p, there is some Φ such that $\blacksquare\Phi$. But how could p contain such a proposition? Φ could not be the thesis of absolutism itself, for *ex hypothesi* there are perspectives in which absolutism is not true. On the other hand, Φ could not be the thesis of relativism, for *ex hypothesi* there are perspectives in which relativism is not true. Other candidates for Φ are in no better shape, since – given the assumption that relativism is true in some perspectives – it must be the case that the truth-value of every proposition Φ will vary across perspectives. Thus, no proposition is true in all perspectives since each proposition is true in some perspectives and not in others. But it follows that relativism is true in all perspectives. This entails that relativism is not true. Relativism can be neither absolutely nor relatively true and so the claim "everything is relative" must be false (*Relativism*, 101). Of the argument just described, Hales writes that

> we considered the option of relativism being relatively not true. Therefore, in some perspective there was a proposition Φ that was absolutely true. Formally: $\blacklozenge\blacksquare\Phi$. Yet it turned out that there could not be such a proposition since the assumption of relativism prevented any proposition from being true in all perspectives. In other words, there could not be a Φ such that $\blacksquare\Phi$. This is why $\blacklozenge\blacksquare\Phi$ could not be true. The form underlying this argument is modus tollens. The conditional relied on is none other than the S5-like principle P: $\blacklozenge\blacksquare\Phi\Rightarrow\blacksquare\Phi$. The preceding argument does not constitute a formal proof that P is true; rather it is a set of semantical considerations designed to uncover the intuition that P. It is a tacit acceptance of P that I suspect undergirds many rejections of "relativism is absolutely false" as being merely true relatively. (*Relativism*, 101, 102)

Thus, global relativism is false and the self-refutation objection to global relativism is undergirded by P.

Is the relativist to give up on relativism? Hales says, no, at least not for that reason. Just as one shouldn't give up on possible world semantics because one rejects "everything is possible," one shouldn't give up on relativism because "everything is relative" is false. Just as "everything is possible" runs afoul the theorem that $\Diamond\Box\Phi\Rightarrow\Box\Phi$, "everything is relative" runs afoul P. But "everything true is possibly true" does not run afoul $\Diamond\Box\Phi\Rightarrow\Box\Phi$, and neither does "everything true is relatively true" run afoul P. Hales writes:

> There is nothing self-contradictory or paradoxical about the claim that everything true is relatively true, just as there is no puzzle engendered by the claim that whatever is true is possibly true. As in the case of alethic modality, it is entirely consistent for the new-and-improved relativist to hold that some propositions are absolutely true and that perspectival truth is every bit as decent and upstanding as "real" truth. Indeed, "real" truth is just truth in this perspective, just as actual truth is truth in this world. Absolute truth turns out to be truth in all perspectives, just as necessary truth is truth in all worlds. For the relativist it will be nonsense to talk about truth outside of the structure of perspectives ... However, this stricture should be no scarier than forbidding talk of truth outside the structure of worlds, once we have accepted possible world semantics. (*Relativism*, 102–3)

This limited relativism does not fall prey to self-refutation.

Hales notes that some relativists might be loath to accept P for it shows that their view is false. But P's rejection leaves the relativist to answer the self-refutation problem. The relativist ignores the problem at her peril. Furthermore, some relativists might be bothered by the fact that Hales's view is consistent with all truths being absolutely so, including P. But, says Hales, relativists should be pleased that the view is consistent with many propositions being merely relatively true. Finally, Hales notes a further advantage, viz., relativism's truth doesn't just fall out of the logic. Relativism needs defence.

2 PHILOSOPHICAL PROPOSITIONS AND RATIONAL INTUITION

Hales describes and defends a relativism of "philosophical propositions." Basically, his position claims that "[p]hilosophical propositions are true in some perspectives and false in others (*Relativism*, 1)." Philosophical propositions are typically either necessarily true or impossible. Hales passes over what separates philosophical from mathematical propositions and says that "all that matters is that we can pick out philosophical propositions ostensively (*Relativism*, 21)." He lists a number of examples of philosophical propositions including moral claims, knowledge claims, free will claims, etc.

Philosophical propositions derive from a "different methodology, namely, through an appeal to common sense, 'what we would say,' or a kind of intellectual intuition (*Relativism*, 9)." He calls this "rational intuition." Rational intuition provides philosophers with basic or noninferential propositions known to be true. Hales claims that "on pain of contradiction, we are compelled to accept that 'the method of intuition justifies some propositions' is self-justifying. In other words, a form of foundationalism must be true for intuition-driven philosophy to get off the ground (*Relativism*, 3)." He rejects the notion that philosophy should be thought of primarily as conceptual analysis and suggests that rational intuition provides philosophers with a means of acquiring beliefs or, more particularly, with a means of evaluating the truth or acceptability of propositions (*Relativism*, 19).

It's worth noting that Hales's is a modest foundationalism, eschewing indubitability for foundational propositions. Reflective equilibrium is also central in reaching knowledge via the method of rational intuition. I do not consider those features but turn to the defence of his modest foundationalism. Hales identifies the "Problem of Intuition" and suggests that its solution leads to foundationalism. The Problem of Intuition (PI) is as follows, quoting Hales:

1 If a proposition is epistemically justified, then it is justified either a priori or a posteriori. (Premise)
2 If a proposition is epistemically justified a priori, then its justification depends on the method of intuition justifying some propositions. (Premise)
3 If the proposition "the method of intuition justifies some propositions" is epistemically justified, it is not justified a posteriori. (Premise)
4 "The method of intuition justifies some propositions" is epistemically justified. (Premise)
5 Nothing is self-justifying. (Premise)

6 If "the method of intuition justifies some propositions" is epistemically justified, it is justified a priori. (From 1, 3)

7 If "the method of intuition justifies some propositions" is epistemically justified, then its justification depends on the method of intuition justifying some propositions. (From 2, 6)

8 The justification of "the method of intuition justifies some propositions" depends on the method of intuition justifying some propositions. (From 4, 7)

9 Thus "the method of intuition justifies some propositions" is not epistemically justified. (From 5, 8)

10 "The method of intuition justifies some propositions" is and is not epistemically justified. (From 4, 9)" (*Relativism*, 26, 27)

After considering premises 1–5 in some detail, Hales summarizes his position in this way:

[T]he five premises of PI form an inconsistent set. I have argued that there are only two ways to avoid commitment to the elements of this set: 1 become a radical empiricist/naturalist, give up the a priori, and abandon the use of rational intuition; or 2 accept that a modest foundationalism is true and that "the method of intuition justifies some propositions" is epistemically justified on the basis of nothing other than the method of intuition itself. The only way for a proponent of traditional a priori philosophy to avoid the problem of intuition is to reject premise 5, and by so doing, endorse a modest foundationalism. Here, then, is our choice: either a form of foundationalism is true or philosophy grounded in the use of rational intuition is bunk. (*Relativism*, 33)

Hales rejects radical empiricism/naturalism as unviable. I agree with the majority of his criticism. If Hales is right, that leaves us with rational intuition and modest foundationalism.

According to Hales, however, competitors to analytic philosophy and rational intuition exist and these competitors also provide justification for the truth of philosophical propositions. Unfortunately, philosophical propositions justified as true by the competitors conflict with those of rational intuition. Since conflicting philosophical propositions are justified as true, relativism must be the case. I very briefly turn to Hales's account of the competitors.

3 ALTERNATE SOURCES OF PHILOSOPHICAL PROPOSITIONS AND THE CHALLENGE TO PHILOSOPHICAL KNOWLEDGE

Hales argues that both Christian revelation and the ritualistic consumption of hallucinogens are sources of philosophical knowledge. He writes of the mainstream traditions in Christian theology and scholarship that

> 1 revelation is an epistemic method that yields beliefs about a class of philosophical propositions; 2 the beliefs generated by revelation are foundational ones, upon which reason then operates to produce a more elaborate theology; and 3 revelation and rational intuition are apt to produce inconsistent results – that is, one method might produce the belief that *p*, whereas the other might produce the belief that not-*p*. (*Relativism*, 50)

Hales develops a long and detailed argument for these claims, an argument we needn't enter here. Suffice it to say that he makes a good case that these three claims are true.

Hales then turns to other cultural groups. One of his examples is an Ecuadorean cultural group, the Jívaro. The Jívaro ritually use hallucinogens to discover religious truths, including philosophical ones. We needn't go into details about the use of hallucinogens for spiritual purposes, but it is fair to summarize Hales's claims by saying that the quotation in the last paragraph applies as well to the use of hallucinogens as to Christianity.

Hales considers four arguments defending rational intuition over the other methods generating philosophical propositions and finds each wanting. I'll skip these arguments and instead turn immediately to Hales's claim that the three epistemic practices are not only sources of knowledge but sources generating conflicting truths. Thus we face a trilemma:

> Given an inability to show the relative superiority of rational intuition over the two other methods we have been discussing, there are three possible responses. The first is purely epistemic: skepticism. Since we don't know which of various competing methods is the best one to use to gain justified beliefs about philosophical propositions, if we pick the best method, it is merely a matter of

luck. Therefore we have no *knowledge* of philosophical propositions. The second two responses are metaphysical: nihilism and relativism. Perhaps our failure to vindicate rational intuition over the
competition is evidence that there are no properly philosophical
propositions to be known at all. It is our attempts to acquire
justified beliefs about the nonexistent that is the problem. The final
alternative, relativism, is the idea that there are knowable philosophical propositions, but which ones are true is somehow dependent on method. Given the methodology of the Jívaro, there are
nonphysical spiritual souls, but given the methodology of rationalist, analytic philosophy, there aren't. (*Relativism*, 91)

In short, given the epistemic and metaphysical stand-off among the
three methods of reaching knowledge, we have to choose between
skepticism, nihilism, and relativism. He opts for the last.

Hales rejects "nihilism" thus: Nihilism suggests that philosophical propositions are either not philosophical or not propositions.
The former is correct if naturalism is right, for philosophical propositions are reducible to scientific claims. As already noted, Hales rejects naturalism and I agree. The latter approach says philosophical
sentences are at best akin to poetry or art and should be rejected, an
approach that Hales basically ignores, as well he should.

4 SKEPTICISM AND HALES'S
ARGUMENT FOR RELATIVISM

Hales suggests that since all attempts to show the relative superiority
of one of the three epistemic methods fail (a point with which I
agree), the skeptic might suggest that we simply can't know the deliv-
erances of the methods. Hales hazards that "skeptical arguments are
generally based on the notion that S doesn't know P because S's true
belief that P is improperly dependent on good luck (*Relativism*, 90)."
In applying this approach to putative knowledge of philosophical
propositions, suggests Hales, "we have no defensible reason to prefer
one basic method of acquiring beliefs about philosophical propositions over another basic method that gives different results. Any true
beliefs we have about philosophical propositions are accidental – it is
just good fortune if we pick the right method (*Relativism*, 91)."

Hales believes the skeptical position is too strong because it de-
feats itself. He writes that

accidentally true belief is not knowledge, and ... some similar idea is behind most familiar skeptical arguments. Yet the proposition that *accidentally true belief is not knowledge* is justifiably believed only on the basis of intuitions about the sort of [Gettier-type] cases discussed [earlier in Hale's book]. The conclusion of the skeptical argument is that we can't know any philosophical propositions as the result of rational intuition. If that is correct, then we can't know that accidentally true belief is not knowledge as the result of intuition. (*Relativism*, 91–2)

Hales schematizes the argument thus:

1 If skepticism about philosophical propositions is true, then we can't know the truth of any philosophical proposition. (Definition of skepticism)
2 Skepticism is a philosophical proposition. (Premise)
3 Therefore, *p*: if skepticism about philosophical propositions is true, we can't know it. (From 1, 2) (*Relativism*, 92)

Note Hales's claim that "it does not matter how we analyze skepticism, whether we understand it to involve accidentally true belief as presented above or in some other way ."[4] I think Hales's generalization leads him to overlook some problems with his argument.

Hales defines skepticism as follows: "If skepticism about philosophical propositions is true, then we can't know the truth of any philosophical proposition." What kind of "can't" is Hales using here? What is the force of it? Furthermore, is it that we can't or that we simply don't know any philosophical proposition? Additionally, why does he repeat the phrase "the truth of?" Does he mean to assume that the item in question is true but knowledge of it is not possible (that is, knowledge of it is impossible) or is it that we can't adjudicate whether we know, since justification (warrant or what have you) never guarantees truth and hence what we think we know may or may not be true? Obviously our thinking we know some p does not entail that p is true, or even that p is known. But these are perhaps quibbles.

The most pressing issue comes out when we take the same approach to skepticism as Hales does to global relativism and global "possibilism." One of the plausible moves Hales makes is to back off from a global relativism to a more modest one, paralleling what we generally do in backing off from overly ambitious claims about what is possible. Hales claims that "everything is possible" is false and yet that doesn't lead to a rejection of alethic modal logic. In a parallel manner he claims that "everything is relative" is false and yet that doesn't lead to a rejection of a limited metaphysical relativism and the logic Hales develops. The two global claims founder because of self-refutation whereas the less global claims do not. But then it seems natural to ask why the falsity of "everything is unknowable" must lead to a rejection of skepticism. Isn't there some parallel means out of the apparent self-refutation of skepticism Hales presents?

While rejecting "everything is possible" and "everything is relative" we can make sense out of "everything true is possibly true" and "everything true is relatively true." If we reject "everything is unknowable" (because it leads to self-refutation) why can't the skeptic retreat to "everything true is unknowably true?" This is not a path Hales considers, nor should he if he wants his overall argument for modest relativism to work. The reason is not far to seek, for the logics of possibility and relativism are different from the logic of skepticism. The former two can be given an account in terms of truth alone whereas skepticism deals not simply with truth but justification (or warrant, etc.). When we think of skepticism (about some range of propositions) as simply the claim that some range of propositions is unknowable, we often confuse the unknowability of Φ with the fact of Φ's not being known. These, of course, are not the same thing and in fact the former is definable in terms of the latter. Consider first knowability. To claim that Φ is knowable is simply to claim that Φ is possibly known, that is, Φ is known in some possible world. Of course, Φ's being possibly known does not entail Φ's truth (in the actual world) but only its truth in the possible world in which it is known. Now it could turn out that the possible world in which Φ is known is also the actual world, but one cannot presume to know that on the basis of what's been described thus far. What then is unknowability? If Φ were unknowable then there is no possible world in which Φ is known. Assuming Φ is not necessarily false, then this account of the unknowability of Φ is a very strong sort of skepticism. It is, however, the kind on which Hales's argument depends. We of course hold the truism that Φ's being known is sufficient for Φ's being true and of course reject the contrary, viz., that Φ's being true is sufficient for Φ's being known. Not only is something's being true not sufficient for its being known but by obvious extension, something's being true is not sufficient for its knowability.

Let's take this strong skepticism and ask why "everything is unknowable" (for all Φ, Φ is unknowable) is false. Why is it self-refuting? Let "skepticism is unknowable" be a substitution instance of Φ. If everything is unknowable, then so is skepticism unknowable. There is no possible world in which skepticism is known. This is more or less the conclusion Hales reaches: "if skepticism about philosophical propositions is true, we can't know it." But what exactly follows from that? Surely not that skepticism is false. Skepticism could be true and we not know it which is of course much weaker than the claim that skepticism could be true and we can't know it.

Let's now turn to consider the more cautious version of skepticism, parallel to the more cautious versions of possibility and relativism. Consider:

1 Everything true is unknowably true.

Consider also:

2 Everything true is knowably true.

While it might seem at first that 2 is true and 1 is false, in fact the opposite holds, for knowledge has to do with more than truth. For 1 to be the case, it would have to turn out that there is no possible world in which a given proposition is true in which it is also known. While this seems perhaps a little wild – surely in some possible world where Φ is true it is also known – we simply have to remember that something's being true is not the same as its being evidenced, justified, warranted, and so forth (so long as one holds a nonepistemic or realistic view of truth, at least). To avoid the potential ambiguity found in 1 I propose that

3 Everything true is unknowably true (in virtue of its truth alone).

But then similarly, 2 should be clarified by

4 Everything true is knowably true (in virtue of its truth alone).

Thus we see that 1 is true and 2 is false because 3 is true while 4 is false. These clarifications simply make explicit that to achieve knowledge, one has to add justification (warrant, etc.) to a proposition's positive truth status. Here the skeptic has the upper hand, for she never has to claim to know that skepticism is true. Skepticism's merely being true is enough to entail that we don't have knowledge, even if we don't know that we don't.

Let's briefly apply this reasoning to skepticism about philosophical propositions. According to Hales, the truth of "every philosophical proposition is unknowable" is problematic, for it itself is a philosophical proposition and thus unknowable. But why is this a problem? Its unknowability does not entail its falsehood. There is no self-refutation at this point (unlike with global relativism and global "possibilism"). Skepticism about philosophical propositions might be the case and one doesn't have to claim to know that it is in order for Hales's argument for relativism to be undermined. Hales's expectation for knowledge is perhaps too grand a goal for philosophical propositions.

In short, the consequent of Hales's first premise (the premise giving Hales's definition of skepticism) says "we can't know the truth of any philosophical proposition." What if it said simply: "we don't know whether any philosophical proposition is true or false." Furthermore, let us say this consequent is not known but only rationally surmised or believed. This skepticism is unscathed by Hales's argument and hence his overall argument for relativism fails.

Hales might reply as follows: It might be the case that skepticism is true but if we can never know it's true then it doesn't do any positive work against the argument for relativism.[2] In reply, I suggest that this simply misses the point. Hales's claim is that skepticism is self-refuting and hence isn't true and not a viable alternative to relativism. I've shown that it's not self-refuting and therefore could be true. Since it could be rationally believed (even if not known), it is a viable alternative to relativism.

5 AN ALTERNATIVE TO HALES'S MOVE TO RELATIVISM

Suppose one is not inclined toward skepticism (which I, in fact, am not). Does philosophical relativism lurk at the door? Fortunately, an alternative response to Hales is possible. Merely discovering apparent alternate ways of knowing does not provide sufficient reason to admit that all apparent ways of knowing are actual ways of knowing.

In his extended defence of the doxastic practice (DP) of the Christian, William Alston considers the challenge of religious diversity and the apparent fact that the Christian mystical practice (CMP) is on an epistemic par with many other religious doxastic practices (for example, the Hindu practice).[3] He assumes the worst case scenario wherein there are in fact no good reasons to prefer one such practice over the other. Given this embarrassment of riches, what is the Christian to do? Well, Alston certainly does not admit that all the practices give us knowledge and hence truth about ultimate reality. He does not become a relativist about religious (or philosophical) truth. Instead he argues that the Christian is rational in continuing to engage in CMP. While Alston is not speaking directly of knowledge, I think the extension is easy enough to make.

The typical means, Alston says, by which we form beliefs about the world around us is what he calls sensory practice (SP), one of many doxastic practices. SP, he argues, can only be shown rational from the "inside" much in the same way that CMP can only be shown rational from the inside. But what if there were competing sensory practices? He writes:

> Suppose that there were a diversity of sense perceptual DP's as diverse as religious experiential DP's are in fact. Suppose that in certain cultures there were a well established "Cartesian" practice of construing what is visually perceived as an indefinitely extended medium that is more or less concentrated at various points, rather than, as in our "Aristotelian" practice, as made up of more or less discrete objects of various kinds scattered about in space. Let's also suppose that in other cultures a "Whiteheadian" SP is equally socially established; here the visual field is construed as made up of momentary events growing out of each other in a continuous process. Let's further suppose that each of these practices serves its practitioners well in their dealings with the environment. We may even suppose that each group has developed physical science, in its own terms, to about as high a pitch as the others. But suppose further that we are as firmly wedded to our "Aristotelian" mode of conceptualizing what is visually perceived, as we are in fact. The Cartesian and Whiteheadian *auslander* seem utterly outlandish to us, and we find it difficult to take seriously the idea that they may be telling it like it is. However, we can find no neutral grounds on which to argue effectively

for the greater accuracy of our way of doing it. In such a situation
would it be clear that it is irrational for us to continue to form
perceptual beliefs in our "Aristotelian" way, given that the practice is proving itself by its fruits? It seems to me that quite the
opposite is the case. In the absence of any external reason for
supposing that one of the competing practices is more accurate
than my own, the only rational course for me to take is to sit
tight with the practice of which I am a master and which serves
me so well in guiding my activity in the world.[4]

Alston is here concerned only with whether such a situation shows that
engaging in a DP that has (or possibly has) real competitors that generate conflicting beliefs is irrational. Hales is not telling us that it is irrational to engage in rational intuition or the alternatives. Instead, he
reaches the much stronger conclusion, namely, that no matter which of
the three means of generating philosophical propositions one uses,
each gives us truth (relativized to perspectives, of course). So to have
Alston's counterfactual suggestions do any work against Hales's
claims, we have to say something like this: The existence of competitors for the proper way to go about reaching philosophical truths
(which give us deeply conflicting results) doesn't necessarily lead to
philosophical relativism. Why not just say that one of the three (at
best) gives us truth? We don't know which one. Yet it is rational for
me, as someone who engages in rational intuition (or Christian practice or the ritualistic use of hallucinogens) to continue to do so, even
knowing there are alternatives. I do not have to accept the competitors'
results (nor they mine). I can go on my path, assuming that my way is
what I have and that I have no external reason to worry myself about
their ways. This is an existentially bothersome position, for not knowing which perspective is the right one leaves us, perhaps, in some philosophical discomfort. Perhaps some day a philosophical genius will
show us how to adjudicate among the alternative but apparent ways of
knowing. Until then, it seems more reasonable to stick with the means
of knowing one has than to leap to Hales's philosophical relativism.[5]

6 A FINAL NOTE ON EPISTEMIC
ACCOUNTS OF TRUTH

Hales spills several bottles of ink showing that relativism is compatible
with certain epistemic accounts of truth, noting that such compatibility

is not entailment (*Relativism*, 131–42). He also argues for relativism's compatibility with various nonepistemic accounts of truth. While I think Hales is right on both matters, I think his time is not well spent on those issues. The real question is, does Hales's *defence* of philosophical relativism entail an epistemic account of truth? The answer, I believe, is "yes."

From the point of view of my criticism, Hales's defence of relativism comes down to a choice between relativism and skepticism. He thinks skepticism is not viable and hence we are left with relativism. The relativism is generated out of the fact that there are several knowledge-generating epistemic practices giving us conflicting propositional results. But Hales writes a curious thing:

> It is truth that is relative to perspectives on the present account, not epistemic properties like justification or warrant. Justification is wholly intraperspective; with respect to philosophical propositions, one gains new beliefs as a result of the methods indigenous to a specific perspective, and does not employ or take seriously basic methods from other perspectives. (*Relativism*, 133)

I find it odd for Hales to claim that justification and warrant are not relative and yet that the competing means of generating philosophical propositions are wholly intraperspective and basic (where basicality includes there being no way outside the mechanism to show it superior to the other mechanisms). If the epistemic practices are not interpespective, then one expects justification and warrant not to be interperspective. But if they are not interperspective then they should turn out to be merely intraperspective and hence relative to perspectives. I don't see how warrant or justification will not be deeply shaped by the epistemic practice itself. Thus, it seems that if truth is relative to perspectives and those truths are dependent upon the very means by which competing propositions are generated then Hales's defence of relativism forces his position into an epistemic notion of truth. Whatever perspective I'm in, I use the native generation of belief and its native approaches to justification or warrant to know my beliefs. The justification, according to Hales, is strong enough for knowledge, which in turn entails that the beliefs are true. If this doesn't slouch toward an epistemic account of truth, I don't know what does. Since I reject epistemic accounts of truth, I find Hales's position problematic on the grounds of its implied epistemic alethic theory.

7 BUILDING BLOCKS FROM HALES

What do we take away from Hales? Some negatives first. His argument, based as it is in epistemic shortcomings, is unsuccessful. Generalizing from this point, I believe we should reject any argument for pluralism rooted in human epistemic shortcomings. Second, and related, I think a solid pluralism should reject epistemic accounts of truth, something Hales does not clearly avoid. A third negative, and its importance becomes clearer below, is that God certainly cannot be merely relative to human conceptual schemes unless God's existence is positively relative to all human schemes. The main positive building block is that Hales's approach to the logic of relativism is a good one, in general at least. To say that everything true is relatively true is the right approach, an approach I take below, once some other building blocks from Lynch are added.

3

Lynch's Ontological Pluralism

Michael Lynch's pluralism is broader than Hales's relativism. Unlike Hales, however, Lynch provides no argument for his position. Rather his work is largely an explanatory view, a way of thinking about ontological pluralism.

1 WORLD VIEW

Lynch develops an understanding of world view that we can take as a starting place. A world view is

> an organic whole whose parts – one of which is what I'm calling a conceptual scheme – can best be understood in relation to their functions inside the whole ... Like our eyes, our worldview is a complex system with various components, each of which must work together if we are to see anything at all. Our worldview includes not only our *beliefs and the concepts we employ in forming our beliefs, but the interests we have that help explain why we have those concepts, the values that guide those interests, and the underlying practices and capacities that limit and define our cognitive production and intake.* [italics his][1]

Lynch's account of a world view is helpful. Indeed, that there are many world views and hence many ways the World is is very much at the heart of a viable pluralism. From our world views we make worlds.

Although Lynch is committed to pluralism, talk of making worlds is too much. Consider:

Concepts, no more than styles of painting and sense of humour, cannot come and go at will. There are causes, often beyond out control, for changes in such things. This is why it would be gravely misleading to describe metaphysical pluralism in general, or relativistic Kantianism [Lynch's view] in particular, as a view according to which we can construct (or deconstruct) reality. To construct something, either literally, as in the case of a house, or metaphorically, as in the case of a new law or statute, is to engage in a conscious, deliberate process of creation. The ebb and flow of our concepts more often takes place well beneath the surface of our thought.(*Truth*, 74–5)

For Lynch, we construct neither reality nor concepts. We cannot make a world at will. I wonder if perhaps Lynch suffers from a small lack of imagination in this matter. His worry about the "gravely misleading" language of constructing or deconstructing reality is, I think, a tempest in a teapot.

I'm more attracted to Nelson Goodman's response to a similar challenge. Goodman writes:

Scheffler also objects to the idea that we make worlds, and he is not alone in this. Much of the usual resistance can be attributed to one of two complexes. The first is the-world-is-so-wonderful-I-couldn't-do-that-well complex, otherwise known as the only-God-can-make-a-tree complex. The other is the-world-is-so-terrible-I-don't-want-to-be-blamed-for-it complex. Both rest on the fallacy that whatever we make we can make any way we like. The source of the fallacy is hard to perceive. We make chairs, computers, books, planes; and making any of these right takes skill, care, and hard work. A chair I make is likely to wobble; a book takes endless pains; I can't make a computer at all; and no one has been able to make a plane that flies far on batteries. Making right world-versions – or making worlds – is harder than making chairs or planes, and failure is common largely because all we have available is scrap material recycled from old and stubborn worlds. Our having done no better or worse is no evidence that chairs or planes or worlds are found rather than made.[2]

Goodman, although not as explicit as possible, doesn't worry about radical distinctions between making things with our hands vs our concepts. He is right about this, *pace* Lynch. However, I think Lynch is partly right when he says the "ebb and flow of our concepts more often takes place well beneath the surface of our thought." But, it seems also often to take place at the surface when we theorize, make art, or invent.

2 CONCEPTUAL SCHEMES

After rejecting both a Kantian and a Quinean model of conceptual schemes, Lynch attaches himself to what he (reluctantly) calls a Wittgensteinian model (WM). After approving of Peter Strawson's notion of a basic concept, Lynch shows how WM fits the bill for ontological pluralism. Basic concepts are

> those whose grasp is presupposed in our employing a large extent of our other, more specific concepts. These concepts are *highly general*, presumably, in that many other concepts naturally fall under them without them falling naturally under any other concept. And they are *irreducible*, Strawson says, in that they "cannot be defined away, without circularity, in terms of those other concepts to which [they] are necessarily related [Strawson's *Analysis and Metaphysics*, 23]. I would add that they are *significant* in that they play important roles within our conceptual scheme. A concept will not be basic, in other words, unless it matters to me, that is, unless going without such a concept would severely limit and reshape our conceptual life to the point of unrecognizability. [italics his] (*Truth*, 44)

Such concepts are what make up the "riverbed" propositions of Wittgenstein's notion of a conceptual scheme, viz., those that play a normative role within one's world view. According to WM, then, there are four central aspects to conceptual schemes. First, "conceptual schemes are schemes of concepts" (*Truth*, 44), that is, a conceptual scheme is "a network of general and specific concepts used in the propositions we express in language and in thought" (*Truth*, 45). It is a functional notion of concepts open to various ontological interpretations about what plays the role of concept. Second, "schemes differ to the degree that they do not share basic concepts" (*Truth*, 46). Insofar as basic concepts are not shared, the schemes allow for different specific concepts. Third, "conceptual schemes are consistent with nonsharp, fuzzy analytical/synthetic and related distinctions" and fourth, "schemes are only structurally foundationalist" (*Truth*, 46, 47).

3 CONCEPTS AS MINIMAL AND ROBUST

I suggested in chapter 1, following Alston, that alethic realism is compatible with noetic irrealism. Lynch fleshes out Alston's thought. For the pluralist, the nature of existence and objects is central, specifically when one holds an alethic realism but a noetic irrealism about the worlds. As we know, the alethic realist holds, minimally, that the content of the truth-value bearer itself gives us everything we need to specify what it takes for the truth-value bearer to be true: "'p' is true iff p." There is no noetic contribution to the truth of "p" from the person holding that p. Rather, "p" is made true by the way the World is. But how is that related to which objects exist, specifically when an object exists in one world and not in another? How can there be different objects (in different worlds) but alethic realism hold?

Lynch contends that metaphysical pluralism is consistent with alethic realism. To develop relativized Kantianism he introduces two distinctions. The first is between the crystalline and the fluid pictures of concepts and the second between minimal and robust concepts. First we need his account of concepts. Lynch writes that

> the minimal concept of a concept ... [is that] concepts are the constituents of propositions, whatever they turn out to be. Concepts compose our thoughts; in short, a concept is a particular way of thinking about something or other. So to *have a concept* involves understanding or "seeing" something a certain way, and moreover it implies the possession of certain abilities. [italics his] (*Truth*, 56)

Following Christopher Peacocke, Lynch further suggests that, "trivially, one possesses the concept F when one can correctly apply F, and one can't correctly apply a concept unless one possesses, or grasps, that concept. To grasp a concept is just to know how to apply it correctly, and to apply it correctly entails that one grasps it."[3]

The crystalline picture of concepts, according to Lynch, holds that concepts are quite clear and clearly applicable. When a concept is absolutely determinate, following Frege and the early Wittgenstein, its boundaries are always and everywhere precise. The crystalline picture of concepts is behind the notion of necessary and sufficient conditions for the application of a concept. In contrast, the fluid picture suggests concepts are not absolutely determinate but elastic and flexible. "Concepts on this view are more like sculpting clay. Unlike crystal, which breaks easily, you can stretch and pull a piece of clay in radically different directions before it tears apart. Concepts too are always subject to radical changes in shape (*Truth*, 59)." Fluid concepts are open to future application and need not be absolutely determinate. The pluralist, in saying concepts are fluid, is not saying we are confused about their application. "Rather the point is that concepts are not absolutely determinate or closed; they do not have a fixed use in every possible situation. This does not imply, however, that no concepts have determinate uses in all *actual* situations. Some concepts may be perfectly determinate in actual situations but not in all possible situations [italics his]" (*Truth*, 61). On this picture, it makes little sense to talk of "the" concept of one thing or another. Inconsistent applications of a concept occur regularly in everyday discourse.

Hales criticizes Lynch's settling on the fluid over the crystalline view, suggesting that Lynch offers no argument that the fluid view fits better with the Wittgensteinian Model. He continues: "I am not sure why [Lynch] feels the need to distance himself from [the crystalline] view."[4] Hales also suggests that the crystalline position could be used in Lynch-style pluralism by taking conceptual shifts to be changes in basic, determinate concepts. However, Hales misses an important aspect of Lynch's position, namely, his belief that two people working with two different conceptual schemes share minimal concepts (more below). The crystalline notion would require giving up basic concepts and replacing them with others, at which point the two people would potentially not share minimal concepts. If there were a criticism to make, I would point out a tension between Lynch's claim that the differences between conceptual schemes are differences in basic concepts and his claim that we share minimal concepts.

The problem is Hales's, not Lynch's. Part of the latter's motivation in keeping shared minimal concepts is to leave us all in the same World with different conceptual schemes rather than different Worlds created by the different conceptual schemes. Hales is likely to suggest not different Worlds but rather different perspectives within the World. I find his view problematic because one perspective contains

God while others don't. That seems too great a difference between perspectives within one World and certainly seems to point us toward different Worlds entirely. The latter is problematic on theism as well, for different actual worlds, which multiple Worlds seem to be, leave God a distinct entity in each World, contrary to traditional theism. More on this in chapter 6. For now I just register that Hales's position doesn't take theism's claims seriously enough. Since pluralism makes sense using Lynch's concept-based position, I'm happy to start there.

Lynch continues by distinguishing between minimal and robust concepts.

A minimal concept of F is a concept whose ordinary use "floats free" of metaphysical questions (or most metaphysical questions) surrounding Fs. It is a way of thinking about something that is neutral with regard to issues about its ontological nature ... In contrast, what I will call a *robust concept* of F is a concept whose ordinary use consists of a commitment to some particular ontological view of Fs. (*Truth*, 61)

He says, for example, that we can use the term "mind" minimally whether we are materialists or dualists. In dialogue between two philosophers, it is clear that while they disagree about what the mind is, they agree they are speaking of the same thing. Further, epistemic justification (its minimal concept) deals with what it is, plus truth, that gives us knowledge, while operative notions of epistemic justification are spelled out in internalist or externalist ways, giving a more robust concept. Robust concepts are enrichments or extensions of minimal ones.

4 OBJECTIONS TO OBJECTS: TRUTH AND EXISTENCE

How are these two distinctions – crystalline vs fluid, minimal vs robust – applied to objects, existence, and truth? These three concepts are fluid, says Lynch, and this resolves a number of issues for the pluralist holding alethic realism. First, objects and existence. The absolutist says the concept of an object must be absolute and determinate since the concept of existence is absolute and determinate. Thus, metaphysical questions about what there is can be given absolute answers. So the absolutist, driven by a crystalline picture, claims that our notions of objecthood and existence are fixed and determinate. All future circumstances of use are determined by the crystalline concept. Lynch writes: "In the case of the concept of existence, this implies that there is always one and only one correct answer to the question of whether something exists ... On the metaphysical level, it implies that everything to which the concept correctly applies shares a unique common property. Such a property would be what distinguishes existing from nonexisting objects" (*Truth*, 84).

Lynch will have none of that. The problem with distinguishing existing from nonexisting objects is that there is no property all existing objects share, for there are no objects that do not exist. Since there can be no nonexisting objects, there could be no property that would distinguish existing from nonexisting objects or exclude some objects from the class of existing objects. "Therefore, the idea that there is a property that all and only existing objects have in common, a property that distinguishes existence from nonexistence, is an idea with no content. Existence neither has, nor could have, an essence" (*Truth*, 84). But then if existence is not an absolute concept, neither is the concept of object absolute. Both existence and object are concepts flexible, fluid, and open. We learn them by reference to certain paradigms but we extend them beyond. Each of the following statements (supplied by Lynch) appeals to a different paradigm, yet all appeal to existence: 1) There are no more cookies: you've eaten them all. 2) Santa Claus does not exist. 3) There are rules in this house, young man! 4) Once upon a time, there was a very good prince. Lynch claims that in each of these, one concept is used correctly but in different paradigmatic ways. There is no way to single out one of these as "the" way to use the concept of existence. As a final point, says Lynch, he is not using the term "existence" (and by extension, the term "object") equivocally.

To summarize, Lynch claims that his argument makes Kant's point, viz., existence is not a property. "The concept of existence is that most basic of concepts. It is not a characteristic of something but is what must be presupposed for us to make sense of there being any characteristics at all" (*Truth*, 85). Not only is there no essence to existence but existence is not a property. The upshot of Lynch's discussion is that what exists – what objects there are – can be dependent upon the conceptual scheme one has without undermining a fairly stable, although fluid, concept of existence and objecthood. The latter are open and fluid, but not arbitrary or equivocal.

The question now before us is truth. Does the fluidity of "object" and "existence" apply to "truth?" One significant difference between truth and existence is that truth, according to Lynch, is a property that some propositions have and others don't. While there are no nonexistent objects, there are nontrue propositions. Truth being a property is required for a realist account of truth, according to Lynch. He says that the

T-Schema: The proposition that p is true if and only if p

should be taken as a necessary truth (*Truth*, 112). Further, "if we combine the T-schema with the intuitive principle that things are as the proposition that *p* says they are if, and only if, *p*, we get MR (minimal realism)" (*Truth*, 126).

MR: The proposition that p is true if, and only if, things are as the proposition that p says they are.

Lynch distances this minimalist view from any deflationary theory, claiming that instances of the T-schema and minimal realism are conceptual truths and yet that does not entail truth's not being a property or that "p" and "the proposition that p is true" are synonymous. "The minimal realist can hold that instances of the T-schema are *weak conceptual truths*. On this view, the two halves of a T-proposition are not identical in content, but they are necessarily equivalent (true in all the same worlds) in virtue of the concepts involved [italics his]" (*Truth*, 126). Truth, in short, is a real property.

Furthermore, MR is minimal in that it lacks the grander metaphysical implications of the correspondence theory, a more robust version of the minimal account. While the correspondence theory suggests an absolutely strict structural relationship between propositions and scheme-independent facts, MR does nothing of the sort. Hence, MR is compatible with a correspondence theory but does not entail it. Nor does MR conflict with metaphysical pluralism, for it is open to there being truths under different conceptual schemes.

Finally, note that this metaphysically "thin" account of truth requires an equally metaphysically thin account of proposition and fact. Lynch writes that "If we take any instance of the T-schema as necessarily true (e.g., the proposition that the pool is open is true if, and only if, the pool is open), then there are propositions if there are any truths at all. But granting the existence of propositions doesn't force one to take a stand on their metaphysical nature" (*Truth*, 127).

Likewise with facts. The minimal alethic realist will admit that the

F-Schema: It is a fact that p if, and only if, p

together with the T-schema, gives us:

It is a fact that p if, and only if, it is true that p.

But again, the truth minimalist can remain neutral with regard to the ontological nature of facts. A fact turns out to be whatever is the case and what is the case is so within the confines of a conceptual scheme.

Yet truth is a property. Lynch turns to Alston for aid. Alston marks the distinction between the property of truth and the concept of truth. Thus, "'deep theories' of the nature of truth are consistent with the minimalist conception" (*Truth*, 129). One can grasp the minimalist concept of truth and see its consistency with a richer, more substantive account of the property. "Alston introduces the distinction by appealing to Putnam's and Kripke's view of natural kinds, which implies that kinds (or properties) may have certain features not reflected in the concept. Just as facts about gold or anger may outrun our ordinary concepts of gold or anger, so it may be with truth" (*Truth*, 129). So, says Lynch,

Armed with the distinction between concept and property, it would seem that we can make sense of alethic pluralism. Simply put, the minimal realist can hold that there is only one concept of truth but allow that there may be more than one property that fits the constraints marked out by the concept. In this way, the nature of truth can vary across conceptual schemes even as a single, univocal concept of truth is being shared in those same schemes. (*Truth*, 130)

Adding a note of caution, Lynch says that when it comes to truth, the concept/property distinction is not as clear as with gold or anger. One can investigate properties associated with gold or anger empirically, but how does one investigate the property of truth? An a priori approach seems no better. Nevertheless, "the suggestion in [Alston's] ... account is worth retaining: the property of truth may vary from context to context. We need only add that a single minimal concept of

truth may vary as well, in the sense that it can be extended or enriched differently across contexts ... Two strikingly different and even
incompatible 'robust' concepts can both be enrichments of the same
'thin' or minimal concept" (*Truth*, 131). The MR account of truth is
both fluid and stable: fluid because it can be enriched in a variety of
contexts and stable because even the more robust accounts are extensions of the basic, minimal account. Finally, "since even robust concepts of truth have the minimalist concept as a necessary element,
realist truth will be 'preserved' across contexts. Logical inference is a
function of our minimal concept of truth (as we would expect from
the ubiquity of our basic logical concepts)" (*Truth*, 132).

In summary, Lynch says truth is a property some propositions
have while others don't. The minimal concept of truth gives us that
much. It does not give us the nature of truth, or what the property's
"fleshed out" account will be in any given conceptual scheme.

5 CONTENTS AND FACTS

Pluralism has two faces. The first is content relativism. Assertions
have content. The pluralist will say that an assertion's content is relative to a world view *cum* conceptual scheme. Lynch writes:

> On my understanding, the underlying position here is that the con-
> tent of an assertion is intrinsically related to a conceptual scheme ...
> [O]ne can distinguish propositions by their truth conditions; so an-
> other way of putting the point would be to say that truth conditions
> are determinate only within a conceptual scheme. There are no de-
> terminate propositions independent of schemes; content is internal.
> In effect, propositions, true or false, are implicitly indexed to some
> conceptual scheme or schemes ... In sum, content relativism about
> some domain is the view that if one were to give a complete and
> comprehensive analysis of a proposition in that domain, one would
> have to refer in that analysis to the conceptual scheme in which that
> proposition is expressed. (*Truth*, 21).

In contrast, content absolutism says that "what we say or think on
some occasion – the proposition we express – is not relative to any
worldview, perspective, or conceptual scheme" (*Truth*, 14).

Pluralism's second face is fact relativism, most easily introduced in
contrast to fact absolutism which says that "the totality of facts,

should it exist, is necessarily unique and nonrelative. Facts are external to worldview. Necessarily (in the strongest, most metaphysical sense of the word), there can be one and only one totality of facts; there is one and only one way the world is" (*Truth*, 15). In contrast, fact relativism says facts are "internal to conceptual schemes, or ways of dividing the world into objects, among which there can be equally acceptable alternatives" (*Truth*, 22). Since Lynch uses a neutral notion of facts, he adds that we could equally well talk of states of affairs or objects being relative to conceptual schemes. In short, what there is in the World is there only within the context of a conceptual scheme. "For the metaphysical pluralist ... every reporting of an ontological fact is done within a conceptual scheme or metaphysical perspective. There is no scheme-neutral way of making a report about the world. It would be a mistake to search for the scheme that tells it like it 'really' is – there is no such thing" (*Truth*, 22).

Lynch importantly observes that although no contents or facts are free from a conceptual scheme, conceptual schemes can overlap. They need not be incommensurable. Schemes are incommensurable "only to the degree to which they do not share concepts, basic concepts in particular" (*Truth*, 53). Thus people speaking from one scheme to another can understand one another.[5] Further, there being no absolute facts or contents is compatible with facts or contents showing up relative to every conceptual scheme. He writes that "it is rarely, if ever, noticed that metaphysical pluralism is consistent with there being some *virtual absolutes* – facts that do not obtain independently of conceptual schemes but that *do obtain within every scheme*. Pluralism is similarly consistent with virtually absolute propositions, or propositions that are relative to every scheme [italics his]" (*Truth*, 142). This last insight is, I think, very important and a key building block in showing how theism plays a central role in a better pluralism.

6 A PROBLEM FOR PLURALISM: THE CONSISTENCY DILEMMA

A major issue facing any ontological pluralism is what Lynch calls the "consistency dilemma." This challenge claims that pluralism is entirely unmotivated and, in fact, not even possible. Lynch writes:

The pluralist alleges that there can be more than one true account of the world. Now consider two such metaphysical perspectives,

A and B, that meet whatever criteria the pluralist requires for perspectives to be "equally" true. Either these perspectives are consistent with each other or they are not. If not, then by virtue of
her statement that A and B are equally true, the pluralist is in
danger of being committed to the truth of contradictions. [The]
... pluralist avoids this ... problem by relativization. On her view,
facts and content are relative: A can be the case relative to C_1,
and –A relative to C_2 without contradiction. But ... this move
fails to get the pluralist off the hook. The real problem for pluralism is not the *inconsistency* but the *consistency of schemes*. In
other words, given the consistency between A and B that the relativization of fact apparently implies, the pluralist must explain
how it is legitimate to talk about *incompatible* but equally true
schemes in the first place. Specifically, if A and B are consistent,
then either (1) A and B are expressing the same absolute truths in
different languages (they are "notational variants") or (2) A and
B are simply concerned with different subject matters altogether.
But even the most hard-headed absolutist could grant either possibility, for both (1) and (2) are consistent with absolutism! [ital-
ics his] (*Truth*, 129)

That was the "content" version of the dilemma, but there is a "fact"
version as well. It issues in the "many-world" problem in which

the pluralist is committed either to the existence of many worlds of
facts – one world for each conceptual scheme – or to the existence
of the one world of facts that all conceptual perspectives are perspectives of. If the former is the case, if there is one world for each
conceptual scheme, then not only has the pluralist adopted a bi-
zarre ontology on which worlds are like bubbles insulated from
each other by the fragile barriers of concepts, she has apparently
committed herself to absolutism. On such a picture, there will be
one true story (an absolutely true account) of each individual
world. (And the conjunction of those stories will be an absolute account of every world.) On the other hand, if the pluralist holds that
there is only one world that all schemes represent, then presumably
there will also be one true account of that world. (*Truth*, 29–30)

The consistency challenge is thought by some to be the death blow
to pluralism.

The consistency challenge and a straightforward reply are made intuitively clear by Putnam's example, repeated by Lynch. Consider Smith and Johnson. Smith and Johnson, let us say, are purveyors of marbles who toy with ontology on the side. Looking in a bag containing three marbles, Johnson, who holds to mereological objects, counts exactly three objects while Smith, who is no mereologist, counts only but exactly seven objects. How is a pluralist to handle this situation? The pluralist, says Lynch, needs to affirm all four of the following propositions:

1 Smith and Johnson are expressing distinct propositions.
2 Smith and Johnson are expressing incompatible propositions.
3 Smith and Johnson are expressing true propositions.
4 Smith and Johnson are not employing completely different concepts of "object" or "exist" or "number"; they are not talking past one another.

The first proposition is true because "exactly three" implies "not exactly seven" and hence two distinct propositions are being expressed. Four is true because both ontologists share the same concepts of object and existence even though they are extending the concepts in two different, if quite incompatible, directions. Three is true because "just as it can be true that x is a game in relation to one paradigm example of a game and false relative to another paradigm without this fact causing so much as a whisper of cognitive dissonance, so too is the same move completely acceptable with 'exist' or 'object.'" (*Truth*, 92).

That, of course, leaves 2. The consistency dilemma and its reply enters at precisely this point. Quoting Lynch,

> According to the pluralist, [Smith and Johnson] are (or could be) extending their shared minimal concept of an object differently. Thus the propositions they are expressing are relative to different conceptual schemes and are therefore logically consistent. At the same time, there is a clear and important sense in which the pair of propositions *are* incompatible: *if these propositions were relative to the same scheme, they would be inconsistent*. This fact is necessarily true of that pair of propositions: in every possible world where these propositions are relative to the same scheme, only one is true. And it is in precisely this sense that Johnson and Smith are

rightly said to be expressing consistent but incompatible propositions. [italics his] (*Truth*, 93)

Thus is the consistency dilemma overcome.

The consistency dilemma claims that pluralism is unmotivated
and cannot, in fact, even be stated as a distinct view. The absolutist
claims that insofar as two propositions are relative to more than
one scheme, there must be some absolute framework in which they
can both be handled. If they are not relative to more than one
scheme but only to their particular schemes, then they "talk past
each other" and are not really inconsistent. But as Lynch argues, the
propositions involved are not absolute propositions. The truth of
the propositions being relative to more than one scheme does not
entail that they are independent of all schemes. Minimally a proposition can be relative to more than one scheme, although robustly it
cannot. In short, Lynch allows for a minimalist, alethic realism with
a pluralist ontology and the consistency dilemma is resolved by appeal to possible world talk. It turns out to be a necessary truth that
in every possible world where any two contradictory propositions
are relative to the same scheme, only one is true. He can admit this
sort of necessary truth precisely because he hasn't lost a realist account of truth. Even though truth is only construed minimally, it is
still construed realistically.

7 OTHER CHALLENGES

Several other challenges have been laid at Lynch's feet. Steven Hales
notes two things. He writes: "Lynch's entire motivation for metaphysical pluralism was the idea that metaphysical debates are intrac-
table. Yet here he is coming down on one side of the metaphysical
debate over concepts."[6] While Hales goes on to suggest that Lynch
might take the position that some metaphysical debates are tractable
and some are not since the entire motivation toward pluralism is the
intractability of such debates, and since there is no way to tell which
are tractable and which are not, no absolutist will accept the apparent arbitrariness in picking the fluid notion of concepts.

I think Hales's argument goes astray here and the reason is not
far to seek. Hales attributes to Lynch what Hales calls the "Intractability Argument for Pluralism." But I do not see an argument of
this sort in Lynch's book. In fact, it seems pretty clear that Lynch is

merely trying to make pluralism coherent rather than showing it to be true. While he does mention the intractability of metaphysical argument, he does not use that intractability as an argument for pluralism but rather simply as a kind of puzzle to which pluralism, by Lynch's measure, provides a coherent response. Yet Hales reports that "I confess it is a bit disappointing when an author writes a whole book showing that his thesis has every virtue short of truth."[7] It seems to me, however, unfair to ask Lynch to do something he never set out to do. While Hales may be right that that is not enough (and in the end I agree with Hales that we need a reason to be pluralists), Lynch cannot be faulted for doing something he never tried to do. I don't think Lynch's position runs into "deep" trouble, at least on this point.

Hales brings another criticism. In order to get a significant pluralism off the ground and avoid the consistency dilemma, Lynch has to show that Smith and Johnson are expressing distinct propositions, that the propositions are incompatible, that the propositions are true, and that Smith and Johnson are not employing completely different concepts of "object" or "exist" or "number." In short, Lynch has to show that Smith and Johnson are not talking past one another. Lynch's solution involves the fluidity of the concept "object." Hales suggests that we arrive at a picture like this

The left circle is Smith's "there are exactly seven objects in the bag" while the right is Johnson's "there are exactly three objects in the bag." The shaded area is the shared content. Hence, according to Lynch, the consistency problem is overcome. But Hales finds a problem here.

Either this shared content is absolute (minimal propositional content is the same in all conceptual schemes) or it is not. If it is not absolute, then, sticking with the example above, there are conceptual schemes in which the sentence "there are exactly three objects in the bag" expresses completely different propositions with no overlapping content. If Smith and Johnson possess such conceptual schemes, then this throws us back to the consistency dilemma ... Suppose then that shared content is absolute. This means that there is no conceptual scheme in which the concept of an object does not entail an object being whatever exists. Put another way, if shared content is absolute, then no conceptual scheme can countenance nonexistent objects. Not only is this dubious ... but it hardly seems congruent with metaphysical pluralism.[8]

As I will argue below, I think Lynch is wrong in taking the position that "objects are whatever exists," so that there are no nonexistent objects. But more telling against Hales's criticism is the fact that Lynch introduces the notion of virtual absolutes in which case some minimal concepts can hold in every conceptual scheme, along with some propositions. Hales rightly quotes Lynch when he says "every proposition is relative but not every concept." Lynch goes on to claim that his minimal concept of truth is not relative but absolute and this, says Hales, is inconsistent with pluralism. While Hales may be strictly correct given what Lynch actually says, Lynch's potential reply is not far to seek and his position easily redeemed.

Lynch claims that pluralism is consistent "with virtually absolute propositions, or propositions that are relative to every scheme" (*Truth*, 138, 142). So while he is comfortable saying that every proposition is relative, with some of them being virtually absolute and hence relative to every scheme, he is apparently, given the sentence Hales quotes, not comfortable with the concept of truth being a virtual absolute. But I fail to see why Lynch feels this discomfort. If some propositions can be virtually absolute, that is, relative to every conceptual scheme, why can't some concepts be virtually absolute? And if they can, then it seems Hales's criticism fails to meet its mark. This minor, although important, adjustment to Lynch's position overcomes the inconsistency challenge brought by Hales and does not seem to undermine anything important in ontological pluralism.

A third criticism, also related to minimal vs robust concepts, comes from Gregory Ganssle. He writes:

Now if Lynch is claiming that the physicalist and the dualist share the same minimal concept of mind but not the same robust concept, then their disagreement is one about the robust concept of the mind. Starting from the shared minimal concept, it is the beliefs each has about the mind that pushes this minimal concept of mind in one of two different directions. Lynch does not elaborate how this extension of the shared minimal concept works. Presumably, the physicalist extends his minimal concept so that it includes the claim that the mind is entirely a physical thing. The dualist does not include this item in his concept of the mind. It may be the case that the beliefs that push their concepts in opposite directions are not about the mind in particular but about reality as a whole. The physicalist may believe that there are no non-physical objects. This belief will push his concept of the mind in the physicalist direction. If extending the minimal concepts does not work in this way, then it is not clear how it is that the disagreement is about the robust concept of the mind. If the disagreement is a conceptual one, then for the physicalist, it turns out that it is a conceptual truth that the mind is physical. This is a conceptual truth, though, only because the physicalist has wedded his concept with this metaphysical position.[9]

Ganssle goes on to suggest that "it would be more clear to drop the distinction between the minimal concept and the robust concept and to think rather in terms of our *concept* of something (e.g., the mind) and our thoughts about the *nature* of that thing [italics his]."[10] Ganssle then suggests that in fact the physicalist and dualist disagree not at the level of concepts but at the level of beliefs.

I think the right response here is to note that Ganssle correctly describes how concepts are extended from minimal to robust. It occurs basically through the larger metaphysical position held by the physicalist or the dualist. Of course the physicalist has wedded his concept of the mind with a physicalist position. That is one of the functions of world views in Lynch's overall approach. It turns out then to be no substantial criticism to suggest that Ganssle's approach is more clear. While it may be more conducive to an absolutist metaphysic, that is no reason for Lynch to take Ganssle's approach.

However, we do need a real motivation, some sort of argument, to move us toward ontological pluralism. Lynch's book was not written to argue for the conclusion of pluralism but such an argument would perhaps give critics such as Ganssle a reason to see why Lynch is doing what he is doing rather than simply respond with what appears to be a more or less typical absolutist reply: "Surely the dualist or the physicalist is wrong about the nature of the mind. Perhaps they both are mistaken."[11] If there is a reason to think pluralism the best way to understand the World, then we need it in front of us. I'll return to such an argument in chapter 7.

Ganssle raises another criticism. In short, he says Lynch's solution to the consistency dilemma isn't much of a solution. To Lynch's proposed counterfactual approach, Ganssle replies

> I want to say, "So what?" If Smith and Johnson agree about mereology, they would both think there were only three objects in the bag. This counterfactual analysis of inconsistency is wrong-headed. It seems clear that Johnson rejects Smith's theory and their theories are incompatible. How they answer the question is partially dependent upon what they hold. One theory is better than the other and Smith (or Johnson) ought to rethink his whole view. I do not think that Lynch can have it both ways. If there is real disagreement, both statements cannot be true. If both statements are true, they cannot be in real conflict. Counterfactual disagreement is not real disagreement.[12]

So far forth, it appears Ganssle has only restated the absolutist position and that is no challenge to pluralism. Furthermore, that counterfactual disagreements are not real disagreements seems to need further explanation. Why isn't counterfactual disagreement enough to deal with the consistency dilemma?

Lynch replies to this issue directly in his rejoinder to Ganssle but it is worth noting a later argument by Ganssle that is also resolved by Lynch's response. Ganssle writes:

> If [the] pluralist must be able to hold all four propositions about the dispute between Smith and Johnson, Lynch may find himself in trouble. If we grant Lynch his compatibility argument, then how many objects are in the bag is relative to conceptual scheme. Smith and Johnson both assert true propositions. What makes each of these propositions true is the facts about the number of objects. Since Smith and Johnson are standing in *different* schemes, they are talking about *different* facts. Fact S is the fact, according to Smith's scheme, that there are exactly seven objects in the bag. Fact J is the fact that there are exactly three. If these are each facts, then propositions about these facts cannot be in

conflict simply because the propositions are about different facts. [italics his][13]

Ganssle concludes that Smith and Johnson are talking past each other on Lynch's view because even though they may have very similar concepts Smith and Johnson are talking about different facts.

In reply to Ganssle's charge about the counterfactual analysis of inconsistency, Lynch writes,

> So on the view I defend in [*Truth in Context*], we can understand the dispute between Smith and Johnson either minimally or robustly. Robustly speaking, they don't disagree, since they are using distinct concepts, and their propositions are indexed to distinct schemes. Minimally speaking, however, they do disagree, for they are applying the same minimal concept of an object in inconsistent ways. *Further, this latter fact can be stated in both schemes.* Consequently, there remains a real sense in which our metaphysicians' assertions are incompatible – even when relativized to distinct schemes. For it is true from both perspectives that were Smith and Johnson to enrich the concept of an object in similar ways – that is, *were their propositions relative to the same scheme – they would be inconsistent* [italics his].[14]

But we can also see that this handles Gannsle's argument about Smith and Johnson talking about different facts. If, minimally speaking, they are applying the minimal concept of an object in inconsistent ways, then surely they are uttering propositions about facts that are also inconsistent and this can be stated in both schemes. In the end, I don't believe either Hales's or Gannsle's criticisms do much damage to Lynch's position.

4

Goodman's Irrealism

I move now to consider Nelson Goodman's position. Once again, I make no attempt to be exhaustive, presenting only what I take as needful to develop my own position below. However, Goodman is not nearly as clear as Lynch or Hales. So, on occasion I force some clarity where, in fact, there is none in Goodman's work itself, or sometimes I simply make pronouncements about what I think Goodman is after or should have been after. Before we begin, recall the terminological point that I refer to Goodman's worlds as "G-worlds" to distinguish them as extensionalist actual worlds (with no World "underneath") from the sense of worlds that I propose whose status is rooted in the singular actual World.

1 PLACING GOODMAN ON THE REALISM/ IRREALISM MAP

Goodman is not easily placed on the realism/irrealism map, for many reasons. The main one is his own rejection of the terms of the discussion. Perhaps better stated, he simply sits askew the issues. Of *Ways of Worldmaking* he writes,

Few familiar philosophical labels fit comfortably a book that is at odds with rationalism and empiricism alike, with materialism and idealism and dualism, with essentialism and existentialism, with mechanism and vitalism, with mysticism and scientism, and with most other ardent doctrines. What emerges can perhaps be described as a radical relativism under rigorous restraints that eventuates into something akin to irrealism.[1]

As this description indicates, placing Goodman's views is difficult. He does, reluctantly, use the label "irrealism." In fact, I take the term from his work. Irrealism, says Goodman, is a "radical relativism under rigorous restraints." What kind of relativism and what kind of restraints? His answer is neither simple nor straightforward, for at least the following reasons. First, he says that his "world-versions" and "worlds" (G-worlds) are not all truth-related. So it isn't that various G-worlds (or world-versions) simply contradict one another (and hence generate a relativistic pluralism) but that some G-worlds are not even truth-relevant. Second, his commitment to nominalism – sometimes taken by critics to undermine his claims to relativism – is not, Goodman reports, logically connected to his irrealism. Third, Goodman qua irrealist finds both realism and idealism deplorable as well as acceptable. What's to be made of that? Isn't irrealism just a kind of idealism? Finally, Goodman's writing does not always lend itself to easy interpretation. I'll consider the first three of these reasons below, generally leaving the fourth to its own fate.

The first thing to note about Goodman's position is that while truth is important, it is not the only important thing. Truth, for Goodman, is only one of many "rightnesses." We know that truth is fundamentally connected to the linguistic or what is expressed or expressible by the linguistic. Sentences, utterances, assertions have each been suggested as the bearers of truth, although the proposition is the most popular candidate. The reason is not far to seek, for sentences, utterances, and assertions all communicate propositions. To communicate propositions, we use the linguistic.[2] Pictures, gestures, or dances, in contrast, do not communicate propositions and hence are not true, at least not in the sense of sentences or assertions. While dances, gestures, etc. can perhaps be true in some sense, they are not in the literal sense most of us consider when we say a proposition is true.

Many pluralists cash out their positions only in terms of truth and the linguistically expressible. Lynch, for example, says concepts are the constituents of propositions and then spells out his view in terms of concepts and conceptual schemes. While propositions themselves are not linguistic, whatever they turn out to be, we know they are expressed linguistically. Propositions are not expressed by pictures, gestures, or dances. Although we can utter truths about pictures, gestures, and dances, they are not themselves true (or false). Language is the realm in which truth is expressed, not paint or motion. Since truth, in the end, seems to be fundamentally connected to the linguistic, it perhaps is odd to understand pluralism in terms other than truths and their linguistic expressions.

But this is precisely what Goodman does by not limiting the conceptual to the linguistic, although he of course admits that many of our concepts are linguistically expressed. Inspired by Goodman and Catherine Elgin, I briefly introduced several non-linguistic accounts of concepts in the first chapter. My suggestions were rooted in taking cognition broadly so that we construe any type of symbol system (including, but not limited to, the linguistic) as a means of conceptualizing things. In the opening of their book Goodman and Elgin give a partial account of concepts by writing that

> reconception is not confined to correction, and does not always result in replacement; it may yield illuminating and important alternatives to, rather than substitutes for, a standing conception. Nor are concepts and conceptions exclusively linguistic; they may be pictorial, diagrammatic, gestural, kinaesthetic or of any other sort. Musical variations are reconceptions that are neither verbal nor replacements for the original version. Moreover, whether the concepts involved are verbal or not, reconception does not always amount to alteration in what is named or described or otherwise denoted; it may be in what is exemplified or is expressed or is alluded to indirectly. Thus a change in style or even in vocabulary may sometimes effect a significant reconception.[3]

Concepts are not merely linguistic and although always symbolic in some way, many more kinds of symbols and symbol systems exist than the merely linguistic.

Goodman and Elgin point out that human culture is rich in symbol and we need to pay attention to the many varieties of ways in which we symbolize. Once we do so, we notice that some symbol systems allow little room for talk of truth. Once again, statements are true (or false) but pictures and gestures are not. Yet the latter symbolize in a variety of ways. Thinking is not always linguistic. So while it may be true, as Lynch says, that "concepts compose our thoughts," it is less obvious that concepts are the constituents of propositions, at least if we take his meaning as partly definitional of what a concept is.[4] Concepts are sometimes the constituents of things other than propositions. For Goodman, irrealism is a kind of pluralism where there are many ways things are, some that literally conflict with each other (linguistically based G-worlds) and others contrary to each other on grounds other than truth.

So Goodman's view is irrealistic in the same general way Lynch's position is, viz., it rejects the notion that the things in the World are independent of significant human noetic (qua linguistically expressible) contribution. Stated positively, Goodman holds that human noetic feats significantly contribute to the way things are in the various and sundry G-worlds. Yet Goodman's view is richer and broader than Lynch's insofar as Goodman takes the noetic to be not simply linguistically expressible but more broadly symbolic. Linguistically expressible conceptual schemes are only one kind of symbol system. Since many symbol systems exist, we cannot countenance only the linguistic.

2 CONFLICTING PAIRS AND FRAMES OF REFERENCE

Goodman is never shy about philosophical matters and, like a gutsy gambler, places his bet, betting "the World" against a handful of pairs. But this is no bluff, for his pairs take all. He provides pairs of statements that are commonly held as true, even though, when taken as pairs, they are apparently contradictory. There are, he says, many pairs of conflicting claims that are true descriptions of the way things are. One of his favourite examples is the pair "the sun is moving" and "the sun is not moving." Goodman says both these claims are true. But how can they both be true, since they seem, straightforwardly, to contradict one another?

The problem arises only if we assume there is some one thing having both properties, "moving" and "not moving," said of it and that what is said of the object is said in the same way, referring to the same time, etc. Truth is truth, so if some thing A is moving and A is also not moving (and we mean the same thing by "moving" in each statement, "A" in each statement, etc.), we get a contradiction. To avoid contradiction, Goodman concludes that there is no fact of the matter independent of frames of reference. Both "the sun is moving" and "the sun is not moving" are true, and if they are, they must be true in different G-worlds, and hence of different things.

Goodman further claims that no resolution is found by saying that one statement is true in one frame of reference while false in some other frame of reference, if one takes these frames of reference to exist in a singular realist "World." This kind of relativization doesn't help us resurrect a singular "World," that is, a singular fact of the matter about the sun. The reason?

> Frames of reference ... seem to belong less to what is described than to systems of description: and each of the two statements [the sun is moving, the sun is not moving] relates what is de- scribed to such a system. If I ask about the world, you can offer to tell me how it is under one or more frames of reference; but if I insist that you tell me how it is apart from all frames, what can you say? We are confined to ways of describing whatever is described. Our universe, so to speak, consists of these ways rather than of a world or of worlds. (*Ways*, 2–3)

Frames of reference are part of the world-version, the thought, the ideas, the structure for how we organize a G-world and not part of that G-world itself. It's not as if a frame of reference is built into a G-world, we discover it, and then describe the world-version. If any frame of reference is so discovered, all are. Rather, we have a world-version and behold, the G-world correlated to it is configured a certain way. Thus, relativizing motion to frames of reference won't, says Goodman, give us a way out.

In this quotation, the "what is described" (the sun) is in the (described) G-world or just is the G-world itself. The "systems of description" are (in these two cases, "the sun is moving" and "the sun is not moving") linguistic constructions used to describe, in this case, the sun but more generally, one presumes, many other things as well. The frames of reference that are supposed to resolve the conflict between the two statements are not in the (described) G-world but in the linguistic constructions. In short, Goodman keeps the ontology (what actually is) distinct from what determines the ontology (the frame of reference embedded in a descriptive system).

Goodman and Elgin introduce the following terms:

> In describing an object, we apply a label to it. Typically that la- bel belongs to a family of alternatives that collectively sort the objects in a domain. Such a family of alternatives may be called a *scheme*, and the objects it sorts its *realm*. Thus "B-flat" be- longs to a scheme that orders the realm of musical tones; and

"elephant" to one that orders the realm of animals. A *system* is a scheme applied to a realm [italics theirs]. (*Reconceptions*, 7)

Some related claims are 1 "The alternatives of which a scheme consists need not be mutually exclusive." 2 "A scheme typically orders a realm in terms of implicit alternatives." 3 "A scheme need not be exclusively associated with a single realm." 4 "A single realm is subject to alternative schematizations." 5 "Systems are not to be identified with languages" nor are all systems linguistic.

So the sun is an object to which we assign the label "sun." It is one of a family of labels we use collectively to sort the things in the domain of astronomical entities. So the scheme of astronomical labels sorts the realm of astronomical entities. "Sun" belongs to a scheme that orders the realm of astronomical entities. Thus we have a system of astronomical terms applying to astronomical entities. But there can be more than one system. One system has a heliocentric frame of reference, the other geocentric. (Goodman elsewhere refers to frames of reference as precepts of systems, but notes that the line between a precept and a belief is neither sharp nor stable (*Ways*, 17).) Thus whether the sun is moving or the sun is not moving depends on the system. What makes "the sun is moving" true is that the sun is moving. But how could one describe whether the sun is moving, independent of a frame of reference, indeed, the whole scheme and system?

The heliocentric frame of reference and the geocentric frame of reference are part of a system for Goodman. In this case the system is linguistic and fairly literally (rather than metaphorically) so. Both linguistic frames of reference are equally legitimate ways of constructing G-worlds, for we can choose which one to use for one purpose or another. If the linguistic constructions are actually in "the World" then conflicts ensue. To avoid such conflicts, we must understand the (various) G-worlds to be made out of various ways of description. Statements within G-worlds are true (supposing the world actually is the way the description says it is) but to avoid contradictions, the G-worlds themselves must be kept separate ontologically from one another. Furthermore, since no one would deny both the geocentric and the heliocentric frames of reference, and since they are both perfectly meaningful, useful, and true, there must be some way of avoiding contradictions within "the World."

The only way, says Goodman, is to break "the World" asunder and announce the plurality of G-worlds. There is no one, singular way "the World" is, but multiple actual G-worlds.

But with Goodman, the story is almost always more complicated. The point isn't just that frames of reference are part of a system that is itself linguistic. Some world-versions are not linguistic at all, and hence some G-worlds are not linguistically describable. He writes:

> The alternative descriptions of motion, all of them in much the same terms and routinely transformable into one another, provide only a minor and rather pallid example of diversity in accounts of the world. Much more striking is the vast variety of versions and visions in the several sciences, in the works of different painters and writers, and in our perception as informed by these, by circumstance, and by our own insights, interest, and past experiences ... Here we have no neat set of frames of reference, no ready rules for transforming physics, biology and psychology into one another, and no way at all of transforming any of these into Van Gogh's vision, or Van Gogh's into Canaletto's. Such of these versions as are depictions rather than descriptions have no truth-value in the literal sense, and cannot be combined by conjunction ... The dramatically contrasting versions of the world can of course be relativized: each is right under a given system – for a given science, a given artist, or a given perceiver and situation. Here again we turn from describing or depicting "the world" to talking of descriptions and depictions, but now without even the consolation of intertranslatability among or any evident organization of the several systems in question. (*Ways*, 3)

Goodman's overarching point is the existence of various symbol systems, some linguistic, some not. These systems can generate not only apparent contradictions (for linguistic systems) but other ways of being disparate as well (for artistic systems or perceptual systems). One can avoid neither the contradictions nor the disparatenesses by discussing frames of reference. World-versions come in all kinds and hence provide for all kinds of disparateness. Thus we can't easily compare paintings and their worlds to novels and their worlds to the sciences and their worlds. Even within each of these "categories" one finds difficulty in comparing.

Goodman vacillates between G-world talk and world-version talk. Sometimes he seems more interested in world-versions than G-worlds: "Our universe, so to speak, consists of these *ways* rather than of a world or of worlds" (*Ways*, 3). At other times he seems interested in G-worlds rather than their versions, as when he claims that the G-worlds are actual and not merely possible worlds. In addition, he talks about "right" (or in other places, "true") versions.

> Yet doesn't a right version differ from a wrong one just in applying to the world, so that rightness itself depends upon and implies a world? We might better say that "the world" depends upon rightness. We cannot test a version by comparing it with a world undescribed, undepicted, unperceived, but only by other means … While we may speak of determining what versions are right as "learning about the world," "the world" supposedly being that which all right versions describe, all we learn about the world is contained in right versions of it: and while the underlying world, bereft of these, need not be denied to those who love it, it is perhaps on the whole a world well lost. For some purposes, we may want to define a relation that will so sort versions into clusters that each cluster constitutes a world, and the members of the cluster are versions of that world; but for many purposes, right world-descriptions and world-depictions and world-perceptions, the ways-the-world-is, or just versions, can be treated as our worlds. (*Ways*, 3–4)

Goodman never tells us which is more important, G-worlds or world-versions, nor is he apparently interested in doing so. When what's really important is world-versions, he talks of them as linguistic and hence descriptive, or painted and hence depicted, or seen and hence perceived. Sometimes we might want to talk about "the World" and that, too, is fine with Goodman. At other times we get along well with just versions or ways. But Goodman always avers that there simply is no way things are (independent of a symbol-system context).

Systems of description are thus ways of conceptualizing things, whether in scientific or empirical theorizing or just everyday descriptive talk. Yet there are other symbol systems too. These involve artistic expression (which involves not truth and falsity but other kinds of rightness of rendering such as metaphorical truth, appropriateness of purpose, fittingness to a canvas, etc.) or even seeing (which involves perceptual rightness.) Goodman is not simply an epistemizing irrealist but a conceptualizing, emoting, and perceiving irrealist as well.

Goodman's vacillation among talk of universe, world, ways, and world-versions is rather cavalier. His attitude seems to imply that there are no important differences. This appears intentional on his part, for in the final analysis, all these terms are conventional for Goodman. There is no one right way to use them. From Goodman and Elgin: "Our talk of a world amounts to talk of a true or right world version" (*Reconceptions*, 51). Yet Goodman speaks in other places as if there are many actual (G-)worlds. I'll return to this in section 4.

3 IRREALISM, NOMINALISM, AND OTHER "ISMS"

Let's begin this section by considering Goodman's response to the following challenge. As he puts it, some have said that his nominalism is "incompatible, or at least uncomfortable, with my irrealistic relativism. Why should such a relativism not be as open to platonistic as to nominalistic world-versions? Since for the thoroughgoing irrealist everything, including the individual, is an artefact, why does Goodman not find classes or classes of classes, for example, as admissible as individuals?"[5]

On the surface, Goodman easily handles this challenge. If he thinks, as he does, that his irrealism is consistent with various kinds of realism and idealism (a point I'll return to below), it is not a reach to see that it is consistent with nominalism and platonism. But it is worth getting a clear picture of his nominalism, for I later argue that there are greater problems here than Goodman admits. In *Of Mind and Other Matters* Goodman writes,

One thread of a [realist] argument ... [is this:] that "white" applies to certain things does not make them white; rather "white" applies because they are white. Plausible enough but misleading. Granted, I cannot make these objects red by calling them red – by applying the term "red" to them. But on the other hand, the English language makes them white just by applying the term "white" to them; application of the term "white" is not dictated by their somehow being antecedently white, whatever that might mean. A language that applies the term "blanc" to them makes them blanc; and a language if any that applies the term "red" to them makes them red.

Goodman writes further that the realist "seems to hold that a predicate applies initially to a property as its name, and then only derivatively to the things that have that property." But, says Goodman, "the nominalist cancels out the property and treats the predicate as bearing a one-many relationship directly to the several things it applies to or denotes" (*Of Mind*, 49). He continues: "Thus I think that in one clear sense things are white because they are so-called, that the application of a one-place predicate to many things requires no supporting properties, and that predicates classify (and I should even say *make*) and sometimes order individuals rather than naming properties or denoting classes or sequences [italics his]" (*Of Mind*, 49). Goodman's nominalism thus denies properties, affirming individuals as they are made, classified, and ordered by predicates. Properties and classes are not necessary.

A helpful comparison is Quine's position. Quine's nominalism countenances nothing abstract but only concrete physical objects; Goodman's countenances no classes but only individuals. Goodman continues:

[T]he matter is more complex than that. A physical object is not in and by itself, apart from all systematic construction, an individual or a class or a class of classes. A football may be construed as an individual or as a class of molecules or as a class of molecule-classes of atoms, etc. Nominalism for Quine is thus better described as barring all but physical objects and *also* barring treatment of physical objects otherwise than as individuals [italics his]. (*Of Mind*, 51)

Goodman demurs from Quine's abandonment of nominalism. There are two restrictions: one bars all but physical objects and one bars treatment of physical objects as anything other than individuals. The first excludes entities of certain kinds, the second certain ways of constructing. Quine drops the second but retains the first.

Goodman will not have it. To limit the way things are ahead of time is not a complete nominalism. He allows only individuals but puts no limits on what can be taken as an individual. His nominalism, in other words, "bars the composition of different entities out of the same elements" (*Of Mind*, 52). Within a given nominalistic system, for example, one in which A, B, and C are indivisible individuals, only four (at most) other entities may be admitted under that system, viz., those composed of A + B, of A + C, of B + C, and of A + B + C. One can never have more than $2^n - 1$ entities, when the initial number of atomic individuals is n. Whatever one calls these compositions – wholes, sums, or even classes – does not matter, so long as none contain exactly the same atomic individuals. This, says Goodman, is a nominalism with only individuals. In contrast, a platonism that allows the same individuals to make up two separate compositions (as when A is used with A + B to make a new composition and then B is used with A + B to make a new composition) violates nominalism constrained only by individuals. There is no reality of classes or properties, but only individuals.[6]

·How does this nominalism fit with irrealism? Goodman writes:

> The answer should be evident in the very formulation of nominalism as free to take anything as an individual but not to take anything as other than an individual. My sort of relativism holds that there are many right world-versions, some of them conflicting with each other, but insists on the distinction between right and wrong versions. Nominalism, leaving choice of basis wide open, imposes a restriction on how a right version may be constructed from a basis. A right version must be well-made, and for a nominalism that requires construing all entities as individuals. (*Of Mind*, 52–3)

In short, "Irrealism and nominalism are independent but entirely compatible. Indeed, nominalism neither conflicts with nor implies nor is implied by my other philosophical views" (*Of Mind*, 30). As such, Goodman's irrealism, on his own account, can be taken in a number of directions: a restricted platonism, idealism, and even realism! Since all these terms are purely conventional, there is no restriction vis-à-vis irrealism, as to what is allowed.

Goodman says a great many things, not all of them in much detail or clarity, about how his irrealism is happy with these other "isms." I will not take the space to consider his views on many of these matters except to say that the best sense I can make of them is to take his position as a sort of meta-theoretic view. In other words, Goodman's position is not simply a noetic irrealism to be contrasted with noetic realism. His irrealism sits askew these two.

Nevertheless, as I read Goodman, I'm left with the nagging suspicion that insofar as noetic realism is concerned with "the World" being a singular way independent of human noetic contributions, Goodman's irrealism cannot truly be consistent with noetic realism. Even Goodman states that

> if we abstract from all features responsible for disagreements between truths we have nothing left but versions *without things or facts or worlds*. As Heraclitus or Hegel might have said, worlds seem to depend on conflict for their existence. On the other hand, if we accept any two truths as disagreeing on the fact, and thus as true in different worlds, the grounds are not clear for discounting other conflicts between truths and mere difference in manner of speaking. [italics mine] (*Ways*, 119)

There is, in short, no singular "World" underlying our attempts at describing G-worlds. G-worlds, instead, are made with the descriptions. As the descriptions conflict, we make new G-worlds.

Goodman's nominalism is one way of making a G-world. Platonism is another, idealism another, and realism another – but only within the particular G-world as made. But there are numerous G-worlds we can make and we can move back and forth among these worlds quite simply and happily. As he writes,

> So if there is any world, there are many, and if many, none. And if none, what becomes of truth and the relationship of a version to what it describes? Parmenides ran into this trouble long ago: because truths conflict, we cannot describe the world. Even when he said "It is" he went too far. "It is" gives way to "They are"; and "They are" to "None is." Monism, pluralism, nihilism coalesce. (*Of Mind*, 32)

Irrealism appears to be the focal point of this coalescence.

One more indicator that Goodman thinks of irrealism as a sort of meta-theoretic notion is the following. He notes that the trouble occurs when we stretch terms too far. If we stay within a version, the terms "world" and "totality" are clear. It's only when we start considering the multiple worlds that we run into trouble and get the paradoxes. "This sometimes leads to utter resignation, sometimes to an irresponsible relativism that takes all statements as equally true. Neither attitude is very productive. More serviceable is a policy common in daily life and impressively endorsed by modern science: namely, judicious vacillation" (*Of Mind*, 32). He continues, "We usually think and work within one world-version at a time ... but we shift from one to another often. When we undertake to relate different versions, we introduce multiple worlds. When that becomes awkward, we drop the worlds for the time being and consider only the versions. We are monists, pluralists, or nihilists not quite as the wind blows but as befits the context" (*Of Mind*, 32).

What, then, is his view? So far forth, he is an irrealist (rejecting both realism and idealism, yet allowing talk of both within their own G-worlds) who thinks that world versions are ways of describing things, a constructive activity that eventuates into the G-worlds or the ways things are. He is also a strict nominalist, taking neither his nominalism to be implied by his irrealism nor his irrealism to be implied by his nominalism.

Nevertheless, I cannot see how Goodman can keep irrealism at the kind of distance from the realism/nonrealism debate that he apparently thinks he can. For example, frames of reference, linguistically construed, surely are the results of human noetic feats. As such, Goodman's irrealism functions at least some of the time in contrast to realism. He repeatedly tells us that "the World" is a "World" well lost. We cannot say how things are independent of the saying. In the end, Goodman's irrealism cannot be consistent with both realism and idealism. So in what follows I treat Goodman's irrealism as a theoretical position, one that rules out noetic realism.

4 A PLURALITY OF ACTUALITY

I return now to explore the claim that there are many actual (G-) worlds. Goodman writes:

> Why then ... stress the multiplicity of worlds? In what important and often neglected sense are there many worlds? Let it be clear that the question here is not of the possible worlds that many of my contemporaries, especially those near Disneyland, are busy making and manipulating. We are not speaking in terms of multiple possible alternatives to a single actual world but of multiple actual worlds. How to interpret such terms as "real", "unreal", "fictive", and "possible" is a subsequent question. (*Ways*, 2)

Once again, we see the apparent meta-theoretic nature of Goodman's irrealism, including the view that there are many actual worlds,[7] which requires terms such as "real" or "unreal" to receive further analysis. The terms "real," "unreal," "fictive," and "possible" turn out to be relative to the actual G-worlds (as we construct them).

Such talk makes strong ontological claims. There are many actual G-worlds and we can move back and forth between them as easily, sometimes, as simply changing our purposes. This flitting back and forth seems easier to take, somehow, when Goodman talks as if the G-worlds are really just world-versions. Yet he persists in referring to actual worlds. So how can world-versions also be actual worlds? I think the answer, for Goodman, is pretty clear. In the final analysis, an actual world just is a (right) world-version and a right world-version just is an actual world, or at least as near as makes no significant matter. The difference is merely in emphasis. Just as we can go between one G-world and the next by simply changing our purposes, so we can go from G-world to world-version.

Goodman is somewhat cautious, at least on occasion, when it comes to talking about the actual worlds.

> But where are these many actual worlds? How are they related to one another? Are there many earths all going along different routes at the same time and risking collision? Of course not; in any world there is only one Earth; and the several worlds are not distributed in any space-time. Space-time is an ordering within a world; the space-times of different worlds are not embraced within some greater space-time. Worlds are distinguished by the conflict or irreconcilability of their versions; and any ordering among them is other than spatio-temporal. (*Of Mind*, 31)

So G-worlds are not physical, space-time worlds. The worlds are "no where," to answer his initial question. But in answer to the second question, he writes,

> A world is a totality; there can be no multiplicity of totalities, no more than one all-inclusive whole. By assigning conflicting versions to different worlds, we preclude composition of these totalities into one. Whatever we may mean by saying that the motion of the Earth, or of different earths, differs in different worlds, we rule out any more comprehensive whole comprising these. For a

totality cannot be partial; a world cannot be a piece of something bigger. (*Of Mind*, 17)

So G-worlds themselves are not related to each other in a manner where one can be added to another, as if one can get outside the totality in the first place. G-worlds are totalities. Versions are not. We will see later that various versions can be united, although not ever reduced to one or placed "within" a common underlying "world."

Are we any wiser, knowing now what a G-world is? The best we can say is that when Goodman is speaking of G-worlds he is speaking of actual worlds. More details follow in subsequent chapters, but Goodman's commitment to the actuality of G-worlds is simply his commitment to extensionalism. He is ardently opposed to intensionalism and hence to any talk of possible worlds (with one exception but I'll leave that for below.) The G-worlds we live in are determined ontologically on the basis of the world-version one chooses to work with for a given purpose. In short, he is an ontological pluralist.

If we restrict our attention to G-worlds in which language is used to construct true statements, we find that the ontological differences between worlds are related to how we conceptualize things and epistemize claims in those G-worlds such that some p is truly asserted in one and $-p$ is truly asserted in another. To avoid contradiction in a single "World," it follows that the two G-worlds must be kept ontologically distinct.

5 BEARING TRUTH: WHAT MAKES A TRUE WORLD-VERSION TRUE?

Typically, one looks to truth to understand how conceptual schemes are connected to the world. In Goodman's case, we should ask how a statement in a world-version is made true by a G-world. But this suppresses a significant set of assumptions about world-versions. Goodman says not all G-worlds can be thought of in terms of truth and falsity. So we need to cast the net more broadly and ask not merely about truth but rightness.

The statement "a mother bears her child" is ambiguous between "a mother carries her child in her arms" and "a mother gives birth to her child." Goodman's use of the word "truth" is ambiguous in a parallel way. On the one hand, to say some statement or other is true is to say "'p' is true iff p." Thus a statement bears truth, as if the statement carried its truth in its arms. On the other hand, when

Goodman speaks of true world-versions he speaks of G-worlds being made, and thus realities created. This ambiguity can lead to errors in interpreting Goodman, for when he speaks of a true world-version it is natural to think he speaks only of world-versions containing or made of true statements. Lynch, for example, reports Goodman as saying that each G-world contains its own true story. But for Goodman, not all G-worlds contain true statements. Only linguistically based true world-versions do. So it is vital to see that not all true world-versions are descriptive and hence the relationship between true statements and true world-versions is not some sort of one-to-one matching. Not all true versions are collections of true statements.

It is best, I think, to reserve the phrase "right world-version" for "true world-version" or to attach the adjective "generative" to "true world-version." So, a right world-version, understood as one that makes a G-world, is a generatively true world-version. Alternatively we can say that a right world-version has generative truth. However, it is appropriate to claim that along with a rightly rendered descriptive G-world, various statements are made, and thus truths come into being with the G-world made. Here, however, truth (of statements) is secondary (what is made is a G-world and the descriptions are true because of that G-world). Thus we can allow for a noetic irrealism (a G-world is made via noetic contributions) with an alethic realism (what makes a description true is the G-world as made). Descriptive world-versions, when rightly rendered, bear truth in a generative sense (a G-world is made or generated) as well as in the sense that truths are born along with the world (one doesn't make truths directly, but one makes a G-world and that brings with it certain truths). The result is that certain statements (beliefs, propositions, etc.) within a version bear truth based upon the G-world as made. However, in thinking of a world-version as generatively true, we must think more broadly than in terms of statements, for some right (generatively true) G-worlds are not descriptive.

Goodman writes that "insofar as a version is verbal and consists of statements, truth may be relevant [to the criteria for a successfully made world]. But truth cannot be defined or tested by agreement with the world; for not only do truths differ for different worlds but the nature of agreement between a version and a world apart from it is notoriously nebulous" (*Ways*, 17). Note, first, that this applies strictly to descriptive G-worlds, not depictional or presentational ones. Also note that truths vary from one G-world to the next so there is no way to test agreement between some truth-value bearer and the singular "World." I've suggested that this does not preclude testing a world-version-bound truth-value bearer by agreement with the G-world made by that world-version. But even this, Goodman proposes, is difficult, for the notion of testing a world-version against a "world apart" is nebulous. Part of the challenge here rests in what Goodman picks out by the term "apart." G-worlds and world-versions are so closely intermingled that it is difficult to say which is which.

An illustration. Some sentences refer to themselves. If the sentences in a language are uttered, they are uttered in a G-world. When someone says "This sentence is short," is that part of the world-version or part of the G-world? What makes the sentence true is the sentence itself. One doesn't go "outside" the language to discover the truth. But if a world-version is linguistic, and statements uttered in expressing that world-version are true not because of the world-version but because of the G-world, then are such self-referring statements part of the world-version, part of the G-world, or both? Goodman's claim that "the nature of agreement between a version and a world apart from it is notoriously nebulous" is not itself nebulous. But in his sometime characteristic obfuscation, he tells us simply that the right approach to the problem is context-dependent. Separating a world-version from its world is just an issue of being careful in talking about these matters where it might be important. He writes:

> Somewhat like the physicist with his field theory and his particle theory, we can have it both ways. To say that every right version is a world and to say that every right version has a world answering to it may be equally right even if they are at odds with each other. Moreover, talk of worlds and talk of right versions are often interchangeable. Let's begin by acknowledging that a right version and its world are different. A version saying that there is a star up there is not itself bright or far off, and the star is not made up of letters. On the other hand, saying that there is a star up there and saying that the statement "There is a star up there" is true amount, trivially, to much the same thing, even though the one seems to talk about a star and the other to talk about a statement. (*Of Mind*, 40–1)

To make sense of the relation between descriptive world-versions and G-worlds, we must stop thinking about truth in traditional terms in which we separate the real from what is made true by the real. We can as easily say "that's the reality" as "that's true."

What I mean to call attention to is that in thinking of truth, we must note both sides of the formula: "p" is true iff p. Let me hasten to add that I do not deny or question alethic realism or the basic formula claiming that "p" is true iff p. But as Goodman puts it, "saying that there is a star up there and saying that the statement 'There is a star up there' is true amount, trivially, to much the same thing, even though the one seems to talk about a star and the other to talk about a statement." Note that he says "amounts to *much the same thing* [emphasis mine]." He doesn't say they are the same thing. He is not, I think, proffering a disquotational account of truth. Nevertheless, the difference between saying that p and saying that the statement "p" is true amounts to little more than an emphasis of perspective.

6 ONE KIND OF PICTORIAL RIGHTNESS

In order to clarify some issues surrounding truth, I shift from truth to another kind of rightness. As noted, not all concepts are linguistically connected. Some are pictorial, gestural, or emotional. We think in concepts but not all thinking is linguistic or even linguistically describable, even if all concepts are symbolic. When I say, "the dog has fleas," I use linguistic symbols to refer to the dog, some fleas, and a certain relationship among them. In each case, the language refers to something outside the statement, that is, outside the language symbols used. When a painter paints a red triangle on a white background, it is tempting to say that she too is referring to something independent of the painting, namely a red triangle, abstract triangularity, thoughts in the mind of the painter, or something else. Of course, she may very well be referring to or denoting something outside the painting. But she may not be, either. The problem of representation in painting is as old as Plato. With the invention of the camera, representation became more "realistic" and art became more abstract. Not all art imitates or represents. So what is it doing? A painting need not refer to, imitate, or represent anything outside the painting. Sometimes the painting may simply exemplify something, as when a paint chip exemplifies the color we want to paint my wife's office. Sometimes, and this is what I turn to briefly, a painting can exemplify itself.

To help us out, let's say this painting is a G-world, albeit, a limited one.[8] Let's call the painting "untitled 22." Now this G-world is certainly not descriptive, for the painting describes nothing. Nor is the painting true or false, for it makes no statements. Yet we have the concept via the symbol, just by looking at it.[9] It is important that we not confuse a potential description of the painting in words, viz., "there is a white background containing a red triangle," with the painting itself. If I describe the painting in English, when you do not have the painting in front of you, I've not given you the concept presented in the painting but rather the concept of the painting. For the former, you have to experience the painting, for the painting is both the thing itself and the symbol. In short, there is a strict overlap – an identification – between the symbol and the thing symbolized. Indeed, the G-world of the painting is not separable from its symbol. The two are identical. In this G-world, the difference between the thing symbolized and the thing itself is nonexistent.

This is paralleled in descriptive symbol systems by "This sentence is short." Here the sentence refers to nothing beyond itself by exemplifying itself. There is no difference (in this one respect, at least) between the G-world and the world-version. They are identical, just as with "untitled 22." The truth of the sentence just is the sentence, just as the rightness of the painting just is the painting. Of course, as with most statements, there is an apparent gap between the statement (to which we apply the predicate "true") and the fact that makes the statement true. This is reflected in Goodman's comment that saying that p and saying the statement "p" is true amount to nearly the same thing. The more general point is that generatively true descriptive world-versions (the symbol systems) and their G-worlds amount to nearly the same thing. The even more general point is not just about descriptive symbol systems but symbol systems of all types: world-versions (be they descriptive, notational, pictorial, gestural, or depictional) and their G-worlds amount to nearly the same thing. The purest examples of this occur when what is being symbolized just is the symbol itself or, put alternatively, the thing itself just is the symbol. Under these conditions, the gap between G-world and version is nonexistent.

7 TRUTH AGAIN

The point I want to make is that linguistic symbol systems, although functioning in terms of truth and falsity, work in ways parallel to nonlinguistic symbol systems. Sometimes the G-world and the world-version can be separated (as when a painting is a painting of something else and thus can be said to denote) and sometimes they cannot (as when the painting exemplifies itself). What's often not noted is the closeness of thing and symbol in the relationship of true statement to G-world, even when thing and symbol are not identical. This is a core insight of Goodman's work. I want to take this as a major building block.

Truth is important. Our being aware of, or knowing, the truth enables us to get around in the world(s) in which we live. Too often, however, we separate truth from world in such a way that truths (the symbols) are more valued than what the reality actually is (a world). As I've said, we can as easily say "that's the reality" as we can say "that's true." Alston says that facts and truths, although not exactly the same, come in a tightly bound package.[10] I submit that our desire for truth is a desire for getting things right; and truth just is a getting things right. When we get things right, we arrive at the truth. Notice the active, even constructive, nature of both the "getting" and the "arriving" language. I think these are important ways we talk.

We can say that snow is white and we can also say that "snow is white" is true. Insofar as we separate these two, we typically say truth is a property attaching to a truth-value bearer. We might say we emphasize this within a world-version or at least within a linguistic world-version. Looked at from the other side, however, what is important is not just that the truth-value bearer presents the world well, but that the world itself is present to us. We want reality to be within our access. We can accomplish this philosophically by proposing that we make reality with our noetic feats and hence we have worlds. That reality seems to be within our access is an epistemological issue rather than an ontological one. However, the stand one takes on the ontological issue influences one's stand on the epistemological. Strictly in terms of the issue of truth, however, what is important is giving an account of truth such that saying that p and saying the statement "p" is true amount to much the same thing. I believe that the world-version (to which we attribute all kinds of rightness, including truth) and what reality is are very close to one another. Indeed, we can say the two are identical so that whether we say that the world-version is right (generatively true) or that the world is such and such way is, as near as makes no matter, the same. If we can give such an account of truth and rightness, then we will have grasped the importance of truth (and other rightnesses), viz., we will have gotten things right.

Goodman writes:

> What is ... important is that we cannot find any world features in-dependent of all versions. Whatever can be said truly of a world is dependent on the saying – not that whatever we say is true but that whatever we say truly (or otherwise present rightly) is nevertheless informed by and relative to the language or other symbol system we use. No firm line can be drawn between world-features that are discourse-dependent and those that are not. As I have said, "In practice, of course, we draw the line wherever we like, and change it as often as suits our purposes." If I take advantage of the privi-lege to speak sometimes as if there are only versions and other times as if there are worlds for all right versions, I often do it just to emphasize that point. (*Of Mind*, 40–1)

Note again the apparent sidelining of truth. Truth is nearly trivial (but not quite). But this is truth within the world as made, not gen-erative truth (that is, world-making).

In some sense, it is a common intuition that truth is trivial. What could be more obvious than the claim that "Snow is white" is true iff snow is white? But the statement is opaque, too, for we all know the difficulties in formulating a rigorous theory of what truth is, let alone providing the appropriate tests for it. How are we to explain the apparent oddity of the obviously right common intuition of the basic formula and yet the challenges of developing a deep theory? How do we understand the connection between worlds and world-versions? Isn't Goodman just stuck on the world-version side, building one mental sand castle out of another?

Put another way, and more pressing for my concerns here, we should ask Goodman exactly how truth is supposed not to col-lapse into the epistemic creativity of the human mind. How do we get the objectivity Goodman wants to have? Part of the answer lies in Goodman's telling us what truth is not. The other part lies in what Goodman believes is necessary beyond truth. Unfortunately he doesn't develop a detailed positive account of truth. But accord-ing to Goodman a world-version is generatively true (whether de-scriptive, depictive, notational or what have you) just in case it makes a G-world. True statements are true not because of other statements but because the G-world is the way it is. But how do statements carry truth?

True statements are not true because they "cohere" or are "acceptable" or "epistemically warranted." For Goodman, "p" is true iff p. A G-world is the way it is for it results from a rightly rendered world-version (a generatively true version). Hence what statements are true in that G-world are so because certain things exist in that G-world. It is in virtue of the G-world, then, that the statements are true, even though the G-world is the way it is because of the version. In my terms, noetic irrealism does not preclude alethic realism. In allowing for alethic realism, however, one does not, or need not, affirm anything like a full-fledged correspondence theory of truth. In regard to a minimal account of truth, we've already seen Goodman recount that "saying that there is a star up there and saying that the statement 'There is a star up there' is true amount, trivially, to much the same thing, even though the one seems to talk about a star and the other to talk about a statement." But Goodman also writes,

Some of the trouble [with how apparently universal terms apply to things] traces back to Alfred Tarski's unfortunate suggestion that the formula "'Snow is white' is true if and only if snow is white" commits us to a correspondence theory of truth. Actually it leaves us free to adopt any theory (correspondence, coherence, or other) that gives "'Snow is white' is true" and "snow is white" the same truth value. (*Of Mind*, 48–9)

Does Goodman think his irrealism is capable of supporting a correspondence theory of truth? Well, he at least thinks his view is compatible with the formula in question, in the following sense. He writes that

the familiar dictum "'Snow is white' is true if and only if snow is white" must be revised to something like "'Snow is white' is true in a given world if and only if snow is white in that world", which in turn, if differences between true versions cannot be firmly distinguished from difference between worlds, amounts merely to "'Snow is white' is true according to a true version if and only if snow is white according to that version." (*Ways*, 120)

So Goodman allows a minimalist account of truth in the first quotation and then limits it further to holding only within "a given world." In the first instance, his minimal account of truth is compatible with a correspondence theory. In the second, it is limited to a correspondence between a given G-world and a given statement within that G-world. He certainly doesn't give any real leeway to the correspondence theory elsewhere. He repeats in many places that with the loss of "the World" we lose correspondence as well. So if there is any possibility of correspondence, it will certainly be within a given world. But ultimately he rejects correspondence. I think he does so for the reason that a full-fledged correspondence theory, even within worlds, requires truth to be a property and he rejects properties.

Goodman also rejects coherence. He avers:

> When the world is lost and correspondence along with it, the first thought is usually coherence. But the answer cannot lie in coherence alone; for a false or otherwise wrong version can hold together as well as a right one. Nor do we have any self-evident truths, absolute axioms, unlimited warranties, to serve as touchstones in distinguishing right from among coherent versions; other considerations must enter into that choice. (*Of Mind*, 37)

Now if coherence won't get us truth, what about some sort of epistemic account of truth–warranted acceptability, perhaps?

Here Goodman simply finds the bounds of "truth" too much. The more general notion of "rightness" enters the picture in a variety of ways. If coherence won't give us truth, it is not because truth is problematic but because truth is not enough. Among the many coherent versions one might find, some are right and some are not. Truth alone cannot decide this for coherence itself is the proposed test for truth. Here we must wonder about rightness of the world-version. What counts as a right world-version? In part, that depends on what our purposes are. One brief, but important, example illustrates.

In talking of valid inductive inferences, Goodman introduces his rightly famous predicate "grue."

> Validity of inductive inference, though a property of a relation among statements, requires truth neither of premisses nor of conclusion; a valid inductive argument may even yield a false conclusion from true premisses. What, then, is required of inductive

validity? Certain formal relationships among the sentences in question *plus* what I shall call right categorization. [italics his] (*Of Mind*, 37)

Further, a category or system of categories is not true or false – not sentential. Nevertheless, using wrong categories will make an induction invalid no matter how true the conclusion. Here's why.

For example if an emerald is said to be grue just in case it is either examined before a given time and determined to be green or is not so examined and is blue, then the same formal rules that lead from evidence-statements about green emeralds to the hypothesis "All emeralds are green" will also lead from evidence-statements about "grue emeralds" to the hypothesis "All emeralds are grue"; but the former inference is valid, the latter not. For although the evidence-statements are true in both cases, and the truth of both hypotheses is as yet undetermined, "grue" picks out a category wrong in this context, a nonrelevant kind. (*Of Mind*, 37)

So, says Goodman, valid induction is constrained by right categories and not just truth. We must distinguish right categories from among classes in general so we can distinguish valid from invalid induction. What makes a category the right category? "Very briefly, and over simply, its adoption in inductive practice, its entrenchment, resulting from inertia modified by invention … Rightness of categorization, in my view, derives from rather than underlies entrenchment" (*Of Mind*, 38).

Thus truth, although important, is not enough. A variety of other constraints on world-versions are central to making right versions, even within world-versions largely oriented around a true description of things. Truth even within a world is often not the main goal, for even when it is important, it relates to rightness in a variety of complex ways, in part to acceptability. Is truth then a kind of acceptability? To return to induction and its relation to truth, Goodman says that inductive validity is both an example of rightness other than truth and also one of the criteria we use in the search for truth. Why take the acceptability of one inference as better, vis-à-vis truth, than another? He answers:

Obviously, we cannot equate truth with acceptability; for we take truth to be constant while acceptability is transient. Even what is maximally acceptable at one moment may become unacceptable later. But *ultimate* acceptability – acceptability that is not subsequently lost – is of course as steadfast as truth. Such ultimate acceptability, although we may seldom if ever know when or whether it has been or will be achieved, serves as a sufficient condition for truth. (*Of Mind*, 38)

Goodman sets up acceptability as a sufficient condition for truth rather than a definition. In fact, in a footnote clarifying some passages in *Ways of Worldmaking*, Goodman is very explicit that he is not proposing a definition of truth by introducing acceptability as a criterion of it (*Of Mind*, 38). Neither, one can surmise, is coherence or correspondence (within a world) a definition of truth but rather they are tests for truth that, according to Goodman, fall short of generating rightness.

The closest Goodman comes to defining truth is captured, one supposes, with his claim that the formula "'Snow is white' is true iff snow is white" commits us only to a theory wherein "'Snow is white' is true" and "snow is white" both have the same truth value. Any theory of truth must be compatible with this minimal formula, so one supposes that the formula isn't about the criteria for truth per se but what makes a truth-value bearer true. As we have seen, to be more accurate about the formula we must relativize it to worlds.

5

Irrealism, Nominalism, and Properties

One of the most difficult challenges to ontological pluralism is the consistency dilemma. As noted, I take Lynch's reply to be successful. Recall that his solution rests on a counterfactual. I propose that the appeal to counterfactuals, however, commits the irrealist to both a realist theory of truth and a fairly rich modal semantics. I'll return to the latter issue in the next chapter. Note, however, that these commitments bring along a third, namely, that properties exist. If properties exist, then no pluralist irrealist should be a nominalist. Enter Goodman. How can a pluralist irrealist be a nominalist?[1] Furthermore, if the noetic irrealist appeals to counterfactuals, it appears that existence should be understood as a property. I illustrate the problems with nominalism using Goodman's position in the first half of the chapter. The second half argues for significant modifications in Lynch's account of existence.

I GOODMAN'S NOMINALISM

Goodman claims that his nominalism is logically independent of his irrealism. Indeed, he says an irrealist can be a platonist. How can a platonist, who affirms the existence of properties, also affirm that properties are simply made by the human mind? Such properties certainly aren't noetically real.

Note first that any platonism Goodman might admit will be no stronger than a Quinean platonism. Quine's platonism, recall, says that the world should be thought of only in physicalist terms. The major Quinean/Goodmanian difference is that Quine countenances properties, for he says that insofar as individuals exist they are physical.

Quine in no way allows for intensional properties. Both Goodman and Quine remain extensionalists. For Quine, what properties there are, are (physical) properties found in experience but rooted in the way the World actually is (phenomenally). Properties are found in the objects that actually exist. For Goodman, there are no such properties and hence no preset way the World is. At best there are what Goodman calls "relevant kinds" or "relevant classes." These classes are not noetically real. Rather they are historical classes or kinds, made for the convenience of reference or for their usefulness or out of the habitual role they play in ontological constructions. Goodman thus claims that irrealism is neutral vis-à-vis nominalism and platonism.

So classes are ontologically suspect, not noetically real, and definitely not based on intensional properties. Here some important questions arise about the notion of individuals, for what is the notion of an individual if not a class of things? Is being an individual a property for Goodman?

Goodman, as a world-maker, is committed to individuals, almost as if no G-world could contain anything but individuals. He insists all property talk can be reduced to talk about individuals. The building of a G-world of Quinean physical objects resting on extensionalist properties is merely conventional. Quine's commitment to physicalism cannot come about because of some "prior" way the worlds are. Is Goodman's commitment to nominalism any better off in this regard? One supposes that in any G-world created by Goodman only individuals exist. But one can't say that they must exist, or that only they must exist, for nothing exists "ahead of time." Although Goodman's admitting that an irrealist could be either a nominalist or a platonist seems the right way to go for a pluralist, why should one take a nominalist stance over a platonist stance, and if the latter, what kind of platonist could a noetic irrealist be? What kind should she be?

2 EXTENSIONALISM AND INTENSIONALISM

Goodman is also committed to extensionalism. In fact, his commitment to extensionalism is more basic than his commitment to nominalism, for he says any platonism must be consistent with extensionalism. He writes that

in this general discussion of worldmaking I do not impose nominalist restrictions, for I want to allow for some difference of opinion as to what actual worlds there are. [And from his footnote:] (In the same spirit, although *The Structure of Appearance* is committed to nominalism, its criterion for constructional definitions and its measurement of simplicity were, for comparative purposes, made broad enough to apply to platonistic systems as well. On the other hand, neither there nor here is any allowance made for departures from *extensionalism*.) That falls far short of countenancing merely possible worlds. The platonist and I may disagree about what makes an actual world while we agree in rejecting all else. We may disagree in what we take to be true while we agree that nothing answers to what we take to be false.[2]

Extensionalism is thus central to Goodman's enterprise.

Extensionalism supposes that the use of terms is completely determined by what falls under the terms in the (or an) actual world. An extensional meaning or sense is given by listing or otherwise indicating the (actual) things referred to by the term. Since "Morning Star," "Evening Star," and "Venus" all refer to the same thing, the extensional meaning of those terms is identical to the thing referred to by each, which in this case, is one particular extraterrestrial object.

Goodman wants to give an account of what exists solely on extensional grounds, assuming that the only things that exist are individual things. Goodman can thus say, "No difference without a difference of individuals." However, platonism can be compatible with extensionalism, says Goodman, if the properties, kinds, classes, etc. countenanced by the platonism admit no more than what actually is. The nominalist and the platonist differ here simply in that the nominalist recognizes only individuals while the platonist also recognizes classes, kinds, and properties. For an extensionalist platonist, however, each of these – classes, kinds, and properties – exists (only) in the actual G- world(s). There are no intensional objects.

On Quine's extensionalist platonism, there is only a property of being a football in virtue of footballs being actual. Merely possible footballs won't do it. Goodman, in contrast, remains open to all sorts of things counting as individual objects, including the physical, the phenomenological, and so on. He writes:

I am sometimes asked how my relativism can be reconciled with my nominalism. The answer is easy. Although a nominalistic system speaks only of individuals, banning all talk of classes, it may take anything whatever as an individual; that is, the nominalist prohibition is against the profligate propagation of entities out of any chosen basis of individuals, but leaves the choice of that basis quite free. Nominalism of itself thus authorizes an abundance of alternative versions based on physical particles or phenomenal elements or ordinary things or whatever else one is willing to take as individuals. Nothing here prevents any given nominalist from preferring on other grounds some among the systems thus recognized as legitimate. In contrast, the typical physicalism, for example, while prodigal in the platonistic instruments it supplies for endless generation of entities, admits only one correct (even if yet unidentified) basis.[3]

Thus goes Goodman's extensionalism.

In contrast, intensionalism says there are uses of terms beyond what is determined by the actual world (or G-worlds or worlds). Intensionalism is thus a (more or less rich) platonism which countenances classes, kinds, and properties that may or may not have actual things falling under them. Thus, unicorns as possible objects (unicorns exist in some possible world) have the property of unicornness attached to them, and thus the class of unicorns, although empty in the actual world, still exists, as does the property "being a unicorn."

3 EXTENSIONAL NOMINALISM, NOETIC IRREALISM, AND REALIST TRUTH

What relationship holds between Goodman's noetic irrealism and his extensional nominalism? The former says that what exists depends in some more or less explicit way upon the noetic feats of the human. There is no mind-independent reality. So, not only do classes and kinds not rest on any ready-made (set of) properties (within Goodman's account, kinds are at best "relevant kinds") but neither do individuals rest on any ready-made base. Individuals can be furniture-sized objects, physical particles, phenomenal experiences, ghosts, or minds. But how can Goodman talk either of kinds, classes, or individuals without talking about properties?

Properties, given his nominalism, don't exist. Why not? It can't be because of extensionalism, for he admits that some platonisms are compatible with extensionalism. It can't be that the worlds are "premade" containing only individuals, for that denies noetic irrealism. It

appears to come down solely to Goodman's preference for talking
that way or for making G-worlds that way. Nominalism is a limit
with which he happens (by choice) to work.

Extensionalism too is a controlling factor in world-making, but
why? Why not an intensionalist view? For all Goodman's talk
about limits on the ways we can make worlds, there seem in the end
to be few, if any, constraints. Except, of course, the ones that he as
world-maker chooses. Once we've removed the constraints of "the
World," what is to keep us from a very radical and extreme relativism – more radical than Goodman admits? His extensionalism is
one way to avoid an extreme radical relativism but I don't think it is
up to the job, for extensionalism is chosen no less than nominalism
or platonism.

If the irrealist is to allow for limits in world-making, it appears
she needs something beyond a self-imposed extensionalism or nominalism. The reason seems clear: an irrealist cannot make worlds
containing only individuals without introducing kinds, classes, and,
finally, properties. Goodman's commitment to ontologies of individuals alone keeps him from admitting not only Quinean extensional classes and kinds but intensional classes and kinds, for on a
strict nominalism, properties do not exist. These claims need an argument, the goal of the next section.

4 THICK AND THIN INDIVIDUALS

According to Goodman, as we move from one G-world to another,
only different individuals show up. If there are no properties, what
makes an individual an individual? Using Lynch's terminology, I suggest Goodman has a robust view of objects. That is, he takes the minimal notion of an object and fills it out in such a way that objects can
only be individuals. Things that exist (objects) are never classes,
kinds, or properties, no matter the G-world in which they appear.

Here a challenge to Goodman's account of pluralism arises. Because of Goodman's extensionalism, we know no G-worlds contain
merely possible objects. As such, each G-world is an actual world.
Furthermore, as a nominalist, he is committed to each and every
G-world containing only individuals. While his noetic irrealism
seems to allow for extensionalist properties (a platonism), his extensionalism limits the kinds of G-worlds the world-maker can create. I
believe his nominalism also limits the ways things can be. Just as

Quine's commitment to physicalism demands platonism, so Goodman's commitment to G-worlds of individuals requires platonism. His commitment to G-worlds of individuals alone requires properties that hold across all G-worlds.

So either the concept of individual is minimal or it is robust. If it is minimal, it appears not to be distinct from the notion of object. For the pluralist, what counts as an object varies world to world, conceptual scheme to conceptual scheme, ontology to ontology. Given noetic irrealism, objects can turn out (within a given world robustly conceived) to be individuals or classes or kinds or some combination of these. But Goodman says that only individuals exist, no matter what G-world. The upshot is that just as there are objects in every G-world, so there are individuals in every G-world. In any G-world where there is anything at all, there are objects qua individuals and thus not only are there no nonexisting objects but there are no nonexistent individuals.

If the concept of individual is not distinct from the concept of object, then the thinness of the concept "individual" (or "object") must remain open to there being classes and kinds of individuals, for what objects there actually are, given irrealism, turns out to depend on how one chooses to thicken the concept of individual (or object). Goodman can't be a strict nominalist – can't require it "ahead of time" – if he takes this branch of the dilemma. He must allow that objects can be classes or kinds. So says his irrealism. But this undermines his commitment to nominalism for all worlds. In short, by standing fast with nominalism, Goodman affirms a platonism of individuals.

If he takes the other branch of the dilemma, viz., if the concept of individual is robust from the start, then it is already filled out by an explanation of what the properties of individuals are. A thick notion of the individual already brings with it some sort of platonism for we know that no matter what world we consider, it will have only what we might call "true individuals," that is, no classes or kinds. Yet by Goodman's admission, what relevant or historical properties things have (how the properties are thickened) varies G-world to G-world. Hence one would expect nominalism (that is, that only individuals exist) to hold in some G-worlds but not in others. However, it appears that he can't actually allow for strict nominalism, since then the concept of individuals already is a robust class, a class filled out with certain properties. The properties demanding individualism in fact entail at least one class or kind, viz., the class or kind "individual." And if we suppose, *per impossible*, that the concept of individual is minimal but turns out to hold only in one world, then Goodman must spell out why there are individuals in one world but not in another.

It looks as if noetic irrealism and nominalism taken together are a bad mix. There are (robust) properties attached to the concept of individual and hence nominalism holds across the entire universe of G-worlds. But that is inconsistent with irrealism understood as open to extensional platonism. Goodman is not just open to platonism; he is forced into it.

5 EXTREME AND UNRESTRAINED RELATIVISM

Goodman describes his position as "a radical relativism under rigorous restraints." In the end, it appears unrestrained and hence more radical than he admits. We might say it is an extreme relativism with no, or just arbitrarily chosen, constraints. Left this way, the concepts the irrealist uses in making a world will not themselves be fixed ahead of time by any way "the World" is. What replaces the "World" in providing for limits? Goodman might suggest extensionalism. But why pick extensionalism over intensionalism? Isn't extensionalism created on the noetic side, just as nominalism is, or Quinean platonism?

Here Goodman might demur, saying that intensionalism introduces talk of terms that don't have actual referents but which nevertheless exist. In particular, intensionalism introduces the notion of essential properties. But intensional essential properties will undermine alternative ontological G-worlds by claiming that things are by essence one way and not another. However, perhaps intensionalism can be understood in such a way that Goodman's pluralism is allowed. In fact, perhaps allowing for intensionalism, or at least some version of it, will help the irrealist avoid Goodman's extreme relativism. I return to this in the next chapter.

For now let me say this. If the noetic irrealist continues to work under the limiting claim that there are no properties, there is a straightforward argument to the conclusion of extreme and unrestrained relativism. Since there are no real properties, truth turns out not to be real property. A singular (read: realist) account of the concept of truth (at least on a minimal level) is necessary to make sense of logical terms being constant. Thus there is no reason to assume even the limits of logic and hence no limit on world-making.

But in addition to the apparent arbitrariness of choosing the basic framework of world-building, including the logical framework, I think it is a mistake to believe that a strict extensionalism can even allow for noetic irrealism and its concomitant pluralism. To see why, we have to return to the response to the consistency dilemma.

6 TRUTH, EXISTENCE, AND PROPERTIES

Lynch argues that alethic realism is consistent with ontological pluralism. His position is actually stronger than that, I believe, for I think his argument can be extended to show that pluralism requires a realist account of truth. This extension revolves around the consistency problem. If pluralism is to get off the ground, then the consistency problem must be resolved. The solution to the consistency problem is built on the notion of possible worlds. If possible world talk is up to the job of solving the consistency problem, then there needs to be a commitment to some sort of intensionalism. The question arises, what makes modal statements true, if not intensional entities? Various options are proposed here, but when it comes to the solution to the consistency problem, only intensional accounts will do the trick. But it seems that intensionalism requires a realist account of truth. Or so I argue below.

Alston distinguishes between the property and the concept of truth. Lynch rightly notes, in discussing Alston, that our having the concept of gold does not necessarily entail our understanding the richer, more robust set of chemical properties of gold. In contrast, it is not obvious that we can have the concept of truth without having some details about the property of truth. What is it to have the concept of truth unless we understand its most basic properties, for example, "'p's being true iff p?" This formula itself indicates the minimal properties of truth. In having access to the minimal concept of truth, we have access to the fact that truth is a property. We are not thereby committed to all the richness of more robust accounts of truth.

Truth is a property, says Lynch, but existence is not. Truth has an essence while existence does not. I think Lynch is wrong about existence or at least if he is right, the consequences are more sweeping than he realizes. The reason he gives for his claim is that there are no nonexisting objects. Existence is not a property because if it were, then one could divide objects into two kinds, those that exist and those that do not. But objects that do not exist, he says, aren't objects at all. In virtue of existence not being a property, says Lynch, we can take existence to be a minimal concept, along with object, and hence the various ontologies we might make by filling out the concepts of existence and object more robustly are profligate.

Lynch's argument rests on the following "fairly basic" principle: "If there could be no properties that individuate some alleged kind of things from other kinds, then there is no sense talking of a 'kind' at all. The very idea of an object in the metaphysical sense ensures that this is the case for 'existing object.' Hence there is no kind marked out by any application of the concept of existence. Thus existence has no nature."[4]

I believe the principle that "if there could be no properties that individuate some alleged kind of things from other kinds, then there is no sense of talking about 'kinds' at all" is problematic. First, what does Lynch mean by "could" in this principle? He seems to suggest that it is a conceptual truth that there are no nonexisting objects. Of course, not everyone agrees with the claim that there are no nonexisting objects (or at least the phrase is somewhat ambiguous). Is the claim a conceptual truth? It is not obvious that there could be no property distinguishing existing from nonexisting things. Furthermore, "distinguish" is ambiguous between an epistemic and an ontic use. While it's clear we don't have any easy epistemic access to a property that distinguishes the existing from the nonexisting, it doesn't follow that there is no ontically distinguishing property. Indeed, Lynch considers one possibility and rejects it. He writes:

> Of course, there are objections that can be made against the conception of existence I've been discussing. To begin with, one might try arguing that there *is* a property shared by all and only existents. For instance, one might point out that the property of self-identity is shared by all existing things. That is, everything is necessarily identical with itself. Could not this be the essence of existence? If so, then the concepts of existence and objecthood would be shown to be absolute after all.[5]

His reply to this suggestion seems simply to beg the question for he says, "to take the property of self-identity as the defining essence of existence seems to commit one to the view that existence itself is a property, which is false."[6] Yet what we were exploring was whether existence is a property. He continues in his consideration of self-identity:

> Of course, it might be objected that the original point was meant as a conceptual claim only: the idea is that "*x* exists" and "*x* is identical with itself" are somehow conceptually connected. This is also implausible, however. First, to say that something is self-identical is not to say that it exists, if only because one can suppose that a person might not exist without supposing (incoherently) that he might not be self-identical. Second, from the fact that every thing is identical to itself, it follows that Santa Claus is identical to Santa Claus, but it is certainly not a conceptual consequence of "Santa Claus = Santa Claus" that Santa Claus exists.[7]

To the first point, one can simply suggest that if a thing doesn't exist then of course it isn't self-identical – it isn't anything at all. To the second point, one can equally simply point out that, in fact, Santa Claus is not a thing at all, and therefore Santa Claus is not identical to Santa Claus. Self-identity might very well turn out to be the property in virtue of which all existents exist.

Of course self-identity is not an empirically manifest property in virtue of which we can pick out the existing from the nonexisting. Nevertheless, existence could have an essence and itself be a property. Plantinga writes, in contrast to Lynch, "Among the properties essential to all objects is *existence*. Some philosophers have argued that existence is not a property; these arguments, however, even when they are coherent, seem to show at most that existence is a special kind of property. And indeed, it is special; like self-identity, existence is essential to each object and necessarily so."[8]

It is, perhaps, no coincidence that self-identity and existence are found together in every object. Perhaps, indeed, self-identity is conceptually connected to existence and as such is the essence of existence. But we need not take a stand on that here. My concern is only that Lynch's argument fails to convince.

I'm inclined to the view that existence is a special kind of property, viz., an essential property of objects. On such a view, all objects exist. With this, of course, Lynch agrees. What doesn't follow is that existence is not a property but, as Plantinga notes, rather that it is a special sort of property. This does not undermine Lynch's pluralism. Lynch seems guilty, when it comes to existence, of some all-or-nothing thinking, arguing that if existence is a property or has an essence then absolutism must be the case. But why think that? What if existence were a thin property? Were existence a thin property and hence fluid enough to be filled out robustly in different worlds, pluralism would still work. After all, if truth is a property and can be thinly taken in general but thickly filled out in different worlds, I don't see why existence can't be just as well. And if existence, then surely objects also.

Irrealism is helped, too, by the further suggestion that the concept of a property is fluid, with a minimal concept of property and (potentially) many robust accounts. Two directions can be taken with this suggestion. First, just as existence is not (it is supposed) a property, so are properties not properties. The second is that properties are properties. The former sounds like an explicit contradiction while the latter merely tautological. A rephrasing solves these problems. We can say that properties considered minimally are not real (intensional) properties and properties considered minimally are real (intensional) properties. The first view is problematic and therefore we are left with the second view.

Before we enter that discussion, however, an observation about the relationship of noetic realism/irrealism to intensionalism/extensionalism should be noted. Extensionalism says only actual things exist. Intensionalism suggests that merely possible things exist as well, that is they exist but aren't actual. Now whether properties are intensional or only extensional seems connected to the noetic realism/irrealism discussion in this way. If there are intensional objects that are merely possible then in some respects they must be noetically real objects. If not, then they depend upon some actual human (or other world-maker) for their being and so far forth the objects are not intensionally merely possible but the merely possible is built up out of some sort of concepts rooted in the actual thought of some actual human. The merely possible is no longer existent on its own as the intensionalist wants but a sort of nonmodal actualism (such as we find in Nicholas Rescher).[9] But Rescher-like accounts of possibility intend to do away with intensional properties, that is, to make possible worlds talk consistent with extensionalism. Extensionalism seems to fit better with irrealism than does intensionalism. But we shouldn't hang too much on this last observation, for the fact that intensional objects, when merely possible, are noetically real does not entail that actual objects are noetically real.

Returning now to properties, the first position noted above – that properties are not real (intensional) properties – could be motivated by the move that properties, like objects, are tied to what exists, so that just as there are no nonexisting objects, so there are no nonexisting properties. The minimal concept of a property might be "the features that makes objects what they are" but since, on our assumption, filling out what an object is depends on its properties, there will be robust concepts of properties as well. On the minimal understanding of properties, there is no property of being a property, just as there is, for example, no property of being an object or no property of existence. Nevertheless, we have a concept of property, a minimal one, (just as we do with object and existence) which will be filled out in a variety of ways in the many worlds we make. One robust account of properties is an intensional account (read: "noetically realist account"). Another account is more noetically nonrealist and therefore a merely extensional account of properties.

But if we make this move – to (minimal) properties not being (intensional) properties – and hence leave open how to fill in the ontology of properties in various conceptual schemes, there are limits if one is to remain a pluralist. Too strong a realist account on the robust level will entail there being only one way "the World" can be, viz., the singular way it is. This is parallel to filling out minimal realism about truth with too strong a correspondence theory. Taking the concept of truth that way undermines any claims to truth being compatible with various sorts of noetic irrealism. But a limit exists in the other direction too, for a radical noetic irrealism about properties undermines the pluralist's distinction between minimal and robust properties, for anything could then count as a property. Anything will go and we are left with an extreme relativism, the charge I laid against nominalism. In the end, the notion of minimal concepts itself seems to rely on there being some property, no matter how thin, that makes a concept a concept. It seems we can never be free of properties, and real ones at that. Not only must properties be real (intensional) properties but being an object and existing too must be properties, even if minimal ones, should pluralism have any chance of avoiding extreme relativism.

This struggle appears in Lynch as he discusses the distinction between truth as a concept and truth as a property. How do we investigate the property of truth, via a posteriori or a priori methods? Unlike gold, of which we can have a concept without knowing its true makeup, it's less clear that we can have a concept of truth without knowing something about its properties. In fact, Alston and

Lynch both say robust accounts of truth will fill in the properties of truth but that any realist account of truth, even the minimal realist account, views truth as a property. This property must be a realist property – a property to which no human noetic/epistemic contribution is made – which both Lynch and Alston admit. But then doesn't the minimal concept of a property face the same issue? How is one to have the (minimal) concept of a property without its being a noetically real property? As such, minimal properties are real. And that implies that existence is a (real) property too. And as intensionally real, then noetically real as well.

Does pluralism require that existence is not a property? No, not any more than pluralism requires truth not to be property. One can be a minimal realist about truth, and a minimal realist about properties and existence (in the sense that each is a minimal property), and yet there be many actual ways the World is (that is, many worlds). These worlds, of course, are filled out as the properties of objects are filled out beyond the minimal accounts. Recall that although merely possible intensional objects are noetically real, actual objects can be irreal.

Recall Lynch's commitments to necessary truths and the usefulness of possible world talk. Once it's admitted that even the minimalist account of truth requires real (intensional) properties then we are committed to existence being a property. Lynch is wrong that existence is not a property. Existence is a property, if a special one, such that all objects have the property of existence. What then is the ontological status of objects in merely possible worlds, and in particular the objects on which the solution to the consistency challenge depends?

6

Possibilities of the Actual

Any irrealist denial that existence has a nature and the concomitant denial that existence is a property are problematic when it comes to the reply to the consistency challenge. I've suggested that existence is a property, a property essential to all objects. To be precise, it is necessary that all objects exist. Furthermore I've suggested that existence understood as a minimal property is a real (intensional) property. But are there nonexisting objects? That there are no nonexisting objects seems fairly obvious, yet it is not uncontroversial because of potential ambiguity. This is nowhere more obvious than in discussions of possible worlds and their objects. What status should the pluralist irrealist give the merely possible objects of possible worlds, given the dependence of the solution to the consistency problem on possible worlds? In particular, we need to pay attention to the notion of a nonexisting object.

I HALES, LYNCH, AND GOODMAN ON POSSIBILITY AND NECESSITY

To build toward a more robust pluralistic irrealism, I begin with a few, mostly undeveloped, comments on modality offered by Hales, Lynch, and Goodman. Each one raises the subject in a different context and none have the goal of fleshing out the implications of their claims about modality and how their suggestions interact with their pluralisms. Nevertheless, what little they say is worth considering.

Hales very briefly raises the question of how possible worlds are related to his (relativistic) perspectives. The context for Hales's comments is a discussion of perspectives as abstract intensional objects. He writes:

Perspectives themselves I propose to treat in the same manner as possible worlds, namely, as abstract intensional objects. They are ways of knowing. This characterization does not beg the question in favor of relativism, as one might consistently maintain that all propositions have the same truth-values in all perspectives. Thus the existence of perspectives as ways of knowing is perfectly consistent with global absolutism.[1]

He shortly thereafter says,

Merely trotting out the Quinean chestnut about intensions being creatures of darkness … is not enough to dismiss this approach. So far we have seen that there is much to be gained by treating relativism as a kind of modality analogous to possibility and necessity. Perspectives as abstracta is the natural continuation of this analogy. Opinions vary tremendously as to what possible worlds are – sets of propositions, states of affairs, properties and so on. Still this deliberation does not mean that there are no possible worlds, or that we should be skeptics about possible world semantics. Similarly we should not take a lack of nice and neat individuation criteria for perspectives as sufficient grounds for skepticism.[2]

Hales's noncommittal attitude about which description of modal semantics is the best one aside, it is clear that he holds perspectives to be intensional abstract objects akin to possible worlds. But he clearly does not want to identify the two. He continues by saying that

one may argue that, given the similarities between perspectives and possible worlds, perhaps there is no difference between the two. Maybe relativism is just another manifestation of ordinary alethic modality. This objection raises a good question (viz., what are the ontological differences between possible worlds and perspectives?) but gives a bad answer (viz., there are none). The considerations that motivate the belief in possible worlds are completely distinct from those that motivate the belief in perspectives. A skeptic about perspectives will need to do much more work to show that these two concepts are "really the same" or that one is reducible to the other.[3]

While I agree that the motivations for possible world talk are certainly dissimilar to Hales's motivation for introducing perspectives, it doesn't follow from that fact that possible worlds are distinct from perspectives. Suppose I have a wood splitter that works wonderfully for splitting wood. Suppose I later discover that the woodsplitter does a great job on pumpkins too. What we have is a piece of equipment that does more than one thing. The equipment is still of a piece.

Hales, in *Relativism*, says little else about this matter. But it is worth pursuing and in a sense broadening out from Hales's perspectives to include the status of, say, Goodman's G-worlds or Lynch's actual (but conflicting) ways the World is. What differences are there between possible worlds and various irrealist proposals?

We have a glimpse into what Goodman thinks in the following:

recognition of multiple worlds or true versions suggests innocuous interpretations of necessity and possibility. A statement is necessary in a universe of worlds or true versions if true in all, necessarily false if true in none, and contingent or possible if true in some. Iteration would be construed in terms of universes of universes: a statement is necessarily necessary in such a super-universe if necessarily true in all the member universes, etc. Analogues of theorems of a modal calculus follow readily. But such an account will hardly satisfy an avid advocate of possible worlds any more than spring water will satisfy an alcoholic.[4]

Here we see Goodman provide a framework for an extensionalist account of possible world talk. Possible truths would not, on his suggestions here, be intensional entities. Possibilities and necessities are just what fall out naturally from the ways various G-worlds are constructed by us.

Although he doesn't claim that his actual G-worlds are possible worlds (let's say in something like the sense proposed by David Lewis),[5] it seems as if the overlap is too close to overlook. A statement is necessary when true in all G-worlds (descriptive G-worlds, at least), necessarily false when true in none, and possible when true in some and not others. However, it is important to note that Goodman's G-worlds are not fixed in some sort of logical space "out there." Rather, they are built by us. These actual G-worlds are G-worlds we both create and inhabit. But once again, Goodman says little beyond this tidbit.

Finally, consider Lynch on how to handle necessity, recalling that his comment is a suggestion rather than a developed account. In an article in which he takes up whether ontological pluralism is consistent with metaphysical realism Lynch proposes that one aspect of metaphysical realism is the notion that "the World" exists independently of the mind. In particular, Lynch notes Michael Devitt's claim that the pluralist cannot accept truths such as "were there no conceptual schemes, there would still be stars in the galaxy."

Part of Lynch's reply is that the claim that "Relative to every scheme, if there were no conceptual schemes, there would still be a world"[6] might be understood as a necessary truth. But what are necessary truths on Lynch's pluralism? He writes:

The rough picture is this.

> IM: It is impossible that p if, and only if, it is inconceivable that p given our conceptual scheme.
>
> And since our conceptual limits preclude us from conceiving that two and two make five, that proposition is rightly impossible.[7]

Thus modal notions may be understood as limited by what we can conceive given the conceptual scheme we actually have. Lynch further says that

> [t]hese are deep waters. But the following remark seems relevant. The pluralist can grant that IM entails (A) [Were our conceptual scheme different, then it would not be impossible that two and two equal five] but argue that *when the basis for the modal concepts is considered,* (A) does not entail (B) [Were our conceptual scheme different, then it would be possible that two and two equal five and thus (C) It is possible that two and two equal five, the latter being absurd]. For where we are considering a counterfactual situation in which the elements of a conceptual scheme which ground our modal concepts are different from what they actually are, the correct inference from IM is not simply (A) but (D) Were our conceptual scheme different, our modal concepts would be inapplicable.[8]

Lynch's comments seem to imply that there is no fixed account of necessity and possibility but that such notions should be entirely unpacked from within the relativized truths of our various (competing) conceptual schemes. This is a remarkably Goodman-like comment. On Goodman's view, given the extensionalist account of pluralism, possible world talk must be decided after the fact. This makes talk of possibility and necessity, as Goodman notes, innocuous. It seems fairly clear that Goodman's possible world talk will not be nearly deep enough to provide the framework for a solution to the consistency dilemma. Is Lynch's?

There is also an important difference between Goodman and Lynch, viz., the former thinks our noetic creativity brings with it alternative actual (G-)worlds whereas Lynch denies this, there being only one actual World and yet many different and conflicting ways the World is. But even with this additional bit of information, one should wonder whether Lynch's view enables the pluralist to solve the consistency dilemma.

2 THE CONSISTENCY PROBLEM AND POSSIBLE WORLDS

The solution to the consistency problem depends on possible worlds. But not just any old notion of possible worlds will work in this setting. In particular, the pluralist needs an account of possible worlds in which a proposition A describing objects that exist (in one conceptual scheme C_1) can be, so to speak, brought together with a proposition -A denying that those objects exist (in another conceptual scheme C_2) where being relative to distinct conceptual schemes makes A and −A consistent without thereby admitting that the two, A and −A, remain compatible. How is this to work? How does one make A and −A relative to the same scheme? When A and −A are brought together in the same conceptual scheme (in a possible world) what status do they have? Do these possible objects exist or not, and in what sense do they exist, if they do?

Philosophers approach possible worlds and their objects many different ways. We need not rehearse them all but instead consider a few representative and central examples as they touch on the solution to the consistency problem. Let's begin with the extreme possibilism of David Lewis and suggest that possible objects do, in fact, exist because all the possible worlds containing them are actualized. The pluralist irrealist wants the possible world language used to resolve the consistency dilemma to pick out not the actual world but possible worlds other than the actual one. Of course, she can admit that the actual world is one of the possible worlds, but we needn't worry about that here since in the actual world A and −A are kept sealed off from one another by the conceptual schemes that allow for their truths and the existence of the objects to which they refer. The propositions A and –A, embedded as they are in their own respective conceptual schemes, are, after all, in our actual world and not some merely possible world distinct from ours. The actual world in which we live (with all its pluralistic complexity) is not merely a possible world but the one possible world that is actualized.

Or is it? Not if the irrealist were to take a Lewis-inspired line on possible worlds and their objects, for on Lewis's view, there are as many actual worlds as there are possible worlds. Could the irrealist then understand the possible worlds to which she appeals as Lewisian possible worlds?[9] No. Transworld identity is a major issue for Lewis's understanding of possible worlds and it becomes a vitally important matter given the specifics of the solution to the consistency problem. Basically the problem of transworld identity is generated by the fact that an object actual in one world cannot be (numerically) identical to any object in another actual world. Since all Lewis's possible worlds are actual, there is no object actual in one world that is strictly speaking identical to an object in another possible world. Lewis gets around the problem of transworld identity by introducing counter-part theory, namely the position that while no object in one possible world is strictly identical to an object in another possible world, there are objects – what he calls "counter-parts" – similar enough in the two worlds to allow all the powerful uses of possible world semantics.

How would this apply to the counterfactual found in the solution to the consistency challenge? The counterfactual, recall, is this: "If A (true in conceptual scheme C_1) and –A (true in conceptual scheme C_2) were relative to the same scheme, they would be inconsistent." Restated in possible world language this comes to the following: It is a necessary truth that in every possible world where any two contradictory propositions are relative to the same scheme, only one is true. Are the objects referred to by the propositions A and –A (relative as they are to two different schemes in what we can call "Our World" – the only actual world there is, according to Lynch), when thought of as being relative to the same conceptual scheme in some possible world (but not Our World – call it World*), really the same objects as the ones in Our World or only their counter-parts? And if only their counter-parts, has the irrealist shown how A and –A can both be true yet incompatible? Hasn't the ground shifted here?

On Lewisian terms, it appears that while A and −A in Our World appear to be contradictory (until we realize that they are relativized to different conceptual schemes), when the propositions are considered in World* (where they are relative to the same scheme), then the objects referred to by A and −A are "replaced" by their counterparts, which are picked out by propositions we could call A* and −A*. Now it may be that the propositions referring to the counterparts in the same scheme are contradictory, as the pluralist might suggest, but we are no longer talking about objects identical to those in our World. No matter how similar the objects referred to by A and −A might be to those in World*, the contradiction between A* and −A* is in World* and not in our World. A Lewisian approach to possible objects and worlds won't work for the resolution to the consistency problem. Counter-parts, in this instance, don't seem close enough to the objects in our World.

The pluralist will have to go elsewhere. Let's consider the non-modal actualism proposed by Nicholas Rescher.[10] Here possible worlds are constructed out of actual, but nonmodal, notions, that is, out of the concepts we actually have (hence this is a kind of actualism). There is no commitment to significant modal notions at all. Such views are typically intended to give us possible world talk and its powerful mechanisms without resorting to the existence of properties or kinds and the associated intensionalism. But this clearly won't help the pluralist irrealist insofar as she is committed to truth being a real property.

I think Lynch's suggestions from the last section belong in this camp. He says our modal terms are limited by what we can conceive given the conceptual scheme we happen to have. This position is based in what is (the actual set of conceivings) found in a conceptual scheme.[11] In this context, Lynch introduces the particular notion of necessity and possibility he does in order to protect pluralism from ending up admitting absolutes all the while allowing for claims such as "relative to every scheme, if there were no conceptual schemes, there would still be a world" to be necessarily true. This last claim is intended to show that pluralism can be consistent with metaphysical realism, or at least that aspect of metaphysical realism demanding that reality is independent of the mind. One question to ask is why Lynch feels the need to show pluralism consistent with metaphysical realism. This is especially pressing given that doing so forces pluralism into the situation where the account of possible worlds is such that it's not clear that the solution to the consistency problem will find success. Let's say, for example, that I operate in C_1 and hence A is true. A's being true, of course, is inconsistent with −A's being true in C_1. But of course, on pluralism −A is true in C_2. But to show that A and −A really are not compatible, and hence show that pluralism has some real bite to it, there has to be a possible world in which A and −A are relative to the same scheme. But how is that going to work, if possible worlds are only built out of the way I conceive things in my conceptual scheme? Can I conceive of A and −A being relative to the same scheme? If I can, is that because I can get outside my conceptual scheme to do so? And what does that come to when we are speaking of possible worlds? Lynch says that one cannot, in the end, reply to the question whether something is possible if one leaves once's conceptual scheme behind. He says that

> ordinarily, inference from *it is not impossible that p* to *it is possible that p* is valid. But in this case [whether the inference from (D) "were our conceptual scheme different, our modal concepts would be inapplicable" to (B) "were our conceptual scheme different, then it would be possible that two and two equal five" is a good one], we are considering the basis of our modal concepts. When we consider if our scheme were different in that respect, we can say neither that p would be possible nor that it would be impossible. Rather, p is not possible and it is not impossible. Why? On the pluralist understanding of modality under consideration, what is possible or impossible is a matter of conceivability relative to our scheme. And I cannot say what would or wouldn't be conceivable relative to another scheme since any answer to that question presupposes my own.[12]

The upshot here is that some modal questions cannot be answered, specifically ones that deal with our modal concepts. A good example here would surely be any question dealing with how things are modally in other conceptual schemes. The question of whether there is a possible world in which A (which is true in my conceptual scheme C_1) and −A (which is true in your conceptual scheme C_2) are relative to the same scheme is not, it would seem, a question to which I can ever have an answer. So I believe Lynch's proposal about necessity and possibility is not strong enough to disallow the challenge from consistency.

Modal actualism is a third way for the irrealist to understand possible worlds and objects. Robert Stalnaker and Alvin Plantinga suggest two distinct but related modal actualisms. Michael Loux explains their views well and tersely when he writes,

> On [t]his view, possible worlds can be identified with actually existing objects or with constructions out of actually existing objects. One version of actualism is grounded in the Platonic insight that there are objects – things like properties, relations, kinds, and states of affairs – for which there is a clear-cut distinction between existence and instantiation. This version of actualism goes on to identify possible worlds with instantiable entities of one of these categories.[13]

Stalnaker and Plantinga present the notion of an existent but unexemplified or uninstantiated property or essence or state of affairs as coherent. So there are many possible worlds, worlds that could be but are not instantiated. Hence many possible worlds exist. However, only one possible world obtains or is instantiated – the actual world. We can thus distinguish, on the one hand, between objects that exist – say the possible object unicorn – but whose essences or properties are not exemplified or instantiated and, on the other hand, those that exist – the actual object horse – but whose essence or properties are exemplified or instantiated.

One is tempted to say that here we have some nonexistent objects (merely possible ones) that exist. That, of course, isn't properly stated for there is an important distinction between actuality and existence, one that leads to the distinction in the modal actualism just described between existence and exemplification or instantiation. What status would merely possible objects have were existence not a property but modal actualism the right way to think about possibility?

Let's reconsider the notion that existence has no nature. The problem, as I see it, leading to the claim that existence has no essence and the concomitant claim that existence is not a property is that the reasoning often begins with the notion of existence rather than with the notion of object. This is in fact how Lynch argues. Were one to begin with object rather than existence one could (and I think should) say that to tell the difference between objects and nonobjects is just to note that objects exist (and thus have the essential property of all objects, viz., existence – without existence, objects would not be objects) and nonobjects do not. One need not look for some further feature or property all existing objects have that nonexisting objects do not have. Of course it is wrong-headed to talk about nonexisting objects, since nonexisting objects are not objects at all and hence have no other (positive) properties.

Existence is, of course, very controversial. Of particular importance for this discussion is the question: do we start with existence or with actuality? An actual existing object (horse, horseness) is distinct from a (merely) possible existing object (unicorn, unicorness) in virtue of the fact that while both the property of horseness and the property of unicorness exist, only the former is instantiated – and hence only the horse is actual, whereas the unicorn is not actual. So one might say that in some sense, there are nonexisting objects whereby one means that there are merely possible objects (nonactual existing objects). Are such things objects or not? The irrealist should just say that these objects exist but are not actual. This allows her to say that all objects exist (there are no nonexisting objects) without giving up the idea that actual objects are distinct from nonactual objects, even though the latter do not, in some ordinary sense, exist.

Plantinga claims that all objects have the essential property of existence and I see no reason why pluralist irrealists can't also affirm this (and thereby admit that existence is a property). Perhaps the worry is that by doing so, one has to admit that existence is a crystalline property. But I don't see why the irrealist need think this, unless the possible world talk that attaches to Plantinga's view forces the crystalline account of concepts, and hence forces a crystalline concept of existence, onto the irrealist's position. I don't see why anyone should think this either.

To summarize, the irrealist can't take a Lewisian approach for possible objects (because of the problem of counter-parts) nor can she take a nonmodal approach (because nonmodal approaches eschew intensional objects, such as properties, and the irrealist needs properties for a nonepistemic account of truth). Neither will understanding possible worlds in terms of our conceptualizing (in Lynch's fashion) help the irrealist (for judgments about modal issues depend on his conceptual frameworks). So that leaves a modal actualist approach. This position doesn't commit the irrealist to a crystalline notion of concepts, and in particular to a crystalline account of the concept of existence. Existence could have both a thin account as

well as various thicker accounts without giving up the notion that
objects can exist in one conceptual scheme but not another, even in
the fullest sense that the objects from each conceptual scheme are
actual objects.

So I think the irrealist who avails herself of a possible world solution to the consistency problem – and I don't see any other good
possibilities – is committed to some sort of modal actualism about
possible worlds. This further commits her to existence being a property or having an essence. But I do not think this undermines pluralism. In short, the most direct route out of the consistency problem
seems to require real properties, some of which are not instantiated
or exemplified, but might have been. The property of existence is an
essential property of all objects. The objects there are, however, include properties. If the irrealist wants to solve the consistency problem, she needs the World to be modal. This modality needs enough
power to do what the counterfactual solution needs it to do. In
short, it seems to require that existence is a real property of things.

It is worth reiterating that pluralism qua pluralism is not committed to nominalism or the extensionalism that often attends nominalism. In particular pluralism is not committed to a nominalism about
existence. There is no need to deny as a pluralist that existence is a
property. If the pluralist irrealist claims that existence is a property,
she does not have to admit that it is a robust property and thus give
up pluralism, any more than her claiming that truth is a property
forces her to admit that there is only one way "the World" is. There
could be a minimal concept of existence shared across all possible
worlds and all actual conceptual schemes and more robust, richer
accounts as well, accounts that are not shared across possible
worlds or actual conceptual schemes, except counterfactually. As
such, she can talk about possible objects existing, and counterfactuals being true, without caving in to there being a single way "the
World" is. Intensionalism (with its commitment to existence being a
property) and pluralism are compatible.

3 EXTENSIONALISM, INTENSIONALISM, AND PLURALISM

Hales asks the question, what are the ontological differences between
possible worlds and perspectives? I want to broaden the question and
ask, what are the ontological differences between possible worlds, on

the one hand, and Halesian perspectives, Lynchian ways the world are, and Goodmanian worlds on the other? I pursue this not so much to provide a definitive answer but rather because important things can be learned from observations made along the way, and they prove useful in building a theistic irrealist pluralism.

The issues surrounding extensionalism, intensionalism, and possible worlds are quite complex. It matters whether one takes an extreme possibilism in which all possible objects are, in some world or other, actual, or a (modal) actualism in which only the world we live in is actual and other possible worlds are nonactual (because not exemplified) but nevertheless existent. Of course, one slice of the pie is a radical actualism in which possible objects and worlds are rejected altogether. This is Goodman's position following from his commitment to extensionalism. Possible worlds are not G-worlds at all, for they are empty.

Goodman believes that only actual things exist. There are no merely possible objects and no merely possible worlds in which they exist. This might be all well and good, perhaps, if there were only one world. But Goodman denies that and hence his pluralism seems to put pressure on the notion of the actual. How can there be many actual worlds? What relationship holds between them?

It is worth noting that Lewis's view of possible worlds sounds vaguely like Goodman's position, at least insofar as Goodman affirms many actual G-worlds. But of course Goodman flat-out rejects possible world talk except in a way that is compatible with extensionalism. Lynch, on the other hand, eschews Goodman's many actual G-worlds talk. Yet one can also see potential affinities between Lewisian possible worlds, which can be read as an ontological pluralism of sorts, and Lynch's conceptually based ontological pluralism. Lynch's alternative ontologies are to be taken as actual ways the World is, however, and not simply possible ways it is or as alternative possible worlds. But one might suggest that Lynch's many actual ontologies are provided a basis in the total number of possible conceptual schemes there are. The number of different ways in which the World actually is (when shaped by our conceptual schemes) depends only upon the number of ways in which it possibly might be. But Lynch is not saying that the actual ways the World is are simply possible ways it could have been. Conceptual schemes are actual frameworks from which the ways the World is are made. Unlike Lewis, his actual ways the World is are about a singular World, not the many worlds of possible world talk.

Returning to Goodman, one way to think about the relationships among his multiple actual worlds is to press them into a Lewisian mould and propose that Goodman just didn't go far enough. Had he pressed on, perhaps he would have admitted, in reverse order to Lewis, that because there are many actual worlds, actuality and possibility begin to merge. Lewis, in trying to uncover the nature of possibility, suggests that all possibilities are actualities. Goodman, in trying to uncover the nature of actuality, could have suggested that the many actualities are identical to the many possibilities. Goodman, unlike Lewis, simply failed to see that all possibilities are actualized.

The difference – and it is a significant one – is that Goodman's view is radically dependent on human noetic contribution. Hence the actual G-worlds we construct are built out of conceptualities. They are mind-dependent in a way the possible worlds of Lewis, Plantinga, and others simply are not. One way to put this point is that all Goodman's G-worlds contain human conceptualizers. This, of course, puts severe limits on which actual G-worlds can be built. This is a limit intensionalism and possible worlds based on it simply do not face, for surely there are possible worlds where humans are not actualized.

Lynch, who eschews talk of plural worlds, nevertheless affirms a plurality of conceptual schemes and hence a plurality of ontologies or ways things are in the actual World. Because he admits only one actual World, it seems allowable for him to appeal to intensionalism – in principle, at least – to resolve the consistency problem. There are other ways the (singular) World could have been. But having allowed intensionalistic possible worlds into the picture does nothing to shed light on the fact that for the actual World to be the various ways it is there must, in fact, be human conceivers. Like Goodman, Lynch proposes a relativism rooted in how humans think about things and hence, we need an explanation of the status of the human. Where do human cognizers fit?

Goodman is concerned to claim that there are quite strict limits on what G-worlds can be made. Is the presence of human cognizers one such limitation? We are told that G-worlds come from world-versions and world-versions from human noetic activity. Is there a G-world in which humans don't exist? The answer is surely "no." G-worlds are noetically irreal and extensionalistic. Without people creating G-worlds, no universe of G-worlds would be at all. In contrast, for the intensionalist there are possible worlds in which no human exists.

So there is something deeply unsatisfying about Goodman's suggestions about necessity and possibility. As long as one holds to noetic irrealism in an extensional sense, one is left with only the actual. One can't get the intensionalism one needs for a full-blooded modalism, for talk about possible worlds beyond those actually made by humans simply makes no sense. Perhaps one way to put the point is that nothing "forces" necessity on any statement for Goodman's actual G-worlds. The modal structures simply are not present to allow for real (beyond-how-humans-construct-them) essences, properties, kinds and classes. Without these, all that is (even if there are many actual G-worlds) is what there is, not what there might have been. Any necessities for Goodman are necessities "after the fact" and not real in the sense the intensionalist wants. Since intensionalism is taken as false, all the possibilities there are are restricted to the actualized G-worlds coming from actual cognizers. What turns out to be necessary is just what happens to be the case in all the actual G-worlds. We discover what is necessary only by looking in each and every G-world to see what carries across them all.

Since we make G-worlds noetically, Goodman seems committed to the view that it could turn out that there are no statements true in all the G-worlds. So, if there is something true in all the G-worlds, it appears to be so contingently and hence we do not have real (intensional) necessity. This, of course, is no surprise to Goodman, nor should it be to us. Goodmanian worlds are all human creations and since humans are contingent, it is tempting to say that possibly, there are no G-worlds at all. But whence this possibility? Doesn't noetic irrealism commit us either to the claim that human beings are necessary beings (at least in Goodman's sense of necessity) or to the claim that, since humans are contingent, if there were no humans, there would have to be some other conceptualizers for any G-world to be?

Goodman consistently claims there are limits to which G-worlds can be built. One such limit seems to be the existence of human beings in each and every G-world. We can't make a G-world in which no humans exist simply by conceptualizing. We know we can't make ourselves simply by our own noetic feats.[14] Why there is anything at all and, in particular, why there are human persons at all are age-old questions of philosophy. Perhaps the answer lies in another direction, viz., God exists and is the ontological foundation of everything, including humans. And God made the latter to participate in world-making along with God's own self. I'll return to this matter in chapter 11.

Goodman also tells us that all the G-worlds humans create are actual worlds. We know from considering Lewis's extreme possibilism that some account must be given of transworld identity. One supposes on Goodman's view that the person who exists at some point in an Aristotelian world and at some other point in a Whiteheadian world is the same person in each world. Here Goodman faces a parallel issue to Lewis, viz., how to understand individuals across G-worlds. It appears that individuals are G-world-bound. Lewis introduces counter-part theory to allow our modal intuitions to be captured in his account of possibility. But this seems out of reach for Goodman, for on Lewisian grounds I can't move, so to speak, from one world to another. As such, I cannot be understood as making a new world and moving to it.

Lynch's pluralism avoids this problem, for he does not claim that there is more than one noetically constructed world but simply that there is one actual world whose ontologies are plural. An individual does not have to leave the actual world to enter another actualized World in order to move from one way the world is to another way it is. Indeed, Lynch's main criticism of Goodman's multiple world talk is a normative criticism that if we live in our own (G-)worlds literally, then why should I care what happens to another person in another (G-)world?[15]

One final matter. Lynch's introduction of the notion of virtual absolutes (truths that hold in each and every conceptual scheme) is a very important one. What is the relationship between virtual absolutes and necessary truths? Lynch himself asks, "how can the pluralist account for the intuition that certain truths, including PMR [Relative to every scheme, if there were no conceptual schemes, there would still be a world], are necessary truths, without granting that there are absolute facts?"[16] While his main concern in this context is to show that pluralism is consistent with metaphysical realism and hence his focus is on the question of absolutes, he nevertheless goes on to provide an account of modality as dependent upon what is conceivable given our conceptual scheme. And this, we've seen, appears not to be the best direction for a pluralist to go.

Virtual absolutes, with propositions true in every conceptual scheme but independent of none, seem quite in line with certain aspects of Goodman's suggestion that even within his extensionalism, one can give an account of possibility and necessity. Goodman's necessities, of course, are truths that hold in every actual G-world (but

not independent of all the G-worlds, there being no truths independent of G-worlds). And on Lynch's view, necessities hold across all
possible worlds only because we conceive of modalities in the way
we do given our conceptual scheme.

In Lynch's various conceptual schemes, not only what there is but
what can possibly be appears limited only by what humans can actually conceive of. But then, whatever is possible in that sense is, in
fact, built up out of the actual. All this is done within the one actual
world, however, and there is no talk of multiple noetically made actual worlds. Hence there is no transworld identity problem.

PART THREE

How and Why to Be an Irrealist

7

An Argument for Irrealistic Pluralism

Steven Hales, in writing of Lynch's *Truth in Context,* says, "I must confess it is a bit disappointing when an author writes a whole book showing that his thesis has every virtue short of truth."[1] I wish to avoid similar charges against this book. I've already noted, *pace* Hales, that Lynch never claims to be giving an argument for the truth of his version of pluralism and so I think Hales's charge against Lynch needs no reply. Hales, on the other hand, does supply an argument for relativism. I've shown that his argument fails. I think Goodman's argument also fails, as we'll see shortly. It fails in an interesting manner, however; one that points us toward a more successful argument. My main goal in this chapter is to present that argument.

I WHY BE AN IRREALIST PLURALIST?

One typical kind of argument given in defence of irrealism goes as follows. Since we don't have access to the World that is free of conceptual or epistemic dealings with it, then the World can't itself be free of our conceptual or epistemic dealings with it. Put affirmatively, all our access to the World is conceptually and epistemically influenced, so the World itself must be conceptually and epistemically influenced. In short, there is no "World."

This argument, the realist typically says, is dressed up in any number of complicated ways by various irrealists. But being well dressed isn't enough to make something attractive. There is simply no evidential connection between the fact that we access the "World" via concepts and epistemizing to the conclusion that the "World" itself is

determined by our concepts and epistemizing. Epistemology is one
thing, metaphysics another. So says the realist.

If the irrealist is right, then epistemology and metaphysics are not
so easily separated as the realist assumes. Looked at from the point
of view of irrealism, how the World is is inseparable from how we
think about, know about, or conceive it. The conceptual and
epistemic are enmeshed with ontology. On the other hand, the realist seems right intuitively to claim that one's failure to be able to
gain access to the "World" without appealing to the noetic does not
show that the "World" is shaped by the noetic. And it certainly
doesn't show that the "World" is more than a singular way. So why
move to irrealism or to pluralism?

Lynch claims that one motivation for the move toward pluralism
is the apparent intractability of metaphysical debates. More specifically, he writes, "the intuition that these debates are incapable of
being absolutely resolved is not simply due to the fact that there is
wide disagreement. Rather, it is the *nature of the disagreement* that
fosters the relativist intuition: the metaphysical concepts themselves
seem to be responsible for the suspicion that there is no absolute
way to resolve the dispute [italics his]."[2] But a suspicion is not an
argument, nor does Lynch say it is.

A suspicion won't convince us. We need to see what it is about
the nature of the disagreement that leads to pluralism. Lynch falls
short here, giving no real evidence that the metaphysical concepts
themselves are responsible for the problem. In what follows, I attempt to do what Lynch does not, viz., provide a reason to think
that the intractability of metaphysical debates is not merely a problem with epistemological shortness of breath. The irrealist pluralist
needs a good reason falling on the metaphysical side. That's what I
aim to provide. Irrealism thus accounted for brings pluralism along
with it.

2 WHAT GOODMAN SHOULD HAVE SAID

I discovered the argument below when exploring what Goodman
should have said in response to Nicholas Wolterstorff. Wolterstorff's
way of putting Goodman off led me to see that he couldn't be put off
so easily if his basic insights were presented differently. The gist of
Wolterstorff's argument is that all Goodman's examples of conflicting
truth claims can be explained away by alternative frames of reference.

Short of that, we can simply note that if two well-evidenced claims contradict each other, the solution is to admit our epistemic shortcomings, assuming our evidence is limited rather than the world plural.

Goodman argues that we make contradictory claims where both claims seem true to us. In order to maintain the truth of both claims, we must admit that truth is relativized to worlds. Hence, pluralism is the case. Thus, on the surface Wolterstorff qua realist is right in his response. We can either find ways to show the apparently conflicting claims to be consistent or hope someday to do so. The problem here is Goodman's favourite examples, such as "the sun is moving" and "the sun is not moving." The examples leave his position vulnerable to the realist challenge for there are seemingly fairly obvious ways to make these "conflicting" claims consistent.

So let's start with different examples. Consider the claims, "humans are metaphysically free" and "humans are not metaphysically free," where we fill out "metaphysical freedom" with the richest account of freedom we want. The difficulty with using these as examples is that it is obvious to us that only one can be true whereas both "the sun moves" and "the sun doesn't move" certainly seem to be true. In other words, my example doesn't have the prima facie epistemological pull of Goodman's "the sun is moving" and "the sun is not moving" example.

Consider the law of noncontradiction. It is fixed, apparently. Goodman never gives it up. Indeed, it is wrong-headed for any irrealist qua pluralist to give it up. Given its fixedness, Goodman's example has whatever plausibility it has because both "the sun is moving" and "the sun is not moving" appear true. Goodman appears to think, therefore, that they are contradictory. Unfortunately for Goodman, as Wolterstorff points out, we also believe they have dyadic components and the contradiction can therefore be paraphrased away. Goodman seems alone in his denial of this.

With my freedom example there is not even the slightest temptation to take both statements as true. So, from that point of view, it is a more difficult example with which to start. The critic will just say that obviously the two freedom statements are contradictory and one of them, therefore, false. So not only are these statements not ones we must believe (as it might seem with Goodman's original example), but there is little motivation even to wonder if both are true. The explanation for this reaction is not far to seek. We are far more convinced of the truth of the law of noncontradiction and that the two freedom statements cannot both be true than we are of even the possibility of pluralist irrealism. In other words, there are all kinds of epistemic weightings going on in our judging how to handle the case.

Wolterstorff writes: "Not only has Goodman not presented us with a pair of statements that we *must* take as both true and irreconcilably conflicting; he has himself pointed out how the *apparent* conflict can be resolved without appeal to the relativity of truth [italics his]."[3] The "must" in this statement is a term of epistemic success. But wherein lies the epistemic "must" for any statement? With the freedom case, no one is ever tempted to hold both of the statements true. Contradictions are not possible and therefore we know that metaphysical freedom can't both exist and not exist. Therefore, we know one statement is false and no one feels an attraction to both these controversial statements being true. But that's just to note that we think the "must" of believing in the law of noncontradiction and a singular world is stronger than any "must" that we might attach to controversial freedom statements, or any other pair of controversial metaphysical claims.

What pluralistic irrealism needs to get an argument off the ground are two statements that are true and contradictory. Only such a case will split the World asunder. But what might those be? I suggest that we try to shed all epistemic success terms and just talk about raw truth. How would the argument look then? Continuing with the freedom case, the argument is succinctly stated.

1 Contradictions are impossible.
2 Metaphysical freedom exists.
3 Metaphysical freedom does not exist.
4 Therefore, there are at least two worlds, one in which metaphysical freedom exists, one in which it does not.
5 Therefore, truth is world-relative.

(I use the term "world" in lower case here, dropping the Goodmanian notion that there are many G-worlds each of which is actual). I'll refine this argument in the next section but for now we can simply reiterate that the realist is going to say that 2 and 3 cannot both be true. After all, the World is a singular way, contradictions are not possible, and therefore we can reject 4 and 5. The irrealist, the response will continue, is asking us to suppose that 2 and 3 are equally epistemically justified. Why should we realists accept that, if it gives us an absurd conclusion? And even if we do accept it, it doesn't follow that both are true. That our epistemic or conceptual abilities can't help us decide between two claims doesn't entail that both are true. Epistemology isn't metaphysics. This is the common irrealistic error of confusing epistemic limits with the world itself.

The irrealist will readily admit that, yes, this argument indicates that our epistemic activity, our "epistemizing," contributes to the World – or worlds. Here we should remind ourselves of the distinction between noetic realism/nonrealism and alethic realism/nonrealism. Is the irrealist meaning to talk about truth or about the ways the World is (worlds are)? Since I want to retain alethic realism, we'll have to say that our epistemizing contributes to the World rather than to the truth.

I believe noetic realism entails alethic realism. It would be odd to claim that the world is in no way shaped by noetic feats but then say that truth is so shaped. But the reverse is not the case. Alethic realism does not entail noetic realism. We can say, then, that what makes something true in an irrealist world (at least those containing truth-value bearers) is the way the world is. That is, the content of the truth value bearer itself gives us everything we need to specify what it takes for the truth-value bearer to be true. We can say, too, that there are many truth-value bearer worlds, each with its own truths. But we can also affirm that strictly speaking it is not the epistemizing of the truth-value bearers that makes the worlds separate. Instead, it is variables in our symbol systems and/or conceptual schemes that make the separate worlds. Pluralism enters at the level of language, not epistemology or, more exactly, pluralism enters at the level of symbol system and concepts, of which language is one kind. Of course, our systems and schemes, having influenced the way the various worlds are, will influence how we epistemically rank-order truth-value bearers within those worlds. So although the argument is most easily cast in terms of epistemizing truth-value bearers, it is what is behind the epistemizing that is important. We can't get away from epistemizing truth-value bearers the way we do. The reason is that the worlds we construct are the way they are because of our conceptualizing feats (rather than our epistemizing feats).[4] Once a world is conceptualized, any truth-value bearers within a world are true according to the way that world is and not something else (some epistemic contribution).

To summarize, truth is not epistemologically conditioned but truth is world-relative. Worlds are what they are because of noetic feats. The world-relativization of truth occurs because the symbol systems (especially linguistic conceptual schemes) influence the way the World is (worlds are). Our epistemizing itself does not change what is true. That is to move from epistemology to ontology. The proper move is from a (world-realtivized) ontology to epistemology. The ontology of the world(s) influence(s) our epistemizing. But the ontologies of the worlds are what they are because of other non-epistemizing conceptualizing that we do.

So, truth is relativized to the worlds. However, it is vital to get the order right. Truth is relativized to worlds not because we can simply choose to epistemize one way rather than another. That would land us in the truly crazy position that because I believe the world is thus-and-so-way, it is. That gives humans immense powers of creativity, powers we obviously don't have. Instead, we must think of the situation thus: we epistemize (and hence come to believe) the way we do because there are different and distinct worlds and the one in which we live supports the particular truths it does. Thus the noetic realist who insists that epistemology and metaphysics be kept separate can't actually pull it off, without giving in to irrealism and its many worlds.

3 THE CORE IRREALIST ARGUMENT

We can now move to explain and defend the main irrealist argument. To get started, I urge us to continue taking the line that epistemology and metaphysics – that is, our cognizing and the way things are – are two different things and not slip and slide between them. Let's admit that, at first blush, it certainly seems as if both our epistemizing and conceptualizing activities are distinct from the metaphysics of the world. Let's admit, too, that, prima facie, to say that p is true is not the same as saying that p is believed, justified, known, taken to be true, thought to be true, accepted, and so forth. While truth is a metaphysical term, the other terms are epistemological. They are terms of epistemic evaluations or weightings. The alethic realist wants to keep these things completely separate when it comes to the account of truth. Epistemizing does not a truth make. The noetic realist wants to do the same, putting epistemizing and conceptualizing on one side of a divide and the "World" on the other. Given that noetic realism entails alethic realism but not vice versa, it seems that the noetic *cum* alethic realist case rises and falls not with alethic realism but with noetic realism. Can the noetic realist pull both realisms off?

I believe the answer is "no." Let's try applying the strict separation of epistemology and metaphysics to the argument laid out above. What happens when we strip 1, 2, and 3 of epistemic evaluations and weightings? What follows logically, given the truth of 1, 2, and 3, is 4 and 5. A strict keeping of the dichotomy between epistemizing and reality puts pressure on the notion that the World is a singular way, independent of human noetic feats.

Now the realist might say that the reply is easy to see. We should simply take some one of 1, 2, and 3 to be false. The laws of logic demand it. In particular, 2 and 3 contradict each other; one must be false. In discussion, Peter van Inwagen gave a straightforward argument against the position argued here: First, if some possible world W_1 is actual, then free will exists. Second, if some distinct possible world W_2 is actual, then free will does not exist. Third, it is not both the case that free will exists and that free will does not exist. Therefore, it's either not the case that free will exists or it's not the case that free will does not exist. In effect, van Inwagen said that 1, 2, and 3 cannot all be true. Since contradictions are impossible, either 2 or 3 must be false. It makes more sense to reject as false one of 2 or 3 than to reach the absurd conclusion that there is more than one world.[5]

I think van Inwagen's response, and in fact the realist response in general, misses the point. First, van Inwagen's third premise ("it is not both the case that free will exists and that free will does not exist") rests on an interpretation of the law of noncontradiction, viz., a realist interpretation. That realist interpretation rests on a realist conceptualization of the laws of logic, viz, that the world is a singular way. This conceptualization in turn leads to a realist epistemizing of the premises. But without the realist interpretation, van Inwagen's third premise doesn't go together with his first and second to give his conclusion. Furthermore, his argument is legitimate only if we epistemically value the negation of 4 or 5 more highly than the affirmation of 1, 2, or 3. But then he slips in some epistemic rankings again, precisely what we agreed to keep out of our discussion.

But one wonders why van Inwagen, and realists in general, slip in these epistemic rankings. Their reply to the argument begs the question against nonrealist positions. The realist assumes that the World is the (single) way it is, and that our epistemizing has nothing to do with it. Thus they set aside any role for epistemic weighting or ranking. But when the irrealist wants to agree with the realist and actually set aside epistemic rankings, the realist slips in the epistemic rankings through the back door. The realist cannot say that epistemizing must be set aside when doing so favours realism and appeal to it when it does not. Either we can use epistemizing to decide metaphysical issues or not. If we can epistemically rank-order the premises and thereby decide metaphysical issues, then our epistemizing, resting as it does on conceptualizing, contributes to the way the world is and irrealism wins. If we cannot, then the irrealist argument above goes through, pure logic wins, and there is more than one world. Either way, irrealism wins. Here the "common sense" stranglehold that realism seems to have in the debate is broken. Realism is not the obvious default position.

This raises all kinds of nasty questions about the role of epistemic warrant or reasonableness or what have you in doing metaphysics. These are questions the irrealist pluralist should avoid. Instead, she should stick to the epistemic neutrality the realist proposes in the first place and push hard on the realist's own appeal to epistemic terms in the realist defence of realism, for it is precisely with these epistemic terms that the difficulty for realism begins. If we try to avoid epistemic terms as realism demands, but then go on to defend realism, we are forced to reintroduce the epistemic terms. The only other alternative is not to avoid them, in which case we are back in irrealist territory before we begin. In short, the realist's strategy forces her to admit that she epistemizes the descriptions of reality and that such epistemizing is rooted, ultimately, in the way we conceptualize. A world is the way it is, and we epistemically take it to be so, because we have already conceptualized the world.

Wolterstorff uses two strategies against Goodman, but we can generalize the case. As it turns out, neither even applies to the argument constructed here. The first strategy is to admit that both conflicting statements are true, but to provide paraphrases in which one is true and the other false under two distinct interpretive frameworks. Both statements turn out to be true but contradictory in the same world. Wolterstorff surely won't take that strategy in the freedom case because he won't admit that the statements in question have any chance of both being true. There is no need to look for paraphrases. Wolterstorff's other strategy suggests that we know the statements are not contradictory, even if we can't provide paraphrases to show it. There's no need to take this second strategy, since it is obvious that the two statements are contradictory. They don't even seem to both be true.

If the realist were to press either of these responses on my form of the argument (either by providing paraphrases of 2 or 3 to show that they are not contradictory or by simply stating that 2 and 3 must not be contradictory), she would run the risk of simply admitting that no two statements should ever be accepted as contradictory. Surely that approach to the matter would undermine more than it would resolve. Both strategies use epistemic success terms. They thus move from talking about truth to making judgments or holding beliefs (or some other equally epistemic task) about whether the statement is true. What the strategies do, in effect, is to rank 1, 2, and 3 epistemically, so that we recognize that we are more certain that 1 is true than 2 or 3. We can then admit that either 2 or 3 is false. But then our epistemic ranking decides our metaphysical conclusions.

But there is no reason to rank the law of noncontradiction higher on the epistemic scale than the freedom statements when we have truly set aside epistemology. In addition, not only are we ranking 1 more highly than others, we are slipping in another premise, a premise that tells us how to apply 1. We end up not only with 1 true but with either 2 or 3 false. But how do we end up with that? Why not say both 2 and 3 are true, and conclude that 4 and 5 follow? The easiest way to avoid this apparently unsavoury result is to slip in a premise claiming realism to be true, that is, that there is a singular "World" and our epistemizing simply doesn't contribute to the way the "World" is. But that, of course, begs the question we are asking. If we want to challenge the irrealist intuition, we can't do it by appealing to the separation of metaphysics and epistemology without admitting the use of epistemology in metaphysical accounts of the world.

The irrealist argument I've presented, and the realist argument against it, share a propensity to separate epistemology and metaphysics. But there the similarity ends. The irrealist suggests that if we take two controversial and contradictory metaphysical statements along with the law of noncontradiction, we end up with irrealism. The realist says no, even though epistemology and metaphysics are entirely separate enterprises, we do and must epistemically rank-order the three statements. Who is more philosophically righteous? Since realism is always demanding that we keep epistemology and metaphysics hermetically sealed from each other, irrealism wins. We always use our epistemizing to decide which metaphysical path to take. Doing so lands us in irrealism.

The critic might note an apparent ambiguity in the irrealist argument thus far developed. There are two senses of the term "decision." One is an epistemic sense of "decide," as in "I decide which statement is true." In this case, I decide which way to believe. The other is a metaphysical sense, as in "I decide which way the world is going to be," that is, the world is constituted the way it is by my believing it to be so. If one takes the latter, metaphysical meaning, then the argument as presented might find success. Here alethic realism/ nonrealism and noetic realism/irrealism need not be conflated or confused. My believing there are trees in the world does not cause it to be true that there are trees in the world. That would be to affirm an epistemic account of truth, an alethic nonrealism. It is important to note, however, that one believes p is true only because of an ontologically prior commitment, viz, that the world is conceptualized a certain way. The decision, if one is made at all, is made on the level of conceptualization, language, symbol system, etc., and the beliefs follow from the world. To say that truth is world-relative is not, in short, to deny alethic realism. It is only to admit that different noetic-qua-conceptualizing feats generate different worlds. Truth is thus fixed in that world and alethic realism still holds. But decision language here is potentially misleading and better left out of the conversation. We epistemize statements within a world one way rather than another because we conceptualize a world one way rather than another. We don't typically decide at all, but are raised up into, trained and educated into, one way rather than another. It is not believing that the world is such and so that makes it such and so. Rather, it is the prior conceptualizing. So the argument requires us to move beyond talking just of epistemizing one way rather than another.

Many philosophers note that we don't, in fact, choose our beliefs. The best we can do to control our beliefs is to put ourselves into situations where our beliefs may change. Bernard Williams makes some astute observations about this. He notes, for example, that while finding out that a statement is false does not entail that we won't keep asserting it, such a discovery is fatal to our actually believing it. In virtue of the discovery that the content of one's belief is false, one abandons the belief. In contrast to assertion, we don't ever say, upon discovering that our belief is false, "I ought not have believed it." Yet we might say, "I ought not to have asserted it."[6] I'll return to this issue in the next chapter, but want to suggest here that the intimate connection between how we conceptualize the World and what we believe about it may explain much of the puzzle about belief's apparent involuntary nature.

Returning now to the other way of taking "decision," that is, to the epistemic understanding, we can see that it allows that the World is what it is with noetic contribution, all the while keeping our discovery of the World a substantially independent enterprise. We can take our best epistemic shot at the World, but our believing one way rather than another has no causal or creative link from belief to World at all. We can say that at best the realist is left with only being able to discuss worlds as we epistemize them and not the World itself. Realism seems then to preclude ever getting at "the World," and we are left with a potentially very radical form of skepticism. The World known (reasoned about, argued over, etc.) is the World epistemized/cognized and not "the World" as it is in itself. Realism can never claim to know or, for that matter, rationally surmise that "the World" itself is a realist "World." One can never talk about "the World" itself but only the World as it is epistemically rank-ordered. And that is what the irrealist is saying: there is little difference between the World we talk about and the World as it is. To suggest that "the World" is a singular, fixed way is to assume something we cannot show without epistemizing via conceptualizing. Either there is no significant difference between "the World" and the World epistemized by me (or us), or "the World" is simply beyond our means and we cannot talk about it.

But perhaps the irrealist argument should be recast to avoid any decision language. Consider this way of putting the irrealist argument:

1 Contradictions are impossible.
2' p
3' −p
4' Therefore there is more than one world, one in which p is true, another in which −p is true.
5 Therefore, truth is world-relative.

Consider also this supporting argument, remembering that epistemizing results from conceptualizing a world and thus we epistemize

because of a prior creating of a world rather than simply epistemizing a statement on its own, so to speak, and therefore making it
true. I've added alternative ways of putting the point to keep this issue in front of us. This caution in place, we can say

A Either our conceptualizing-epistemizing premises 1–3′ contributes to 1–3′ being the case or it does not. (Alternatively: our conceptualizing the world makes 1 and 2′ the case or 1 and 3′ the
   case but not both.)
B If our conceptualizing-epistemizing 1–3′ contributes to 1–3′ being the case, then irrealism obtains. (Alternatively: if our conceptualizing the world makes either 1 and 2′ the case or 1 and 3′ the
   case but not both, then irrealism obtains.)
C If our conceptualizing-epistemizing 1–3′ does not contribute to 1–
   3′ being the case, then the irrealist argument is successful, and irrealism obtains. (Alternatively: if our conceptualizing the world does
   not make either 1 and 2′ the case or 1 and 3′ the case but not both,
   then the irrealist argument is successful and irrealism obtains.)
D Therefore, irrealism obtains.

Taken straightforwardly, premise B simply gives us irrealism.
Suppose we epistemize 1–3′ according to one conceptual framework rather than another. That is, suppose that we conceptualize
the world such that either 2′ or 3′ turns out true. The antecedent of
B then is either true or false. If it is true, then the truth of 1–3′ depends somehow on our conceptualizing-epistemizing them. That,
in turn, rests on our conceptualizing the world one way rather than
another. In which case there is surely more than one way the world
is and no reason apart from our conceptualizing the world(s) to
pick one over the other. For there is more than one way to conceptualize-epistemize 1–3′. Truth thus is world relative. Irrealism obtains. On the other hand, if the antecedent of B is false, then the
truth of 1–3′ has nothing to do with conceptualizing-epistemizing
and it is thus irrelevant to the irrealist argument presented above.
This irrelevance drives a large wedge between epistemology and
metaphysics. Thus C comes into play.

The antecedent of C says the truth of 1–3′ is in no way shaped by
our conceptualizing-epistemic stance toward 1–3′. So, if we do not
conceptualize-epistemize the premises in the irrealist argument, we
cannot appeal to reasons to reject any of the premises. That leaves

three possibilities with regard to the truth or falsity of 1–3′. However, before exploring those possibilities, it is important to note that the discussion is not focused on defending the truth of 1–3′ (that would be to rank them epistemically) but rather on understanding what actual epistemic neutrality looks like in regard to this argument. So the issue isn't whether we have evidence for or against the truth of any of the premises. If we had such evidence, it would be because we had already conceptualized the world one way rather than another. We must first have a conceptualized world in order to have reasons. The real question is, since we aren't allowed to appeal to such evidence, how we are to treat 1–3′? It looks like the position claiming all the premises are true is at least as viable as any other position – in fact superior to some – and therefore the argument goes through.

Let's consider the possible combinations of truth values for the premises. First, let's suppose all the premises are false. No solace for realism is found here. Because all three are false, 1 is false. But then contradictions would be possible and that is a fate worse than irrealism, for then anything goes, leaving us with a true and complete antirealism, a totally unconstrained extreme relativism. So if we get irrealism if 1–3′ are true, we get a radical and irresponsible kind of antirealism if 1 is false. Taking this route won't help the realist. The second possibility is that some of 1–3′ are true and others false. But which ones? One won't be false, on pain of rendering the World completely relative. What of 2′ and 3′? While it is possible that one is true and the other not, without introducing some reason to pick one over another (which, by assumption, we cannot do) we look to be on shaky ground. Why take the situation one way rather than another? According to the realist dichotomy between epistemology and ontology, believing, knowing, taking, accepting, and so forth have nothing to do with the way reality is. In remaining epistemically neutral, we cannot, by supposition, epistemically rank-order the premises. That leaves the third possibility, that 1–3′ are all true. But then 4′ and 5 follow, and irrealism obtains.

One could marshal evidence against 1, 2′, or 3′, but to marshal such evidence is to epistemize the premises, for we will have already conceptualized the world. Again, we can't do that, by supposition. Hence, if we are consistent in not introducing epistemic rank-ordering, the irrealist argument is successful, and irrealism obtains.

A particularly recalcitrant realist may still say that the world is the way it is completely independent of the way we relate to it epistemically. In particular, he may admit how the first and third possible combinations of truth values go, but not admit the second. Why not just retreat to the position that we don't know which of 2′ and 3′ is false, but that one must be true while the other is false? There is no need to introduce epistemic rankings but just admit that one isn't true. The irrealist response to this is simple and direct. The realist must admit that he is stuck, on the one hand, between the rock of admitting that conceptualizing-epistemizing contributes to the metaphysical nature of the world, and hence what turns out to be true or not, and, on the other hand, the hard place of skepticism.

Actually the irrealist can press another issue here, pushing the realist into an even worse position. As it turns out, there is no noncircular way of being a realist, once the realist retreats to the position of admitting that realism could be wrong about the way the world is. Premise 1 is actually metaphysically neutral between there being a singular world and multiple worlds. That is, although 1 is taken to be true, there is no built-in commitment to a singular-world realist interpretation of the law of noncontradiction over against an irrealist interpretation. An irrealist can hold 1 as well as the realist. One difference between the two, however, is that the irrealist can truly remain open to where the argument might go. The irrealist who remains epistemically neutral about 1 through 3′ actually doesn't beg any epistemic questions about them. By remaining neutral in this way, the irrealist gets the conclusions, 4′ and 5. About this, the irrealist is quite sanguine.

How can the realist avoid these irrealist conclusions? What reason can the realist proffer to defend the single-world interpretation of 1? None, except, perhaps, to assert that there is only one "World," along with the singular-world realist interpretation of the law of noncontradiction. But that is the realist thesis itself and begs the question against the irrealist. Realism is not the default position on these matters. Irrealism is on ground just as solid. In fact, irrealism is, I submit, on better ground.

The realist might say, in a final defence, that on the grounds of the irrealist argument circular reasoning is acceptable. We know that a proposition follows from itself, if we stick to logic. " p therefore p " is perfectly valid, deductively. "Realism is true" follows from "realism is true." So what's wrong with begging the question against the irrealist position? The irrealist retort is simple: Go ahead, but that appeal to logic stripped of epistemology proves the irrealist point and doesn't help the realist at all. There are many odd things about deductive logic, stripped of all epistemic concerns. One of them is that logic alone cannot tell us anything about the World – or the worlds. Logic is at best neutral vis-à-vis these matters. The irrealist does not end up in the same skeptical boat because at least the irrealist has provided an argument. The irrealist provides 1, 2´, and 3´. And it looks like one can substitute whatever one wishes for p and –p. Perhaps that humans have rights based in our natures and that humans do not have rights based in our natures. Or that abortion is acceptable and abortion is not acceptable. And so on. (Some very important limits on this are considered in later chapters.) Pick your favourite metaphysical issue and take from it two contradictory claims. All the irrealist needs is some argument with contradictory statements substituted for p and –p. She need not offer them as epistemically ranked propositions. She need only offer the bare logic of the situation. She needs no other reason. The strict separation of epistemic concerns from metaphysical ones opens the door to irrealism, just the opposite result from what a typical realist might suspect.

4 A REPLY TO GANSSLE

In an exchange over a paper that covers much of the same material as this chapter, Gregory Gannsle criticizes my argument and I reply.[7] Both positions are worth noting.

First, Ganssle suggests that I overlook an Alston-style distinction between the content of a position and what it takes to defend a position. In fact, I don't overlook the distinction at all. In the essay to which he refers[8] and in chapter 1 of this book, I make explicit various types of cognizings of which epistemizing is only one. While it is true that epistemizing does often involve defending a position, it does not always do so. Epistemizing, as I say, includes "some sort of grasping, understanding, or ranking of truth-value bearers ... in regard to their being true or rationally acceptable." To epistemize, however, can be a state one is in (as in being justified or having epistemized) or showing that one is in that state (as in justifying or epistemizing). I can recognize the distinction to which Ganssle refers and simply sidestep the charge as inaccurate. More importantly, epistemizing is not the only kind of cognizing I've noted. Conceptualizing does not involve showing anything (and hence the Alston-style distinction doesn't apply). But I've suggested that even to state the realist position conceptualizes the world a certain way (namely as real). Ganssle's charge falls short and, once again, the argument for irrealism goes through. If I were guilty of ignoring the Alston-style distinction, I could simply state my argument more circumspectly.

Second, Gannsle notes that I draw existential claims from propositionally structured premises and therefore the argument is not valid. I plead guilty. However, I believe the spirit of my argument is correct and Ganssle's reply is helpful in showing why. He provides two versions of the argument that are valid, one of which he thinks I'll have to reject on my own terms, the other he wants to reject for reasons he provides. I'll take these in order.

My version of the argument is as follows:

1 Contradictions are impossible.
2 p (where p stands for nearly any metaphysical claim).
3 –p
4 Therefore, there is more than one world, one in which p is true, another in which –p is true.
5 Therefore, truth is world-relative.

Ganssle rightly points out that the existential claim in 4 simply doesn't follow from the propositional structure of the premises. He suggests that 4 and 5 might possibly be replaced with

     4* p v q (where q stands for any proposition)
     5* q⁹

Ganssle thinks I have to reject this new argument because it shows too much, viz., that anything goes, resulting in an extreme relativism. I think Ganssle is correct about this. Nevertheless, the reasons he gives for thinking the argument shows too much are questionable. This version, he claims, does not involve a realist interpretation of noncontradiction. Here our intuitions are quite different, but what is important is the reasons for the difference. I believe Ganssle is using a realist interpretation, having cognized the world in a realist manner, and therefore he doesn't see that he is. I made this point above, noting that often the realist provides no argument for realism because she or he simply assumes the framework of realism and therefore sees no need to provide an argument. The notion of a purely formal argument (one stripped of all interpretation) is assumed to be part and parcel of realism. The argument is assumed to be without interpretation because it's "just the (realist) facts." But the irrealist wants to know what "stripped of all interpretation" means. An argument stripped of all interpretation (conceptualizing, epistemizing, etc.) is merely ink marks on the page. So although Ganssle may be right that his first version of the argument for irrealism shows too much, he seems on shakier ground when he claims his argument is purely formal (and hence lacking any realist interpretation). The irrealist simply rejects the notion of a purely formal argument, if that means that no ontological assumptions are made.

Gannsle's second proposed version of the irrealist argument goes as follows:

6 It is impossible that both p and –p be true in a single world.
7 If p and –p are both true, then there is more than one world such that p is true in one and –p in another.
8 It is possible that both p and –p are true.
9 p.
10 –p.
11 Therefore both p and –p are true.
12 Therefore, there is more than one world such that p is true in one and –p true in another.
13 Therefore, truth is world-relative.

He then suggests that, really,

13* Therefore, what is true is world-relative

is the proper conclusion, or at least the one I mean to support.

Ganssle thinks this version is valid but rejects it for the following reason.

It is clear that the irrealist holds that if *p* and *-p* are claimed or asserted in a single world, they cannot both be true. The reason the irrealist holds this view (rightly) is that, in a single world, *-p* is the denial of *p*. The irrealist also holds that, in different worlds, both may be true. If so, it must be that *-p* is no longer the denial of *p*. It turns out that *-p* is not the denial of *p* because *-p* makes no claim about the world in which *p* is true. Nor does *p* make a claim about the world in which *-p* is true. The proposition *p* is a claim about or within world$_1$ and *-p* is a claim about or within world$_2$. We might be able to say that *if* the propositions *p* and *-p* were about or within the same world, then they would be contradictory and they could not both be true. As it stands, they do not conflict with each other. So if p is true in world$_1$, -p cannot be true in world$_1$ but it may be that -p can be true in world$_2$. This approach implies that the proposition p in world$_1$ is not the same proposition as p in world$_2$. The first proposition is incompatible with -p in world$_1$ and the second is not. If two propositions have different entailments, they cannot be the same propositions. We no longer have a case of the *same* proposition being true in one world but false in another. [italics his][10]

This is a version of the consistency challenge. Once again, the initial problem for the pluralist is that p and -p are inconsistent with one another. The pluralist solves the problem by relativizing the two claims to different conceptual schemes or worlds. But then the problem isn't inconsistency but consistency. p and -p turn out to be consistent with one another on some other scale. As Ganssle points out, "If two propositions have different entailments, they cannot be the same propositions." p and -p turn out to be consistent with one another. Since the two propositions in question, p and –p, turn out to be consistent, the nonpluralist can simply say that there is no real contradiction and there is therefore no need for all the talk of plural worlds or conceptual schemes. Absolutism rather than pluralism wins.

My response is the one already covered in chapter 3. I won't repeat it here. But it is worth noting that Ganssle hints at the solution in his own criticism, viz., "We might be able to say that *if* the propositions p and -p were about or within the same world, then they would be contradictory and they could not both be true." Ganssle never returns to this possibility. However, as the reader knows by now, I think the strategy a good one, so long as the appropriate theoretical structures (realist truth and a substantial modal account of possibility) are in place.

8

Idealism and Irrealism

I earlier raised a question about Goodman's irrealism, viz., isn't he just building mental sandcastles? We can raise the question more generally about any irrealism. Before doing so, let me note that in this chapter I ignore questions surrounding single-World irrealism vs pluralistic irrealism since most of what I have to say easily carries over from the former to the latter and the exposition is much less cumbersome without having to worry about permutations of the term "World."

Now to the question. Isn't any theory claiming that the World is the way it is because of human noetic feats open to the challenge that the World just collapses into the world-version? Put another way, what happens to the independence of the World from the human mind? There are really two issues here. First is noetic irrealism and second, alethic irrealism.

In some sense, the World's independence from the mind is simply not a problem for the irrealist. The World's dependence on the mind is, after all, the point. But how dependent? Here we face the "spectre" of idealism in more or less radical versions. One concern with more radical idealisms is that no doorstop exists between the way one thinks or conceives of the World and the way it is; there is no World independent of the mind in such a way that there is some limit on what will work as a properly constructed World. This, of course, is only a problem if one fears the metaphysical doctrine of idealism. Many do, and not all of them are noetic realists. Lynch attempts to show that ontological pluralism is consistent with metaphysical realism, making the point that ontological pluralism does not commit one to idealism, at least in the form of some deep causal sort of dependence of the World on the mind.[1] One goal of this chapter is to consider how the irrealism being built here relates to idealism.

The second issue raises a question not about the World per se but about truth. The question is, what is the nature of truth? Is something true because the mind makes it so or is something true because of some mind-independent relationship between a truth and what makes it true? In a realist alethic theory the truth-value bearer is made true by something independent of it, a truth-maker. In irrealistic accounts of truth, truth-makers tend to dissolve into the truth-value bearers, the latter being thought to make the World one way rather than another.

I've held fast to the notion that a realist alethic account is compatible with noetic irrealism. I plan to make good on that claim, beyond the general suggestions I've made. I'll postpone the discussion until the next chapter. It's important to note, however, that the two issues, idealism and truth, sometimes are conflated.

In idealism, the World is the way it is because of the way the human mind makes the World. But then since in the end the only thing we really have is the mental, truth must be contained purely within the mental. Hence, truth must be epistemic or otherwise mentally brought about by humans. However, as Lynch and Alston have argued, a realist theory of truth is not incompatible with idealism or any other sort of ontology on the market. So it is best if we keep the two issues separate from one another as much as possible in what follows.

1 IDEALISM

Idealism is often contrasted with metaphysical realism. Metaphysical realism can be thought of as having three conjuncts: that there is only one true description of the World, that truth is some sort of correspondence between the World and our beliefs (propositions, etc.), and, finally, that the World is mind-independent. I concentrate on the final conjunct.

Irrealism can certainly seem to entail idealism and perhaps in its most radical forms, it does. Recall the distinction between the World being the way it is in virtue of a conceptual scheme and its merely being the way it is relative to a conceptual scheme. Recall also that the former seems clearly to entail that there would be no World were there no human minds, for the World is caused, in some fairly strong sense, by human noetic feats. A clear case of idealism.

The latter, however, only commits one to the view that the World is shaped by human noetic feats and it is therefore less likely to be accused of idealism. There could still be a World even if not shaped by noetic feats.

My position is that human noetic feats make the World the various ways it is. This suggests some sort of causal relationship between the conceptual scheme and the way the World is. When I make a table, I cause the table to be only in a secondary sense. Likewise, when I make a tree using concepts, I make it only in a secondary sense. Human noetic feats are a secondary cause and we do not create *ex nihilo*. Only God can do that. There are limits on what we can make with our concepts. One starts with the materials at hand and shapes them into things. So questions such as, "would there be stars if there were no humans?" can have a definitive answer. On my account, the answer is "no." That negative answer, however, does not entail that there would be nothing at all if humans didn't exist. The irrealism I'm proposing doesn't entail idealism in the strong sense objected to by so many metaphysical realists. On the other hand, it does presume that there are causal connections between what is and the conceptual scheme that supports what is. These connections are not *ex nihilo* causal connections. God sustains the World along with the ways we make it even though the ways we make it cause the World to be the way it is. Irrealism itself does not rule out some sort of mind-independent World. But neither is the World free from significant influence by our ways of thinking about it.

2 MCDOWELL'S *MIND AND WORLD*

I briefly noted in chapter 1 that John McDowell's claims about the role of conceptualization in experience can help explain how concepts make the World. I want to return to that promissory note and talk more about McDowell's work. McDowell denies that his position commits him to idealism, a claim I think is false. Since I appeal to a McDowell-like move in the next chapter, it is important to explain how his position, as I see it, falls on the idealist side.

I also want to note McDowell's denial of the need for and the reality of the supernatural. I think this denial makes his position all the more interesting for it provides an apparent alternative to a World "shot through" with God (as I believe the World to be). So in some ways, McDowell's position is a foil (although after the fact[2]) for the position I am developing here, all the while being a position from which I have learned a great deal and with which I agree in some significant ways.

At the risk of overdone brevity, let me provide a summary of McDowell's work in *Mind and World*. The medieval mind "enchanted" the natural world with meaning. The new science and the move toward representationalism in epistemology fostered by Descartes led to the following understanding of experience: there is a perceiving subject and the disenchanted world, and experience is understood to be a causal force in our sensibility and also a source of epistemic justification for our beliefs.[3] This understanding of experience, however, is problematic, for nature is understood to be strictly law-like, inexorably marching on in its own blind way, whereas the mind is the realm of the normative and rational (spontaneity), dancing to the tune of a reasonable piper.

McDowell thinks this picture is wrong and that it leads to two dilemmas. First, there is an oscillation between the Myth of the Given and coherentism. The former takes experience to be foundational with a nonconceptualized content that nevertheless is supposed to provide justification for our beliefs. Of course, it is not clear how that is to work. The latter holds that beliefs alone can justify other beliefs and forfeits any chance of objective, external constraints. The second dilemma is birthed from the first. We are apparently left with a choice between "bald naturalism" (that dispenses with spontaneity talk completely or reduces it to purely scientific talk) and "rampant platonism" (that suggests a "space of reasons" separable from nature that comes tied to supernaturalism).

McDowell rejects the terms of the discussion by denying that nothing natural can be shaped by conceptual capacities. This is too narrow (and superstitious) a view of nature. McDowell proposes, in the Kantian spirit, that experience is a deeply entwined combination of passive receptivity and spontaneity wherein external affairs can be directly presented. Experience is already conceptually shaped; spontaneity extends all the way out to the world. Experience, says McDowell, has conceptual content as a natural phenomenon. This is a modest re-enchantment of nature, a naturalized platonism. Aristotle recognized this naturalized spontaneity in his view that the normative flows from the natural. This "second nature" develops as a response to human maturation in a socially structured setting.

We grow up in a *Bildung* – our background culture and education that is itself the way in which humans are natural.[4]

In short, McDowell sees the world as impinging on our minds in a way that does not leave us blind to the World. Rather the impingement of the World – our experience – is already bound up with concepts and those concepts, although passively received, are actively used in making judgments, forming beliefs, and providing reasons. This is an entirely natural occurrence, seeing beyond bald naturalism (that leaves us without meaning) but drawing in short of rampant platonism (that might give us meaning but is disconnected from nature).

3 IDEALISM AGAIN

What I reject is McDowell's suggestion that the supernatural is best left to the dung-heap of medieval philosophical history. Supernaturalism is not something we ought to leave out of the philosophical view of human nature and its relationship with the rest of nature. What I accept is that experience comes to us bound up in the conceptual already. I reject McDowell's rejection of idealism, at least in some sense. I accept his deep-felt need for something beyond belief to provide a doorstop for our beliefs.

It seems to me that idealism, in the strong causal sense, is often rejected these days as if it were obviously false. In fact, it is often treated with a sort of disdain. To be blunt, it is often treated the way supernaturalism is treated – as if no educated, thoughtful person could believe it, or continue to believe it, once having thought about it. I think idealism is treated this way because of a relationship that once was thought to hold but is no longer accepted. Culturally, at least among the intelligentsia, we simply don't like the idea of God – some sort of mysteriously spooky force – sustaining the World "behind the scenes." Idealism, so long as God was sustaining the World, seemed acceptable. Since theism is now thought patent nonsense, and since idealism without theism leaves humans with far too much power – indeed, the power to create the World – then idealism is assumed false.

As a Christian philosopher, I have no philosophical fear either of God or of idealism. Indeed, McDowell's "relaxed naturalism" or "tempered platonism" seems an attempt to have one's cake and eat it too; to have meaning and meaningfulness without having to admit that there is something beyond the natural world. I'm inclined to claim simply that the reason various meanings and meaningfulness exists is because God exists. In a way, this essay is about showing how that works.

As noted, McDowell deals with the Kantian antinomies and the apparent challenge of allowing for an external limit (from experience) on our thought. This external limit is supposed not to admit of the myth of the given (information that arrives passively to the mind without being cognitively shaped). At the same time he recognizes that, on the cognitive side, we have a range of freedom that seems unconstrained, left alone without "external" constraint. McDowell's reply to dilemmas created by understanding nature too stringently is to argue that the conceptual is unbounded so that the very same concepts appealed to in spontaneity (our freedom in believing and judging) are already embedded in passivity. One result is that the World itself is immediately present to the mind without, he says, falling into idealism.

McDowell writes:

> But to say there is no gap between thought, as such, and the world is just to dress up a truism in high-flown language. All the point comes to is that one can think, for instance, *that spring has begun,* and that very same thing, *that spring has begun,* can be the case. That is truistic, and it cannot embody something metaphysically contentious, like slighting the independence of reality. When we put the point in high-flown terms, by saying the world is made up of the sort of thing one can think, a phobia of idealism can make people suspect we are renouncing the independence of reality – as if we were representing the world as a shadow of our thinking, or even as made of some mental stuff. But we might just as well take the fact that the sort of thing one can think is the same as the sort of thing that can be the case the other way round, as an invitation to understand the notion of the sort of thing one can think in terms of a supposedly prior understanding of the sort of thing that can be the case. And in fact there is no reason for a priority in either direction.[5]

The very thing that is thought is the thing that is in the World. One merely thinks the World as it is, at least when one thinks a true thing.

The proposal, says McDowell, is not idealism in some mysterious sense where the World is merely a mental stuff. McDowell notes that there is no clear issue of priority here. Why assume that the thought comes before the World rather than the World before the thought? But to further distance his position from idealism he writes,

> If we say that there must be a rational constraint on thought from outside it, so as to ensure a proper acknowledgement of the independence of reality, we put ourselves at the mercy of a familiar kind of ambiguity. "Thought" can mean the *act* of thinking; but it can also mean the *content* of a piece of thinking: what someone thinks. Now if we are to give due acknowledgement to the independence of reality, what we need is a constraint from outside *thinking* and *judging*, our exercises of spontaneity. The constraint does not need to be from outside *thinkable contents*. It would indeed slight the independence of reality if we equated facts in general with exercises of conceptual capacities – acts of thinking – or represented facts as reflections of such things; or if we equated perceptible facts in particular with states or occurrences in which conceptual capacities are drawn into operation in sensibility – experiences – or represented them as reflections of such things. But it is not idealist, as that would be, to say that perceptible facts are essentially capable of impressing themselves on perceivers in states or occurrences of the latter sort; and that facts in general are essentially capable of being embraced in thought in exercises of spontaneity, occurrences of the former sort.[6]

McDowell is concerned not to "slight the independence of reality" and so is careful to distance his position from the idea that the World is identical to the action of belief – made up, so to speak, simply by one's believing something. In order to protect both the spontaneity of the mind's response to the World, as well as the independence of the World from thinking, he must keep the World (the content of belief or the content of thought, more generally) separate from the action of belief. Otherwise, the spontaneity of belief or thought would make the World.

My irrealism is not a radical sort of idealism suggesting that there would be no World at all if there were no human conceptualizers, but rather that there would not be the sorts of things there are were there no human conceptualizers. In other words, things are what they are relative to concepts but not in virtue of them. There is no *ex nihilo* creation of things by human conceptualizing. In this, I believe, I'm in line with aspects of McDowell's position. Yet it seems to me that if it is idealist to hold that what counts as a thing is shaped by the concepts humans have in play, and there is no explanation for the human itself outside the *Bildung*, then McDowell is an idealist. And this notwithstanding his claims that there is friction applied to spontaneity from outside thinking and that this friction need not be outside thinkable contents.

In order to show this in a little more in depth, let me quote again the two passages with which I introduced McDowell in chapter 1. In speaking of how receptivity works, he writes,

> The relevant conceptual capacities are drawn on *in* receptivity ... It is not that they are exercised *on* an extra-conceptual deliverance of receptivity. We should understand what Kant calls "intuition" – experiential intake – not as a bare getting of an extra-conceptual content. In experience one takes in, for instance, *that things are thus and so*. That is the sort of thing that one can also, for instance, judge.[7]

He adds,

> The conceptual capacities that are passively drawn into play in experience belong to a network of capacities for active thought, a network that rationally governs comprehension-seeking responses to the impacts of the world on sensibility. And part of the point of the idea that the understanding is a faculty of spontaneity – that conceptual capacities are capacities whose exercise is in the domain of responsible freedom – is that the network, as an individual thinker finds it governing her thinking, is not sacrosanct. Active empirical thinking takes place under a standing obligation to reflect about the credentials of the putatively rational linkages that govern it. There must be a standing willingness to refashion concepts and conceptions if that is what reflection recommends. No doubt there is no serious prospect that we might need to reshape the concepts at the outermost edges of the system, the most immediately observation concepts, in response to pressures from inside the system. But that no-doubt unreal prospect brings out the point that matters for my present purpose. This is that

although experience itself is not a good fit for the idea of spontaneity, even the most immediately observational concepts are
partly constituted by their role in something that is indeed
appropriately conceived in terms of spontaneity.[8]

According to McDowell, the concepts passivity draws into experience are the same concepts used in the activity of the mind in judging
and believing. These concepts are linked to other concepts in a large
network of concepts embedded in the rational network that is the
space of reasons. Given these last claims, and given the spontaneity of
the space of reasons at the upper end, it seems to follow that the
lower end "use" of concepts is influenced or determined by the upper
end. No matter how many times McDowell denies that the activity of
thought (judging, believing, and so forth) is what is at stake in receptivity, his linking of the two – indeed, the essential linking of the two
– seems to undermine his denial. Every time we adjust our rational
network of beliefs, judgments, and concepts, we adjust the way experience occurs via the concepts we use. Here McDowell's reliance on
the notion of *Bildung* comes into play. The educational and cultural
context in which we are raised is itself historical and is itself a result
of the free activity of the human mind. But then isn't the whole of the
human being itself in need of some sort of explanation from the outside if, indeed, there is going to be friction? This, I believe, pushes
McDowell into idealism. Which type? While I think he'd be comfortable with things being relative to our conceptual scheme (without
thereby admitting pluralism) he would not be happy with the stronger notion where what is is in virtue of the conceptual scheme. But
what's to keep him from slipping into the latter? The whole enterprise of experience qua conceptualized and its being related to the
very concepts we use in judgment and belief seems free-floating of
anything beyond our thought. It seems that there would be no World
if there were no humans.[9]

My view does not fall prey to this type of challenge because God
is the ultimate source of all that is, even the irrealistic aspects of the
World that humans make. God provides for the World in the first
place and humans are not somehow evolved out of the unknowing,
meaningless primordial soup. Any *Bildung* we have is rooted, ultimately, in God's creative activity and is not, therefore, a natural or
even second nature product of what it is to be human where this is
thought to develop all on its own, without anything extra-natural.

On this view, there is a World because there is a God who makes it. But that God makes the World does not entail that humans don't contribute to it noetically. I believe irrealism need only commit us to a limited sort of idealism but that that sort of idealism only makes sense if God exists. More on this below: chapters 11 and 14 to 17. I turn now to consider questions about truth-value bearers and their relationship to the World and truth.

9

Toward a Theory of Truth

The last chapter introduced two closely related questions, dealing there with concerns about idealism. This chapter picks up the second question, concerning itself with truth. My goal is to sketch a theory of truth that is plausible in general but in particular plausible for the noetic irrealist. Once again, in order to avoid awkward linguistic constructions I typically speak only of the World (rather than the permutations used earlier).

I TRUTH-VALUE BEARERS

In exploring a theory of truth, it is natural first to consider truth-value bearers. Richard Kirkham rightly points out a "good turn" in the discussion of what kinds of things bear truth.[1] Perhaps many different kinds of things bear truth – sentences, propositions, utterances, beliefs, and so forth. Indeed, he suggests the following:

It is a mistake to think that there is only one kind of entity or only a very small class of kinds of entities that can bear truth values, for there are no restrictions *in principle* on what kinds of entities can possess truth or falsity. If this is right, there is no "correct" answer to the question of what kind of thing can possess truth values. The matter is one of *choice*, not discovery. In any philosophical drama where the concept of truth is a principle character, we may cast any sort of thing we please in the role of truth bearer. To be sure, our choice will be guided by the goals of the theoretical enterprise at hand ... [T]he key word here is "useful," for when we rule out some entities as an inappropriate choice of truth bearers, we ought to do so only when *in the context at hand* the choice would make it difficult for the theory under construction to do what we want it to do.[2]

I think Kirkham is right. We certainly go back and forth among assertions, claims, sentences, propositions, utterances, and beliefs in speaking of their truth. And it seems sometimes as if not much hangs on which of these one picks, so long as it does the job required of it by theoretical considerations. In this section I simply make some general observations about the "usual suspects" and indicate which seem most central.

The usual suspects are typically some sort of representation of the way the World is (or chunks of the World are). By "representation" I mean either a physical or a mental entity that stands for the World or aspects of it. Of course, even the physical representations need somehow to be related positively to the mind. The representational nature of truth-value bearers minimally requires some sort of mental accessibility. Typically, on a realist account of truth, there is a truth-value bearer and a truth-maker, the latter being the World and the former being the (ultimately mental or mentally accessible) representation. So, except perhaps for strict physicalisms, the truth-value bearer is mental or at least mentally "conditioned" so the mind can access it more or less directly. On irrealist accounts of truth one finds the maker and the bearer merging. Here I just consider the typical alethic realist sort of case.

The representations under consideration are either mental entities themselves or the sort of thing to which the mind has access – for example, the content of a belief or physical entities such as sentence tokens. Of course, something's being the content of one's thought does not make the content itself mental. Consider when sentences are taken as truth-value bearers. But it is equally true for the propositional analysis of belief where the content of a belief is taken to be a proposition. Propositions need not be mental. Propositions could exist independent of minds of any sort. To take a position on whether truth-value bearers are mental or something else requires some argument. But at the least, in the typical case (in a realist account of truth) truth-value bearers are understood as distinct from the World itself, that is, distinct from truth-makers. This holds whether the truth-value bearer is mental or not, some sort of platonic, free-floating entity or not, or something else.

In suggesting why someone might be attracted to what he calls "creative anti-realism," Alvin Plantinga notes strong intuitive support for the role of the mind in "holding truths."

> How could there be truths totally independent of minds or persons? Truths are the sort of things persons know; and the idea that there are or could be truths quite beyond the best methods of apprehension seems peculiar and *outré* and somehow outrageous. What could account for such truths? How would they get there? Where would they come from? How could the things that are in fact true or false – propositions, let's say – exist in serene and majestic independence of persons and their means of apprehension? How could there be propositions no one has ever so much as grasped or thought of? It can seem just crazy to suppose that propositions could exist quite independent of minds, persons, or judging things. That there should just *be* these truths, independent of persons and their noetic activities can, in certain moods and from certain perspectives, seem wildly counterintuitive. How could there be truths, or for that matter, falsehoods, if there weren't any person to think or believe or judge them?[3]

Plantinga's queries illustrate the attractiveness of a position in which truth-value bearers are understood to be, if not mental entities themselves, at least accessible to and perhaps dependent on the mind for their existence. He rejects this position insofar as it suggests that humans create the World, although Plantinga happily rests truths in the mind of God.

What then are representations? I won't take on this huge subject here except to say that representations minimally stand for something else. In this context, representations stand for bits of the World. Furthermore, representations are related to what goes on in the human mind and the related semantic structures that allow for informational content in our thoughts. So when we say that truth-value bearers are representations we bring truth-value bearers into the realm of the mind. It does seem odd, as Plantinga notes, that truths (his example is propositions – we can say representations) exist independent of the mind. Even sentence tokens, perhaps the most material of the candidates, are representations. But sentences surely in the end depend on mental work as they don't just crop up out of nonmental nature. Sentence tokens, as ink marks, have meaning

only in the context of human thoughtfulness. This inclines us toward thinking of truth-value bearers as dependent on the mind, if
not toward thinking of them as mental entities themselves. But here
a deep struggle begins, for the question then is, in what sense is a
sentence token, an assertion, an utterance, or a proposition mental?
No obvious answer leaps to mind.

Moving now to the most popular candidate for these representations as truth-value bearers, the proposition, we can take Kirkham's
characterization as a starting place. He says propositions are abstract
entities that are the informational contents of declarative sentences or
the thing named by the noun clause in statements predicating mental
attitudes, such as the italicized part of "I believe that *George is tall*."
Given this account, is there something about propositions that makes
them peculiarly representational? Taking representations, for the moment, to be purely mental, perhaps the idea is that propositions are abstract entities (like numbers) and perhaps all abstracta are mental
objects. But that is certainly controversial. Or take propositions to be
the informational contents of declarative sentences. Perhaps because the
very notion of information seems dependent upon the activity of the
mind, propositions are dependent upon the activity of the mind. Or
perhaps it is simply that whenever we talk about propositions we are,
in fact, talking, that is, we are using language and language is dependent on the mind. But aren't there more propositions than there are
constructed sentences, thereby putting propositions themselves outside
the realm of the linguistic and merely their expression (as sentences)
within the linguistic? Finally, perhaps it is that propositions are expressed when we attempt to describe our mental attitudes, such as belief, hope, or perhaps fear. But then isn't it the mental attitude that is
mental, and not the proposition, which could be entirely free-standing?

Let's switch now to taking representations not as strictly mental but
rather as the sort of thing to which the mind has access. If propositions
are this sort of representation, how should we understand them? Are
propositions the sort of thing that, as Plantinga says, "exist in serene
and majestic independence of persons and their means of apprehen-
sion?" That is, are propositions something in addition to the World,
representing it, but not mental entities themselves? Bertrand Russell
somewhere referred to propositions as shadowy entities distinct from
facts. One supposes that this is the kind of worry that led W.V.O.
Quine to reject propositions as truth-value bearers and instead, allowing only a strictly extensionalist ontology, claim that sentences are the

truth-value bearers. The status and nature of propositions remains an open question.

Some other typical candidates for the role of truth-value bearers are beliefs, assertions, utterances, and statements. Of this list, beliefs are the most purely mental since all the others have a clearly public (and linguistic) aspect. I can state, utter, and assert my beliefs, but beliefs themselves, unless brought into the public sphere in one of these ways – by being stated, uttered, or asserted – remain strictly mental and therefore private. So, beliefs seem the most likely candidates for truth-value bearers, if one is considering strictly mental possibilities, with perhaps propositions taking second place. In fact, on the standard propositional analysis of belief, what one believes (the content) just is a proposition, and so belief (the act of believing) is thought of as a propositional attitude, a mental state.

This brings us to the commonly made observation that each of beliefs, assertions, judgments, statements, and utterances falls prey to act/object ambiguity. On the act side, we have some action taken toward the object side, so we can say "I believe this belief," "I assert this assertion," "I utter this utterance," or "I state this statement." In each case, there is content to our believing, uttering, asserting, or stating, and in each case, we can substitute "proposition" for the object of the act. In some of these, the act aspect is public, such as in asserting, stating, and uttering. As noted above, the act of believing need not be public. Indeed, it cannot be public itself, for among the acts listed here, only believing is a purely mental action. Furthermore, there is something fundamental about beliefs, for unlike statings, utterings, or assertings, believings are more intimately connected to truth. I noted earlier that Bernard Williams observes this point when he says that discovering a belief is false is fatal to our believing it, while discovering an assertion is false is not fatal to our asserting it.[4] One can assert an assertion, knowing it is false, but one cannot believe a belief, knowing it is false.

I would add to Williams's observation the following. The connection between belief and truth is so strong that while one can assert, state, or utter one's belief so long as one takes it to be true, one cannot assert, state, or utter one's belief once it's known to be false. The belief ceases to be one, once known to be false. Yet one can assert the assertion that expresses the (former) belief, now taken to be false. There is something special and central about belief that does not attach to the other candidates.

The most important of the other candidates for truth-value bearer are sentences, either types or tokens. Just as a proposition can be understood as the content of belief, assertion, utterance, or statement, perhaps so can a sentence. I can, it seems, believe, assert, utter, or state a sentence. However, sentences seem to fall into a different camp, for whereas one can say "I believe a belief" or "I assert an assertion," one cannot say "I sentence a sentence" (whether a type or a token). Sentences – at least tokens – are physical objects, either ink marks or airwaves.[5] There is no act/object ambiguity attached to sentences. So I can assert or state a sentence but I cannot sentence a sentence. As such, these truth-value bearers are not mental, and are more attractive to those inclined toward physicalism or extensionalism. Sentences are purely public.

The act of holding a sentence to be true nevertheless is a mental act. But what is it to hold a sentence to be true? Do we believe it? Perhaps – we sometimes say we do. If we do, then either sentences or propositions are the primary bearers of truth, since either can be common to all the acts of believing, uttering, stating, and asserting. Once again it's worth noting that we believe a sentence only if we take it to be true, whereas we can assert, utter, or state a sentence we take to be false. And this leads me to suspect that the issue of which candidate is the best cannot be settled quickly. Since sentence tokens are physical entities, it seems clear enough that I can utter, state, or assert them (with my mouth or my hand). But do I believe sentence tokens? I'm not convinced. I don't think I believe ink marks or airwaves. Sentence types, then? Perhaps, especially if sentence types are taken as Wilfred Sellars suggests, as a set of sentence tokens, each of which plays the same role as the others or, in other words, each of which has the same meaning.[6] But again, do I believe a sentence type when I believe that snow is white? Do I believe a set of sentence tokens, all of which mean the same thing? This seems stranger yet. Perhaps sentences have a content I believe, but then what is the content of beliefs? This returns us to propositions.

I think propositions are the most popular candidate for truth-value bearer because they can do everything sentence types can do (capture the meaning of sentence tokens, handle contents of sentences across languages such as "snow is white" and "la neige est blanche"), and yet still exist even if no sentence is ever found to express them. Likewise with the other linguistic candidates – the object aspects of assertions, utterances, and statements. Propositions can do whatever they

do. Indeed, propositions seem to be at the ontological root of assertions, utterances, and statements. We assert, utter, and state propositions. And when we assert, state, or utter something, it is as a sentence
with, arguably, a proposition underneath.

I think the best candidates for truth-value bearers from among
the one's I've discussed are propositions, with sentences, assertions,
statements, and utterances being truth-value bearers in a secondary
way. The astute reader will have noticed that beliefs are not on the
list. That is because I believe they play a more central role than do
sentences, assertions, statements, and utterances. Yet I also believe
that one cannot, in the end, separate propositions from beliefs.

2 BELIEFS AND THEIR CONTENT

Propositions are not only the most popular candidates for the role
of truth-value bearer but also for the content of beliefs. But not everyone is happy with this latter idea. One of the core doctrines in
Richard Rorty's complex pragmatic antirealism, for example, is the
denial of representations. Since he takes propositions to be representations (they are understood as intentional, mental objects), in
denying representations, he is denying propositions. But if propositions are not the content of beliefs, what are?

Rorty says the content of beliefs is other beliefs. What does this
come to? I see only two options. Either a belief's content is other
beliefs themselves or the content of those other beliefs. The first of
these generates a kind of infinite "passing around" of beliefs about
beliefs, where the content of belief p is belief q, and the content of q
is the belief r, and so on.[7] So when I say I believe p, I ultimately believe things only about other beliefs. Thus are beliefs cut off from
the World and certainly won't help an irrealist make out a connection between the World, our thinking about the World, and truth.
But this is not what we think of when we think of the contents of
beliefs. When I say I believe the table is brown, I mean to say not
just something about other beliefs of mine, but about a nonbelief
content of the belief or, indeed, something about a bit of the World,
viz., the table and its relation to the colour brown.

The second approach, where the content of beliefs just is the content of other beliefs, only raises the question again: what is the content of beliefs? It appears that the contents of beliefs must be
connected to the World. But how? Rorty says our beliefs are shaped

by the World by means similar to those by which, on a Darwinian model, the World shapes our bodies.[8] What content results for our beliefs? Our bodies adapt to the environment through interactions with it. We have the hands we do because we mutated and the result worked. But our hands could have evolved may ways – other mutations could have worked – and we would have survived just as well. There is no single right way. So it is with beliefs. As our bodies have evolved to help us get around and survive in the World, so have our beliefs. But there is no more truth involved with beliefs than there is truth involved with the adaptations of our bodies. One way might work as well as another, although not all work equally well.

On Rorty's account, to say that a belief's content is true in virtue of the way the World is, is simply to misrepresent what goes on in the formation of beliefs. The content of beliefs is caused by the World, but there is no such thing as a justification (aimed at truth) and no true way for our beliefs to be. Belief formation is purely pragmatic. So in Rorty I see no proper account of the content of our beliefs, only that experiences with the World form beliefs. Beliefs themselves, as Rorty indicates, have no content but themselves, even though beliefs are caused by the environment. There are no representations, no mental, intensional entities, no propositions, standing between us and the World. Thus, says Rorty, there is no truth and no objectivity.

I think Rorty's position wildly antirealist and wildly relativistic. On the other hand, introducing something between the World and us doesn't seem promising either, as we learn from McDowell. We are suspicious of both pure platonism and pure anti-platonism. The notion of there being propositions "out there," independent of mind altogether, is odd. On the other hand, the notion of nothing having being unless constructed by the human mind is equally odd, if not more presumptuous. Is there a middle ground? Is there a way of giving beliefs content without propositions understood as mental entities? The question is, what is that content if not representational?

3 THE CONTENT OF BELIEFS AS CHUNKS OF THE WORLD

My suggestion is that the content of beliefs is the World itself. Call this the "worldly theory of belief." So far forth, we could be talking about a noetically real World, as seems to be the concern of McDowell and several philosophers who propose an identity theory of truth. In the end, of course, I propose that by the term *World* one should be thinking *irrealist world* – and where the irrealist is a pluralist, one should be thinking of one of the many worlds available to us. So, the content of our beliefs does not represent a world, it is a world (restricting the worlds under consideration to linguistically descriptive ones).

Yet, a whole world is not contained in our beliefs. I mean, first of all, that any given belief contains only chunks or bits of a world, not the whole thing at once. A belief that snow is white contains the chunk or bit of the world that snow is white. I mean also that some existing things are things about which I have no beliefs – there are whole worlds that exist of which I have never thought. That I haven't thought of them doesn't entail they don't exist. Some things that exist are things about which I have no beliefs. Are there things that exist that no human has beliefs about? If there are, these would be, one might surmise, the worlds of which God, let's say, is the singular source and knower. The contents of our beliefs, whether mine, yours, or ours together, need not total to a whole world, let alone the-World-the-singular-way-it-is. That is, the universe of worlds is bigger than our particular set of worlds and the beliefs attending to them.

The worldly content theory of belief does not imply a strong antirealist noeticism. Not everything in our beliefs is purely internal to our beliefs in the sense that we make it up. Thus, the view in question need not imply that nothing exists outside our human minds – what Plantinga calls "creative antirealism" and what many might call "radical idealism." In other words, some things appear in our beliefs from the outside. I do not mean that what appears from outside appears as part of the Given, as unconceptualized information. Yet such bits of the World need not be simply made up by me or us. I propose that these things are aspects of the World God brings to the table at which our minds feast. So in saying that the content of one's belief is just such-and-such part of the World, one is not "slighting the independence of reality."[9] To argue that the mental and the World are the same thing or that the World is an effect of the mental, a sort of *ex nihilo* creation of the human mind (as the radical idealist might want to do) would require another and separate argument, one that I think cannot be based solely on the worldly content theory of belief.

The worldly content theory of belief does not imply noetic realism either, although the former is perhaps compatible with the latter.

Some philosophers who hold to the identity theory of truth, and therefore hold a position close to the one I'm suggesting, struggle to explain how their theory does not imply (radical) idealism. I'll return to this shortly. For now, let's simply note that the worldly theory of belief need not commit us to either a totalizing noetic realism or a totalizing (Rortian-like) antirealism. It neither denies the independent status of (some) objects out there (independent, that is, of human noetic feats) nor denies the determinativeness of things created by our noetic feats, whether fictional (such as unicorns) or natural (such as stars and rocks).

4 THE IDENTITY THEORY OF TRUTH

I turn now to propose a theory of truth proper. Let's consider first the identity theory of truth (IT) that I believe, on the ground laid out so far, to be correct and that I believe meshes well with noetic irrealism. I say "on the ground laid out" because, as I will argue, IT focuses on propositions as truth-value bearers which are not as well suited as they could be for a noetic irrealism. But IT is important, for propositions are what we typically take to be bearers of truth-value. I suggest, however, that propositions and things that express propositions are secondary bearers of truth and hence we need a theory of how they are true when they are.

The identity theory is currently undergoing something of a revival, but its roots go further back. Something like the contemporary versions of the identity theory are found in G.E. Moore and G. Frege,[10] although the former rejected the view shortly after suggesting it and the latter said, finally, that truth is indefinable. It is also found, perhaps, in F.H. Bradley and other nineteenth-century idealists.[11] We find hints of the theory – or at least the set up for the theory – in John McDowell, and fuller treatments of it in Jennifer Hornsby, Stewart Candlish, Michael Lynch, and Marian David. I concentrate on Hornsby, Lynch, and David, with McDowell's position looming large in the background.

Marian David discusses but does not defend the theory. He puts IT this way: For every x, x is a true proposition iff x is a fact. IT is supposed to follow, he says, from a propositionalist treatment of "that"-clauses (where "that p is true" is the deeper grammar – the logical form – of "it is true that p") and the two schemata, (a) It is true that p iff it is a fact that p and (b) That p is true iff that p is a fact. David goes on to explain in detail how IT is supposed to work and how it contrasts with correspondence theories.[12]

Michael Lynch argues for IT in the following way. Propositions are objects such that they have the property of being true or false. The truth or falsity of propositions rises and falls with the reality of facts. Lynch writes: "If we take any instance of the T-schema [the proposition that p is true if, and only if, p] as necessarily true (e.g., the proposition that the pool is open is true if, and only if, the pool is open), then there are propositions if there are any truths at all."[13] Truth is sufficient for the existence of propositions. Propositions, of course, are true just in case the facts are the way they are. The facts are the way they are because of the objects that exist. Lynch claims that the F-schema (it is a fact that p if, and only if, p), in conjunction with the T-schema, generates this truth: "It is a fact that p if, and only if, it is true that p." Lynch says that a fact can be given an account by saying that a fact is a true proposition. The identity theory is summarized, according to Lynch, in the claim that "*the proposition that p is true if, and only if, it is identical to some fact* [italics his]."[14]

Both accounts take propositions to be the bearers of truth and facts to be truth-makers, although in the end, true propositions just are facts. I say more about this below. I turn first to Jennifer Hornsby's account of IT and her gloss on McDowell. After quoting McDowell where he denies the ontological gap between the sort of thing a person can think and the sort of thing that is the case, Hornsby writes,

> Someone who objects to this supposes that, by denying any gap between thought and the world, one commits oneself to a sort of idealism. But such an objector confuses people's thinking of things with the contents of their thoughts. If one says that there is no ontological gap between thoughts and what is the case, meaning by "thoughts" cognitive activity on the part of beings such as ourselves, then one is indeed committed to a sort of idealism: one has to allow that nothing would be the case unless there were cognitive activity – that there could not be a mindless world.[15]

Hornsby goes on to argue that the identity theory of truth is consistent with what she calls "a perfectly common sense realism."[16]

Hornsby suggests that we use the term "thinkable" to avoid the confusion between one's thinking and what one thinks. "Thinkable" stands in for the more familiar "proposition," "content," or "thought." She argues for a version of IT, a theory that, she says, contrasts with the correspondence theory. Identity theory, according to Hornsby, is "encapsulated in the simple statement that thinkables are the same as facts."[17] The identity theory is not vacuous, she says, because it "takes a stand on what the bearers of truth are, calling them thinkables."[18]

Frege called attention to the fact that two perfectly corresponding things must be the same thing and argued accordingly against the correspondence theory of truth.[19] After quoting Frege's argument, Hornsby writes,

> Putting this only slightly differently, we hear Frege saying: if truth were explicated in terms of any relation, it would have to be identity, since anything less than a candidate for truth's coincidence with a putatively corresponding thing would lead to the intolerable conclusion that there is no truth. Someone who takes herself to think that true thinkables correspond to the facts has it right, then, only if she actually means that any true thinkable is the same as some fact – which is what the identity theorist says.[20]

In short, there is a kind of *reductio* against correspondence theories of truth. When a correspondence theory holds that correspondence is something less than identity, then nothing is true. Only identity between truth-maker and truth bearer is enough for truth. And thus the identity theory takes a metaphysical stand and as such is a real competitor among theories of truth.

Here I wish to return to Hornsby's explicit, and McDowell's implicit, emphasis on the notion that such a theory of truth and its concomitant theory of thought content do not put realism in danger. McDowell is concerned to note that what we need is a constraint outside of thinking, a constraint that, he says, need not be outside thinkable contents – what Hornsby calls "thinkables." And Hornsby argues for a similar conclusion – that the identity theory is compatible with a perfectly commonsense realism – by arguing that there are more thinkables than thinkings.

> Here one thinks of thinkables in connection with expanding knowledge. And it might then be supposed that the facts are to be circumscribed by reference to what is known by an ideal knower, at the limit, as it were, of an inductive series of more and more

knowledgeable beings. But acceptance of unthought thinkables, some of which are facts, requires no such supposition. The supposition requires an understanding of the ideal situation for arriving at knowledge. And this can only be a situation in which all sources of error are eliminated or taken account of – a situation, that is to say, in which one is sure to believe what is *true*. Perhaps we can gesture towards such an ideal. But since we can explain it at best in terms of an antecedent notion of truth, the style of thinking used here to uncover a conception of facts can lend no support to an epistemic theory of truth.

The conception of unthought thinkables elicited here does not depend upon any settled opinion about human ambitions or limitations, but only upon an idea of intelligible others from whom one could learn. It evidently yields a generous conception of facts, to which an identity theorist is entitled. I hope, then, that the identity theory emerges as a defensible theory of truth, in keeping with our commonsensically realist view about the extent of facts independent of us. [italics hers][21]

But here I must ask, what does it matter if the identity theory is compatible with a perfectly commonsensical realism, if that commonsensical realism doesn't hold? What if irrealism is the case rather than realism? Of course, I have argued for just that in chapter 7. In the present context, the question isn't how the identity theorist can avoid idealism but rather whether the irrealist can use the identity theory. If she can, what story is to be told?

The emphasis of both McDowell and Hornsby on distancing the notion of thinkables being bits of the World from idealism is notable. But what sort of idealism? In Hornsby it is clearly idealism understood in such a way that were there no human thinkers there would be no World. One supposes McDowell intends something similar. I've already argued that McDowell doesn't easily escape the idealist's label. Minimally it seems that he must hold that what there is is relative to a conceptual scheme. In his case, it is the scheme deriving from our *Bildung* – our cultural education and training. Is he committed to the stronger view, viz., that there would be no World if there were no humans? Without God in the background, it is difficult for me to see how McDowell, or the many irrealists who try to build an irrealist account of the World, can explain the deep role of our conceptual frameworks in experiencing the World. Yet McDowell's falling into idealism is not the same as his falling into an irrealist theory of truth.

Reading McDowell from the point of view of the irrealist provides a reason to embrace the worldly content theory of belief and, in fact, IT. Identity theory, however, can easily be misread as an irrealist alethic theory, especially when connected to idealism. In this regard, let's return to Lynch's claims about IT and connect them to something McDowell says. McDowell notes that what he says is neutral in regard to whether thought comes first and then the World or the World comes first and then the thought. He is right about this. Although not specifically speaking of a theory of truth in this quotation, his point is relevant to something Lynch says about IT. Lynch writes:

Is IT a realist theory of truth? At first glance, it may seem that the answer to this question depends on how we interpret IT itself. When a philosopher or scientist makes an identity claim, for example, "Water is H_2O," it is usually thought that one of the terms in the claim is meant to be more explanatory of the phenomenon in question than the other. In other words, in the present example, "H_2O" is more revealing of the nature of that stuff that fills our lakes than "water"; hence "H_2O" has *explanatory priority*. Whether IT is taken as a realist view of truth seems to depend on which term, "proposition" or "fact," has the explanatory priority. If it is "proposition" and propositions are taken to be mental entities (such as "thoughts"), then to say that facts are true propositions smacks of idealism. This in turn might seem to tell against interpreting IT as a realist view of truth in my sense. In truth, however, it does not. For suppose that we take propositions, and thus facts, as mental entities. That means that the existence of propositions (and hence facts) will depend on minds. But it doesn't imply that a proposition's *being a fact* depends on our minds, and it is the latter that IT takes to be the essence of truth. On the other hand, if it is "facts" that have the upper hand from an explanatory view and facts are entities of the external world, then IT does not stand as a barrier to one's being a realist in any sense. [italics his][22]

Lynch's point is about causality. The existence of propositions (and hence facts) will of course depend on the human mind if and insofar as propositions are mental entities. Since Lynch's position is a noetic irrealist one, propositions (and hence facts) will be mentally conditioned. But where does the contribution of human noetic feats play in? According to the view I'm proposing, noetic activity makes the World, but truth lies in the relationship between the World as made and the belief-value bearer. Truth is one thing, the World is another, when it comes to their nature. It appears, then, that on the level of the content of belief – the proposition – of course there is a mental *aspect*. That is nothing unique to an explicit noetic irrealism, however. McDowell and Hornsby, who reject idealism, both admit that bits of the World are thinkable. But doesn't that make them mental? Well, not without a fight. Neither McDowell nor Hornsby would admit that propositions are representations in the mind. No. Instead, bits of the World are directly present to the mind. It doesn't follow that a particular proposition's being true depends directly on (the activity of) the mind, even though the fact itself – the way the World is – is made in some way by the mind. A truth is true simply in virtue of the relation of identity.

The identity theory does not entail an irrealist account of truth. So I think the identity theory of truth is a good one for the noetic irrealist to hold, at least insofar as propositions are understood to be truth-value bearers. I think, however, there are some issues to consider. According to Hornsby's gloss on McDowell, what can be thought just is the World. The notion of a thinkable replaces (or incorporates) the notion of a proposition. According to Lynch and David, true propositions just are facts. But what are propositions or, more broadly, what are thinkables? Are they bits and pieces of the World or are they mental entities? Certainly McDowell and Hornsby don't think that propositions are strictly speaking mental entities (propositions are not simply ideas, for example) for each thinks that the World itself, while thinkable, is independent of the mind's activity. That is, they both reject the notion that bits of the World are identical to thinking (what we might call "act-thought" as opposed to "object-thought").

According to the versions of IT noted above, to avoid the Fregean problems with correspondence theories of truth, the relation between truth-maker and truth bearer must be identity. But if a proposition just is a fact, or a thinkable just a bit of the World, then how can we really separate the truth bearer from the truth-maker? Propositions and thinkables are what is thought and what is thought is not, on their view, a mental object but a bit of the (independent) World. This protects the view, supposedly, from collapsing into idealism.

So truth doesn't lie in a matching between the mental and the World. In what sense then are propositions true? Only in the sense that they are facts. But then since the content of my thoughts, according to IT, is the World itself, doesn't the phrase "is true" come to the same thing as "is real?" It appears so, and thus it seems that propositions or thinkables are the bearers of truth only in the sense that propositions take the explanatory priority in the claim that propositions are facts, just as H_2O takes explanatory priority in the claim that H_2O is water. But there is no difference between the proposition and the fact. They are one and the same and they are not, in the end, mental objects. Here, we find a reverse to a kind of idealism where the World collapses into thought. Instead, thought collapses into the World. Avoiding just this kind of charge, it seems to me, is part of Hornsby's motivation in noting that IT is not vacuous because it "takes a stand on what the bearers of truth are, calling them thinkables." But a thinkable is just what can possibly be contained (so to speak) in the mind. Apparently many things can. But those things are facts or bits of the World itself and not some separable (mental) thing.

Ultimately, we want to capture how linguistic entities such as sentences, assertions, and statements are true. Something's being true explains how our claims accurately present the World. But note that it is a presentation (the facts qua proposition) rather than a representation (merely a thought) that is true.[23] I'm not sure, then, why Hornsby's "taking a stand on what the bearers of truth are, calling them thinkables" helps. Thinkables just are bits of the World. Truth bearers and truth-makers turn out to be the same thing, even if there is some explanatory priority in speaking of one rather than the other.[24]

So whether one calls the thing believed a proposition or a thinkable, it turns out just to be (an aspect of) the World itself and not some mental object standing between the believer and the World. Rorty is, I think, right when he says there are no propositions in the representational sense. Propositions do not, in the end, represent the World. Instead, they are bits of the World. But Rorty is wrong when he says that the content of beliefs is just beliefs. The content of beliefs is the World itself.

These considerations point to some problems with taking propositions to be the primary bearers of truth, problems to which I return in the next section. Nevertheless, I think we need such a notion to help us talk about these matters. I think that "proposition" provides us a term that picks out an explanatory entity for the notion of truth. Furthermore, "proposition" picks out the entity found underneath assertions, utterances, statements, sentences, and beliefs. That is, it is a term picking out the content of these various linguistic representations (all of which, save beliefs, are public). That content, however, is just the World itself and nothing more. However, I also believe that based on these things, we can be comfortable in accepting that propositions are truth-value bearers. Since the proposition is a convenient way to do all the things I just noted, I think we should affirm IT with its understanding of propositions as the truth-value bearers underlying all of these. But in the end, just as water's being H_2O reports on a feature of the World, with one term having nothing more than explanatory priority, so a proposition's being a fact or a bit of the World reports on a feature of the World, with one having nothing more than explanatory priority.

5 ACT-BELIEFS AS TRUTH-VALUE BEARERS

I noted earlier that propositions and beliefs seem to be the best candidates for the mental aspect of truths. I've now suggested that propositions can be considered truth-value bearers only in a secondary sense, for they turn out, on IT, to fall on the worldly side of the explanation of truth. What then are the primary truth-value bearers?

Unlike assertions, utterances, statements, and sentences, beliefs seem to have a peculiarly private and therefore mental aspect. Assertions, statements, utterances, and sentences are all public and fall on the worldly side rather than the mental side. So it seems these public entities are all secondary (or perhaps tertiary) bearers of truth-value as well. As linguistic representations of the World, assertions, utterances, and sentences all, finally, express propositions, which in turn just are bits of the World. As such, we don't yet have anything connecting the mental with the World in a way we need for a realist theory of truth combined with a noetic irrealism.

So let's consider beliefs a little more. It is important to note that on a propositional analysis of belief, one can't have beliefs without propositions. Given the central role of belief in our cognitive lives, it would be rather suspicious if we didn't give an account for the truth of beliefs. But the reader might ask whether I haven't done that already by giving an analysis of the truth of propositions. My answer is no.

I've proposed the worldly content theory of belief. I've also noted that "belief" is notoriously ambiguous between its act and object senses – the act-belief and the object-belief. I also left unstated which I was referring to in the worldly content theory of belief. Insofar as we are happy with propositions (understood as bits of the World) being the content of beliefs, then we can say that propositions are the content of object-beliefs. Of course many philosophers take such a position and go merrily on their way.

Such a merry trip, however, overlooks an important issue. To ask about the content of the object-belief p seems simply to ask what p is. But the answer seems to be, if we follow IT coupled with a propositional analysis of belief, that p is just a bit of the World. The object-belief is what is believed. What is believed is a bit of the World. But then to ask about the content of the object-belief is just to ask about the object-belief itself. In other words, it's just to ask, what is the content of the content of a belief? That seems a rather unhelpful question.

When we ask about the content of a belief, aren't we asking about the content of the act-belief rather than the object-belief? Here I have visions of receiving the "incredulous stare" response made famous by David Lewis. So, I admit, my view will raise some suspicions about the worldly content theory of belief. Doesn't the fact that one's act-belief contains the World or bits thereof entail idealism, and a rather crude sort of idealism at that? I think the right answer is that the theory of truth I'm suggesting does not entail idealism but rather is simply compatible with it, and that the idealism itself is not crude.

The question boils down to this: does my believing p cause p to be the case? Recall from chapter 7 my claim that it is not the epistemizing of the truth-value bearers that make the worlds separate but, instead, the variables in our conceptual schemes that make the separate worlds. Even if the World is monistic, the way the World is enters at the level of symbol system and concept and not at the level of epistemology or believing. Our systems and schemes, having influenced the way the various worlds are, influence how we epistemically rank-order truth-value bearers within those worlds. Furthermore, not only do our systems and schemes influence how we epistemically rank our believings but they influence which believings we in fact have. That our freedom is involved in coming to hold one set of act-beliefs over another does not show that we can just "make up" a world to our own liking. That is one of the important lessons we learn from McDowell. But one needn't buy McDowell's commitment to realism about the World to gain the insight that our conceptualizing goes all the way down to a world, and that such a world, indeed, influences our believings. But there is no causation from our "freely chosen" believings to the worlds. Rather, the conceptual framework makes a world be what it is and, in that context, we come to believe as we do. The worlds we construct are the way they are because of our conceptualizing feats (rather than our believing feats). Once a world is conceptualized, any truth-value bearers within that world are true according to the way that world is and not some epistemic or spontaneous contribution. Worlds are what they are relative to noetic feats. The proper move thus is from a (world-relativized) ontology to our believings and the epistemology that goes with them.

More pertinent to my concern, however, is this. Doesn't the worldly content theory of belief, where beliefs are understood as act-beliefs, make it impossible to have anything but an irrealist account of truth? Doesn't it just make my believing something sufficient for its being the case, leaving no distinction between the mental action and the world itself and, perhaps worse, opening us up to the wildest sort of relativism? I think not.

I want to take a rather long route to the explanation of why I hold a negative answer. The route begins with my reply to the "incredulous stare" response to the apparently counterintuitive nature of my proposal. Act-beliefs are, of course, typically understood as propositional attitudes – attitudes toward some content or other. Since an attitude can't be true or false, it is thought, it is object-beliefs that are true or false. This corresponds to the generally held notion that it is propositions, statements, assertions, utterances (understood in the object sense, once again), sentences, and so forth that are the bearers of truth-value. Object-beliefs in fact just are propositions or object statements or sentences, etc. Consider this from Marian David:

> But the noun "belief" harbours an "act-object" ambiguity: at times it is used to refer to the state of believing something; at other times it is used to refer to what is believed. On a traditional understanding of the propositional analysis of belief, belief *states* are, strictly speaking, not truth bearers at all. We say "What she believes is true"; we do not say "Her believing it is true". The form "Her belief that *p* is true" is to be construed along the following lines: "The

proposition that *p* is true and is believed by her". So this view denies that there is an intelligible sense in which beliefs (thoughts, judgments, etc.) are truth bearers in addition to propositions.[25]

I'm obviously taking a different position and proposing a different tack. I reject the propositional analysis of belief where propositions are considered a sort of mental entity except in the relatively innocuous sense that they take an explanatory prior role to facts. I hence reject the notion that belief states (act-beliefs) are not bearers of truth. I also reject the notion that propositions are abstract entities independent of, but related to, bits of the World in any way other than identity. That is, I reject the notion that propositions represent the World.

Once we grasp IT, we see that propositions or thinkables are not somehow distinct from the World itself. The so-called proposition that snow is white just is the fact that snow is white. Snow's being white is not an abstract entity but a concrete bit of the World. In rejecting the propositional analysis of beliefs I am, I think, only pushing the insights of McDowell and Hornsby into a kind of honesty with their observations about thinkables and facts. When the thinkable is just a bit of the World, what is it about the thinkable that is mental or independent of the World? The thinkable isn't independent of the World – it is the World. The only thing independent of the World is the believing (the mental action). But in order to avoid lapsing into some sort of idealism or antirealism, McDowell and Hornsby hold that the content of thought is a bit of the World and that bit of the World is not identical to any mental *action*. Well and good. But then the proposition or thinkable is just a bit of the World and not mental or if the proposition or thinkable is mental, then so are facts, and idealism is at the door.

What is clearly mental is the attitude one takes toward the World – in this case, the act-belief. It is only the mental that has actual content. The proposition or the thinkable just is a bit of the World itself and cannot, as such, have content. It can only be what it is. To say that something (the "thinkable") is thought comes to what? What is the "thought" that is attached to the "thinkable" if it is not the act of thinking? Since thinkables are on the worldly side, they cannot themselves be something mental. What is on the mental side is the thinking.

How does all this affect IT as compatible with noetic irrealism? McDowell says that "It would indeed slight the independence of reality if we equated facts in general with exercises of conceptual capacities – acts of thinking – or represented facts as reflections of such things; or if we equated perceptible facts in particular with states or occurrences in which conceptual capacities are drawn into operation in sensibility – experiences – or represented them as reflections of such things."[26] Limiting my comments to propositions as a kind of thought, we can state McDowell's concern in this way. If instead of facts (or bits of the World) being identical to propositions they were identical to acts of thought (e.g., believings), then it would appear that the World is brought about by our noetic activity and the World cannot, so to speak, simply impress itself upon our thoughts. Furthermore, we can extend this concern beyond mere idealism to include an irrealist account of truth. If facts were identical to believings, let's say, then truth would be constructed by human noetic activity.

This is a reason for the noetic irrealist to abandon IT as the theory best compatible with noetic irrealism, even if it functions just fine for analyzing linguistically expressible presentations of the World (e.g., sentences expressing propositions) and their connection to the World (the fact). Because I reject the notion of propositions as mental entities, if I wanted to retain IT I would have to say that facts or bits of the World are identical to believings. But McDowell is right about the identification of acts of thought with bits of the World entailing idealism of the more radical sort. Furthermore, such a position entails alethic irrealism as well.

Here's more detail. If believings are purely mental entities, and if believings are identical to facts, that would mean that the existence of believings (and hence facts) would depend on minds in a most radical way. But does that imply that a particular believing's being a fact depends on the mind? Unlike in Lynch's argument, quoted above, defending IT as a realist alethic theory, the answer here seems to be yes. Lynch speaks of the explanatory priority of propositions over facts. But when it comes to believings where believings are identical to facts, it seems clear that if someone act-believes x, then x would turn out to be a fact. That is, x's being believed not only makes believings and facts dependent on the mind but the truth of some claim, say p, would be caused by the mind. My believing p is identical to p's being a fact. A Lynch-type argument cannot get the identity theorist who holds that believings are identical to bits of the World off the alethic irrealist's hook. So I do not wish to identify acts of thought with facts or bits of the World. However, I do wish to connect true believings with the content of those believings. I will do so in the next section.

There is a further argument for why it is strictly act-beliefs rather than object-beliefs (or any of the other things on the object side of the act/object ambiguities) that are true. The move to act-beliefs as truth-value bearers makes a great deal of sense of some things we typically hold about beliefs and their relationship to truth, in particular that falsehood is a fatal objection to belief. We can grasp the relevant issues here by noting that belief functions quite differently in regard to truth and falsehood from, let's say, assertion. As I noted above, not only belief but assertion has an act/object ambiguity. There is both a content of an assertion and the asserting of it. Taking note of these ambiguities, Bernard Williams suggests that act-assertions can be rude or tactless or revealing of a secret and hence objectionable. He continues: "Falsehood is certainly an objection to an assertion; intuitively it seems to be a more basic objection than these others ..."[27] But why think this, Williams asks. One answer might be that falsehood is a property of the content and not the act. This is not correct, however, for "[w]hat A asserts, the content of his assertion, may equally be what B supposes or C denies; it is just a content ... If it is false, it is false in all these connections or presentations, but its falsehood is an objection only in A's case, not in B's or (least of all) in C's. Though the objection to A's assertion is grounded in a fact about its content, the objection is to his asserting it."[28]

An alternative explanation for the intuition that the falsehood of an assertion is more basic than its rudeness or tactlessness is just that it is the only universal objection, the one everyone must either approve or deny just because it is an assertion. Williams writes,

> is it the only absolute objection, the others being variously relative to audience, circumstance, and so on? What is tactless or rude if said to one listener is not if said to another, but what is false is false whoever is listening. But now everything turns on what counts as "an objection." No-one can hold that if A's assertion is recognized to be false, it follows that he ought not to have made it. He may have made it in good faith, on convincing evidence, and so on.[29]

So far, so good. But in the case of belief, we conduct ourselves very differently. Williams continues:

Indeed, there was no such implication in the case of belief: if what one believed turns out to be false, it does not follow that one ought not to have believed it. What does follow is that if one recognizes the falsehood, one does not carry on having the belief – that is what it was for the objection to be fatal. So will the objection of falsehood be fatal to an assertion in this sense, that if a person recognizes that an assertion of his is false, he cannot go on making it? No, since it is a sad truth that he can. Perhaps he ought not to, but that merely reminds us of what we knew already, that falsehood is one kind of objection to assertions, and does nothing to show that it is fatal.[30]

An assertion can go on being asserted (the object-assertion can be act-asserted), even if the object-assertion is false, but the logic is different with belief. A belief cannot go on being believed (the object-belief cannot be an act-believed), if the object-belief is (thought to be) false. In dealing with beliefs, there is an important psychological-*cum*-epistemological-*cum*-ontological feature: upon coming to hold that an object-belief is false, one's act-belief automatically changes. There is a kind of necessity here, but it is not exactly a logical necessity. To believe that p but also admit that p is false is, while odd (we simply don't find people doing this, ever) it is not clearly logically impossible to act-believe an object-belief thought to be false. Why is this? It seems to me that our act-beliefs, once emptied of content, simply stop – cannot help but stop (in that psychological-*cum*-epistemological-*cum*-ontological way mentioned above) – being actions.

6 THE WORLDLY CONTENT THEORY OF TRUTH

Building on the worldly content theory of belief, I propose the following – what I call the "worldly content theory of truth" (WCT) – viz., beliefs (that is, act-beliefs) are true just in case the content of the belief is actually in the belief. Or alternatively, act-beliefs are true just in case the content of the belief is (part of) the way the World is.

The worldly content theory can be stated (more formally) in either of the following ways, where I take the first and the second versions to be substitutable for one another. These two versions can be stated as

WCT1 For all x, x is a true (act-)belief iff the content of x is actually in x.

and

> WCT2 For all x, x is a true (act-)belief iff the content of x is (part of) the World (or part of the world) itself.

The phrase "actually in" in WCT1 is meant to emphasize that it is the act-belief (the attitude of belief itself) that is in touch with some aspect of the actual World (or an actual way the World is – a world) and thus it is the act-belief (rather than its supposed content) that is true. So WCT1 says the same thing as WCT2 because to be actually in a person's act-belief is simply for the appropriate chunk of the World (or world) to be the content of a person's act-belief. If the belief that snow is white is true, then the chunk of the (or a) world that snow is white is actually the content of the belief in question. That is, the content of the belief "snow is white" is (part of) the way the World is (or a world is). In the same way, if the belief that Huck Finn has a friend named Jim is true, then the chunk of the world in which Huck Finn has a friend named Jim is the content of the belief. That is, the content of the belief "Huck has a friend named Jim" is part of the way the (in this case fictional) world is. WCT1 and WCT2 are meant to present the same feature of true beliefs.

Understood in this way, truth is a metaphysically rooted, and not an epistemically rooted, notion. The truth-maker is a bit of ontological furniture and not how we know, believe, cognize, etc., about that furniture. A belief is true just in case the belief has as its content the relevant part of the world or the World. This theory is alethically realist, but not a correspondence theory or an identity theory. A realist alethic theory says that the content of the truth-value bearer itself gives us everything we need to specify what it takes for the truth-value bearer to be true. If the content of the belief is a world or the World itself (or appropriate parts thereof), we've got what it takes to meet the minimal requirements of a realist alethic theory.

The worldly content theory is not an epistemic notion of truth. There are no requirements that the believer be justified, warranted, or stand in any other positive epistemic position in regard to the belief, in order for the belief to be true. It is, in short, compatible with a minimalist realist alethic theory. The content of the truth-value bearer gives us everything we need to specify what makes the belief true. In our case, the belief not only lets us specify what would make the belief true, but it actually contains what makes the belief true. One can hardly get more specific than that.

7 ON WCT AND IRREALISM

So there is a way to sidestep representations as mental entities and yet have something other than other beliefs themselves as the content of a belief. In the case of the irrealism defended here, the content of beliefs is not simply a World found but rather beliefs have an irrealist world content, namely, chunks of that world itself where that world is constructed by noetic, that is, conceptual feat. At least true ones do. If my suggestions rightly render the world, then at least some of Rorty's issues can be resolved without giving up the distinction between the world and beliefs about it. As well, we have set the stage for developing a noetically irrealist account of things and worlds without giving up alethic realism.

Act-beliefs are the fundamental truth-value bearers, as truly mental entities. But we can act-believe a fact, for facts just are true propositions. What then are propositions, act-statements, act-utterances, and the like? They are pieces of a world in and of a world but also in and of the mind, at least when they are true. We can say they bear truth because they are real. As such, they are truth-value bearers, but derivatively so. What bears truth primarily is the act-belief – one's attitude toward the content, that is, the world itself. Truth is getting things right (in our attitudes – our act-beliefs) and as such there is a close relationship between generative truth (world-making) and the truth of statements (the world as made). But it is a connection through concepts, construction of a world, experience of that world, and believings that grow within that world.

What of McDowell's fear of idealism? The concern seems to be clearly stated by Hornsby when she identifies idealism with the position that "nothing would be the case unless there were cognitive activity – that there could be no mindless world."[31] But the kind of idealism I'm developing here is more modest and does not claim that there would be nothing at all without human minds. It's just that there would be a lot less. The fact that there are humans with minds is itself something that needs explaining. But I see nothing in

what I've said in this chapter that sets loose a radical noetic antirealism such as one finds in Rorty.

8 THE CHALLENGE OF BEING CONTENTLESS

I'll close this chapter with a few comments about false beliefs. The
critic may have a problem with the notion that false act-beliefs have
no content. Perhaps the intuition is this: Since we can distinguish
among act-beliefs, including false ones, the implication is that there
is a content of the beliefs in virtue of which we can so distinguish.
Surely, for example, we can distinguish between the false act-belief
that snow is green and the false act-belief that the Empire State
Building is the tallest building in the world in 2008. While it is the
case that we can distinguish among beliefs, what has that to do with
what makes them true or false? Truth is a metaphysical notion not
an epistemic one. The issue here isn't whether I can know or judge
or reliably believe that some belief is true or sort it out from false
beliefs. The issue is whether it is true. This has nothing at all to do
with our ability to distinguish among beliefs. The suggestion that
what makes a belief true is that it has the content it does may simply have the result that false beliefs cannot actually be distinguished
from one another in any way that matters vis-à-vis truth. So, while
we need to distinguish among beliefs in order to tell which ones are
true, we do not need to distinguish among beliefs in order for them
to be true. Perhaps we need to consider alternative ways of thinking
about epistemology rather than to reject the suggestion in order to
keep our epistemologies.

Yet we do seem to be able to distinguish among even false beliefs,
and how do we do this, if false beliefs have no content? A variety of
suggestions are possible here. One is that when we consider false
beliefs we distinguish them from one another not in virtue of their
content but in virtue of the sounds or marks that fill in the blank "I
believe _____." It is rather like distinguishing among squig-
gles drawn by a monkey. We can tell one from the other, but they
have no real meaningful content. The linguistic terms we use to talk
about the supposed content is just talk. It refers to nothing, exemplifies nothing, symbolizes nothing. An alternative suggestion is
that we can distinguish among false beliefs on the basis of what
they purport to have as their content, even if, as it turns out, they

don't have this content. The false belief that snow is green purports to be about green snow, but, there not being any green snow, the belief can't be true.[32] "True" is a positive term while "false" is a negative one. An analogous situation is found in discussions of finite and infinite, the former being positive, the latter negative. While we have a decent grasp of the finite, we have a less firm grasp on the infinite. And while we can talk well enough using the term "infinite," what the term refers to is less than clear.

Make/Believing What Is,
and Other World Renderings

I've presented three contemporary irrealisms, each of which describes how the mind's creative symbolism is related to the World. I've argued that noetic irrealism is the right way to think about the relationship of the human mind to the World and provided a realist account of truth compatible with noetic irrealism. I've further suggested that we "make/believe" various irrealistic worlds. These various ways the World is (the worlds) result, in part, from various noetic feats including the conceptualizing involved in believings, contemplatings, perceivings, and picturings. A world-version is rightly made when it makes an actual way the World is (a world). To say that p is true iff p is to admit that facts and truth come in a tightly knit package. To say that p is true iff p is also to admit that facts, truth, and believings come in a tightly knit package. For descriptive worlds, one of the markers of a rightly formed world-version is that our act-beliefs are true, that is, the attitude of belief bears truth. What makes our believing true is the world, the right side of the "iff." It is the attitude toward the world that is true, and the object-belief (or proposition) just is (a bit of) the world.

I need to clarify the relationship of world-making (via our concepts) to a world made. In making a world, we come to act-believe some things, reject others (as not act-believable), and withhold our act-belief from others. This process of taking on, rejecting, or withholding believings provides the core of our interaction with the world we are making. It is our way of being in the world, if you will, and the world's way of being in us. Yet our believings are rooted in the concepts we use in making the world and those concepts run all the way out to our experience of the world. The world provides the doorstop for our believings via a realist notion of truth. But of course the World is the way it is because of the conceptual schemes we use. There are a number of issues on which to comment. Let us begin with the role of choice.

I CHOICE AND WORLD-MAKING

Recall McDowell's concern with human spontaneity, our freedom in judging and believing things about the world. The same concepts used in judging and believing are those via which, in passivity, we experience the world. This enables McDowell's position to explain how it is that we have friction that keeps our system of beliefs and judgments from running wild. Recall also McDowell's requirement that our rational network always check and recheck the appropriateness of the connections it's making. "There must be a standing willingness to refashion concepts and conceptions if that is what reflection recommends,"[1] says McDowell. He continues, and here I repeat the quotation to have it freshly in view:

> No doubt there is no serious prospect that we might need to reshape the concepts at the outermost edges of the system, the most immediately observational concepts, in response to pressures from inside the system. But that no-doubt unreal prospect brings out the point that matters for my present purpose. This is that although experience itself is not a good fit for the idea of spontaneity, even the most immediately observational concepts are partly constituted by their role in something that is indeed appropriately conceived in terms of spontaneity.[2]

On McDowell's model, concepts, even the most immediately observational ones, are open to development from within the "higher" level concepts used in judging and believing. So the interaction between the world and the world - version, or the world and conceptual scheme, involves a reliance – in both directions, I believe – between the concepts in play and the beliefs we have and judgments we make. In what follows I assume this kind of give and take, ebb and flow between believings and judgings, on the one hand, and concepts in play, on the other hand.

But do we freely choose our concepts? Are believings in our control? If not, how then can we make a world? The beginning of an answer is that even if our beliefs and the use of concepts are not in our direct control, we can still do some things to influence our beliefs and concepts. Although Lynch speaks here only of concepts and not beliefs, we can quote Lynch again as a starting place. He writes:

> Concepts, no more than styles of painting and sense of humour, cannot come and go at will. There are causes, often beyond our control, for changes in such things. This is why it would be gravely misleading to describe metaphysical pluralism in general, or relativistic Kantianism [his own view] in particular, as a view according to which we can construct (or deconstruct) reality. To construct something, either literally, as in the case of a house, or metaphorically, as in the case of a new law or statute, is to engage in a conscious, deliberate process of creation. The ebb and flow of our concepts more often takes place well beneath the surface of our thought.[3]

Lynch obviously disagrees with the notion that we actively construct or make worlds. I think Lynch's concerns are not well founded, at least in part.

The concepts with which we think, and the beliefs we therefore hold, are historically rooted. Lynch is right about that. My concepts and beliefs do not generally change at my will. Yet they do change in my circumstance and my circumstances come about, in large measure, because of the way I will. Because I decide how to live, much of what I believe ends up different than it otherwise would have. I wind up with one set of beliefs rather than another, using one set of concepts rather than another. It is important to note the role of other people as well. As a child, I learn how to think about things as I learn language from those around me. I attend school and am taught certain theoretical ideas – the tables aren't really solid but made up of tiny particles. Or I take a philosophy class and learn that Aristotle thought the world made of discrete things, while Whitehead thought it made of events. With each new exposure, my repertoire of realities, so to speak, becomes larger. Typically, I settle into one or the other of these. I don't create my own. But I can choose to go into advanced physics or philosophy programs and as a researcher at least contribute to (as opposed to entirely make) the ways the World is. I do so by my thinking creatively, by theorizing about physics or ontology. But even in these circumstances, I build out of the materials at hand. Worlds are built out of other worlds. To paraphrase the ancient wisdom of Israel, "there is nothing (entirely) new under the sun."

Much of what I believe and many of the concepts I use are shared beliefs and concepts, inherited from others. If I go on to contribute to the World (to make a world) then I build on those shared concepts. But I want to emphasize that we all do this, at least on a minimal scale, simply by living and making choices. I choose to work hard at school – my world changes. I choose to apply to college – my world changes. I get in (the result, too, of other people's choices) and I am further educated, being exposed to new concepts and ideas. I choose to marry – again with another's contribution – and we make, together, a new thing – a marriage. I vote liberal rather than conservative. And so forth. Some people contribute in larger theoretical or creative ways than others, but we all contribute.

So we build worlds by the choices we make in living our lives. In my varying circumstances I find my beliefs changing. This is true both of my act-beliefs and their corresponding objects, that is, chunks or bits of the world. What makes a world and its facts is a large complex of inherited and created concepts, beliefs, attitudes, precepts, perceptions, and so forth – a world-version. My act-beliefs are a small part of that complex and as such are responsive to the complex and to the world the complex makes. The difference between the world and the world-version is thus one of perspective or emphasis rather than two distinct realms. Worlds just are versions, and versions worlds.

My decision to live one way rather than another generates the circumstances in which I live and hence the act-beliefs I have. Falsity is a fatal objection to a belief, but falsity is fatal to my act-belief only because the world is not as I act-believe it to be. But then the world is not as I act-believe it to be in part because I don't act-believe it to be so.[4] Sometimes this is because of direct choices I make to construct the world with one set of concepts rather than another. Most times it is less directly a choice. Which it is depends on many factors, including the complexity of the situation, the goals or purposes toward which I'm aiming, the amount of attention I'm paying, what I value, and so forth. Here are two examples.

The first you've already seen in the beginning chapter where a young son announces, "that is a great boat" as an object floats by him in the bath water. To make that announcement, and for the father to go along with it, is to choose to live in a certain world, at least for a while. The object is no longer a bar of soap; it is a boat. What changed? The act-belief changed, which changed the ontology of the world, which changed the object of belief "that's a bar of soap" into a false one (an empty bit of the world) and a previously false belief "that's a great boat" into a true one. Of course, there are all the related things the "soap" is as well, such as a mess of molecules or another parcel of particles.

A more complicated example is a change of belief from an Aristotelian ontology to a Whiteheadian one. Suppose I discover, in the course of philosophical discussion, that my Aristotelian act-beliefs have no connection to the world. That is, I discover that I no longer believe that discrete entities but rather events are the basic ontological building blocks. The facts of the universe have changed for me.[5] Now was that a choice? If it was, on what side of the iff did the change occur? I leave one world and enter another. Perhaps for a while, I entertain both. Perhaps I decide to throw in my lot with Whitehead. Then, my beliefs are embedded in my choices and my choices in my beliefs. It is possible, though, that I don't decide but just find myself believing the Whiteheadian story. Sometimes, living our lives "steadies the mind" and its content, as Williams suggests.[6] Our beliefs change in historical and social context, sometimes directly involving choice, sometimes only indirectly. But we do make worlds out of other worlds. We call this history. We work hard to make theories and hold beliefs that make sense out of the data but our theories, perspectives, values, and experience influence the data.

We sometimes discover our act-beliefs as we live and will to be one way rather than another. On the other hand, sometimes we just choose which way to believe. Of course, a lot of the World is "permanent," or so it seems. It is inherited from the past and from other things we believe. But we change what we can and what seems right to change, and our believings change with the choices (sometimes very slowly). Because we make our worlds by living, thinking, and acting, we influence how our beliefs are. To discover that a belief is false is fatal to it, but not simply because of something outside the influence of our minds. It is fatal because we don't believe it. The psychological feature of coming to disbelieve (the act) because the belief is false (the content), cannot be separated, on irrealism, from the belief being false (the content) because we come to disbelieve (the act). We change our minds, or our minds become more stable, in history. Lynch is right, so far forth, that concepts generally don't come and go at will. But what we will in history can surely make the concepts and their co-relative beliefs come and go.

2 STATEMENT TRUTH AND GENERATIVE TRUTH

This brings us back to world-making (generative truth) and truth and falsity within and across worlds. An act-belief false in one world can be true in another.[7] To some degree, as my beliefs change, they change because my world changes. Versions and worlds rise and fall together. What relationship holds between true and false beliefs and true and false versions? A generatively true descriptive version, one presumes, includes all the act-beliefs true in the world of which the version is (generatively) true. A generatively true world, in my terms, is a historically rooted world – an actual way the World is. Since a (generatively) false version is true in no world, one can presume that it contains only false beliefs, that is, beliefs with no content.

I've said little about worlds or versions in transition, that is, worlds as they are being constructed. Neither do Goodman, Lynch, or Hales say much about these worlds. Most of Goodman's talk, for example, seems to be about true versions or false versions, versions as if they were transfixed in some final sort of way. There is little talk about worlds only partly made. Yet it seems our worlds are always under construction. We are finite beings striving toward a complete story.[8] One supposes when a world is completely made, all one's beliefs would be true. God seems the only likely candidate to pull off complete worlds, and perhaps not even God can do that, if God is self-surpassing creativity. Our world-making is full of false starts, blind alleys, and wishful thinking. Some of our beliefs are false. When we discover that our world is other than we believed, our beliefs change to embrace the new. But, most importantly, even if my or your world-version is not complete and contains many empty and hence false beliefs, it remains that if a descriptive world were complete, all the beliefs would be true (in that world). Alternative worlds, if they were complete, would also contain only true beliefs.

A false version, given the fact that it generates no world at all, is a world in which no one really lives. It is not historically rooted – not actual. Hence it contains no beliefs. This raises all kinds of questions about false beliefs. Since a belief false in W_1 can be true in W_2, it seems that while generatively false versions must contain only false beliefs, some of those beliefs, (which are false because there is no chunk of the world to make them true), are still (potentially) true in other worlds. A false version contains, so to speak, only false beliefs, but then, in the literal sense, it contains no beliefs at all, for it isn't a world at all. Such a world, I propose, is logically impossible or perhaps impossible on other grounds. Such a world version is not acceptable to us, for we cannot believe anything in the world it makes because it makes no world at all. However, in partly complete worlds we will find false beliefs. Even in complete worlds we could consider alternative ways things might be. As such, while A is true in W_1, A might be false in W_2. So, some statements (let's say, thought of when building a world) would be false in the world being constructed (W_1) but true in another one (W_2). Such beliefs are just never true in that world (W_1).

All this suggests that whatever is act-believed in a world is true in its world. In other words, there are no false beliefs in a world. But surely, the critic will say, the world in which I live contains act-beliefs that are false. True enough, and the explanation is not far to seek for the world I live in is not complete. So, a belief false in my world is false because it has no content and hence there is no part or chunk of the world on the right side of the iff: "p" is false iff $-p$. The $-p$ is, simply, nothing at all in the world being made. Can a world-version then be true (generatively) and hence create a world and yet I, as a holder of that world-version, have some false beliefs in that world? Yes, because we humans are finite, we always fall short of fully making a world. Of course, we think our act-beliefs true, that is, to have content. Yet they sometimes do not. Such act-beliefs, however, could be true, if another world were brought into being under a different conceptual system.

This is what the irrealist should be striving for when she claims (in a Goodmanian spirit) that true versions, conflicting though they might be, generate actual worlds and not just possible worlds. False versions are simply worlds that contain contradictions. These are worlds that in the end cannot be constructed. They are empty. Generatively true world-versions containing false beliefs correlate to worlds that are not completely constructed. Of course, when I have false beliefs I don't know it. Once I discover a belief is false, I don't believe it any longer. My act-believing p changes when I discover that the belief has no content. I can no longer believe it. But I might be able to imagine how such beliefs could be true. This simply points to the rich possibilities of new world-construction. Such beliefs are "merely possible" from the point of view of the world I'm in. That is, if they were held in an alternate world, they would be true. False beliefs are beliefs about unactualized things, that is, that have no chunks or bits of the actual world (as construed by the world-version in question) as their content. But no false belief is held in a completely rightly rendered world. Insofar as the world I live in is rightly formed, all my beliefs have content from that world. My believings are true when the world is rightly rendered. It is my believings that bear truth, and the generative notion of truth comes together with the truth of statements in a generatively true descriptive world. But most and perhaps all human worlds are only partly rightly formed.

Beliefs are false just in case the content of the belief is not really in the belief. That is, beliefs are false when the world as generatively true (rightly made) does not have the appropriate fact in it and hence neither does my belief. The notion of falsity is metaphysical (and not epistemic or linguistic), in just the way that the notion of truth is metaphysical. Falsity is just as radically nonepistemic as is truth. We see the apparent gap between descriptive world-versions and the worlds correlated with them closing up very tightly, so there is little, if any, significant difference between them. A belief is false just in case the belief fails to have genuine content. Thus, the belief that snow is green is false simply because the belief has no genuine content in the world in which it is held. There is no chunk of the world (in question) in which snow is green and so it cannot be the content of the belief. Likewise, the belief that Huck Finn is a slave is false just because there is no chunk of the world in which Huck Finn is a slave.[9] But of course, what is true or false depends upon the world in which it is uttered. What is true in one might be false in another. Thus, "the sun stands still" and "the sun moves" are both true, depending on the world.

We must note, however, that some beliefs are true in every world – the law of noncontradiction, for example, or that God exists. Likewise, some beliefs are false in every world – contradictions or the belief that God does not exist. But some generatively true versions have not yet been thought of and therefore right now they are true in no world since they are not actualized. They wait our making them. Finally, some versions simply cannot be thought of (contradictory ones). These latter are false versions.

3 RENDERING AND RIGHTNESS

Rightnesses other than truth are important in a variety of ways, but especially to explain the values of beauty and goodness. I move in the remaining sections of this chapter to consider the more general notion of rightness of rendering.

Goodman presses the term "rendering" into use at many places. Unfortunately, his guidance about what it comes to falls short on details. Let me begin by taking the terminology of "rendering" seriously. To render something is to submit or present it for consideration, as when a bill is presented to a customer. Related uses of the term include making something available, giving what is due or appropriate, giving in return, and yielding or surrendering. We can also render fat by melting it down or render something by expressing it in another language or by means of translation. None of these have strictly to do with truth of statements as we typically take it, a "matching" between one thing and another. The closest uses of the term to a kind of matching are, perhaps, the idea of giving something in return and translation into another language, but even they involve much more than a matching. Is a poem translated from English into Hindi the same poem? How many of the metaphors will be the same, how many linguistic nuances? Or what of when you exchange your car for my dollars? These are not cases of matching.

To rightly render, thus, is not to compare two things (a world-version and a world) but to present something, to make it available. A right world is a true world and truth, in this generative sense, is a whole, a unity of world-version-*cum*-world-presented. The task of constructing worlds includes the tasks of describing, representing, expressing, and exemplifying. Some of the worlds are scientific or quasi-scientific and hence tend toward literalism, whereas other worlds are poetic or artistic and hence tend toward the metaphoric or exemplificatory. But in all cases, when a world-version is rightly rendered, the result is a world presented for consideration. Such worlds are meant to help us understand. Goodman writes:

> Representation or description is apt, effective, illuminating, subtle, intriguing, to the extent that the artist or writer grasps fresh and significant relationships and devises means for making them manifest ... And if the point of the picture is not only successfully made but is also well-taken, if the realignments it directly and

indirectly effects are interesting and important, the picture – like a crucial experiment – makes a genuine contribution to knowledge. To a complaint that his portrait of Gertrude Stein did not look like her, Picasso is said to have answered, "No matter; it will." In sum, effective representation and description require invention. They are creative. They inform each other; and they form, relate and distinguish objects. That nature imitates art is too timid a dictum. Nature is a product of art.[10]

There is a way of presenting or making available what is appropriate to the thing or world itself. But what is presented need not be thought of as pre-fixed in "the World" but rather as an emerging thing, worked on and worked out over the course of time. A rightly rendered world is a world well made. Moving beyond anything argued by the three irrealists considered here, let me suggest that a world generated by a rightly rendered world-version is made and presented to others for consideration. We do not, typically, work alone, but more importantly here, we do not work for ourselves alone. Working to present a world to others (as well as to ourselves) is intrinsic to the notion of rendering.

Right rendering is central to noetic irrealism. Generative truth – right rendering – is a presentation, a making available to others. This holds not only for descriptive worlds but for worlds embedded in other symbolic systems as well. Such rendering is constrained – it ultimately needs to be right rendering. To be a right rendering, certain conditions must be met. Not just anything will go, so far as world-making is concerned. There is, in short, a requirement of genuineness for a true world-version. The world made must be an actual way the World is, a genuine world, as opposed to a false, fake, or empty world.

Let's consider one example of rightness from art. Must artistic worlds be realistic? Goodman describes two pictures, one realistic (that is, what we Westerners typically take to be realistic, one that "looks like" nature, whose perspective is "ordinary" and whose colours are "normal") and one in reverse perspective and whose colours are replaced by the normal colours' complements. He then says,

The two pictures … are equally correct, equally faithful to what they represent, provide the same and hence equally true information; yet they are not equally realistic or literal. For a picture to be faithful is simply for the object represented to have the properties that the picture in effect ascribes to it. But such fidelity or correctness or truth is not a sufficient condition for literalism or realism. The alert absolutist will argue that for the second picture but not the first we need a key. [In response,] ... the difference is that for the first the key is ready at hand ... Just here, I think, lies the touchstone of realism [in the arts]: not in quantity of information but in how easily it issues. And this depends upon how stereotyped the mode of representation is, upon how commonplace the labels and their uses have become.[11]

Must a rightly rendered artistic world be a realistic world? No.

However, many rightly rendered worlds leave us with a sense of the realistic and that sense, I believe, is often the source of our sense that "the World" itself must be noetically real. There must to something "there" to copy. Realism in painting is not about the amount of content taken from one world and represented accurately in some preset and expected, habitual way but rather some information taken and presented in a way easy to access. Realism in art thus is habitual and as we learn to understand non-realistic pictures, we learn that such pictures can rightly render a world or aspects of a world. Realism in the arts is about habit and how comfortable we are with a pattern of understanding and reading.

So too, I submit, our being drawn to noetic realism – the notion of a "found World" – is habitual. Any given world is dependent upon habit and how comfortable we are with a pattern of understanding. So we often confuse a cultural fondness with foundness. But there is no singular real way (independent of a symbol system) that a painting – or any given world in general – is or should be. Unfortunately, the confusion between "the World" being noetically real and our habitual sense that "the World" is noetically real makes it difficult to shift, emotionally, if not for other reasons as well, from noetic realism to irrealism.

We are further helped in understanding noetic irrealism by considering a general summary passage on depiction and description where Goodman writes,

Throughout, I have stressed the analogy between pictorial representation and verbal description because it seems to me both corrective and suggestive. Reference to an object is a necessary

condition for depiction or description of it, but no degree of resemblance is a necessary or sufficient condition for either. Both
depiction and description participate in the formation and characterization of the world; and they interact with each other and
with perception and knowledge. They are ways of classifying by
means of labels having singular or multiple or null reference. The
labels, pictorial or verbal, are themselves classified into kinds;
and the interpretation of fictive labels and of depiction-*as* and
description-*as*, is in terms of such kinds. Application and classifi-
cation of a label are relative to a system, and there are countless
alternative systems of representation and description. Such systems are the products of stipulation and habituation in varying
proportions. The choice among systems is free; but given a system, the question whether a newly encountered object is a desk or
a unicorn-picture or is represented by a certain painting is a question of the propriety, under that system, of projecting the predicate "desk" or the predicate "unicorn-picture" or the painting
over the thing in question, and the decision both is guided by and
guides usage for that system. [italics his][12]

Rightness of rendering thus depends on a number of things, not
simply a matching of language to thing or picture to thing. Rather,
it depends on projectibility within a system of symbols and that is
guided by, but also guides, usage within the system. But this is simply one aspect of rightness.

No philosophical pronouncement can provide a general criterion
of rightness. Yet different applications of rightness have in common
the following:

They are all concerned with effecting positive-negative dichoto-
mies or a grading on a preferential scale, and they share other
highly abstract but important features. The question what constitutes rightness in general has to be taken as asking for some
characterization or sketch, in terms of such features, of what the
various kinds of rightness have in common, not for a touchstone
that will determine rightness in every or indeed, any case, nor
even for a formal definition.[13]

But we can say that rightness is a kind of fitting and working. Since
rightness is not confined to systems that describe or state or even

depict, "the fitting here is not a fitting *onto* – not a correspondence or matching or mirroring of independent Reality – but a fitting *into* a context or discourse or standing complex of other symbols [italics his]."[14] Yet rightness is not merely coherence, any more than truth is. Factors such as seniority (dealing with what came before – issues of habit and entrenchment) matter. Fitting is neither passive nor one-way, but "an active process of fitting together; the fit has to be *made*, and the making may involve minor or major adjustments in what is being fitted *into* or what is being fitted *in* or both [italics his]."[15] Furthermore, fitting is tested by the working not just of what is fitted in but of the whole together. But perhaps most importantly the irrealist need not reduce rightness or truth to practicality. The main concern is understanding. Rightnesses of all kinds are about the business of helping us understand things and worlds. Noetic irrealism is a way of providing understanding of things and their worlds.

Examples of rightness include deductive inference where the argument may be valid with false premises, or inductive inference where one can have true premises but false conclusions. One can have a fair sample without reflecting accurately what is sampled: a fair sample can be understood as one that is fairly taken. Categories may be right or wrong: "Having been ordered to shoot anyone who moved, the guard shot all his prisoners, contending that they were all moving rapidly around the sun. Although true, his contention was plainly wrong, for it involved an inappropriate category of motion."[16] With all these possible approaches to rightness, rightness can clearly be seen as something other than a shadowy kind of correspondence between world and belief or world and thought. There are many aspects to rightness and they depend upon the particular symbol system one is using, the purposes for which a world-version is created, and a host of other factors. I think all these issues can be drawn together by focusing on the notion of a world-version presenting a world. It is on the presentational nature of right rendering that noetic irrealism should concentrate.

4 TRUTH AND OTHER RIGHTNESSES

We can learn about nondescriptive rightness by exploring descriptive world-versions. Recall the pictorial world I dubbed "untitled 22" (the red triangle on a white background). As we know, it is a mistake to say that untitled 22 is descriptively true. While we can say of a rightly rendered descriptive world-version that it contains true beliefs, we cannot say the same of untitled 22. What does it mean to say that untitled 22 is rightly rendered?

I begin with a general comment from Goodman about when a version can be taken to be true; that is, when a world-version is right and generates an actual world. Note, however, that he immediately turns to beliefs (and hence linguistically based descriptions) to do his explaining.

> Speaking loosely ... a version is taken to be true when it offends no unyielding beliefs and none of its own precepts. Among beliefs unyielding at a given time may be long-lived reflections of laws of logic, short-lived reflections of recent observations, and other convictions and prejudices ingrained with varying degrees of firmness. Among precepts, for example, may be choices among alternative frames of reference, weightings, and derivational bases. But the line between beliefs and precepts is neither sharp nor stable. Beliefs are framed in concepts informed by precepts; and if a Boyle ditches his data for a smooth curve just missing them all, we may say either that observational volume and pressure are different properties from theoretical volume and pressure or that the truths about volume and pressure differ in the two worlds of observation and theory. Even the staunchest belief may in time admit alternatives; "The earth is at rest" passed from dogma to dependence upon precept.[17]

It is clear that for Goodman virtually everything in a world-version can be challenged.

Similar to Quine's holistic account of epistemology, the ontology qua world-version proposed here allows no safe haven for beliefs and thus, for the things they present: no belief, even a belief about the laws of logic, appears to be outside the reach of potential challenge. As we will see in the next chapter, the suspicion that even the laws of logic are at risk is exactly where a major objection can be lodged against the particulars of Goodman's position. Setting that issue aside for the present, it appears that most beliefs, and thus the ontologies that are brought with them in a rightly rendered world-version, can be modified given enough time and enough reason. Furthermore, precepts (what we might think of as various bases via

which we generate beliefs and trace out their effects on other beliefs
– various ordering principles, sorting principles, etc.) can become
"mere" beliefs and vice versa. But it is important to see that this is
no mere epistemology being proposed. Rather, it is of a world itself
that Goodman speaks.

There is a kind of ontological bootstrapping going on here, for a
version is judged against its own beliefs and precepts. Goodman
seems to suggest a sort of coherence model of world-making. As
one's beliefs and precepts "hang together" a world is generated and
hence true statements emerge. Hence a world and a world-version
are very close to the same thing, but can be variously described depending on the context. But we've already seen indication that they
are not exactly the same thing. In an earlier quotation we saw that a
star is not made of letters nor a version far away. Goodman gives
another example when he writes,

> Yet if all features of a world are creatures of a version, are
> generated and imposed by the version, what can they be imposed
> upon? The question is pertinent but slightly awry. The world of a
> true version is a construct; the features are not conferred upon
> something independent of the version but combined with one
> another to make the world of that version. The world is not the
> version itself; the version may have features – such as being in
> English or consisting of words – that its world does not. But
> the world depends upon the version.[18]

So a descriptive world-version is generatively true (right) if it offends
none of its unyielding beliefs and precepts. A true version generates
an actual way the World is, and that world does not have all the features of the world-version nor the world-version all the features of
the world. World-versions (at least those that describe) consist of
words (and statements, beliefs, principles, attitudes, concepts, etc.)
while worlds do not.

What is presented in a descriptive version is the world itself.
When a descriptive world-version rightly presents a world, the
words are both part of the world and yet not. Which it is is a matter
of emphasis, focus, or perspective. We all know the difficulty of fig-
uring out how words and the world are connected and the challenges of self-reflexive sentences. But as we've seen, to say that that
tree is a long way off and that it is true that "that tree is a long way

off" is, as near as makes little matter, the same thing; "p" is true iff p. Yes, it's true that we can consider and talk about the world, but in the end what is important is the world, for it is the world that grounds any true statement. In short, it is the world that is the reality, not the words about the world. When I say something meant to be true, I am trying to get things right. The truth of a statement and generative truth are very close indeed. Language as public forces upon us a public symbol system. But what is presented (a world) is thought of directly. When we wish to communicate what is on our minds, we can either point (using gestural concepts) or paint (using pictorial concepts) or preach (using linguistic concepts). With language, it seems, we can typically separate the world-version from the world or, as the noetic realist might suggest, the world from the world-version. But I think this is not possible. Language presents the world itself, although the symbols are one step, so to speak, removed, if looked at from the point of view of the world. But looked at from within the world-version, the language simply presents the world. We make/believe the world – all the worlds. The language itself is in the world and the world embedded in language, a fact best illustrated by the self-reflexive "this sentence is short."

What of nondescriptive versions? One world-version is chosen over another for certain purposes. If I want to describe how the World is put together physically, then I may need waves or I may need particles, but I will certainly need words. In contrast, if I want to make a house, then I don't so much need words as I need pieces of two-by-four Douglas fir or clay bricks. Of course, a picture or two will help as well, and perhaps some notations. But here, as with language describing the world, I'm as much making a world as I am describing it. But if I simply want to present a new way of viewing 3-D objects, and I'm Picasso, I paint all the faces of the object flat on the canvas and use no words or notations. Here there may be no gap at all between the symbol and the thing symbolized.

Recall the claim "A true version is true in some worlds, and a false version in none."[19] I agree and thus speak primarily of the truth and falsity of versions rather than beliefs (or other truth-value bearers) within the versions. Nevertheless, what conflicts there are across worlds will certainly be referenced to beliefs or statements within the worlds. When I say a true version is true in some worlds, I imply that a true version can generate more than one world or perhaps that several versions may be present in a single world. What worlds are built by a world-version may depend on the truth of individual statements. So a true version built around "the sun is moving" will generate some actual worlds but not all. There are many worlds in which it is true that the sun moves. There are also many built around the sun not moving. But in order to preserve truth, when two true truth-value bearers contradict, they must be true in worlds distinct from each other, if true at all. But then obviously a true world-version containing the statement –A and one containing the statement A will not be true in the same world.

When we leave the area of descriptive worlds (worlds constructed out of linguistically rooted concepts), then the question of truth within the worlds is moot. In those worlds, say pictorial worlds, a true world version creates an actual way the World is in which truth is not the focus, although there are other rightnesses, in particular the rightness of presentation. Presentation comes in many ways. The Mona Lisa, for example, does many things, including represent. But what or who does it represent? Or perhaps the Mona Lisa is not a representation but rather an expression of love. These things can be discussed and debated. Yet we see in the Mona Lisa (a set of) pictorial concepts that rightly render without appeal to language. The Mona Lisa, we presume, wouldn't be right if the woman's nose had a large wart on its left side. Nor, we presume, would it be right if the woman weren't smiling that famous smile. But now, of what do we speak here, some woman who sat as the model or the woman in the painting?

The limits on world-versions depend on what kind of world one needs. Is it a world for telling us about nature? Then we'll need a descriptive world-version containing true statements. But that is not all the version will contain. Indeed two different true versions will generate two different (physical) ways the World is. The differences between these ways the World is will be in large measure determined by things other than the statements contained in the world-version. The world-version will contain various precepts that enable us to weight one kind of thing as more important than another, or add two things together that were apart in some other world, or order things differently. In contrast, if the world-version is not concerned with the (hidden) nature of physical things (or some other descriptive project), it may generate an art-worthy painting. But in a slightly different world, that painting might not be a painting but rather a sheet of canvas to block the wind from blowing in through

the broken window.[20] Or a world may not contain any literal statements at all but only metaphorical ones.

What I hope is clear is that when it is right to ask about truth depends as much on rightness as it does on truth. A true world-version,
in generating a world, may make true statements true or it may not.
Truth of a world-version is as much about presentation as it is about
true statements, and which is the category of first concern depends on
context. Some true versions simply present new things for us to consider; some true versions simply present true propositions via statements. But what makes the statements true is what is presented in the
world made, and whether a world-version is made simply of language or perhaps includes other symbol systems, and how these
worlds within world-versions are related to one another is difficult at
best to sort out.

Saving Pluralism:
Why Irrealism Needs God

I turn now to bring noetic irrealism into the theistic framework. Goodman says G-worlds are built out of other G-worlds yet the "search for a universal or necessary beginning is best left to theology."[1] Goodman isn't particularly prone to talk about God in general, and perhaps we should take this comment as tongue in cheek. Nevertheless, it is difficult to philosophize without dealing with God. Goodman, should we take him seriously here, is not in a hurry to reject a role for God. Lynch seems to allow for God to show up in some ways the World is, and Hales clearly has God exist in some perspectives. I argue that God must turn up in every way the World is.[2]

I THE ISSUE

Goodman says that many different world-versions are of independent interest and importance, without any requirement or presumption of reducibility to a single base. He continues on:

> The pluralist, far from being anti-scientific, accepts the sciences at full value. His typical adversary is the monopolistic materialist or physicalist who maintains that one system, physics, is pre-eminent and all-inclusive, such that every other version must eventually be reduced to it or rejected as false or meaningless. If all right versions could somehow be reduced to one and only one, that one might with some semblance of plausibility be regarded as the only truth about the only world. But the evidence for such a reducibility is negligible ...[3]

The adversary of irrealism here is not a theistic view of "the World" but a physicalist or materialist view. I agree with Goodman that the pluralist accepts science fully but also that science is neither monolithic nor reductionistic.

Science, just like the arts, presents more than one world for our consideration and, in fact, delights in the plurality of worlds. The World isn't a single way but multiple ways. Yet there are limits, both in the arts and the sciences. Not just anything will go. Some world-versions are right and others not. Some things are truly said in one world and not in another. Some things are appropriately done in a painting, others are not. Some things are done properly by a novel's character, others are not. The concern with rightness of rendering is a concern for the limits on our world-making, limits of logic, of purpose, of design, of metaphor, of canvas, and so forth. These limits enable us to render the worlds rightly.

The limits on world-making provide for a shift in our construal of knowledge or epistemizing as well.[4] In fact, I propose that seeking knowledge is best replaced with an emphasis on understanding. Knowledge and understanding rise and fall with the kind of world under consideration. Because a world is the way it is relative to the symbol system in use, knowledge is much closer to hand – more akin to understanding – than with a realist construal of "the World." The realm of the epistemic *cum* conceptual is not hermetically sealed from the realm of the ontic.

Given that there are right renderings of worlds, one might suspect that, having gathered all these worlds together, one could then reduce them to a singular underlying "World." That is what the physicalist suggests can be done. It is a position we should reject, as McDowell does in his shunning of bald naturalism. The physicalist must reject worlds that cannot be propositionally described – the realms of fiction, art, and architecture. Physicalism may accept the macro-level realm of everyday description. The push, however, is toward reducing the macro-level descriptions to scientific descriptions. Yet the pluralist's "acceptance of versions other than physics implies no relaxation of rigor but a recognition that standards different from and yet no less exacting than those applied in science are appropriate for appraising what is conveyed in perceptual or pictorial or literary versions."[5] One can't reduce the worlds to a singular account, nor can one reject rigorous approaches in what counts as a rightly rendered, nonphysicalist world.

Singularity is not, thus, to be sought in reduction. But one can seek unity, if not singularity. Goodman writes:

> So long as contrasting right versions not all reducible to one are countenanced, unity is to be sought not in an ambivalent or neutral *something* beneath these versions but in an overall organization embracing them ... My approach is ... through an analytic study of types and functions of symbols and symbol systems. In neither case should a unique result be anticipated; universes of worlds as well as worlds themselves may be built in many ways. [italics his][6]

The overall organization embracing the various worlds, the "universe of worlds," should not be expected to be unique for irrealism. Why not? Goodman gives no reason directly, but we can surmise that it is the same as the reasons leading to there being many worlds. The many worlds emerge because there are conflicting but true statements about "the World" taken singularly. So, just as there are apparent conflicts that generate the various worlds with their various contents, so are there apparent conflicts among universe-descriptions that generate various universes of worlds. If this is the case, however, it is hard to see where unity rests.

Why seek unity? Part of the answer is that without it, there is simply no way to get pluralism off the ground. As we've seen with the consistency challenge, there must be some way of linking worlds, not in the sense, of course, of a singularly described world underneath but rather in terms of a realist account of truth and its openness to real properties and real counterfactual analyses. Is this unity enough? I think not. Unity is also needed for the irrealist to avoid the radical relativism into which the more radical antirealists slide. In short, unity needs to provide for limits.

Whence the limits? Goodman seeks to understand the unity of various worlds through exploring the universe(s) of worlds, but admits that we should not expect any unique result. Here his position faces an infinite regress problem, and it is open, in the end, to the challenge of radical relativism with the result that it collapses into a completely relativistic antirealism. Goodman's irrealism goes all the way up, through individual worlds to universes or superworlds of worlds. Since no set way exists to understand the unity, no way exists to provide the sorts of limits on world-building the irrealist needs.

In contrast to Goodman's irrealism, the unity sought is provided in part by the way I've developed pluralism to allow for and, in fact, demand a realist account of truth. With the addition of intensionalism, the consistency problem can be resolved. But still a problem lingers. Goodman thinks the unity lies in part in the nature of symbol systems. Part of the symbol systems are the fundamental laws of logic, especially the law of noncontradiction. In addition, pluralism on my account is motivated partly by an appeal to the law of noncontradiction stripped of epistemic commitments. To get pluralism moving, we must appeal to the law in each and every world or claim that it is external to the worlds. This is where the search for unity comes in. Part of the unity across worlds is in the appeal to the law of noncontradiction. We must look externally to generate the worlds in the first place, but in looking externally to any given world, we open the door to other levels of externality.

2 THE LAW OF NONCONTRADICTION: AN INFINITE REGRESS CHALLENGE

It is often thought that relativists must deny the law of noncontradiction. Otherwise, they can't get the apparently contradictory beliefs to come out true. But as we've seen, a solid reply to the consistency dilemma can be made without giving up logic. The law of noncontradiction applies even for the noetic irrealist, along with a realist account of truth. The law of noncontradiction holds in all the conceptual schemes/worlds. It's no surprise that the law of noncontradiction is important; so important that there is no world in which it doesn't apply.[7]

It is important for the provision of limits. Since the worlds cannot be united via materialist reduction, there needs to be an overarching unity of worlds. This unity of worlds provides the key to the limits on the worlds. The rightness of rendering concern is not simply a concern with "getting things right," since there are presumably many ways of getting things right. Instead, it is a concern with not allowing rampant relativism. So the irrealist needs some objective feature or principle or superworld to which to appeal. One way to do that is, as we've seen, to introduce a realist account of truth. But a new problem shows up when we admit a realist account of truth, for not only does the consistency dilemma itself grant the law of noncontradiction some special sort of status, but so does the appeal to alethic realism. That special status seems initially hard to defend on pluralist terms.

The framework for the limits in world-making thus includes the law of noncontradiction, for it disallows the generation of contradictions within any given world. But how about the universe of worlds and its so-called provision for limits on worlds? Does the law of noncontradiction apply there? The main irrealist argument operates precisely on that assumption. Recall the argument:

1 Contradictions are impossible.
2′ p
3′ –p
4 Therefore there is more than one world, one in which p is true, another in which –p is true.
5 Therefore, truth is world-relative.

Or Gannsle's suggested improved version of the argument:

6 It is impossible that both p and –p be true in a single world.
7 If p and –p are both true, then there is more than one world such that p is true in one and –p in another.
8 It is possible that both p and –p are true.
9 p.
10 –p.
11 Therefore both p and –p are true.
12 Therefore, there is more than one world such that p is true in one and –p true in another.
13 Therefore, what is true is relative to a world.

Premise 1 (or premise 6) is assumed to be true universally. That is, it is true in all worlds. So far, so good. But it appears to be external to the worlds as well – that is, it is true in a uniting superworld. So if there is a universe unifying the worlds, then surely the law of noncontradiction holds there. On that basis, the irrealist can allow for the contradiction between 2′ and 3′ (and 9 and 10) and yet also allow for both to be true. The irrealist argument can do this because it is assumed that there is a superworld of worlds unifying the worlds. Thus the law of noncontradiction holds within each world and holds within the superworld unifying the worlds. If that is right, then the following argument works as a parallel instance of the main argument:

6′ It is impossible that both p and –p be true in a single superworld.

7′ If both p and –p are true, then there is more than one superworld such that p is true in one superworld and -p in another.

8′ It is possible that both p and –p are true.

Then taking "There is only one world" and "there is more than one
world" as substitution instances of p and –p, respectively, we get:

9′ There is only one world.

10′ There is more than one world.

11′ Therefore both "there is one world" and "there is more than one
    world" are true.

12′ Therefore, there is more than one superworld such that "there is
    one world" is true in one and "there is more than one world"
    true in another.

13′ Therefore, what is true is relative to superworlds.

One can easily see where this argument heads. First superworlds,
then supersuperworlds, then supersupersuperworlds, and we are off
climbing an infinite mountain. So here, the realist might say, is the
reason to reject the original argument: it shows too much – too
many worlds, if you will.

   Now the irrealist might suggest that only realists need worry about
infinite regresses. After all, on the realist account, there is to be only
one true description of the world. If the realist allows some sort of infinite regress, there would not only be multiple worlds but an infinite
number of them. Any chance at a singular, uniting world or description
is lost. Furthermore, nothing ever gets explained if there is always one
more description resting at the next step up the mountain. The irrealist,
in contrast to the realist, will maintain that it just doesn't matter
whether there are two worlds or an infinite number of worlds. Once
the metaphysical garden is planted, let a thousand flowers bloom – or
even an infinite number of flowers! There is no logical inconsistency in
superworlds or supersuperworlds, even an infinite number of them.

   Yet doubts remain about an irrealistic garden planted on the side
of an infinitely inflated mountain. Recalling common sense, even irrealism should be more modest, for its ontology is just too bloated.
The reason universes of worlds were introduced in the first place is
that we seek some sort of unity among them. This unity is in part,
at least, what keeps irrealism from collapsing into a truly radical
relativism – a sort of antirealism with a complete denial of truth.

This unsavoury result should be avoided. So the irrealist must avoid the infinite regress no less than a realist should.

A number of alternative ways might be proposed to attempt to extricate irrealism from the infinite regress challenge without giving up on unity. First, irrealism could just deny that superworlds are worlds by suggesting that worlds contain facts whereas a unifying superworld has none. This would stop the regress from getting a foothold up the mountain. But why think that? The law of noncontradiction is true in the superworld and it is true that the superworld unifies all the other worlds. It follows, then, that the superworld contains facts, even if the law of noncontradiction is the only truth. So long as the purpose of the superworld is to unite the others, it appears to function just like a "larger" world and we are off to the infinite races. This strategy is not promising.

Perhaps another way out of the regress for the irrealist is to suggest that by holding so fast to the law of noncontradiction, she has admitted too much. If she really wants to defend irrealism, she must go all the way to an antirealism with a denial of the law of noncontradiction. But this is to give up the climbing party as lost for it just admits to an extreme, no-limits relativism. Beside the obvious fact that this is to give up the climbing party as lost, in denying the law of noncontradiction, the argument that generates the multiple worlds, and hence irrealism itself, turns out not to work. So perhaps the best strategy for irrealism is just to admit that there is an infinite regress of worlds and we are back where we started. Irrealism then loses the unity it seeks and that looks toward failure.

Not only Goodman's irrealism but Lynch's also faces the infinite regress problem, or at least something closely parallel to it. Lynch writes:

> Just as one sketch can be filled in in different but equally correct ways, so [can] one concept – and by implication, one proposition – be employed or used in more than one correct way. Further, in the way in which two painters can paint the same scene differently or fill out the same sketch differently, so two schemes of concepts can fill out the same minimally interpreted proposition differently – even to the point of opposite truth-values. And just as exactly what a sketch is a sketch *of* cannot be determined except in reference to a more detailed filling in of that sketch, so what is said on a particular occasion can only be understood in reference to a particular scheme of concepts. It is in this sense that each proposition can be understood as having an index to a

scheme. Yet we must be careful not to fall into a false absolutism here. For whether the proposition that grass is green is to be understood minimally, and hence as indexed to, or shared between, two concept schemes, or understood robustly, and hence as relative to a particular scheme, is not an absolute fact about it, but is fixed or determined itself by the overall context in which that proposition is being expressed or employed. Independent of the shifting sands of context, there is no fact of the matter. [italics his][8]

In a footnote Lynch recognizes the infinite regress challenge when he writes, "Fact and content relativism hold at the 'meta' level as well as at the 'object' level. Propositions about propositions are also relative. An infinite regress looms, but as we shall see … it is a regress without teeth."[9]

I think there are teeth here, however. To explain why, we need more from Lynch. There is a problem for pluralism combined with minimal realism about truth, a problem falling out from self-reference. He writes:

An example of a self-referring claim is "every sentence is in a language" – including *that* sentence, of course. Such statements must apply to themselves if they are true. Similarly, content relativism states that propositions are relative to conceptual schemes. Presumably, this applies to pluralism itself, including the proposition that every proposition is relative to a conceptual scheme. Some may think that this aspect of pluralism undermines the entire position. If content relativism itself is relative to a conceptual scheme, then there could be a scheme where it is not relative. If so, then pluralism is false, since some propositions would then not be relative to conceptual schemes. On the other hand, if the statement of content relativism were exempt from being relative, again there would be propositions that were not relative to conceptual schemes, and content relativism would be false. Either way, the objection runs, pluralism must be false. [italics his][10]

Lynch's solution to this challenge is based on a distinction he makes earlier in his work but repeats in the present context.

This is a familiar quandary for any type of relativism. The answer to it in this case lies with the distinction between absolute facts and propositions on the one hand and *virtually* absolute facts and

> propositions on the other. An absolute fact is a state of affairs
> that obtains independently of any conceptual scheme. Pluralism
> is committed to denying that there are any such facts. The same
> story obviously holds with absolute propositions – propositions
> that are determinate independently of any scheme. This is famil-
> iar. But it is rarely, if ever, noticed that metaphysical pluralism is
> consistent with there being some *virtual absolutes* – facts that do
> not obtain independently of conceptual schemes but that *do ob-
> tain within every scheme.* Pluralism is similarly consistent with
> virtually absolute propositions, or propositions that are relative
> to every scheme. [italics his][11]

He goes on to note, of course, that a proposition saying that every
proposition is relative to a scheme does not commit the pluralist to
absolute propositions, for the proposition just mentioned could be
relative to every scheme without being independent of any or all.

The regress problem is generated, finally, at this point. While he
thinks the distinction between virtual and absolute propositions
and facts gets pluralism out of the dilemma stated above, it generates an infinite regress. He writes:

> But content and fact relativity would seem to be vulnerable to a re-
> lated problem: an infinite regress. Again the problem would seem
> to arise from the self-referring nature of the pluralist view; content
> relativity is the idea that every proposition is a relative proposition,
> including of course, this proposition. Thus the proposition that
> *propositions are relative* is relative to some conceptual scheme.
> And so is this last proposition. And so on. It may appear that any
> attempt to state content relativism is impossible, since any state-
> ment of it would result in an infinite regress. [italics his][12]

But this regress, says Lynch, is not vicious. First he points out that
the schemes to which the iterated proposition is relative may themselves be the same schemes to which the uniterated proposition is
relative. Once we recognize this, we see that the regress is no more
challenging than the regress entailed by "every sentence is in a language," including that sentence, of course. He points, second, to the
fact that all propositions face an infinite regress of sorts. For every
proposition, if p, then the proposition that p is true. That statement
itself is also true, and the statement stating that statement is true,

and so on. But we simply don't worry about these regresses, and so we shouldn't worry about the regress involved in relativized statements. Stating a logical consequence of a statement is not the same as stating the statement itself.[13]

But I'm not convinced, for pluralism doesn't just claim truth for itself but for multiple, incompatible truths. The infinite regress worry here is not just about what is true being repeated endlessly but rather that what counts as true varies from conceptual scheme to conceptual scheme. As such, I think Lynch faces the same problem Goodman does, viz., how to avoid the iteration of conceptual schemes collapsing into total relativism. What stops us from developing a conceptual scheme in which the law of noncontradiction doesn't hold, or a conceptual scheme in which truth is not understood as real? Furthermore, if truth isn't real or if the law of noncontradiction doesn't hold, then there will be no solution to the consistency problem, for it seems the notion of alethic realism rises and falls with the law.

Will it do for Lynch just to say that the statement of the law of noncontradiction is itself a virtually absolute statement, not true independent of conceptual schemes but true in all of them? Here we face the same challenge Goodman faces with his extensional nominalism. Why hold it to be true in all worlds, other than philosophical preference? For Lynch, why hold the law of noncontradiction – or for that matter, alethic realism – to hold across the conceptual schemes if there is nothing "under" the worlds to support them? Perhaps Lynch can appeal to the fact that, after all, there is only one actual World. However, that World does not itself give us the contents of the competing ontologies. That falls to conceptual schemes.

So both Goodman and Lynch as pluralist irrealists face a trilemma. Either the pluralist irrealist admits the law of noncontradiction, does not admit it, or admits it applies only within a singular world. If she admits the law of noncontradiction, then she admits to a (super)world uniting all the other worlds but that (super)world is only the first in an infinite number of worlds, the unifying feature for the worlds she seeks seems lost, and pluralistic irrealism is headed toward deep antirealism where anything will pass as a world. If she simply denies the law of noncontradiction, she generates a deep antirealism with its extreme relativism rather than pluralistic irrealism with its limited relativism. If she admits the law of noncontradiction within a singular world, that is, if she denies that the law of noncontradiction is external to the singular way "the World" is in the first place, then she gets realism and not irrealism, since the multiple world argument doesn't get off the ground.

It looks as if pluralism is in bad shape. It either collapses into realism, and noncontradiction provides a lever by which to create a singular "World," or it collapses into a deep antirealism, with no fixed law of noncontradiction, and relativism grows with a vengeance. Fortunately, there is a way out, a theistic way. I return to it in the last section of this chapter. We should first consider the other possibility further and explore why accepting the law of noncontradiction within a singular world won't rejuvenate realism.

3 THE EPISTEMIC/ONTIC STATUS OF THE LAW OF NONCONTRADICTION

Does the noetic realist have a lever against the worlds, a bit of noetic realist reality, in the law of noncontradiction? If he does have this lever, then the debate appears to be over. A total irrealism should be rejected. But the realist can't be redeemed so easily and the status of the law of noncontradiction, although complicated, is not, in the end, going to provide redemption. Let's first get clear about why the realist might believe he has a noetically real lever.

The core irrealist argument from chapter 7 assumes a radical separation of epistemology and ontology and thus claims there is no reason to pick a realist over an irrealist account of ontology. If the realist appeals to a separation of epistemology and ontology, he is charged with skepticism and we conclude that there is no reason to hold to realism. On the other hand, if we go ahead and admit that we do cognize-epistemize the law of noncontradiction, along with the other premises of the argument, then the irrealist wins.

The realist will note, however, that there is something unique about the law of noncontradiction. It is betrayed since the irrealist doesn't treat the law of noncontradiction in the same way she does the other premises.[14] One would be right to assume, given the argument's complete epistemic neutrality, that no premise should be ranked higher than or differently from any other. As such, we can't privilege the law of noncontradiction. But that is precisely what the irrealist does functionally. It appears, in fact, that we all privilege the law. This special treatment becomes most clear when it comes to the question of the unification of the worlds.

The starting suggestion of the argument is that we begin from the basis that taking things to be true by assumption, as we do in working logic proofs, is not an epistemic issue. Thus, from the point of view of the irrealist argument, it appears that we all just hold the law of noncontradiction to be true, as if "holding" were not an epistemic stance. The irrealist goes on to argue that we, nevertheless, still epistemically rank-order our beliefs, including the law of noncontradiction. The irrealist's treatment of the law of noncontradiction seems different from the treatment of the other premises in the argument. While we are not sure which of the second and third premises to cling to (whether they be about free will or the stature of furniture-sized objects or what have you), we are quite sure we should cling to the law of noncontradiction. We wouldn't argue this way, for example:

1   The law of noncontradiction is true.
2* There is a world in which the law of noncontradiction is true.
3* There is a world in which the law of noncontradiction is false.
     etc.

The irrealist treats the law of noncontradiction in a special way, different from the other premises, no matter what they are.

But, comes the challenge, the irrealist can't have it both ways. We either epistemize/cognize all the premises the same way or we don't. If we do, then it looks as if the law of noncontradiction has no special status outside the world we create – it's just as much up for grabs as free will or determinism, for example – and the irrealist argument doesn't get off the ground. Hence, we can safely return to realism. If we do not, then we grant it a special real status (and the realist a starting point) by treating the law of noncontradiction in some special manner – as true and fixed. Realism is triumphant.

What all this points out, and this is no surprise, is just how central a role the law of noncontradiction plays in our thinking. Both the realist and the irrealist share a strong commitment to it. At this point the realist is inclined to claim victory because the irrealist ends up appealing to the law in a special way – giving it a special status – and hence admitting a realist feature of the World. In contrast, the irrealist is inclined to claim victory because she has noticed that we epistemize the law the way we do. However, the irrealist takes the law of noncontradiction one way, with many worlds. The realist takes it the other, with only one "World." Who is right?

Alternatively, we can ask whether the law of noncontradiction is an epistemic principle or an ontological reality. In the irrealist argument, we admit that we have to epistemize the law of noncontradiction in order to solve anything. We have to take the law of noncontradiction to be true. Apparently both sides of the discussion admit this. But what is the force of that "have to?" One way to understand the "have to" is this. If we want to describe anything, then we have to take the law of noncontradiction to be true. The law of noncontradiction is then nothing more than an epistemic principle, a way of believing. As such, it tells us nothing about the World itself, independent of our thinking about it, but only what we believe about the World. So we get a kind of conditional necessity. If you want to describe the World, then accept and act on the law of noncontradiction. As such, there is no reason to take the law of noncontradiction as being an ontological account of the World but rather only as a means by which we make sense of the World.

On the other hand, if we start with the law of noncontradiction as an ontological principle – that the law describes a necessary feature of the World itself and not merely a necessity enabling us to think about the World – we've simply assumed that realism is correct or at least that there is one realist feature of the World. In order for this to do us any good, however, we have to then assume that we have epistemic access to this feature of the World. We'd have to know that realism-of-a-sort was the case before we could know anything. Again, we have a conditional necessity. If you want to resolve the realism/irrealism debate, then assume that what we think we know is actually the case, that is, assume that our epistemizing the law of noncontradiction makes it so. But it still doesn't get us a link between the World and what we believe.

The best answer may simply be to "split the difference" and suggest that the ontological status of the principle is its epistemic status. But we should be more than cautious here. It is tempting to say that the law is true if we say it is and false otherwise. But that would suggest an alethic irrealism, which I reject. Instead, we must at this level simply not distinguish between thought and the world(s). The law of noncontradiction rises and falls with the worlds. Does the law of noncontradiction have a status in regard to truth and falsity? Perhaps, but it is not a status that stands free of any or all worlds. Instead, I suggest it is a virtual proposition, true in all worlds but not true independently of them. Epistemology thus converges with ontology, skepticism recedes, and the metaphysical status of the law of non-contradiction is identical to its epistemological status. The law of noncontradiction has the ontological status it has just because it has the epistemic status it has.

So although it seems that realism wins with the law of noncontradiction holding in all worlds, it wins without giving us a feature of the universe independent of our thinking and/or believing it to be so. Irrealism comes through in the end. Yet the problem of the infinite regress remains. Is the approach to the problem just described enough to stop the infinite regress of worlds, enough to provide unity across the worlds without resulting in radical relativism? No. For any pair of worlds or superworlds or supersuperworlds, the law of noncontradiction is present. Thus while the law of noncontradiction puts limits within worlds, it doesn't put limits on how many worlds there might be, and a radical relativism creeps back in. A further issue presents itself as well, viz., why is the law of noncontradiction a virtual absolute? Since, so far forth, it rests in the human mind, we need to ask, whence the human mind? And, given human finitude, whence the universal nature of virtual absolutes in general?

Kant believed in some sort of universality for the rational mind's operations. He proposed the idea of the transcendental ego connected to human thought, a sort of essence we all share. The problem is that Kant's notion of the transcendental ego can be taken in different directions, not all of them good. Without entering into a discussion of nineteenth- and twentieth-century philosophy, we know that we end up with postmodern denials of universal rationality, of the human person itself, and even denials of the basic laws of logic. We need some account of the universality of reason and humankind. The pluralist irrealist generally gives no such account, leaving us with what appears to be a radical kind of happenstance in regard to rationality and human beings. It just happens that some propositions – ones about logic and human rationality – are virtually absolute propositions and turn out true in every world. But why believe that? We see the need for truth to somehow share the same concept in every world. But while we are motivated to preserve alethic realism, it seems contingent upon the happenstance of humans being one way rather than another. One way to put this question is, again, whence the universality of virtual absolutes?

It is strange that most irrealism discussions say little about the source of the humans who contribute to the World. Can there be a noetically irreal World with things in it but no humans? No. The concept of human itself, although a concept we humans hold, doesn't seem to make us in the way we make other things in the World. Humans need a source. Here, of course, it is logical to introduce a role for God.

4 GOD AND THE INFINITE REGRESS

Goodman is right to identify materialism as a poor alternative for providing a unity to the worlds. And McDowell is right in rejecting bald naturalism as not ever giving us spontaneity. In naturalistic reductionism, too much that is meaningful is lost. Likewise, the infinite regress introduced in this chapter can't be stopped by reducing all the worlds to one, for the reductionist projects have failed. What is needed instead is a unifying feature that holds the worlds together without reducing any one to another. The law of noncontradiction seems to be initially plausible as a means of stopping the regress but still leaves one uneasy, especially if it is tied to a human nature that we have no clear reason to say is fixed or objective in itself. Since human nature in an irrealist structure is not completely fixed, what reason have we to think that the law of noncontradiction itself is fixed, given that our minds alone contribute the law of noncontradiction as a special ontological feature of the world(s)? Here the suspicion enters that epistemology and ontology are not radically separable and hence that we could make the World differently than we do. So if there is a way to stop the infinite regress and thus to bring limits to the relativism inherent in irrealism, there must be some other means by which to accomplish it.

Goodman tells us that we build worlds out of other worlds.[15] One might thus suppose that there is a first world. Whence this first world? As noted above, Goodman suggests that the search for a universal or necessary beginning world is best left to theology. Taking our cue from Goodman, but applying the suggestion to the superworld problem, let's turn to theology to help us avoid the infinite regress of worlds.

My proposal is this. First, God is a world-maker – not a big stretch for traditional theism! Second, God's ontological status is different from any other thing. Again, this isn't a big stretch for traditional theism. Third, God provides the unification of all the worlds created by humans. There are some limitations here. God can't be viewed as just one more person making up worlds. God must be a unifying factor without God getting entangled, at least at God's core, in the beliefs, attitudes, and other world-making activities of humans.

Hence, there are certain limitations on the core argument for irrealism found in chapter 7. If God is going to help irrealism, we cannot use statements about God as substitution instances for "p" and "–p" in the argument for irrealism. In other words, not just any two contradictory pairs of statements will get the argument off the ground. We can't use "God exists" and "God doesn't exist."[16] Obviously, if God is the ground of unity, God can't be in one world and not in another. God isn't just another piece of finite metaphysical furniture. God is beyond our worlds and yet in all our worlds. Again, there is no surprise here, God traditionally being understood as transcendent and immanent.

I want to note briefly that Hales's position is no help in solving the problem at hand simply because it is open to theism. On his view, theism is true in only one of several philosophical perspectives. For his position to even begin to help us out, he would at least have to argue that God is a virtual absolute. However, so much of his position is dependent on the contrast between the results of a Christian world view and the results of a nontheistic world view that it is hard to imagine him happily following my lead. However, since his view is open to virtual absolutes, perhaps Hales's philosophical relativism – but not the examples he uses to defend it – might in the end, be made more consistent with my suggestions. As can be seen in the last part of this work, however, I think God is a special sort of virtual absolute.

Returning to the argument, note that God is not part of the World, or any world, in the sense that God is just another thing in the world. God is like Plato's Good – beyond simple being. This is not to say God does not have being but that God's being is only analogous to our being, or rather that contingent being, and human being in particular, is analogous to God's noncontingent Being in something like Aquinas's sense. God is the underlying ground of contingent being, but God isn't a being as we are. God's ontological status is unlike anything else. God is in her core being what she is, independent of any human thinking about God, conceptualizing God, believing things about God, and so forth. God is not just another thing. God is not created. God is the ultimate Reality and hence God is the objectivity in an otherwise nonobjective universe of worlds. Yet God interacts with us and as such is within the conceptual schemes with which we operate. So far forth, God is in community with us and, as part of the process, God's being – outside God's core – is influenced by us. I provide more detail about how this might be best understood in chapters 14 and 15. For now the reader will have to rest content with a promissory note toward an explanation about how God is both noetically real (not dependent on human conceptual schemes) and yet a virtual absolute in the worlds humans make.

The problem with introducing God, the critic might say, is that just as the law of noncontradiction is in danger of simply rising and falling with human thinking and believing, so is God. God appears to be another epistemic-ontic posit and this cannot keep the irrealist position from being just as relativistic as ever, anymore than the law of noncontradiction can.

We should pay attention to the realist's intuition here. The problem with the epistemizing-cognizing of the law of noncontradiction does seem quite parallel to the problem of epistemizing-cognizing God. In either case, the infinite regress is not stopped and we seem launched into a radical relativism that gives humans far too much control over the universe. If I choose not to accept the law of noncontradiction, everything is up for grabs. Isn't the same true for God? In fact, isn't God worse off? It is important to note that we all, realist and irrealist alike, appeal to the law of noncontradiction, thus making the World one way rather than another. We don't all appeal to God.

The reply is as follows. No, God doesn't fall prey to our epistemizing-cognizing control. The argument is quite simple. If irrealism *sans* God obtains, then the World is as it is, or worlds are as they are, simply because of our human noetic contributions. And if irrealism *sans* God obtains, it's possible for us to deny the law of noncontradiction (that is, we can epistemize-cognize the law away, so to speak) and so remove the objective limits on what can be in a world. This is an unacceptable result. We don't have the kind of control that allows us to disassemble the World by denying the law of noncontradiction nor do we have the power to assemble the World any way we want. We are, in short, finite entities.

We can raise the issue another way. If I (or we) make the World, then how do I (or we) get here? What is my source? Well, what else but God? Irrealism provides its own argument for God's existence. One of the oddities of irrealism, at least atheistic irrealism, is that it leaves unexplained, and inexplicable, the age-old question of why there is anything at all. It may be right that I contribute something to the World's being the way it is. But if that's all there is to the story, I am the creator of the World, and even the creator of myself. Yet we are and should be deeply suspicious here.[17] The World doesn't seem to depend in this way upon me. I am simply part of the World, and I can't make myself up. I am contingent. There must be something outside the World, so to speak, to account for it. And the existence of that outside something can't be contingent on me or on anything else. Yet something must be able to bring things about in the World. That is the place for God, the Being beyond simple being.

Let me comment briefly on McDowell's "relaxed platonism." McDowell rejects bald naturalism but suggests an expanded naturalism. Humans have evolved, presumably, in such a way that we naturally take the World to be meaningful and meaningfully understood. Here I part ways with McDowell. While his attempt at a relaxed platonism is admirable, it still leaves us with meaningfulness that comes out of nowhere. I don't see how humans as the people we are can have simply moved from bald nature (bits of organic matter) to thoughtful, reasonable humans with a *Bildung*. Our cultural education and history started somewhere and that, it seems to me, remains the central mystery of philosophy to which theology – and for my money, particularly Christian theology – provides a most cogent answer.

If God made the world, and made us, we don't bear the burden of causing the World or creating meaning. But we can't take God's involvement in our worlds to follow the rules we are used to. If the irrealist argument about our epistemic-cognitive contribution to world-making is correct, we have to allow that God would make us as creative beings who can influence the way the World is as well. But we all recognize that there are limits to what we can do. If I am right here, those limits derive from God, the Being beyond simple being. The power of this theistic suggestion is that we now have a reply to the dilemma (running throughout this work) set between the realist and irrealist, viz., either realism obtains and there are objective limits to the way a world can be, but we are stuck with skepticism about the World, or antirealism obtains and we avoid skepticism, but only at the cost of extreme relativism. The solution goes between the horns. There is a middle position between realism and deep antirealism. It is something akin to the Goodman-Lynch view but theistic. Not only does God provide the first world(s) into which we then enter and build and change and make, but God also is the unifier of the worlds. God controls how things finally are (and here one should not read "the singular way things finally are"). For one thing, God noetically determines the law of noncontradiction,[18] so it isn't just left up to us. But then neither is God's existence left up to us. God is a metaphysical requirement if we want to avoid radical relativism, but God is also a requirement to avoid skepticism about the World.

Skepticism is undercut in this way. First, now that we have God, we have some reason to think that God would make our epistemic abilities conducive, generally, to getting truth about the World. Second, the worlds are, to some extent, the way they are relative to our noetic contributions to them. So there isn't such an extreme gap, so to say, between the ways the World is and one's noetic contribution and epistemizing it. Perhaps we do not even need to worry about the first point if the second is true. Indeed, the first point may be trivial because of the second. But none of this will work without God, and one might say that because God made our epistemic abilities conducive to knowledge, God made us as irrealist contributors to the worlds. But on this kind of theistic irrealism, there are some things, or aspects of things, that are beyond our contributions – the law of noncontradiction being contributed by God to the worlds, for example. And if you want to get beyond the worlds we make (but not beyond worlds altogether), God in God's core being is not made up by us.

Furthermore, God, as beyond and yet in the human-made worlds, can reveal Godself to us through some means other than our typical irrealistic epistemic abilities. For example, perhaps this is what happens in Christian, and perhaps all theistic, mystical experience. There is often no skepticism left in the recipient when God is revealed in this way. A common report among recipients of mystical experiences is that they know God more assuredly than they know anything else. One reason might just be that instead of simply knowing about God, the mystic knows God as God knows Godself, at least in part. That partly explains the mystic's talk of union with God. But the mystic also has a heightened sense of being known by God. But God's knowing is a making of a world, and when God makes a world, it is a world made well. Perhaps in the mystical revelation, God simply lets the mystic experience, even if not understand, how God's knowing the worlds is also the making of the worlds. This extends to the mystic as well. So God's revelation of God's knowing the mystic changes the mystic. The mystic, in some way beyond our usual ken, knows the way God knows, for the mystic is known by God, and in God's knowing, the mystic knows himself and God as well. All other knowledge of worldly things ceases to be of import, except as filtered through the primary knowing granted in the mystical experience. More on this in chapter 18.

In summary, the irrealist claims that human noetic feats influence the worlds in substantial ways. But that comes at the potential price of infinite regress and extreme relativism. The realist contribution is the objectivity that God supplies and that objectivity both stops the regress and the radical relativism while admitting that there is an irrealist aspect of the worlds. God, thus, is needed on the irrealistic vision of reality. To what extent is this a realist contribution? That awaits Part 4. For now, Goodman suggests that the search for a first world is best left up to theology. I've taken his suggestion seriously. What is important is that even if God were to have provided the World out of which we humans have since constructed the many worlds we have, this in no way entails that there must be a singular "World" or conceptual scheme underlying all the rest of the right worlds or conceptual schemes, a "World" or conceptual scheme that arrives ready made for us, a "World" that, no matter how much we conceptualize or epistemize, isn't influenced or changed. Once humans are dealing with the World God makes, and humans begin to interact with it and its myriad objects, new worlds are constructed. So, God simply thinks up the first one, *ex nihilo*, God places free and creative humans in the middle of it, and then lets us in on the secrets of world-making. God doesn't make the World ready-made. We can and do interact with it, creating new and different worlds.

Human creativity is very important on this view. In the Judeo-Christian creation story, one of the first things we learn about God is that God is creative. We are then told that God creates humans in God's image. One way to take the story is that humans are, prior to other things, creators. We also know God makes us free. With free co-creators in the World God made, it seems natural to suggest that God encourages some world-making of our own. So God doesn't fail to make a singular fixed "World" because of laziness. God doesn't do it because we were made free and creative.

Now just as there might be a place for God's creativity at the beginning, so there might be a place for God at the end – the overarching universe of worlds. God stops the apparently infinite regress of organizational universes. How does God help us out here? God is not just one more person making up worlds. God is the unifying factor without getting caught up – at the divine core – in the beliefs and attitudes and other world-making activities. How does God do that? In part, I'm suggesting, by playing the role of limit producer. God will not let just any old world be created, nor will God let just any old world be the final say. For example, we can create and bring evil into a world but this is not a world pleasing to God, and God will show us the error of our creative ways.

In the end, then, the trilemma faced by the irrealist is dealt with by seeing God as the basis of everything there is, including the laws of logic – they are part of God's core being – and humans as creative forces in the worlds. Goodman, Lynch, Hales, and, I daresay, all pluralist irrealists need God.

In the next part I attempt to flesh out some details and make good on some metaphors from these most recent comments on the role God plays in our world-making. I do so via the concepts and doctrines of traditional Christianity.

PART FOUR

Traditional Christianity, Theistic Irrealism, and Pluralism

I 2

The Traditional Christian

Christianity, with its various connections to issues surrounding realism and irrealism, provides no easy terrain. Although the ground has been ploughed many times, rocks, weeds, and other debris remain in need of picking up, cutting down, or sorting through. Just as in Eden, we have to get our names straight before the World can be understood or perhaps before the World can even be fully made! What is truth, what is realism, and what is the World are all fair and open questions. I've provided preliminary answers to these questions in the first three parts of this work. My thesis for the remainder is that traditional Christianity is not only compatible with the irrealistic plurality of worlds I've proposed but that the latter comports well with the former. Traditional Christianity not only does not demand a singular, true ontological account of the World, it can readily embrace a quite radical pluralism. To see this, however, we need a clear account of traditional Christianity.

I THE CHRISTIAN

The distinction between Christian and non-Christian can be parsed in any number of ways. A Hindu is not a Christian, nor is a Muslim, a Jain, a Buddhist, or a Jew, even though a number of beliefs may overlap among the various adherents of these religions. Neither, of course, is a secular person a Christian, for Christianity is a religion and secular people reject religion altogether. Among Christians themselves, there are those who might be thought of as orthodox Christians and those who are not. This line runs, approximately, through the field of belief, along the fence of the major historic creeds. There is also the notoriously difficult question of what makes one a Christian, a question sometimes ferociously debated within the faith. Is it belief, baptism, some combination of the two, or something else again? Is it belief that's important or a relationship with God? In that regard, when one accepts the Word of God, should that be understood as the Scripture or Jesus himself? What role does tradition play? Are the core beliefs of a Christian found in one creed rather than another? What are the core beliefs of a Christian? What if a person believes all but one of the core beliefs?

Another distinction, not captured simply by the notion of orthodoxy, is largely philosophical rather than sociological, psychological, or even theological. Theology is, however, relevant because the distinction relies on the notion of orthodoxy. But I needn't go into details as to the nature of orthodoxy, for one could approach that issue in a variety of ways and still make the case to be made in the remainder of this essay. Nor do I need to say what makes one a Christian in the sense of giving some essentialist account of salvation. To attempt this latter task would be the functional equivalent of making a judgment about who will, and who won't (if anyone), end up in God's presence and what exactly it is that gets people there. Since I hesitate to tread where angels fear to walk, I instead simply distinguish between the traditional and the revisionist Christian.

William Alston, in writing of Christian theology, uses the terms "traditional" and "revisionist"[1] but does not define them for they have a more or less analogous use in other contexts – history, science, and so forth. Alston relies, I think, on our intuitions about these parallel cases to give his readers a general notion of what he means. Like Alston, my motivation in using these terms is to get clear about what Christianity requires vis-à-vis various sorts of realism and irrealism and how those fit or don't fit with Christianity. However, I think the terms need some definition. I use the terms in a somewhat technical manner, but I also want the accounts to reflect the actual practices of Christians.

Before providing the definitions, I note that the division of Christians into such camps is a somewhat "modern" division. No one would have worried about the distinction in the early medieval period, as the Church was still clarifying what it believed. Nor could Luther have been charged with being a revisionist Christian, in the sense I use the term. He would have been, and was, charged with heresy. But it is not clear that revisionist Christians are heretics in a technical sense, for many, if not most, revisionist Christians repeat the creeds at worship with regularity and are quite sincere in so do-ing.[2] There may be a logical space, however, where a revisionist Christian falls too far outside what the traditional Christian takes to be required for actual Christian faith and as such simply ceases to count as a Christian, except, perhaps, in name only. Such judg-ments are no part of my purpose here.

How is the distinction modern? We know that through the ages be-liefs were important. In fact, denying one belief or another could be very dangerous business. But often the required beliefs themselves were in the midst of development and it was very hard to tell who was "right." For example, both Arian and non-Arian Christians, before the Nicene Creed was written, were Christians. It was only a good long time afterward that Christianity became more settled and ortho-doxy triumphed. Even today many Arian Christian groups persist. Orthodox Christians just don't consider Arians to be orthodox – or sometimes even Christian. But no one charges them with being revi-sionist. Arian views of the nature of Christ are as old as the Christian story itself. ·

Anyone who has studied the development of doctrine has ob-served that doctrine does just that: it develops. The idea of the faith "once delivered" being static is a simple misunderstanding of the fact that the "once delivered" nature of the faith includes the con-tinuing development of the faith itself. Orthodoxy is a living thing, not fixed and dead. I'm also not convinced that ancient and medi-eval peoples understood the World and truth in the fairly narrow way we often do now. For example, the practice of medieval au-thors using authoritative pseudonyms strikes many people today as a kind of dishonesty. For medieval peoples, however, truth wasn't so obviously thought of as simply being a match between content and World but a consistency of new with old. The use of a pseud-onym, thus, wasn't dishonest as much as it was a claim to be saying what had been said, a true thing.

Be that as it may, we don't live in the medieval period. We live in the modern or postmodern. Some think postmodernism is really an ultramodernism since it hasn't freed itself from the influence of the cogito.[3] We are at least deeply influenced by the modern period. Our propensity to place our own reasoning power over tradition has changed the way we work theologically and philosophically. Debates about the nature of the World will never be the same after Hume and Kant. Yet the creeds continue to be repeated every Sunday by millions of faithful believers. While I hesitate to say that when the creed was repeated in the fifth century everyone understood it the same way, I suspect that few even wondered, in the way we might do now, whether our cognitive machinations contribute to how the World is constituted. Realism and irrealism, as we now think of them, probably never entered the mind of Augustine, Pope Gregory the Great, Teresa of Avila, or Dame Julian. So it would be odd for Christians to start demanding that we add to the Nicene Creed a footnote that one must take its claims to describe noetically real states of affairs or that one must hold an alethic realism. Nevertheless, there is some overlap between my distinction and distinctions from the past, especially the distinction between the orthodox and the unorthodox Christian.

2 THE TRADITIONAL CHRISTIAN

I proceed now with a description of the traditional vs the revisionist Christian. I cannot provide a completely descriptive account (some stipulation is involved) but the following is a good approximation to what it means to be a traditional Christian. We should think of this account as provisional, for I provide some modest changes to the account as we continue. There are four requirements.

The first requirement for being a traditional Christian is that one be orthodox. Here is the stipulation. Let us say that one is orthodox when one holds to the Nicene Creed. But not to put too fine a point on it, one can hold the Nicene Creed with or without the filioque clause, the major division between the Eastern and Western churches.

The second requirement is that one take the credal claims to be true. Again, there is little new here, for whenever one believes p, one holds p to be true.[4] I suspect there has always been some sense of "matching" what it is we believe with the way the World is, regardless of my earlier comments about medieval believers. But in our present context, to say that a claim is true requires further explanation, for as we'll see, a revisionist Christian can also hold that the credal claims are true and yet understand "true" in a way different from the traditional Christian. Of course, in the context of the realism/irrealism discussion, what counts as true may vary according to whether one is a realist or not, as well as according to the kind of realist one is.

A third requirement is alethic realism. Minimally, the traditional Christian holds that Christian claims are true in the following sense, viz., when the traditional Christian says "I believe in one God, the Father, the Almighty, maker of heaven and earth" and so on, she is not only affirming that she believes these things but that the beliefs are true independent of human noetic contribution.[5] In other words, the traditional Christian is committed at least to a minimal alethic realism. As we've seen, a minimal alethic realism claims that "p" is true iff p, where it is understood that the content of the truth-value bearer "p" gives everything needed to specify what it takes for the truth-value bearer to be true.[6] In other words, human noetic contributions play no role in whether a truth-value bearer is true. Only the way things are tells us which claims are true.

But with Christian claims, things are not so simple. There is a lot of work to be done in sorting out the kinds of truth in the creed. Which claims are literally true of God? Which are analogically true? Which are metaphorically true? The creed claims that God is the Father, the Almighty. While God being almighty seems literal enough (yet even here problems can be raised), what about God's being "the Father"? Is God "the Father" literally or is God "the Father" in some other way? Is Christianity essentially patriarchical? The "Father" language is metaphorical or analogical, although a very important historical metaphor/analogy, and one that is commonly misunderstood in our time, leaving us with a deeply patriarchal view of God. But then when we say that the creed is true in a realist sense are we committed to literal truth or will metaphorical truth do? This problem runs all the way down through the creed. Is Jesus literally the Son of God? While it is central to the creed that the Son of God was made incarnate from the Virgin Mary, which parts of that claim should be understood literally vs metaphorically? Once we decide, if we can decide, we still face the question as to whether metaphors can be true in a realist sense. If they cannot, then certain of the creed's claims cannot be realistically true. And if they are not realistically true, then what keeps the ontology of God objectively the case? What keeps the Son of God from merely being shaped by human noetic feats?

Maybe what the traditional Christian needs is an account of metaphor that reduces metaphorical truths to literal truths. Then the traditional Christian can make the more limited claim that the creed expresses a set of realistic truths in metaphorical language. God is not literally Father, Son, and Holy Spirit but God is literally three persons, co-equal, and each essentially God (but even here, isn't the notion of "person" metaphorical or analogical?).[7] Or perhaps we can say that all the terms of the creed are, in fact, technical terms, with very specific nonmetaphorical meanings. Both these suggestions are fraught with problems. A somewhat comforting point is the fact that these problems, as I noted above, are not unique to irrealism. The history of philosophical theology is littered with the tattered remains of theories of religious language and metaphor. However, theistic irrealism can contribute a framework for understanding language about God, as we'll see below.

Let us assume for now that the problems can be resolved and the traditional Christian can affirm the creed in an alethically real way and hold the beings, things, and events described there to be noetically real (where they are) in a sufficiently strong sense to allow for traditional Christianity. It is important to understand, however, that whatever restrictions there are on metaphors extend to all the metaphors, but only the metaphors, in the creed. Of the credal claims, for example, that Jesus Christ is begotten not made, that he was incarnate from the Virgin Mary, that he suffered death and was buried, that there is one holy catholic and apostolic Church and a resurrection from the dead, and so on, which are metaphorical and which are not? All need to be analyzed in terms of their metaphorical vs literal content. Once done, this will allow all the credal claims to be alethically real or something close enough to alethically real. I'll return to this issue at greater length in chapter 15.

The fourth requirement is that the traditional Christian be committed not only to alethic realism but also to the view that God is not made in God's fundamental nature by human noetic feats. The created do not make the Creator. Does this entail that traditional Christians are noetic realists about God? In some sense, yes. God does not depend for God's fundamental being on human noetic feats. But even on fairly radical kinds of noetic irrealism some things – in particular humans – don't seem to rely on human noetic machinations, at least at their core. So in one sense I think it is fair to say that the traditional Christian typically understands God to be noetically real and hence that no human noetic contribution to God's fundamental nature is possible.[8] But in another sense, traditional Christianity seems open to some significant noetic contribution to God's being. Furthermore, while the traditional Christian may hold a fairly realist view about God, she very often holds noetic realism about most things (save for the obvious exceptions to which everyone agrees). So I want to be a little more cautious. What exactly does the traditional Christian have to hold to remain a traditional Christian?

Clearly the traditional Christian does not and should not think of God as existing in virtue of any of our human conceptual schemes. Idealism of this sort would make nonsense out of traditional Christian commitment. On the other hand, what we know of God's essence, and hence what is alethically true of God's essence, may be quite limited. Here I want to call attention to the long and deep tradition that God is a mystery. Lest this sound like an excuse merely to leave God's noetic reality beyond philosophical reach, let me hasten to add that the noetic realist is in no better shape on this matter than the noetic irrealist. All the major theologians have struggled with language and descriptions of the divine. Ranging from the metaphorical to the analogical, few theologians have been willing to say much that is literal of God. The important point is to have some sort of explanation for how we can say anything helpful and true about God at all.

However, how we know God is not the main focus here but rather the ontological question, is God noetically real? Certainly the history of Christianity would suggest an affirmative answer. God is noetically real. However, perhaps this response is too quick. An important follow-up question is this. Is God therefore simply an absolute fact, existing outside human conceptual schemes? Once again, it would seem that the traditional Christian is committed to an affirmative reply. It won't do for God merely to be a virtual absolute, that is, an object that exists within each and every human (well-formed) conceptual scheme. The reason, briefly, is this. Even if being committed to God as a virtual absolute doesn't commit the irrealist Christian to God's existence being caused *ex nihilo* by human thought, the way God is would depend upon human conceptualizing. This seems counter to traditional Christian thought. So if the Christian pluralist irrealist is to remain a traditional Christian, she must show how God is open to being noetically shaped by human thought at least in some important ways. Furthermore, it would seem she must show how traditional Christianity itself is supportive of such a notion. These two matters are the focus of chapters 14 through 17, but tipping my hand just slightly, noetic irrealists, insofar as they limit the irreal to what humans shape, miss important ways of thinking about the divine. Perhaps God's core is outside the reach of human noetic contribution, but not the way God is within a human world.

3 THE DIVINE AND THE WORLDLY

Certain beings (God), certain relationships (the personal relationships among the three persons of the Trinity), and certain events (some historical and some that will be) are part and parcel of the divine and the divine's activity. I refer to these things simply as "the divine."[9] Human persons turn out to be divine as well, for humans are needed for the making of the various worlds and therefore need to be constant across all the worlds or ways the World is. Otherwise, there would be nothing in the worlds but what God puts there, which on the current proposal is a sort of noumenal stuff which humans then shape.

In contrast, the remainder of things and claims about them, that is, things and claims that fall outside the realm of the divine thus described, I refer to as "the worldly." Let me suggest that, in general, the traditional Christian need accept no particular belief outside the divine, although many other beliefs will be inferable from the ones about the divine. There is a great deal of latitude among Christians in regard to which beliefs are inferable from the creed and which are not. So which beliefs are divine beliefs and which are not is a somewhat open question. For example, just what does it mean to say that God is sovereign? Does God's sovereignty follow from God's omnipotence? Does it imply that humans have no free will? The theories abound. My claim is that a traditional Christian in general is required to hold to the creed only in an alethically real way, and to understand the things to which the creed refers in a (more or less) noetically real way.

Furthermore, everyday beliefs, such as that there is a large rock down by the creek in my backyard, that red maple trees have many-pointed leaves, and that gold has the atomic weight it does, are all worldly facts and need not be accepted by the traditional Christian at all. She could be an existence irrealist (one who rejects the existence of certain kinds of ontological entities) about physical entities but believe in the existence of subatomic particles. Or, like Peter van Inwagen, she could deny the existence of tables and chairs and claim not to be contradicting things the ordinary person says, and all the while still be a traditional Christian.[10] The worldly, so far as traditional Christianity is concerned, need not be noetically real. Subatomic items or physical objects might be purely dependent upon a conceptual scheme and have no independent way they are.

4 THE REVISIONIST CHRISTIAN

So much for the provisional account of the traditional Christian. The revisionist Christian is not too hard to describe, for revisionist Christianity stands in immediate contrast to traditional Christianity. One can be a revisionist Christian in at least three ways. One way is to deny some aspect or other of the creed. That is, one might affirm the existence of God but deny that Jesus is fully divine, or perhaps believe in Jesus' divinity but deny the personal existence of the Holy Spirit, and so on. This, in large measure, is to deny one or another orthodox belief. I said earlier that Martin Luther was accused of heresy. Whether or not he was heretical (and of course contemporary accounts, on both the Roman Catholic and Protestant side, give a negative answer at least so far as the creed is concerned), I'm sure he wasn't accused of being a heretic because he doubted the plausibility of the supernatural as noetically real, as some contemporary revisionist theologians might.[11] In fact, for my purposes here, this first kind of revisionism isn't a pure revisionism but simply old-fashioned heresy (and of course I'm not thereby suggesting in any way that those holding heretical views should be ill-treated). I'll not worry about it.

A more important way for a Christian to be revisionist is to deny that the things described in the creed are fundamentally independent of human noetic contribution – that is, she could be a noetic irrealist about the divine core. Another way of being revisionist is to deny that truth itself is independent of human noetic contributions – that is, a revisionist could be an alethic irrealist of some sort. Either of these ways undermines the ontological status of God as the ultimate source of the universe and hence undermines traditional Christianity. On this score, Alston's analysis of the relationship of realism and the Christian faith is quite correct. I'll return to discuss it in chapter 13.

5 DIRECTIONS

As I've said, I want to take theistic irrealism further by developing a Christian irrealism, an irrealism in which traditional Christianity plays the central role. In general outline, Christian irrealism is global, save for the divine – certain aspects of God and God's direct activities and creations (humans in particular). Some people might suggest that if irrealism is a proper account of metaphysics, then surely the divine is a highly likely candidate to which the noetic contributions of humans should apply. Like morality and aesthetics, religion, it is often suggested, is best understood as a human creation. I've already indicated that this is clearly a bad way to go for the traditional Christian, even the minimalist traditional Christian. There are good reasons to exclude certain aspects of the divine from our noetic contributions.

I also want to note the following result, viz., that instead of religion, morality, and aesthetics being the least "objective," they are more fixed than the physical realm and physics. It seems that many irrealists about religious claims and objects don't feel the same way about physical claims and objects as they do about religious objects such as God. The radically symbolic Paul Tillich, Rudolph Bultmann with his emphasis on the "day of the wireless," the R.M. Hare of "religious bliks"[12] (although this is less clear), and many other theologians and philosophers of that generation, are quite sanguine about the idea that religious issues fall into the irreal while physical issues do not. Realism dealing with claims about the natural order often leaves realism dealing with claims about God vulnerable. This is due, in part, I believe, to the deep and broad acceptance of verificationism of the last century. A look at the long discussion about the status of religious language from the late 1940s through the 1970s will illuminate why. Yet this broad attitude of privileging the worldly over against the divine can be understood as predating the twentieth century by some time as well. Even Kant's treatment of religion leaves God outside the realm of pure reason. Although his treatment of physical objects is irrealist, his treatment of God seems to put God beyond our reach except in quite limited ways.

This attitude is curious to me, as a traditional Christian. Instead of thinking that realism about material objects allows for, or even entails, irrealism about religion, why doesn't irrealism about God imply irrealism in other domains? Materialists merrily go on their way, assuming alethic and noetic realism about the physical realm, as do many irrealist Christians assume alethic and noetic realism for the physical realm. My view is close to the reverse, viz., that irrealism (of any kind, existence, noetic, or alethic) about God, while not entailing noetic irrealism about the physical realm, should be understood as entailing existence nonrealism about the World. But since the World is (even in its noetically irreal way), God exists in a noetically real way. We need a realistic God if we are going to have any chance at realism about the worldly, but realism about God doesn't require realism about the worldly.

The tasks set before us are, from the point of view of traditional Christianity, how to spell out noetic irrealism, the things to which it applies, and how it applies to them. Of course, the first sections of the essay attempt to spell out how noetic irrealism should be understood. The other questions are taken up in the remainder of the book.

Christianity, Realism, and Logic

Although an explicit argument from traditional Christianity to a more or less global ontological monism and noetic realism is difficult to find in the literature, my discussions with many traditional Christian philosophers have left me with the impression that traditional Christianity and metaphysical realism go hand in hand. I admit that when it comes to God, this attitude is fair enough – God makes us and not we God. But is traditional Christianity logically committed to realism about the worldly? I assume in this chapter that God is noetically real, and pose the question: just how far does the realism needed for a traditional notion of God extend into what is typically thought of as the created order?

I GLOBAL REALISM AND TRADITIONAL CHRISTIANITY

Let's say global realism is the claim that God exists and that God's ontic status and structure in no way depend upon human noetic contribution (God makes humans and not humans God), conjoined with the claim that the World exists and the World's ontic status and structure in no way depend upon human noetic contribution.[1] We can recognize various exceptions to global realism, such as thoughts and perhaps marriage and other social constructions, and say that global realism is committed to God's noetic reality and to the noetic reality of (most of) the natural realm along with (most of) the artifactual realm (once made).

What constitutes the natural and artifactual realms? What about the beauty of a sunset, the immorality of murder, or the naturalness of theoretical particles? We need to recognize various compartmental realisms. For example, one can be a realist about physical objects or theoretical particles in subatomic physics but not about aesthetic or moral values. Or one could hold the reverse. It is often thought, too, that one can be a realist about the World (some or all of morals, aesthetics, and physics) but not about religious matters such as the existence of God. Related to these issues, although arising perhaps at a distinct level of reflection, are metaphysical questions. For example, what about the Lockean substrate vs the Humean lack-there-of? Or what of the Aristotelian emphasis on discrete primary substances vs Whitehead's event-oriented theory of the basic metaphysical building blocks? Could the World be both Lockean and Humean or both Aristotelian and Whiteheadian? Ontological pluralists seem to think so. The sort of realism I'm concerned with in this chapter doesn't simply claim that (most of) these things – beauty, morality, physics, and metaphysics – are independent of human noetic feats but says in addition that there is a singular way the World is. An ontological pluralism, in short, is typically ruled out by this kind of realism.

My interest in this chapter is the propensity of traditional Christian philosophers simply to assume that their traditional Christian commitments entail, or at least that traditional Christianity is strongly inclined toward, a monistic, noetic realism about the extra-divine realms. Of course, when the question is raised, it is quickly obvious that a traditional Christian certainly could be a nonrealist about many things. Not every traditional Christian is a realist, let's say, about aesthetic values. My point is that many are. Consider the long tradition of understanding God as beauty itself or at least as the measuring stick against which beauty should be judged. Beauty, thus, is not a human construct but noetically real. And certainly most traditional Christians tend to be realist about moral values. Morality is handed down from God, not invented by human persons. Likewise, many Christians treat the physical realm as if it were obvious that God makes trees and rocks and equally obvious that we do not contribute to their nature. Since God made "the World," the way "the World" is does not depend upon human noetic contributions, independent of the obvious sorts of things like my own mental states or the historical results of my decisions. From a Christian point of view, thus, it seems natural to believe that stars and rocks, water and plants, animals and humans, morals and beauty, do not depend upon human noetic contribution. Does this extend to quarks? Perhaps not, although it seems the tendency remains among traditional Christians to assume that science is discovering, not making, the World even at this highly theoretical level. What about free will or Aristotelian primary substances? Again, Christian theoreticians generally seem inclined to say there is only one way "the World" can be. If Aristotle is right, then Whitehead is wrong, and if humans have libertarian freedom, then determinism is false. In short, God's creating the World indicates that we do not. With some more or less obvious exceptions (thoughts and social constructions), we find "the World" as God made it. We discover, and don't make, "the World."

I want to challenge the idea that there is any substantial philosophical connection between traditional Christianity (God's noetic reality) and the following two claims: 1 "the World" can only be a singular way and 2 "the World" generally does not depend upon human noetic feats. The target here is difficult to give a detailed account of because so few philosophers, if any, make explicit the link between Christianity and various realisms about "the World." Instead, we are left with a sort of presumption that a traditional Christian would not, and perhaps should not, hold a view in which humans are the creators, so to speak, of "the World." Even if we do contribute to certain aspects of "the World," such as our thoughts or historical events, and even, perhaps, to some fields of discourse (such as, let's say, the aesthetic), our noetic contributions do not make "the World," since God does.

The one argument that is, I think, intrinsically relied upon is an argument from creation. Minimal traditional Christianity, as I've presented it, affirms the Nicene Creed. Hence, God is maker of heaven and earth. This claim, it might be thought, is a show-stopper for the claim that irrealism is compatible with traditional Christianity. But I think not. To say God creates "the World" is problematic not just for irrealism but for realism too. Consider, for example, the child's musing: "if God made 'the World,' did God make our dinner? I thought Daddy made dinner." This question and its attached observation present a rather deep problem. For God, while responsible for the raw stuff of "the World" – earth, air, water, and cabbage – did not make dinner. Daddy did. Whatever philosophical complexities emerge in explaining how God is responsible for making "the World" but Daddy makes dinner seem little less complex than those involved in explaining how God makes the World but humans make earth, air, water, and cabbage. How we make artifacts is no less complicated than how we make natural objects, at least in the important sense that while God is the creator, humans are co-creators or pro-creators with God, using material that has its ultimate source from God but its intermediate source from humans.

Since there is no obvious logical connection between theism and nearly global realism, one must wonder how to explain the propensity among traditional Christians to hold onto nearly global noetic realism. I proceed by looking at the arguments of two traditional Christian philosophers, Alvin Plantinga and William Alston. Plantinga appears to be a nearly global realist whereas Alston is a much more relaxed sort of realist. While neither Plantinga nor Alston explicitly develops an argument for any sort of global realism in connection with Christianity, both seem to assume that Christianity involves realism of some fairly strong form about "the World." Both provide arguments that some irrealisms are bad for, or inconsistent with, traditional Christianity. I want to mine their discussions to learn what is really important for traditional Christianity vis-à-vis realism. The nub of their arguments seems to be that insofar as one takes traditional Christianity seriously, God and (what I've called) the divine must be metaphysically (noetically) real and not dependent in any substantial metaphysical way upon human contributions. As it turns out, for the worldly there is no such requirement.

2 PLANTINGA ON TRUTH, REALITY, AND CHRISTIANITY

I'll consider Plantinga's discussion first, returning to Alston's in the remaining sections. After saying that some things in postmodernism are compatible with Christianity, Plantinga writes,

> there is one common post-modern sort of view of truth according to which what is true depends on what we human beings say or think, and that *does* seem incompatible with Christian belief. At any rate it does if we accept the plausible proposition that
>> (1) Necessarily, there is such a person as God if and only if it is true that there is such a person as God.
> For the post-modern claim about truth implies that whether it is true that there is such a person as God depends upon us and what

we do or think. But if the truth of this proposition depends on us, then, given (1) so does the very existence of God. According to (1) there is such a person as God if and only if it is *true* that there is; hence if its being *true* that there is such a person as God depends on us and what we do and think, then so does there *being* such a person as God; God depends on us for his existence ... This way of thinking about truth, therefore, is incompatible given (1) with Christian belief. [italics his]

Plantinga continues:

> The same goes for the idea that there simply *is* no such thing as truth. One of our most fundamental and basic ideas is that there is such a thing as *the way things are*. Things could have been very different from the way they are; there are many ways things could have been, but among them is the way they actually are. There actually are horses; there aren't any unicorns, although (perhaps) there could have been; there being horses, then, is part of the way things are. Now the existence of truth is intimately connected with there being horses if and only if there being horses is part of the way things are. [italics his][2]

Since Plantinga in the main talks about truth, it seems fairly clear that he defends the claim that Christianity and any alethic irrealist theory are incompatible. Two potential incompatibilities exist. One relies on the claim that truth depends on what we humans say or think, the other on truth simply not existing.

There is in Plantinga's account, however, a decided bias toward not only alethic realism but noetic realism also. This is clear enough in his discussion of the first position – truth depends on what humans say or think – but equally true in the second. He argues as follows. The statement

> 1 Necessarily, there is such a person as God if and only if it is true that there is such a person as God

is true. Hence, the claim that truth depends on human noetic feats entails not only that they make it true that God exists but also make God exist. The latter entails that God is noetically irreal. In Christianity, God exists all on God's own – humans are created by God and not the reverse – and therefore the postmodern claim is incompatible with Christianity. So far forth, Plantinga is right. But does it follow that

> 2. Necessarily, there is such a thing as a porch on my house if and only if it is true that there is such a thing as a porch on my house

is true? Well, yes. That just follows from alethic realism. But what if the fact that there is a porch on my house is due to my noetic feats? In fact, there is a porch there because I thought up the design, bought the lumber, and built it. Elsewhere Plantinga notes this kind of irrealism and writes, "Of course creative anti-realism with respect to *some* things is very attractive; your average house, or automobile, or B-1 bomber, for example, really does owe its existence and character to the noetic activities of persons [italics his]."[3] But "the creative anti-realist is not ordinarily content to restrict his creative anti-realism to such things as houses, automobiles, and B-1 bombers ... For their characteristic claim is not that human beings create or structure the World; instead they make a certain claim about *truth* [italics his]."[4]

So Plantinga would admit that true is true, but there being a porch is due more or less directly to my noetic contributions. We can structure or pro-create aspects of "the World," but we cannot create truth epistemically or noetically. So, his concern appears to have two aspects. First, alethic claims cannot merge with noetic irrealism and, second, and most importantly, noetic irrealism cannot extend to the divine. Of the latter he writes,

> Postmoderns sometimes seem to oscillate between a momentous but clearly false claim (there simply is no such thing as truth at all) and a sensible but rather boring claim (there is no such thing as truth, conceived in some particular and implausible way). Taken the strong way, however, as the suggestion there really is no such thing as the way the world is, and hence no such thing as truth, the postmodern claim is incompatible with Christian belief. For it is certainly crucial to Christian belief to suppose that there *is* a way things are, and that it includes the great things of the gospel; it is crucial to Christian belief to suppose that such propositions as *God created the world* and *Christ's suffering and death are an atonement for human sin* are true. [italics his][5]

From the point of view of traditional Christianity, Plantinga ought to be concerned about the second point, viz., a noetically irrealist account of God. But should he be concerned about the first, viz., noetic irrealism when it applies to things such as rocks or trees? Why can't an alethically real account of "'p' is true iff p'" be the right account while it also is the case that p is the way it is because of human noetic contribution? Of course, the Christian shouldn't allow this for God, but why not for rocks or trees?

There are further questions, however. Let's ask about this claim:

3 Necessarily, there is such a thing as the Rustic Tuna if and only if it is true that there is such a thing as the Rustic Tuna

where the Rustic Tuna is a ceramic made by a student in a pottery class. This work of art appears even more rooted in human thought than the porch, since the notion of a work of art is arguably even more "cultural" than physical or practical. We have no general notion of the "Rustic Tuna" as we do with "front porch," the former being (typically) unique among things in the World. Individual art objects are ontologically weird and part of that weirdness seems due to their radical dependence on human creativity and conceptual shaping. What makes a work of art art may be directly the noetic doing of the members of the art world.[6]

The problem is not with noetic irrealisms themselves, but with what we take noetic irrealisms to range over. For the Christian, they don't range over God – God isn't the type of thing that human noetic feats contribute to – but perhaps they do range over some, perhaps most, created things. Although Plantinga is right when he says alethic irrealism is incompatible with Christianity, it doesn't follow that noetic irrealism is, unless extended to the divine. But it doesn't follow from this that it is "crucial to Christian belief to suppose that there *is* a way the world is."[7] First, alethic realism does not entail noetic realism. Second, the realities about many created things can be world-bound in an irrealistic sense whereas the divine realities need not be world-bound, so far as human noetic feats are concerned.

Plantinga's second point, viz., that there being no truth at all is incompatible with Christianity, needs some clarifying. If we shift from truth to truths, we can ask what kind of truths Plantinga is talking about. Truths about God might be fixed and singular but truths across irrealistic worlds need not be. He says that "it is certainly crucial to

Christian belief to suppose that there *is* a way things are," but he adds, I think very importantly, that the way the World is "includes the great things of the Gospel; it is crucial to Christian belief to suppose that such propositions as *God created the world* and *Christ's suffering and death are an atonement for human sin* are true [italics his]."⁸ From a Christian point of view, does there have to be a singular "way things are"? About everything? Plantinga says that "the way things are" includes the great things of the Gospel, that God created the World and that Christ's suffering and death are an atonement for human sin. So far forth, it seems that Christianity does require that there is "a way things are." Yet, does God's creating the World entail that humans have no role at all? Why couldn't humans be co-creators? We humans are, after all, made in God's image – we too are creators. Plantinga doesn't pick out that there are stars or that my mother used a table saw once or that the Rustic Tuna is sitting just outside the kiln. Plantinga recognizes that there are no unicorns but there are horses and that that is part of the way things are. But surely these are not essential to the Gospel or Christianity. He also admits that houses and B-1 bombers are human constructs. Although claims about these latter things are true, are they part of "the singular way things are"? Perhaps there are noetic contributions to various world-bound items in noetically shaped worlds, but not to certain other features of those worlds. Features the Gospel describes for us, for example, could be fixed in all the worlds there are. So perhaps while we humans can make various worlds, all the worlds have divine contributions to them in virtue of which not just anything will go. The existence of humans, for example, seems to be a contribution of God. While irrealists might claim we make the stars, it is tougher to see how humans can make ourselves (except in the obvious sense!).

All of which raises these questions: Which things, which bits of the World, are fixed and which are not? Which bits are noetically real and which are not? Does traditional Christianity tell us? It seems clear enough that for the traditional Christian the divine cannot be noetically irreal. That God exists, that God exists without any core contribution from the created order, and so forth, seem to be clearly needed to hold traditional Christianity together. But what about historical events such as that Jesus was born of the Virgin Mary or that Jesus was crucified under Pontius Pilate? Since these are historical events, how can they be immune from human noetic contribution? I'll return to more detailed answers below, being content to make the point now that noetic realism seems required for God and humans, as well as morals and certain historical Christian events, but that that doesn't force the Christian into noetic realism about anything else. But there is much more explanation and argument needed to see how all this fits together, to which I return in chapters 14 through 17.

3 ALSTON, PURE ALETHIC REALISM, AND ALETHIC REALISM*

In "Realism and the Christian Faith,"[9] Alston attempts to show that certain nonrealist (or irrealist) Christian theologies are subversive of the Christian faith. I want to compare his account of alethic realism in that essay with the one found in his book *A Realist Conception of Truth*. The goal is simply to note, as we have with Plantinga's work, that the real issue with irrealist Christian theologies for traditional Christianity is not noetic irrealism applied in general but alethic irrealism and/or noetic irrealism applied to God. Alston claims that irrealist Christian theologies are subversive of the Christian faith, suggesting that a requirement of the Christian faith is alethic realism. While I think traditional Christianity requires alethic realism, in his essay dealing with Christianity and realism Alston construes alethic realism as including a noetic realist aspect. I suggest that irrealist Christian theologians and philosophers certainly can reject alethic realism and therefore undermine Christianity, but the real issue in Alston's discussion is the application of noetic irrealism to God. Once again, so far as Christianity goes, there is nothing about noetic irrealism as applied to the World that seems problematic.

Alston states, in *A Realist Conception of Truth*, that "alethic realism is largely neutral as between different metaphysically realist and nonrealist positions, though alethic realism can be said to carry a very weak metaphysically realist commitment."[10] This commitment is summarized by Alston when he writes,

Almost invariably the truth value of a statement will depend on something other than features of the statement, or of the belief expressed by the statement, since its content concerns something other than that statement. This being the case, if truth is determined as alethic realism has it, then what determines the truth of almost any true statement, that is, the fact that makes it true, is constitutively independent of that statement. Hence, alethic realism, together with the obvious fact that self-reference in statement or belief is rare at best, implies that (almost always) what confers a truth value on a statement is something independent of the cognitive-linguistic goings on that issued in that statement, including any epistemic status of those goings on. *To that extent*, alethic realism implies that what makes statements true or false is independent of our thought and talk. [italics his] ("Realism," 83–4)

In short, there are facts and there are statements. Statements are made true or false not by the statements themselves (except rarely occurring self-referential statements) but by the facts. Facts generally are independent of the statement-making (and the concomitant thinking or talking that goes with statement-making). These facts provide a weak realist aspect to alethic realism. Alston then adds that "that doesn't alter the main point ... that alethic realism is neutral with respect to virtually all the controversies over the metaphysical status of this or that domain that go under the name of 'realism vs. antirealism,' including the relatively global ones)" ("Realism," 84). In short, what makes most statements true is not the statements and the thought and talk that goes into them but the facts. Facts themselves might be noetically irreal but statements corresponding to the facts will still be true in an alethically real sense. Human noetic feats may make the facts, but the facts still make true statements true.

In "Realism and the Christian Faith," Alston characterizes alethic realism by bringing both alethic and noetic aspects together. He writes: "Alethic realism (concerning putative statements, S's, of a body of discourse D) can be ... crisply presented as a conjunction of the following three theses. 1. S's are genuine factual statements. 2. S's are true or false in the realist sense of those terms. 3. The facts that make true S's true hold and are what they are independently of human cognition" ("Realism," 39). To keep the alethic realism of *A Realist Conception of Truth* clearly demarked from the alethic realism of "Realism and the Christian Faith," let's call the former "pure alethic realism" and the latter "alethic realism*."

But even while Alston names the realism in "Realism and the Christian Faith" "alethic," he is still careful not to confuse the various aspects of his account. Indeed, he writes of alethic realism* that

the principles [1–3] are "nested." A denial of any one of them carries with it a denial of its successors, and an acceptance of any one carries an acceptance of its predecessors. If we deny 1, then since we do not recognize any factual statements in the domain, it is not possible that a realist conception of truth is applicable (denial of 2), since that conception is defined for statements of fact. And if 2 is denied, then the question of the status of facts in terms of which the statements are true or false in the realist sense cannot arise (denial of 3). By the same token, if we assert 3, we are committed to there being statements in the domain (1) that can be assessed for truth or falsity in terms of whether what they assert to obtain actually does obtain (2). ("Realism," 39)

From the point of view of pure alethic realism, it is important that these three theses are simply "nested" and not logically implied in both directions. On the one hand, Alston needs facts for pure alethic realism (it is facts that make statements true), so a denial of facts leads to a denial of pure alethic realism. The denial of either facts or alethic realism leads to a denial of noetic realism. Alston's facts need not be noetically real facts. So we see that both pure alethic realism and its relationship to facts and noetic realisms (of various sorts) are reflected in alethic realism*. But after having gone to such pains in *A Realist Conception of Truth* to keep noetic and alethic realism separate, it is curious that Alston puts them together in "Realism and the Christian Faith" and calls the latter account of realism "alethic realism." I believe his motives are directly connected to the purpose of the essay in regard to Christian faith, viz., to note why noetic nonrealism as applied to God is subversive of the faith.

4 ALETHIC REALISM *
AND THE CHRISTIAN FAITH

Alston seems to slip more into his notion of facts than he indicates. This can be seen by comparing how he treats various kinds of facts. Alston writes,

The realist conception of truth [as captured by 2] can be, and usually is, embraced as fully by metaphysical nonrealists as by realists – by those who deny the reality of abstract objects like properties and numbers as well as by those who accept this, by those who take physical objects to be reducible to patterns of sensory experience as well as by those who deny this. In other words, the usual run of departmental irrealists [or nonrealists], including idealists, take it that their statements are made true or false by virtue of whether what they say to be the case actually is the case. ("Realism," 38)

Just as in *A Realist Conception of Truth*, so here, Alston suggests that departmental irrealists are generally still pure alethic realists (in the narrow sense of holding 2). Also, idealists and phenomenalists can be pure alethic realists because although material objects are ideal, humans do not make the material-qua-mental-object-statements *true*. There are, in short, facts about these objects in virtue of which statements about them can be true (or false), without recourse to something "outside" the basic framework of alethic realism, viz., "p" is true iff p. Thus alethic realism "covers" noetically irreal objects. That is, there could be facts made by human noetic feats aligned with genuine factual statements (thus allowing 1 to hold) and those factual statements could be true or false in the realist sense (that is, where the content of the truth-value bearer itself gives us everything we need to specify what it takes for the truth-value bearer to be true). Yet alethic realism* seems to deny this, by adding 3.

Alston writes, more fully describing 1, that "S's are genuine statements of fact, just what they appear to be, as contrasted with, e.g., expressions of feelings or attitudes, or bits of fictional narrative" ("Realism," 37). The point seems to be that statements that appear to be about domain D are realistically true or false only if they are made true or false by actually being about domain D and not about some other domain. So a statement about God is made true or false by the facts about God and not by the facts of my emotional life, just as statements about my emotional life are made true or false by facts about my emotional life, and not some other domain. That is in line with pure alethic realism. Facts are facts, whether emotional, subjective, or otherwise.

But does this match Alston's actual treatment of the situation? I suggest that 1 is somewhat ambiguous. What if statements of fact about a given domain, say the religious domain, really are about emotional expression or fictional narratives that help us guide our lives? Does that entail that 2 is false? I don't quite see why. If the statement that there is a table in front of me is really about some mental or ideal event, and that doesn't entail that 2 is false, then why should a statement about God really being about an emotional response of mine, or some narrative fiction, entail that 2 is false? "There is a table in front of me" can be given an alethically real account, even if the table is an ideal object. The fact remains: there is a table in front of me. But that doesn't yet tell me what a table is. By Alston's own admission, pure alethic realism is neutral with regard to whether the table exists independent of the human mind or as an "ideal" object. What if what made "there is a table in front of me" true were some emotional state of mine?

According to Alston, 1 rules out "God exists" being factual if it turns out to be about some emotional state that I'm in, and 1 also rules out "Jesus died for our sins" being factual if it turns out to be a fiction about the value of human self-sacrifice. Thus, on the analysis of many nonrealist theologians and philosophers, "God exists" and "Jesus died for our sins" would not be factual statements. But then why does "there is a tree" turning out to be about some set of phenomenal images leave the factuality of the statement untouched? What is there about the emotional or the fictional in particular that drain statements of facticity?

What are we to say of God, then? "It is true that 'God exists' iff God exists" could be given an alethically real account while there is, as yet, no specification of what God is. Maybe God is ideal or a convenient fiction or an emotional expression or made to exist by human noetic contribution. Alston admits, of course, that pure alethic realism and noetic irrealism really can be natural bedfellows. But then it seems that his treatment of facts is somewhat limiting. Why can one type of noetic contribution (let's say a linguistically conceptual one) be acceptable as factual but not another type (the emotional or the fictional)?

Alston, like most realist philosophers who still pick up the scent of verificationism as a cause for worry, appears to regard emotions, at least, and perhaps fictions too, as some sort of noncognitivism. Linguistically construed concepts used in statements make for truth and falsity but emotional expressions or fictional statements do not. However, it is arguable, given a kind of pluralistic noetic irrealism based in a broadly enough construed notion of concepts, that fictional statements such as "Huck Finn is a teen-age boy" are true, given the world of the novel written by Mark Twain. I think, too, that in noetically constructed worlds in which emotions are more central as concepts than linguistic concepts, it makes sense to note the closeness of the expression of an emotion (grunts, groans, smiles, grimaces, oral expressions such as "that's yummy," and "I'm in pain") to linguistic descriptions of the emotions. All the former expressions are (or can be) symbolic, even if they are not linguistic. Linguistic statements are either true or false but the expressions are neither. In a pluralistic noetic irrealism, however, not all worlds need be concerned about truth. There are other kinds of rightness of rendering. There are pictorial rightnesses and gestural rightnesses. If we are willing to act contrary to some long-standing philosophical prejudices about the so-called "noncognitive" nature of emotions and fictions, then what Alston says about facts can be challenged.

In contrast to the broader context for concepts just described, Alston seems to construe facts in a particular, narrow way and then build 2 on that construal. Consequently, Alston seems to slip something more into 1 than he should. If so, what happens to the notion of fact? If 1 can rule out emotional accounts of things putatively about some other domain, then why does it not rule out noetically nonreal accounts of things that seem to be about the noetically real? The notion of fact in 1 seems to go hand in hand with 3 being true (which is a way of keeping the World independent of human noetic activity including emotional or fictional creativity). Alston says that a denial of 1 entails a denial of 2 and 3. But doesn't the truth of 3 force 1 to be construed in the limiting way I've suggested? That is, doesn't Alston force facts always to be noetically real facts? As such, not only does denial run down (1 to 3) and affirmation up (3 to 1), but denial seems to run up too. Denying 3 entails the denial of 1, and that turns alethic realism* into noetic realism. I believe, therefore, that Alston's account of alethic realism*'s 1 and 2 as neutral vis-à-vis 3 is at least suspect. Indeed, it seems that the real issue in "Realism and the Christian Faith" is noetic irrealism as applied to God, especially when the irrealism is of the emotional or fictional constructivist sort. All the talk of alethic realism is in the end misleading. While some revisionist theologian or philosopher could hold alethic irrealism and apply it to claims about God, and that would undermine Christianity, Alston gives no explicit examples of this. Rather he criticizes only various kinds of noetic irrealism as applied to God.

In summary, Alston's concern seems to be the old worry about theistic statements being merely "noncognitive." If so, the real problem seems to be that statements putatively about domain D are really about some other domain, D*: statements about God are really about emotion. From a traditional Christian point of view, that would be unacceptable. But if moving from one domain to another doesn't disturb claims about alethic realism in the case of some irrealisms (e.g., the idealistic account of material objects), why does it disturb alethic realism in the case of God and emotions, or God and fiction? If the emotional or the fictional do drain the facticity out of the statements in D, then surely material statements really being about something purely phenomenal would drain them of facticity as well. So, why tack on 3? Why not leave it at 1 and 2? The answer, it seems, is that a denial of 1 and 3, taken together in the way Alston construes them, runs counter to traditional Christianity. One and 3, it seems, are central to the problems with traditional Christianity raised by some contemporary theologians. One and 3 are specifically set in place to show how various metaphysical or noetic irrealisms run contrary to traditional Christianity. The real problem vis-à-vis Christianity isn't with alethic irrealism but with noetic irrealism or, more specifically, "reducing" God to something dependent on humans. In short, Alston could save us a lot of trouble by identifying more specifically that it is noetic irrealism as ranging over the divine that he finds subversive of Christianity. The conflicts thus can be summarized as follows: Traditional Christianity is incompatible with any irrealism that a) reduces factual statements about God to expressions of emotion or narrative fictions and/or b) reduces facts about God to facts that are "made up" by humans. But neither of these has anything much to do with alethic realism per se. Alethic realism* appears to be just noetic realism (broadly construed) with an alethic realist footnote.

5 ALSTON AND SUBVERSIVE CHRISTIANITY

Why does Alston characterize alethic realism differently in the essay than in the book? One possibility is that the essay is earlier than the book and his ideas were still developing at the point of the essay. This seems an incomplete account at best, however, for Alston clearly attempts to set up the alethic realism* of the essay in such a way that the noetic aspect (that is, 3) need not be true for the other two theses to be true. Rather I think he includes the noetic realist thesis 3 (and what turns out, I think, to be its cousin, 1) because that is what is necessary to combat the irrealisms of contemporary

culture as applied in revisionist Christian theology. Alethic realism
pure and simple is not enough to combat the Christian irrealisms he
discusses, since even the most radical of noetic irrealists might hold
to alethic realism. He needs, instead, the stronger alethic realism*
and its built-in noetic realism. He writes:

> My primary concern in this essay is with alethic realism[*] and ir-
> realism [or nonrealism] in the religious domain. Are what look
> like religious statements, including those that are about putative
> supreme realities such as the Christian God, genuine statements
> that can be assessed as true or false in terms of whether they
> 'match' an objective reality that is what it is independent of our
> cognitive machinations? Or do they have some other status? Is
> their truth ... to be assessed in some other way? ("Realism," 40)

His concern, in short, is to evaluate whether the things to which religious statements refer are noetically real or irreal, and this spills
over into taking the statements to be about what they "say" they
are about, viz., the mind- and creature-independent God, as opposed to an expression of emotion or a narrative fiction that helps
us live our lives.

We have, as yet, not considered any of Alston's arguments that
"nonrealism, though rampant nowadays even among Christian theologians, is subversive of the Christian faith." On this Alston writes,

> I want to consider what hangs on the realism issue for Christian-
> ity. What difference(s) does it make for the Christian life whether
> we take our beliefs to be subject to assessment as true or false in
> terms of correspondence with an objective reality or lack thereof?
> Is something fundamental in the Christian life lost if we abandon
> realism? ... My answer is going to be an unequivocal YES ...
> ("Realism," 45)

His main concern with "reducing" God to something we create is
that such views totally lose divine-human interaction and therefore
lose the heart and soul of the Judeo-Christian tradition. Now I
agree wholeheartedly with this point. I think that a downgrading of
God to something human noetic activity makes does not reflect
what traditional Christianity has held. Nor does reducing God to a
narrative story to help us get through life or, even worse, simply the

reduction of God to an emotional expression. But the problem with these is not that they go against alethic realism per se but that they go against a noetic realism (broadly construed) about the divine.

Alston describes alethic realism* as a view "concerning a putative statement, S, of a body of discourse, D." This implies that for any statements in any body of discourse where alethic realism applies (and Alston would be loath, it seems, to admit that truth should be analyzed differently in different contexts), alethic realism* includes 3 and hence a noetic realistic aspect. But then if I am right that Alston builds more into the notion of fact than at first appears, 1 and 3 go hand in hand. That is, to say that some noetic contributions to things are acceptable (the linguistic-based conceptual contributions) but not others (emotional or fictional ones) is a kind of unfair or unwarranted prejudice. Thus, alethic realism* requires only noetically real things to make up the "objective" facts of the World. But, if noetically irreal things in the World can also be truly described according to alethic realism, then so should noetically irreal things in the divine realm be truly describable according to alethic realism.

But we know from the account in *A Realist Conception of Truth* that noetic irrealism is compatible with alethic realism. Thus, Alston's description of alethic realism in the essay seems aimed directly and only at divine discourse. In the end, that says nothing about the rest of the created order and the role of human noetic contribution to it. Yet his demands when it comes to religious claims seem contrary to his demands about the rest of the World. So nothing in Alston's essay countermands a Christianized irrealism so long as it doesn't range over the divine, the same result we found in looking at Plantinga's work. Although Alston and Plantinga may be allies for noetic realism in general, nothing they say in defence of the claim that traditional Christianity is inconsistent with noetic irrealism entails a noetic realism about much of the created order. We would need a separate argument to show that traditional Christianity requires noetic realism about anything other than God. God's creating the World does not clearly entail or even lean traditional Christianity toward noetic realism about the World. As such, the door is open to the possibility, from a Christian point of view, that there need be no singular, true story about the World, so long as all true World descriptions have it that God exists. Traditional Christianity may be alethically and noetically real so far as God goes, but noetically irreal so far as what's left over.

6 ALSTON'S SENSIBLE METAPHYSICAL REALISM

That was not Alston's final word on realism. In this section I briefly describe Alston's most considered view on the matter as found in his Aquinas Lecture, *A Sensible Metaphysical Realism*.[11] I note some quibbles along the way, as well as point out a number of significant ways in which his view and mine are quite different.

The easiest place to begin is with Alston's contrast between realism and antirealism. He writes, "Antirealism (AR) – Everything, and every fact, exists or obtains, and is what it is, at least in part, relative to certain conceptual-theoretical choices that have equally viable alternatives. Realism (R) – Vast stretches of reality are what they are absolutely, not in any way relative to certain conceptual-theoretical choices that have equally viable alternatives" (*Metaphysical Realism*, 23).

The way in which Alston defines realism and antirealism allows for various resting places between the extremes of "everything is dependent" and "vast stretches of reality are independent." Alston describes himself as a realist, appealing to the stated definition, and so he holds that vast stretches of reality are independent of human noetic contribution.

One of the challenges to antirealism, says Alston, is that the notion of the dependence relation between things and conceptual schemes is incoherent. Alston responds by noting two examples of things that may be dependent on our conceptual-theoretical choices: propositions and beliefs. In describing how they might be dependent, he provides a general picture of the dependency relationship.

> The nature and individuation of propositions and beliefs do not confront us as something ready made, whatever our concepts and theories. On the contrary, these matters go one way rather than another depending on those choices. Hence if we think of propositions and beliefs as part of reality, part of what is involved in "the way things go in the world", ... then we must take them as examples of how the existence and nature of things in the world, including their individuation, are partly constituted by one or another way of conceptualizing them and theorizing them. This is not the *causal* dependence that we have seen to be absurd. Our theorizing clearly does not exercise that kind of influence. It is what we might call *constitutive dependence*. Propositions are

what they are in these respects *by virtue of* our shaping our thought of them in one or another way.[12]

Furthermore, "Let's say that propositions enjoy a particular nature not *absolutely* but *relative* to a certain theoretical-conceptual scheme. For any sort of reality that is subject to this constitutive dependence on our thought, there is no such thing as what it is absolutely, *tout court*, but only what it is *relative* to a certain scheme of thought" (*Metaphysical Realism*, 18).

We must thus index statements about propositions or beliefs to a scheme, thus "In conceptual-theoretical scheme C, propositions are ..." On this point Alston's and my position are not far apart. The real difference is just how far the dependency of the World goes.

As I noted above, between Alston's account of antirealism and realism there are a good many resting places. Alston characterizes his position as a "sensible" realism, claiming realism for "vast stretches of reality" while allowing for some (but limited) latitude in what falls on the side of the antireal. He notes that "since an unqualified conceptual relativity is unacceptable, I feel justified in taking realism to be the default position for any putative entity or fact, taking any such item to be independent of our cognitive activity until it is shown to be otherwise" (*Metaphysical Realism*, 34). But what reason is there for this move? From the fact that some stretch of the world is independent of conceptual-theoretic contributions, it doesn't follow that the default position for any given entity or fact is realism. Indeed, I suggest that just the opposite is true. Given a sufficient reason to move to irrealistic pluralism in the first place, it seems a better move to assume that most entities or facts fall under the antireal with only a few or perhaps just one entity being independent.

Alston further notes:

One may still feel the need for more explanation of the kind of relativity envisaged here. Before doing what I can to meet this need, I should point out a respect in which this is more difficult for me, as a realist, than it is for someone like Putnam or Goodman, who universally generalizes the relativity to conceptual schemes. It is more difficult for me because, recognizing as I do vast stretches of reality that are absolute, not relative to conceptual schemes, the problem of why I shouldn't treat my alleged examples of relativity in the same way is a live one for me ...

> Whereas those who take everything to be relative to alternative conceptual schemes have no contrasting, absolutist mode of reality that, so to say, threatens to swallow up all the putatively relative entities and banish all relativity to the thought side of the thought-reality relationship. (*Metaphysical Realism*, 19–20)

This point, of course, depends on Alston's earlier assumption about where the default position is. If we shift the terms of the discussion to the view that the default position is something close to, although just short of, Alston's described antirealism, then the shoe is on the other foot. The threat isn't that the independent side will swallow up the antireal side but that the dependent will swallow up the real. Alston gives, in short, no good reason for either claim and I believe staying the course I've charted is the best move.

Although my overall argument agrees with Alston's intuitions and argument when he says that *something* must be independent of our conceptual choices, I try to give the impetus behind antirealism its due. I have proposed few things independent of our noetic work rather than Alston's "vast stretches of reality." The main question is, then, what might the independent things be?

One can certainly make allowances for various worlds if one limits pluralism to local matters. Thus it is plausible, Alston argues, that there are some aspects of the World that are simply up to our conceptual choices. This is more or less what he proposes in his claim that although large ranges of the world are independently real, certain aspects of the world are up to us and thus dependent upon our conceptual-theoretical schemes. We've already seen his suggestion that the nature of propositions and beliefs may be relative to various conceptual-theoretical schemes. He also suggests that the number of entities in the universe may vary depending on one's view of mereological sums. He suggests further that perhaps even the fundamental structure of things might vary according to conceptual scheme, so that objects in the world might be either Aristotelian or Whiteheadian in nature (*Metaphysical Realism*, 19, 43). Nevertheless, such pluralism does not, for Alston, extend all the way up – or even most of the way up. He remains a realist about some things – most things, in fact – and hence he remains largely a monist about vast expanses the world, holding that there is only one true description of those expanses. Many, if not most, things have a fixed or absolute nature.

Of course, Alston remains a monist about God for, as we saw above, he argues with some force that various sorts of irrealisms applied to God undermine the very framework of Christian theism. Recall that our social interaction with God is made nonsense if God is no more than a fiction or an expression of human emotions ("Realism"). To this we might add the observation noted above, viz., God made the world and the humans therein and not the reverse. Surely included among the things humans don't make is God. But in the spirit of a more radical pluralism, why draw the line where Alston does? Why not include nearly everything inside the irrealist circle except God? But as I argue below, even if God is independent, God need not be totally independent to solve the infinite regress problem found in radical irrealisms.

Perhaps another way to put the question is to ask what if the Alstonian monistic backdrop is not available? That is, what if for huge stretches of the world the natures of things were dependent on humans? Does God automatically fall inside human noetic machinations? How might we tell? These latter two questions are, I think, more complex than many theists might admit. To the first I think the answer is yes and no. No at God's core being; yes in the ways God is in various worlds or conceptual schemes. I return to details on this point in later chapters. As to how we tell, that is one of the foci of this entire essay.

What reasons are there for proposing that radical pluralism is not the case but that at least some stretch of the world is independent? Alston says realism holds for some stretch of the world on the basis of two arguments with which he shows the incoherence of radical antirealism. I report both of these arguments.

Remember that the antirealism under consideration here is an unqualified generalization of the relativity to conceptual-theoretical schemes I have already acknowledged to hold for certain matters ... The internal incoherence is a direct result of that unqualified generalization. Let's say that we have identified a variety of equally viable conceptual-theoretical schemes (total ones, if you like) such that physical objects and facts have a certain character relative to one or another such scheme. Relative to one of the alternative schemes those objects and facts have one detailed constitution, whereas relative to another such scheme they have a somewhat different constitution. But now what about those conceptual-theoretical schemes themselves? And if we are not thinking of such schemes as abstract objects but only as employed by concrete cognitive subjects, how about those subjects? Do all of these exist and have the nature they do relative to each of a number of different conceptual-theoretical schemes? If not, the unrestricted generalization has been given up. But if so, what about these second level conceptual-theoretical schemes. Obviously an infinite regress looms. The unrestricted generalization is purchased at the price of an infinite hierarchy of conceptual-theoretical schemes. And if the conceptual-theoretical schemes involved must actually be used by subjects, we get an infinite hierarchy of subjects, or at least an infinite hierarchy of employments of different conceptual-theoretical schemes by subjects. (*Metaphysical Realism*, 32–3)

The reader will have noted that this is more or less the kind of challenge I push on Goodman and Lynch. The main difference is Alston's addition of an infinite hierarchy of cognitive subjects. I think Alston is right on both accounts. There is an infinite hierarchy of conceptual-theoretical schemes and an infinite hierarchy of cognitive subjects. I think these two issues are so entangled that they cannot, in the end, be separated. First, it seems to me that the only interesting version of antirealism would deal with concrete cognitive subjects holding concrete conceptual schemes. If pluralism were considered to be held only on some sort of abstract level, and the world were itself monistic, why bother? Presumably God could have made the world differently than God did. But the really interesting question is whether humans actually make the world in concrete but plural ways. The reason why Alston's two issues are entangled is not far to seek, then, for there surely are no conceptual-theoretical schemes if there are no cognitive subjects, and if generalized relativism requires an infinite hierarchy of conceptual-theoretical schemes, then it also requires an infinite hierarchy of (finite) cognitive subjects.

Alston puts his finger on a central issue for the radical antirealist when he raises the question of the cognitive subject. If everything, including every fact, exists or obtains and is what it is, at least in part, relative to certain conceptual-theoretical choices that have equally viable alternatives, then whence the human cognitive subject in the first place? I've already noted my hesitations on this point. But it is worth restating. Do we humans somehow bring our own existence or natures into being with our own cognitive work? This seems a feat that we cannot pull off. Perhaps we get our grounding on which we noetically work from the line of cognitive subjects who came before us, but there looms another infinite regress of cognitive subjects. Since on pretty much every account of the universe, humans have not always "been here" and hence came onto the scene at some point in the past, the chances of an infinite trail of human cognitive activity stretching forever back through time seems both logically and practically unlikely. Could the existence of God stop the regress of conceptual-theoretic schemes and while doing so, explain why there are human cognitive subjects as part of the mix? I believe the answer is affirmative. But let's begin with considering exactly what the problem with the infinite hierarchy of schemes is. Besides the fact that philosophers generally don't approve of infinite regresses, in this case the problem appears to be that given an infinite number of such schemes there simply is no limit on how one might conceptualize a world. Things could go just any old way one chooses. Most pluralists seem to resist such a notion. Certainly each of Hales, Lynch, and Goodman do.

The second challenge Alston brings to the generalized antirealist/relativist is likewise familiar. It is as follows:

The different conceptual schemes must be construed as yielding *incompatible* construals of the entities dependent on them. Otherwise there is no objection to taking the entities to be what they are absolutely, not relative to one or another scheme. But they can be incompatible only if they are construals of the *same* entities. For if they are construals of different entities, they can all happily coexist in one unique reality. But this means that the view presupposes some common object of conceptualization. And just by being the shared object of the different conceptual schemes, it is itself immune from relativity to those different schemes. Thus the view is driven back to something like the Kantian noumena, to which the plurality of schemes of categories is applied. And so the price of maintaining the basic argument for the position is an exception to the universal generalization of relativity. If we try to escape this consequence by taking what is differently conceptualized in different conceptual schemes to be itself relative to different conceptual schemes, and so split it up into different "versions" corresponding to those different second order schemes, we are off on another infinite regress. For what are [we] to say of that which is conceptualized differently in those second order schemes? (*Metaphysical Realism*, 33–4)

I take this challenge to be a version of the consistency problem, or at least related to it. Insofar as my summation is right, then I think the possible world solution can handle the issue. But let's say it is a different problem, one limited to what we might call the problem of transworld identity, mirroring the problem in possible world semantics. Alston's solution, viz., proposing a sort of Kantian noumena, will solve the problem, albeit at the expense of a totalizing antirealism. I have no particular grievance with such a solution, as will become clearer below. Proposing some sort of noumenal basis for the making of items in the world, however, hardly commits one to the position that broad stretches of reality are mind independent, except in perhaps a peculiar way. It's not as if being committed to some sort of noumena commits one to the independence of, say, trees or whales or stars. It is these latter that I understand Alston's realism to take as independent entities, not merely some noumenal independent "stuff."

I argue in what follows that while there are some things that we should take to be independent in significant ways of human noetic work (God and humans in particular), my list of independent things is much shorter than Alston's. I tend to want to include, and I think I'm right in including, nearly everything on the antirealist (irrealist, in my terms) side of the equation. And, in fact, everything, including the divine, is in some sense irreal, although I don't think irreality should be limited simply to human noetic work. So while Alston's view is, I think, rightly called "realism," my view is more accurately called "irrealism," even though we two agree about a good many things.

The Divine, Its Furniture,
and Virtual Absolutes

I've suggested that while traditional Christianity requires God's fundamental being to be noetically real, Christianity remains compatible with noetic irrealism for the worldly. However, I've said that certain aspects of God are open to human noetic contribution and that this is consistent with traditional Christianity. It is time to make good on some specifics of these claims and so I turn to explain how the irrealist can think of God as independent of human noetic feats, at least at God's core. The topic of how God can at the same time be shaped by human noetic work and thus not separable from the worlds as humans create them is taken up in the next chapter. However, it is difficult to speak of the first issue without mentioning the second, so this and the next chapter's topics are intertwined to some extent.

An important analogy exists between God's independence of human noetic schemes and human independence of human noetic schemes. So in exploring divine independence, I also explore human independence. The analogy is between God as the ultimate creator and humans as co-creators. Clearly humans do not fundamentally create our selves by our noetic contributions. God creates us, but that is a different order of noetic contribution with which traditional Christianity is quite comfortable. God, on the other hand, simply is not created but the source of all that is. What's important to notice, however, is that it doesn't follow from the fact that God is uncreated that God doesn't exist within a noetic scheme.

In what follows I first spell out in more detail what counts as divine furniture in the World vs what counts as worldly furniture. Second, I set out the position that God interacts with humans in a number of ways. Not only is God creator but God is also sustainer of humans and the worlds we make. Because God is both creator and sustainer, we share in God's creative conceptual work and God shares in ours. As such, humans can and do contribute to what we can call "God's being in a world," the primary subject of the next chapter. However, since no human would be at all without God, human worldly contributions do not affect God in God's fundamental being (which I'll also refer to as God's "core" or "essential being").

I HUMANS AS DIVINE FURNITURE

First some general comments about the divine and the worldly. I've noted, following Alston, that divine-human interaction is at the heart of the Christian faith. So God is certainly noetically real from a traditional Christian point of view. Since God is obviously part of the divine furniture I say little about God in this section but return to the subject below.

If it is true that God cannot be reduced to a figment of our imaginatively constructive minds, neither can the other side of the equation. Humans cannot, it would seem, noetically create humans, at least in our core being. The reason is not far to seek, for if the worlds depend on humans, then humans must have a source other than ourselves, at least at a level that provides for our creative work. Core human being, I submit, can be and is noetically made by God.

The ultimate source of human being is a continuing puzzle. God's creative work is one long-standing solution. Given God's being, it is odd indeed to think of humans as the ultimate source of things. As Plantinga notes, "there is something initially off-putting, offensive and disturbing about creative anti-realism, as even its partisans admit ... and creative theological anti-realism seems at best a bit of laughable bravado."[1] With Plantinga, I find the notion that humans create God to be laughable bravado. Of course Plantinga also thinks that the human creation of dinosaurs and black holes is laughable too. For the irrealist, the latter sort of human creation is less bothersome. However, that humans noetically create humans seems odd, at best, and laughable, but for different reasons. It seems not quite so arrogant to think we create our selves. And surely we do, in some ways. We make ourselves into the people we will be tomorrow. We choose good or evil, to go to college or not, to marry or not. There is a myriad of other ways that our being-in-the-world seems obviously dependent upon us. Yet there is something incoherent about humans creating our selves in our core or essential being. Self-creation of that sort, one assumes, is a trick not even God can pull off. Minimally, the core being of humans comes from God, so far as traditional Christianity goes, and therefore humans fall into the class of divine things, that is, the noetically real (that is, not made by humans) as opposed to the worldly. God is a divine thing, as noncreated, along with humans, who are divine because God creates us (directly). So humans are not purely the result of human noetic activity but rather also the result of God's noetic activity. We are, at the core of our being, "fixed," whereby I mean that our core being – our social, free, creative, and conscious being – is made by God. Thus we are noetically real. Our core being – our shared essence, if you will – is the way it is independent of human noetic influence, and no amount of human noetic contribution will change it, not even one world or one conceptual scheme to another. Yet I don't believe it follows from the fact that in order for humans to be human we must be social, free, creative, and conscious, that these attributes are themselves fixed. There is a variety of ways in which humans can be social, free, creative, and conscious and these ways can vary across worlds. Humans are placed in the World and we develop and grow our cultures and subcultures, our patterns of thinking and our histories – our *Bildung*. We emerge in our worlds because of the basic core God provides for us but human being can be different in each world, within the bounds of sociality, freedom, creativity, and consciousness.

So we are not completely fixed. Humans have some sort of hand (or mind!) in creating ourselves. Humans have free will and can construct ourselves in a variety of ways, including cultural constructions (consider the gigantic number of cultures and subcultures and their hugely different and distinct aspects, including very different self-understandings), theoretical constructions (Aristotelian vs Whiteheadian metaphysical positions), and more specific or personal constructions (such as making oneself a mother or father, or a good mother or good father, or a lawyer or a school bus driver, or what have you or, on the other hand, not making ourselves any of these). Of course, these are not all exactly the same kind of making. Some could be handled by run-of-the-mill realist accounts (making oneself a bus driver). But recalling that making the world falls on a continuum, we can note that insofar as these constructions of ourselves are consistent with our fixed selves and with the more general nature and will of God, there is much we can do in making our selves. God gives us our free will. What we do with free will, including making ourselves sinners, is up to us. So although we are ready-made, we are not completely so. We are not completely noetically real. Certain aspects are noetically irreal and we make ourselves up as we go along. We have a lot of noetic freedom as to how we interact with the worlds and, indeed, with God.

One way to put this is to say that our core being is what it is in virtue of God's creative work, whereas what we make of ourselves within the bounds of God's handiwork is what it is relative to a given human conceptual scheme. God creates humans *ex nihilo* but we create ourselves in secondary ways. To tip my hand, given the structure of pluralistic irrealism, it makes sense to suggest that God makes humans in virtue of God's conceptual scheme which includes a thin notion of the human person (free, conscious, creative, and social) and humans can thicken up the concept via our noetic work. Unlike the thin concept of, let's say, a stone, which I believe is made up out of whole cloth, the concept of human is not. We inherit it from God's way of thinking of us.

Free will is not the only feature of humans relevant to our making the worlds. Free will requires consciousness, specifically the kind of consciousness that can form beliefs, have concepts, be creative, and use reason. That is, being conscious and, in particular, self-conscious, is what puts us into the space of reasons or makes us capable of spontaneity. To be fully free, one must be aware of one's environment, of one's self and others, and, indeed, have the ability to think and reason about alternatives. Not only our free choices but our very awareness of our environment, self, and others, are what allow us to be creative and to shape and contribute to the worlds in which we live. Yet the fact remains, even though humans are conscious and free, we do not create ourselves *ex nihilo*. Only God can do that, which is precisely what Christianity teaches. So God and humans both count in the divine – that is, neither God nor humans are dependent, at their core, on human conceptual schemes but rather on the divine scheme.

2 OTHER PIECES OF DIVINE FURNITURE

What else might count as divine? Well, angels, perhaps, since they appear to have some sort of consciousness and free will, according to the Christian tradition. That angels could create themselves seems no more likely than that we humans could, and angels and God interact along with humans and God. There are also the devils, perhaps, which are taken to be fallen angels.

What about nonhuman animals? Here the issue is less obvious, since it is hard for us to know to what extent nonhuman animals are conscious or free. Are animals self-aware? Do they reason and form beliefs? Is self-awareness needed to shape the environment? I leave the questions about nonhuman animals for another day, believing that if nonhuman animals are capable of noetically shaping the World, their addition to the list simply makes the interaction of all social creatures more complex. I'm content (and relieved!) to set aside angels and nonhuman animals to concentrate on humans.

Consciousness is profound and God letting humans qua conscious have a noetic hand in the creation of nonconscious things is simply one aspect of that profundity. Does noetic realism extend to anything beyond God and created conscious beings? I see no particular reason to suggest that it does.[2] There are, however, aspects of the World where the influence of God is felt more fully.

If the traditional Christian God is the unifier of human-made worlds, then not only must both the human and divine cores not be dependent on human noetic schemes, but certain elements of the Christian story will not be created entirely by humans either. Certain aspects of history – the Christian story in particular – are dependent upon God's creative work rather than strictly human creative work. Humans do not create history alone, on the Christian account, for God is active in the World as well. Furthermore, given God's unifying power in the universe of worlds, not only logical laws (such as the law of noncontradiction), but certain moral, aesthetic, and historical features turn out to be common to all worlds rightly rendered.

Thus, as I noted earlier, the situation is quite the reverse to what is often thought in our current intellectual culture. Frequently the claim is made that science gives us objectivity and truth, where the objectivity and truth are confused or conflated with the results of a physicalistic program. If religion, aesthetics, and morality can't objectively be allowed for in the physicalist program, then so much the worse, it is thought, for religion, aesthetics, and morality. At best these three are treated as subjective and potentially relative. My view is that, unlike this realism qua materialism, Christian irrealism allows for many different physical worlds. Such worlds are not objective or fixed except in some fairly weak sense. However, there is only one fixed moral and aesthetic version (or at least, a much more fixed set of versions) rooted in God.

From a Christian point of view, history is in certain ways fixed too, insofar as it touches upon the moral and aesthetic nature of things and, by extension, the nature of humankind itself. This is even more the case in Christian salvation history, that is, where God makes history divine because of the incarnation or other direct divine actions. According to theistic irrealism, morality, aesthetics, and religion have the greatest fixedness, rather than the physical realm itself or, more broadly, science and its approaches to the worlds.

3 GOD AND THE WORLD: VIRTUAL ABSOLUTES AND NOETIC REALISM

A virtual absolute can be either a fact or a proposition. The former is a bit of ontological furniture that turns up in every world because it exists relative to every conceptual scheme. The latter is a proposition that turns out true relative to every conceptual scheme. Of course, if propositions just are facts, as I've held, what is true will be believings. Be that as it may, I've suggested that the traditional Christian holds God to be noetically real, and therefore it will be thought that God is no mere virtual absolute but just a plain old-fashioned absolute. As I've suggested, so are humans at their core plain old-fashioned absolutes for their existence is not relative to human conceptual schemes.

However, the situation is more complicated. First, while God is not dependent at the divine's core on human noetic feats, God is nevertheless shaped by every human (well-formed) conceptual scheme. Second, God's own being is relative to God's conceptual scheme. Third, humans are made by God and exist in their core being in virtue of God's conceptual scheme. Finally, insofar as God and humans share conceptual schemes, God is relative to all schemes and hence, while not dependent at the divine's core on human noetic work, God is a virtual absolute based in God's noetic work which overlaps with human noetic work.

Why not just say that everything is scheme dependent except for God and humans? I think there are some good reasons to move beyond this claim. First, typically irrealism is explained strictly from the human point of view. This, I believe, is a mistake. Lynch's virtual absolutes are concerned only with the ways in which humans conceive of things. No mention is made of God, typically, except in passing or perhaps as a sort of heuristic device to explain something. But if Christianity holds, there actually is a God and God doesn't depend on human conceptual schemes. What few seem to notice, however, is that from the fact that God is independent of human conceptual schemes it doesn't follow that God is independent of all conceptual schemes. What about angelic conceptual schemes (although the traditional Christian may be skeptical here) or what of the divine conceptual scheme or schemes? Second, it is arguable that humans are, in certain respects, ontologically different across different conceptual schemes even though the very same persons (in their core being) turn up in every conceptual scheme. The same could be true of God. These themes are worth exploring to provide the most complete irrealism consistent with traditional Christianity.

My proposal that God is different across human conceptual schemes is motivated by the many theological and philosophical disagreements about the nature of God (within orthodox categories) and the depth and seemingly unbridgeable nature of those disagreements. Scholars often give good rational and biblical defences for the various positions. A way to allow these disagreements to be settled without denying the truths on each side would be a good thing. We could, for starters, move a long way toward Christian unity, and away from various internecine battles, on grounds other than thinning the various theological positions down until there is so little to disagree with that what's left is barely recognizable as Christianity. An ontological pluralism allowing God to be different across human conceptual schemes without losing the core nature of God could be of immense value. A parallel issue emerges when it comes to understanding humans and cultures as well. With the obvious need for some sort of understanding of human diversity, a theory that allows humans to share the same core but be different in substantial ontological ways across conceptual schemes would again be of immense help.

My task is to provide some sort of explanation for how God, primarily, and humans, secondarily, can be independent of human noetic feats at their core being and yet different across human conceptual schemes. In order to fulfill this task we need a story of how things might go rather than an argument that things do, in fact, go such and such a way. I've already hinted that the general approach can be found in the notion that conceptual schemes are not limited to human conceptual schemes. To say that humans are noetically real is to say that their being qua human is independent of human conceptual schemes. This does not entail that they are independent of all conceptual schemes, at least at their core being. The one they are dependent on is, of course, God's.

What of God? In an analogous, but not identical, manner, to say that God is noetically real (independent of human conceptual schemes) does not entail that God is independent of all conceptual schemes. God, too, is embedded in a conceptual scheme, viz., God's. The obvious difference is that humans are contingent whereas God is not. This is clearly a significant dissimilarity. The traditional Christian does not think of God as existing in virtue of any of our human conceptual schemes. Idealism of this sort, as already noted, makes nonsense of traditional Christian commitment.

Some might observe that if God exists relative to the divine conceptual scheme then God's aseity is questioned. God exists in God's own right and not because of anything else. The response isn't difficult, however, for while God always is, God cannot be separated from God's cognitive activity. Indeed, on some models God as spirit just is God as thought; on models of God where God is simple, God is identical to all God's properties and as such, God is identical to the property of God's thinking. God's necessity creates many questions about how God is related to various aspects of God. The main point here is just that God is essential to God's own way of being qua necessary and God's way of being includes existing relative to God's conceptual scheme.

If these last claims hold, then everything is irreal without undercutting the essential point that God is the fundamental source of all that is and without making God dependent at the divine's core on humans. But here some terminology needs to be cleared up. If to be noetically real is simply to be independent of human noetic work, then both humans and God are noetically real. But we should distinguish between human irrealism and divine irrealism. If we claim that everything is divinely noetically irreal, including God and humans, we need not claim that God or humans are dependent upon human noetic work itself, at least at their core. Both humans and God are irreal in ways distinct from the limited human way irrealism is typically understood. Humans are what they are at their core by God's noetic work but contingently so, while God is what God is at the divine core by divine noetic work but necessarily so. It turns out, then, that humans are irreal in roughly the way Alvin Plantinga suggests the entire created order is, viz., dependent on God's thoughts.[3] Contrary to Plantinga's view, however, God is irreal in that God exists, and necessarily so, only within the divine conceptual scheme. Humans are created by God *ex nihilo* and hence the irreality that attaches to human being is causal. God does not, strictly speaking, create God (God always is and there is nothing *ex nihilo* about God) and so the irreality that attaches to God is not causal. This suggests that God's being and ours are related by an analogy of being.

Yet that is only part of the story, for I've also suggested that both humans and God are different across human conceptual schemes. I'm speaking here of how God is in a world and not just how God is understood in a world. That is, I do not wish to retreat to a merely epistemic rather than a fully ontological account. Having noted that, please also recall that while a deep sense of mystery about God exists, it is not a mystery of which we can understand nothing. It is a long-standing Christian notion (rooted deeply in the ancient scriptural stories) that our understanding of God is fundamentally reliant on God working in us. One way to put this is that our understanding of God is heavily embedded in the ontology of God's own self. Indeed, part of the Christian account of God's role in the universe is that God provides the means by which humans can understand God. God is one who self-reveals to humans. I'm saying nothing novel in this regard. Even theologians who are noetic realists about God say God is understandable to humans because of God's gracious gift to us.

Elizabeth Johnson writes:

Perhaps no contemporary axiom has been more influential in showing this linkage between Christian experience of God and the mystery of God's own being than the epistemological axiom that "the economic Trinity is the immanent Trinity, and vice-versa," formulated in this fashion by Karl Rahner. *Economic* signifies an arrangement, a plan, or the administration of such social groupings as a household. In this Trinitarian adage it refers to the economy ... of salvation, God's plan to redeem the whole sinful world by lavishing on it the riches of grace ... The economic Trinity signifies God's redeeming relatedness to the world in liberating love, God *pro nobis*. On the other hand, the *immanent* of the axiom refers to God's own being considered in itself, God *in se*.

The axiom expresses the epistemological truth that it is given to us to point to the latter only through the former.

The point of affirming that the economic Trinity is the immanent Trinity is that there are not two Gods, one who encounters us in the world and another different one who is totally other than what we experience. In Jesus Christ God does not wear a mask ... [italics hers][4]

Johnson goes on to note that many contemporary theologians reject Rahner's principle maintaining, in effect, that we can only know God as experienced. I want to claim, as do Rahner and Johnson, that we know God in human experience but not merely as experienced. We see God, so to speak, as God is. Religious experience and the theology built out of it are neither experience "as if" nor theology "as if." Our understanding of God is not based on a "seeing as" construct. So Johnson responds, and rightly so:

Given the triune symbol's rootedness in salvific experience and its intent to point via analogy to the holy mystery so experienced, however, we would lose a great deal if we ceased speaking altogether of the immanent triune God. For this language is not a literal description of the inner being of God who is in any event beyond human understanding. It is a pointer to holy mystery in trust that God really is the compassionate, liberating God encountered through Jesus in the Spirit.[5]

My position lines up with Johnson's but goes beyond. Her claim, following Rahner, is that the God we experience in history is the same God who is beyond our experience. She goes on to say that this is really the language of hope. One of the reasons I believe she puts the issue this way is that Rahner's principle is an epistemological principle. I want to transform Rahner's principle into an ontological one. While I agree with Johnson's claim that her position is one of hope, it is too easy to confuse hope with wishful thinking. In the end I believe hope is wellfounded in ontology. The irrealistic model developed here points to how the God we experience in history just is God in God's own self, all the while leaving God beyond our understanding because beyond our experience – beyond our worlds, if you will. This is God's doing, of course, not ours. God makes us in such a way that we actually contribute to God. Thus we do not merely understand

God-as-experienced-and-conceived, one step removed from the actual God. God is ontologically within our reach, since God permits us – indeed, encourages us – to shape God in certain ways, effectively putting God within our epistemic range.

Johnson speaks in terms of analogy and metaphor rather than literal talk of God. That is as it should be. But it does not entail that we know or understand nothing of God as God is. I'll return to that matter in later chapters. For now I want to consider some further detail on the relationship of God and human conceptual schemes.

4 CONCEPTUAL SCHEMES: HUMAN AND DIVINE

God is beyond human conceptual schemes not in the sense that God exists completely outside them but in a sense similar (but not identical) to how humans exist outside human conceptual schemes. How is this to be fleshed out? First note that we humans do not create ourselves but with our coming to be there is a coming to be of human conceptual schemes. A necessary order and dependency is at work here. Human conceptual schemes do not exist independent of human persons. The former depend on the latter. This order is logical, not temporal or causal. Humans are not placed in the World first and then later become the source of their conceptual schemes. Humans are essentially rational and cannot be human without a conceptual scheme. So, humans do not cause the existence of their conceptual schemes. Yet we can cause some of their structure or details because we are free.

Humans and their conceptual schemes come as a bundle. We are always (logically) attended by our conceptual schemes. So it is true to say that humans always exist within their conceptual schemes. This can sound truistic, coming to nothing more than the claim that to be human is to have a human conceptual scheme, but I mean to claim more than that. For example, no matter what conceptual scheme a human works within, it will always, insofar as it is well formed, include the concept of the human. Hence, we cannot conceptualize away human beings, even though humans are contingent. This contrasts with other things in our conceptual schemes, some of which exist in some schemes but not in others. While humans bring about the stars, they cannot bring about themselves. But theoretically, at least, humans can bring about the demise of stars by losing the concept "star." However, humans can never lose the concept "human" and still have a well-formed conceptual scheme. Thus, although humans always exist within their conceptual schemes, the latter do not cause the former to exist or vice versa. Humans do not create themselves.

Similarly, the divine conceptual scheme does not exist independently of God or the latter independently of the former. Yet the divine conceptual scheme does not create God or God the divine conceptual scheme. The divine scheme is not voluntaristic, although again, some of the structure or details can be determined by God. Just as humans have a conceptual scheme but are not created by it, so God has a conceptual scheme but is not created by it. The reasons, of course, are quite different. Humans are made by God whereas God simply is and necessarily so. In the latter case, perhaps God's being is identical to certain aspects of God's conceptual scheme. In particular I have in mind something like the claim that God's existence just is God's thinking.

The Christian irrealist must maintain that humans do not make God at the divine core being, anymore than humans make themselves at their core being. At the end of the ontological day, both God and humans are required to be causally independent (at their cores) of human noetic work for there to be a human world or a way things are in the human world.[6] Humans cannot create themselves or God on the traditional Christian model. This does not entail that humans and God are independent of God's noetic work. Since I'm trying to develop an irrealism that fits well with traditional Christianity, it is important to note that if a noetically real God in a noetically real universe can support a noetically real human who pro-creates things such as tables and chairs, then a God who is necessarily embedded in the divine conceptual scheme (but not caused by it) can support a human who is necessarily embedded in her conceptual scheme (but not caused by it) who then pro-creates things (such as stars) in her world. In short, the logic of God's creation and human pro-creation for the theistic irrealist is no more difficult than the logic for God's creation and human pro-creation for the theistic noetic realist. When we say God makes everything we don't deny that daddy makes dinner, on either model. Of course, on the Christian story, God's ontic role is more primary than humanity's ontic role in that God is the fundamental creator. Humans are contingent at their core; God is not. God would have being without humans whereas humans would not have being without God. Yet both humans and God are ontological givens (at their core) in world-making. We are humanly noetically real in that we do not create our essential selves via our conceptual schemes. But we are the noetic creations of God and thus divinely irreal.

It is worth noting too that no amount of divine conceptual work can do away with God. I've already noted that no amount of human conceptual work (alone) will do away with humans. That would be to suggest that human conceptual schemes causally bring about humans. I've denied this. Although there is a logical dependency of conceptual scheme on the human, the dependency doesn't go the other way. Nor is there a causal relationship. What of God's case? It is a little different. To suggest that God can do away with God would be to suggest that the divine conceptual scheme causally brings about God. I've denied this but affirmed the notion that God may be part and parcel with certain aspects of God's conceptual scheme. These appear to be logical and necessary connections, however, and not causal ones. Both humans and God are noetically real from the point of view of human conceptual schemes. Humans depend upon God's conceptual work and the *ex nihilo* causal activity of God and God depends on nothing at all, at least causally.

Furthermore, human conceptual schemes are social conceptual schemes, dependent upon the social nature of humans. But God too is social. God is both a Trinity of Persons and, once humans are made, God is inextricably bound up with human social life and being. God's creation of humans entails a new set of relationships for God, relationships in which humans and God together shape the ways things are, including humans and God. This sociality is shared across conceptual schemes. This is a very important point, for both human and divine conceptual schemes are involved. The key to understanding how God can be outside human conceptual schemes and yet in them is found here.

Let's consider first God as immanent. God is self-existent. Humans are contingent. But insofar as God's conceptual framework overlaps ours, God's being is in our frameworks. God makes us and makes us in the divine image. We share, therefore, God's creativity but also God's reasonableness, emotional capacity, and sociality. Insofar as there are divine virtual absolutes – that is, both necessities and entities God brings causally into being – human conceptual schemes share those virtual absolutes. In other words, human virtual absolutes are ontologically enforced by the social relationship of the divine being with the human being. On the other hand, God is transcendent, that is, not dependent on our conceptual schemes for existence at God's core being. That God exists relative to human conceptual schemes does not entail that God exists only relative to, and certainly not in virtue of, human conceptual schemes. God exists qua God and in God's scheme. In effect, God's transcendence is based on God being the ultimate source of both humans and the virtual absolutes found in all our conceptual schemes. God's immanence, in contrast, is not God's causing and sustaining the virtual absolutes but rather simply God's showing up in all the worlds, just as humans do. God is made immanent with humans by our socially sharing the means of making the rest of the things in the various worlds there are. Looked at from outside human conceptual schemes, God and humans are absolutes, not dependent on human conceptual schemes. Without God and humans there would simply be nothing at all. But because God and humans bring conceptual schemes into being (logically), neither God nor humans can be without being virtual absolutes, beings that exist in each and every conceptual scheme, whether human or divine. Since God and humans, in their core natures, are virtual absolutes who, of necessity, exist within the conceptual schemes we humans have, then God and humans are "human virtual absolutes," that is, things that exist relative to (but not in virtue of) every human conceptual scheme, at least so far as existence and core being are concerned. There cannot be a well-formed human conceptual scheme without God. But God and humans are also relative to God's own conceptual scheme and hence God and humans are not merely human virtual absolutes but exist within the divine conceptual scheme as well.

One last point. I noted above that humans cannot do away with themselves conceptually and neither can humans do away with God. It might be thought, however, that God can do away with humans and our conceptual schemes. While this seems possible from a logical point of view, there appear to be moral obligations that come into play here. Once having made humans, God is stuck with us. It follows that God, insofar as the divine is shaped by humans in the various worlds we make, is dependent, relatively, on our conceptual schemes. Thus, God's being ontologically enmeshed with us has a moral ground. Once God makes us, God cannot be free of us. Since God is always revealing God's being to us, we always have God in our conceptual schemes.

5 SOME NOTES ON GOD AND THEISTIC ACTIVISM

What is God's conceptual scheme like and how does it relate to God's being? First, God's conceptual scheme can be thought to include aspects that we typically regard as necessities. There are, on many standard accounts of necessity, a goodly number of abstract entities thought to be necessities including properties, numbers, propositions, and possible worlds.[7] Since these things are necessities, they, like God, have always existed. I've already indicated that they are logically dependent upon God, however, and hence, although created by God, they are created in a special sort of way, flowing out of God's being rather than out of God's free choice. Here we have an indicator that God's conceptual scheme can't be other than the way it is, at least insofar as we are considering necessities.

Second, theologically, Christians say God made the World and, as such, the World is contingent in contrast to God who is necessary. It is easy to go from this sort of theological talk to the conclusion that the philosophical notion of the actual world is identical to the created world of theology. It is not obviously so. The created order is typically thought of as contingent whereas the actual world contains necessities besides God. Here it is valuable to remind ourselves of the two kinds of creation accomplished by God. The first is the freely chosen creation of God making things that could have been otherwise and the second is the necessitated creation of God making things that could not have been otherwise. An example of the former is humans, of the latter, numbers. Humans need not have been actualized. Numbers, on the other hand, are necessities. So in addition to God creating necessities, it looks like aspects of God's conceptual scheme are in some respects freely created by God – made up by God out of nothing. While God must think of numbers because of God's nature and in God's thinking of them they are what they are, God need not think of humans or, more circumspectly, God may think of humans without instantiating them.

A more detailed consideration of the necessary aspects of creation is in order. Numbers, along with properties, propositions, possible worlds, and, of course, God, are thought to be necessities. Of this list, only God is a concrete entity, the others all being abstract. Abstract entities are often thought to have a sort of "in-between" status, being neither contingent nor necessary. For example, what exactly is the status of numbers? Typically it is denied that numbers are mental entities, depending on human thought. It is also typically denied that they are material objects or some feature of material objects. What is their status? More pertinent to the matter under consideration, how should the Christian think of numbers or any of the abstracta?

One way of thinking Christianly about these matters is that God creates all the non-divine necessities. Numbers, propositions, and properties thus exist independent of contingent beings such as humans. Whence the necessity of numbers (or propositions or properties)? Three suggestions are made about this from within theism. First, necessities might be thoughts in the mind of God generated by the divine will (a sort of Cartesian approach). Second, they might be identical to God, following a medieval doctrine of simplicity in which all of God's properties are identical. On this view, God's thought is identical to God and hence numbers are identical to God. A third possibility – sometimes called "theistic activism" – is that abstracta are simply God's thoughts and, given God's nature, some thoughts flow automatically from God's being. So when God thinks, God thinks about necessities, that is, about numbers, propositions, and possible worlds.

Problems exist for all three views. The first seems to imply that necessary truths aren't really necessary since they depend on God's will – necessities could have been otherwise. The second bears the heavy burden of giving a cogent account of the doctrine of simplicity. The third generates the problem that even God's properties, such as the property of being God, seem to be caused by God's thinking them and thus one wonders how God could think God's properties if God's properties need to be there for God to do the thinking.[8]

Problems notwithstanding, I'm inclined to think theistic activism is the best explanation.[9] Given God's necessary but concrete existence, as well as God's nature as rational, some things other than God exist necessarily simply because God thinks them. Alvin Plantinga, Christopher Menzel, and Thomas Morris[10] all hold that abstract objects are "in the mind of God." Plantinga suggests that propositions do not exist independent of God's noetic activity – they are God's thoughts. Menzel and Morris claim that in theistic activism[11] "all properties and relations are God's concepts, the products, or perhaps better, the contents of a divine intellective activity, a causally efficacious or productive sort of divine conceiving."[12] If these philosophers are correct, then the non-divine necessities are best thought of, generally speaking, as aspects of God's conceptual scheme.

The abstracta, of course, all have the status of necessities in the actual world, qua necessities. God, too, exists in the actual world because God is necessary. Could any of these things, qua necessary, exist outside the actual world? Is there such a thing as outside the actual world? I think the answer is no. Not even God exists outside the actual world, at least as we often think of modality. Granting that God is a necessary being and that necessary beings exist in all possible worlds, then God exists in the actual world.

What status does the actual world have? Is it necessary, contingent, abstract, concrete? We need to speak carefully here for, in some sense, God doesn't create (*ex nihilo*) the actual world unless God creates God. Here I want to note briefly the oddity, from one point of view, of talking as if God can select or chose from among possible worlds in terms of which to instantiate. Since the actual world always contains God, then it is odd to talk as if God were outside the actual world choosing among possible worlds to instantiate. While it is true that God is a necessary being and no matter what possible world is instantiated God will be in it, it is also true that, from the point of view of the actual world, the other possible worlds are not instantiated. However, the actual world, although containing contingencies, has never not been, for the actual world always contains God and the other necessities.

Put a little more metaphorically, wherever God is, there is the actual world. There is no free causal relationship between God and the actual world understood from the point of view of modality. The relationship is a logical one. Yet the actual world is concrete and many contingent things are instantiated in it. Because it is true that wherever God is, there is the actual world, it seems true also that the actual world flows out of God's thoughts much in the same way as abstract entities do. But the actual world, taken as a totality, is not an abstract entity. It is a concrete entity, made by God, which contains both necessities and contingencies. God's conceptual scheme or, more broadly speaking, God's thoughts, bring the actual world about. Indeed, God brings the actual world about simply by being God. So is the actual world a necessity in the same sense that numbers are? Not exactly. That there is an actual world seems to be a necessity if there is to be a God or numbers or any other necessary thing. But that the actual world is the particular actual world it is is not a necessity. There are contingencies that need not have been instantiated, for God is free.

The actual world, it seems to me, is best understood as the thoughts of God. Not only are abstract entities God's concepts but the actual world itself is a set of God's thoughts. While God does not depend (causally) upon the actual world, it remains true that there would be no God without an actual world. God's conceptual scheme includes, thus, the way the actual world is. Where the actual world is necessarily the way it is, it is because of God's necessary thoughts. Where the actual world is contingent, God's free will enters the picture. But in either case, the actual world is the result of God's conceptual scheme.

At least a brief note is in order about the major challenge to theistic activism. As noted above, God has properties such as haeceity – the property of being God – that seem to be properties God must have in order to think about properties. How can properties be the result of the causal work of God if God must have the properties in order to think them? Morris and Menzel respond that not all God's creative work is causal. Some is purely logical. Given God's nature there must be numbers and properties and so forth. So the challenge to theistic activism can perhaps be solved along the lines Matthew Davidson develops when he says that God's ability to cause abstracta to exist is logically dependent on God's having certain properties, but not causally dependent.[13]

6 GOD AND VOLUNTARISTIC NECESSITIES

Theistic activism holds that abstracta are God's concepts. However, the view that necessities are voluntaristically rooted in God is worth considering as well. In the end, however, it fails. It is worth considering, nonetheless, for we can learn something about the relationship of God and human conceptual schemes.

Suppose that, instead of necessities flowing out of God's being, they are created by God's free choices. On this model both necessities and contingencies are due to God's voluntary choice from the logical "beginning." This brings us to Descartes. Descartes' view seems to leave us with the absurdities typically pointed out in commentaries dealing with his view of necessity and God. Perhaps these problems can be solved. Lynch writes, leaning on Nagel and Bennett,

> It is instructive to compare relativism about logical truths with Descartes' own rather infamous "voluntarism" about necessary truth, according to which the truth of every proposition, even the propositions of elementary arithmetic or logic, depends on the will of God – a will that could have been otherwise. When pressed on how this could be so, Descartes seemed to claim that

although we cannot conceive of certain facts, for example that twice four makes eight, being other than what they are, we *can* conceive of being able to conceive differently than we do, since God could have easily arranged it to be so. Most philosophers interpret Descartes as claiming that although we can't understand what it would be for twice four to make nine, it is possible anyway because anything is possible for God. Thus Nagel says, "It is impossible to believe that God is responsible for the truths of arithmetic if that implies that it could have been false that twice four is eight." For that would imply the absurdity that God could have made *any* statement true or false and therefore that any statement is possibly true. According to Nagel, "structurally, this argument of Descartes is precisely the same as is offered by those who want to ground logic in psychology or forms of life ... and the same thing is wrong with it." For if the proposition that two and two must make four is relative to, for example, our conceptual scheme, then given that we could have had a different scheme, it seems like it could be false that two and two make four after all.[14]

This path seems closed off as a way to understand necessities. But Lynch argues that this is not the only approach to Descartes. Drawing on Jonathan Bennett, Lynch continues:

Nagel's argument assumes that there is only one way to understand the modal concepts employed in logical and mathematical reasoning. On the absolutist reading Nagel is assuming, to say that some state of affairs is possible is to say something about the structure of ultimate reality. If either the pluralist or Descartes understood modal concepts like possibility in *this* way, then they would be committed to an absurdity. But that is not the only way to understand the modal concepts ... The alternative is to say that something is possible or necessary is not to say something about the way the world is in itself. Instead, "our modal concepts should be understood or analyzed in terms of what does or does not lie without the compass of our ways of thinking." In short, Bennett's Descartes holds that *it is possible that p* is roughly equivalent to the claim that *humans can conceive that p*, where this means that as a matter of psychological causal fact, humans have the capacity to entertain that the proposition is true. In turn, therefore, the proposition that *it is impossible that two and two make five* means that *no human can conceive of two and two making five*. Once we understand the modal concepts in this fashion, Descartes' position begins to make more sense. The modal concepts apply as they do because of certain contingent facts about our cognitive abilities. God made us the way we are with the specific cognitive abilities we have. Yet God could have (i.e., we can conceive that he might have) made us differently than he did. If so, then the contingent facts on which the modal concepts depend would be different and the modal concepts would have applied differently.[15]

As I discussed in chapter 6, Lynch makes use of a similar account of necessities and goes on to claim that this approach (*sans* any role for God) can be used to show irrealistic pluralism consistent with metaphysical realism. I suggested there that his account does not supply the kind of basis for modalities needed to provide an answer to the consistency dilemma. It is too much like the Goodmanian account in which necessities and possibilities are restricted to an insufficiently powerful extensionalism that is, in turn, dependent solely on human creativity. But Lynch has that problem merely because God is not in the picture.

What happens if we take the actual world, with God and the concomitant necessities, to be the result of the way God makes humans at their core? That is, what if the actual world in which God exists simply is one in which God freely chooses to create contingent humans with the stipulation that the necessities that are typically thought to flow from God's free choices come about only if they first are created via human conceptual schemes? Perhaps we create too great a separation between the contingent and the necessary. What is necessary may very well be logically posterior to God's freely creating humans. It is only with the creation of humans that we get necessities, as Bennett's Descartes suggests. On this view, in each and every conceptual scheme humans develop it turns out that the very necessities there are are made by God because God made humans. In making humans with the cognitive abilities they have, God makes modal notions what they are. So necessities and possibilities are not made as part and parcel of a noetically real World – as absolutes that have nothing to do with human noetic work – but as part and parcel of the World as God makes humans.

Is this proposal enough to allow that God freely creates not only the contingent aspects of the World but the necessities as well? Does this make necessities arbitrary? Only if God could make humans differently than God did, in fact, make them, the necessities being rooted, on this suggestion, in human being. Here Lynch's position breaks down. Without God it appears that humans could have developed differently than they did and therefore not only are humans contingent themselves but the way our cognitive machinery works could have been other than it is. As such, possibilities and necessities truly seem limited to the human framework of what we can conceive and that framework is contingent itself.

On the Christian story God makes humans in God's image. Part of that image is rationality. If rationality includes thinking of necessities the way humans do, then could God have made humans differently so that we could have had some other set of necessities with which to work? I think the answer is no. If the necessities are more or less built into the cognitive being of humans, then since God made us in God's image, we should think of the particular shape of human cognitive structure that provides for necessities as something shared with God. Necessities, in the end, are provided for by the shape of God's cognitive life. We are back to necessities flowing out of God's nature rather than being truly contingent on human being. This returns us to theistic activism but with a twist, viz., God's thinking the necessities God thinks is manifest through humans and their cognitive makeup. But we seem no further ahead than we would be with the more straightforward theistic activism *sans* humans. There would still be necessities if there were no humans.

But perhaps that is too quick a response. What if the *imago Dei* has nothing to do with God's rational nature? That would leave the necessities dependent on human cognitive structure and contingently so. We would have something akin to the Bennett-Lynch proposal with the weaknesses it has. What is needed is some way to fix the necessities in human nature without resorting to the necessities being rooted, in the final analysis, in God's thought. It is hard to see what that would be. For the Christian, it is also exceedingly hard to see what being in God's image includes if it doesn't include rationality. On a truly Christian account of things, could humans have been made different than they are, in this particular respect? Could God have made humans not made in God's image? This seems to me to be impossible. If humans were not made in God's image, humans simply would not exist, since God's image in humans is one of the essential properties of humans.

So when we say that God made humans in the divine image and that image brings with it reason and therefore the necessities, we are saying that the necessities are what they are not merely according to contingent human capacities but rather according to the necessary features of human persons. Of course, God need not have made human persons at all. But we know that if God makes human contingencies, then they have the essential cognitive capacities that support necessities as they flow from God. Humans and God share the same fundamental cognitive framework in regard to entities such as numbers, properties, and propositions qua necessary entities. What God can't conceive, humans can't conceive.

The failure of Cartesian voluntarism teaches us a way of thinking about the relationship between human and divine conceptual schemes. Our way of thinking about necessities and possibilities, at least when we get it right, lines up with God's way of thinking of them. Possibilities, numbers, properties, and so forth all rest, as abstract entities, in God's mind. Humans are not responsible, in the end, for how they are, *pace* Lynch. Nevertheless, we can't think appropriately without them. This all meshes well with the requirement that pluralism be consistent with a fairly robust notion of modalities as intensional. Possible objects exist, even if not instantiated. They exist in the mind of God. But we humans, being made rational in God's image, have access to those abstract objects because we, to some extent, have the mind of God.

In sum, God and humans are both social and that sociality is shared. Divine and human conceptual schemes overlap allowing for the World to be fixed in certain ways (the necessities) and yet allowing the World to be made into different worlds by human noetic work. The overlap allows for an intensional account of necessity and possibility (necessities and possibilities exist in God's infinite mind) but gives humans access to think about these things as well. We can say, following the general pattern of this essay, that what is depends on the conceptual scheme in play, including necessities and possibilities.

God's conceptual scheme certainly includes God. Furthermore, since God always exists, the actual world always is. The actual world certainly could contain many necessary beings whose being is nonetheless dependent upon God in a way similar to the way the actual world itself depends on God. Things such as numbers, logical relations, and so forth are all necessities. Those necessities flow automatically out of God's nature as they are correlates of God's being. But it doesn't follow that God simply wills them as necessities in a Cartesian manner so that God could, so to speak, change what is necessary. The actual world contains a good many things independent of the creation of the contingent order. The actual world (independent of the creation of contingent entities) just is the contents of the mind of God and those contents are neither separable from God nor identical to God. They make up the World in which God dwells as it is independent of humans coming on the scene.

What about contingent beings such as humans? Again following the general pattern suggested here, God creates some concepts freely and the actual world now contains beings that don't have to be. If this is right, God's thinking certain propositions to be true simply brings with it the creation of the contingent world. So the world is irrealist, for nothing would be were it not for the thoughts of God. This "divine irrealism" – the position, not the name – is suggested by Plantinga. But divine irrealism, as Plantinga clearly argues, does not entail human irrealism of the kind I'm suggesting, a point he is at pains to stress. And God is clearly a noetically real being, vis-à-vis human conceptual schemes, existing as God does without any noetic contribution from humans.

According to Christian pluralistic irrealism, however, the ways the World is are due to human conceptualizing. But that is only after God's creative work. Humans, too, at their core, are independent of human conceptual schemes. God creates humans *ex nihilo* by a free act of God's will. God makes humans and we are in the same actual world as God. Once humans are made, however, the actual world changes in significant ways. Not only are there contingencies whereas before there were not (I'll ignore the Christian tradition's claims about angels and demons which supposedly existed before humans) but, if Christian pluralistic irrealism is correct, then the World is many ways, conflicting but not incompatible. The worlds humans create by their noetic feats are humanly irreal (as opposed to divinely irreal alone).

7 SOME SPECULATIONS ABOUT GOD AND GOD'S WORLD

What was there "before" God created humans? Was there anything more than God (and any necessities God thinks about)? The typical Christian answer will be no or perhaps, more cautiously, how would we know? Anything along those lines is mere speculation on our part. But speculation can be worthwhile and perhaps the reader will indulge me for a few brief paragraphs.

On Christian irrealism it seems to me possible, if not likely, that given God as a free, creative conceptualizer, there were (or are) many divine worlds before (or alongside) the contingent one containing humans. These divine worlds (note again the lower case notation of "world" and the addition of the modifiers "divine" and "human") have the same sort of status as the divine world that contains humans. In short, not only is the actual world such that it contains God but it is possible that the actual world is many different ways because of God's creative noetic feats, independent of humans being introduced into it. An infinite mind that is infinitely creative would surely make many worlds to "fill" the actual world. God may very well be a divine irrealistic pluralist in God's own way. This is, of course, speculation. But perhaps C.S. Lewis's imaginative picture of God, found in Lewis's fiction, is not so far off.

What I'm after here is that God is always in a world of God's own making. If God conceptualizes in any way beyond God's necessary thoughts, that is, if God freely wills anything outside what is necessary, then not only is there an actual world that is as permanent as God, but there are also many ways that actual world is by God's choice. If I'm right about this, then it is helpful to distinguish between what we think of as the contingent but actual World in which we live, which God made and sustains and to which humans noetically contribute, and the actual world that has always been, what we might call simply "God's World." Of course, the former is merely a continuation – and perhaps only one continuation – of the latter. And what for most of the essay I've called "the World" continues God's World in one direction, viz., in such a way that it contains humans. Furthermore, there is nothing impossible about God's World also being pluralistic in that God might conceptualize God's World in many different ways. Indeed, there might be ways God conceptualizes God's World even now and those divine worlds might be such that humans have no access to them. So there might be God's worlds within God's World. What I've called "the World" throughout this essay would turn out to be only one of the divine worlds so that the divine world in which we live is simply one of many ways God's World is. If this is correct, then God is in the actual world and always in every divine world within the actual world. Parallel to that, God is in every human world and yet not created by humans but rather present in the divine world (that is our World) as its no-etic source.

Is God noetically real? To answer this question, it is important to note that on the view being developed, there are more worlds than human worlds. So God is noetically real in the sense that God is in-dependent of human thought. This is the God who is known only in mystery. And God may very well have God's own worlds in which God is simply beyond human conceptual reach. Perhaps these worlds are bits of fancy on God's part. Perhaps some of these worlds are angelic worlds. But once humans are on the scene God is in human worlds as well.

But how much of God? Does God depend in any way on the con-ceptual schemes of humans? Here the distinction that I've made but not defended, between God's core or essence on the one hand and God-being-in-a-human-world on the other hand, comes to the fore. God's core itself is something over which humans theorize and as such God is always God-in-a-human-world. So insofar as God has being for us, that is, insofar as God is experienced or understood by us, God is noetically irreal. That is, God's being is for us as God is conceptualized by us, at least in a well-formed or right world. God is not any particular way for humans outside the conceptual scheme we have in play. That is, there is no particular way God is (for hu-mans) outside human conceptual schemes.

Again I want to emphasize that this is not to say that we know or understand God only in an illusory manner so that if we were able to peel off the layers of our thinking about God, we'd find the "real" God. We can't peel off the layers. God genuinely is as God is conceived, at least when the conceptualization of God is a right one. But neither is God the way God is conceived in God's World, that is, the World independent of human creation. The ways the World are are noetically irreal not simply because of human noetic activity but because of God's. But that does not entail that God makes up the divine self anymore than God is self-caused. Rather when God thinks, a World is. God has always been and therefore there has al-ways been an actual world. We humans, of course, do not have ac-cess to God's World and, indeed, little can be said of it. But that is not a problem new or unique to theistic irrealism. Many Christian theologians have wondered about God *sans* relationship to humans. In the end, God as God turns up in God's world is a mystery. But in all of this there is no denial that God can and does, according to the Christian tradition, share Godself with humans. On the model presented here, God does that by breaking into our history with God's story or, in more technical terms, God breaks into our conceptual schemes with God's own. None of this entails that God is entirely obscure or unknowable or even entirely mysterious to us. In the following chapter I'll explore in more detail how this might work.

The Many Ways God Is

Although the human and the divine core beings are not made by human noetic feats, throughout this essay I've claimed that both humans and God are within and, to some extent, shaped by human conceptual schemes. This chapter explains how to understand this proposal. It also considers how this view fits with understanding the Nicene Creed as providing a thin notion of God as the basis for thicker accounts of God. In particular, I consider the role of metaphor in world-making.

1 GOD THROUGH THICK AND THIN

God can be understood as different across worlds in two ways, one concerned with external relations and one with the nature of God within a given world. First, suppose God in world A were related to Aristotelian realities and in world B to Whiteheadian realities. God, therefore, both has and does not have the property of being related to enduring entities. Second, suppose God in world A were an Aristotelian entity, the unmoved mover, and in world B a Whiteheadian entity, a dipolar God. In the former approach, God is merely related to different things in worlds that are distinct from one another while in the latter God is different in God's own being across the worlds.

So far as the external relations in conflicting worlds go, God's relation to each world can be indexed to that world. That is, God's relationships to the salient and incompatible features of each world are contingent upon those worlds, in a manner parallel to that of a singular being existing in different possible worlds. The relationships holding between God and items in the various worlds do not reflect anything necessary about God's own being. In world A God deals with Aristotelian entities while in world B God deals with Whiteheadian events. No particular problem arises here, for God engages in the supposedly incompatible relational properties only within a given world and not within Godself. God doesn't, so to speak, carry these contingent relationships from one way the World is to another.

The second notion is more difficult, however, for there God's being is caught up in the Aristotelian or the Whiteheadian world and not merely related contingently to things within various worlds. Let's consider the parallel with humans first. We are created beings. Our natures, although essential to us, are essential after the fact. We are contingent. Yet surely there are different ways of being free or creative or conscious that are cogent and self-consistent. All we need to consider is the possibility that God could make us free or creative or conscious in different ways. I suggest God passes that ability on to us in actuality and thus there is quite a lot of play in how we can be-in-a-world. We could be enduring Aristotelian substances or we could be Whiteheadian events. So long as we are free, conscious, and creative, there should be no problem, and God can bless or not bless our created worlds on the basis of how the suggested world fits with our created natures and/or God's necessary nature and the divine conceptual scheme or even the divine will.

In parallel fashion, are there alternative possible ways God might be? If so, then the pluralist need only point out that insofar as there are alternative ways, and insofar as God may allow and even encourage human participation in shaping God's ways of being in various worlds, then pluralism about God's being is plausible. So, there may be competing and inconsistent ways God is across human conceptual schemes. In an Aristotelian framework, God is an unmoved mover. In a Whiteheadian account, God is dipolar, having both a consequent and an absolute pole.

But perhaps the critic will suggest that the extreme differences between an Aristotelian type of God and a Whiteheadian type rule out the possibility that both accounts could truly describe how God is in two different worlds. Perhaps. But the problem here, if there is one, doesn't seem to be with the basic pluralist suggestion that God is different across human conceptual schemes but rather that there are limits on how God can be across different worlds. In particular, maybe the ontological contrast between the Whiteheadian and Aristotelian worlds is too great. In reply to this concern, my suggestion is simply that where God's core being leaves off and God's being-in-a-world picks up is a matter of debate. But the pluralist account can't be ruled out on that basis alone. The only question is how much of God can vary world to world.

That God changes in response to or in concert with human concerns is true, even on a nearly global realism. For example, when humans sin, God responds. God enters the world and surely God is changed by such an experience and that change is not simply a relational one. Also, the Son takes on a human nature and that is no mere relational change. Yet humans didn't have to sin and God would have, presumably, reacted differently had we not. But the realist doesn't thereby admit that God changes in the divine core when God responds to our failures.

The same is true, I propose, when God moves between one irrealist world and another. God's being need not change at its core, but some features of God change from one world to the next. Let's say Susan has free will but it is construed along libertarian lines in one possible world and along compatibilist lines in another. We still have Susan in both worlds. In the same manner, God might be conceptualized as the unmoved mover in one irrealist world and dipolar in the next and we still have God in both worlds. Here the traditional Christian ontologist will surely balk. First, doesn't traditional Christianity simply demand that God be fixed, unchanging, and not dependent upon human thought or creativity? Second, doesn't the Nicene Creed have to be true, and true not just in one world but in all the worlds? Third, haven't I slipped up by claiming that the essential property of freedom can be different in distinct worlds?

My answer to the first two questions, as a traditional Christian, is a broad yes, but with caveats. To the first question, we can briefly note that even on realism as applied to God and "the World," the traditional theist must deal with God's interaction with humans. The problems generated by God's interaction with the World are not made significantly more difficult by God having to deal with many worlds instead of just one World. So yes, God in God's core is not dependent on humans but God is changed by us, at least as we interact with God.

Before moving to the credal question, I'll consider the third. The critic might say that Susan's being free in one sense in one possible world and in a second sense in another surely is a change in essential properties. But why say that? I think what is at stake here is not a change from one essential property to another but rather how we have an essential property or how we should think of it. Consider another example. While humans are essentially conscious, does consciousness arise out of the particular kind of brain material that we have or could it occur some other way? Surely God could make a stone conscious and that could be our brain. Or perhaps we don't have to have a brain at all. The angels or humans in heaven may not have materiality as we understand it. Can one be said to be essentially A when A is taken thickly toward B in one world and thickly toward C in another? This issue turns out to be the important one.

As to the credal question, two issues arise. First, the Nicene Creed is full of metaphorical description. Metaphors are context-dependent but arguably no less rigorously applied than literal terms. Metaphorical truth is a kind of rightness of rendering just as literal truth is, and as such has its limits. The creed is a context-dependent account of God stated largely in metaphorical terms. These terms are rooted in human history and experience where God reveals the divine self to us. Is God literally Father? No, but God is personal and caring. Second, the very properties we consider essential can be understood in various ways in terms of their actual workings, as noted above. The creed can be taken in a variety of ways across worlds without denying that God is at core the creating, personal, omnipotent, loving saviour of humankind. I'll return to this issue in detail in the next section.

To explore a little more thoroughly how God can be different in different worlds, I return briefly to virtual absolutes and the notion of thin vs thick concepts. A virtually absolute proposition is true across all worlds. On human irrealism, such propositions will depend on the proposition's being built up from the same concepts in every world. But what kind of concepts: thin or thick? I think the typical intuition might be that the concepts will be fairly thick. Otherwise, the absolute nature of the proposition might not have much bite. For example, suppose it were a virtual absolute that there are objects. If this is understood thinly – let's say by thinking of objects as things that are – there isn't much to be gained by claiming that "there are objects" is virtually absolute. But if the notion of object were thickened as the notion that objects are always and everywhere physical and that was claimed as a virtual absolute, there might be some point.

However, I think context makes all the difference. Suppose the proposition "there are minds" is proposed as a virtual absolute where the mind is understood strictly as a thin concept. Suppose the mind is understood as the thing that thinks. That claim, it seems, has some import, for if irrealism (whether divine or human) holds, then the presence of minds in every world is very important. But notice that the virtually absolute nature of "there are minds" does not rule out there being thicker accounts of what a mind is where those accounts vary across worlds. One might suggest a purely spiritual account of minds whereas another suggests a more physicalist-emergentist account.

Finally, if we consider God's role as I've proposed it, some virtual absolutes will be necessities (that do not depend on humans per se). Numbers, the laws of logic, and possible worlds are virtual absolutes because God makes them so. Insofar as we share (as we must) aspects of God's conceptual scheme, then we participate in the virtually absolute nature of these necessities. These virtual absolutes might be based in quite thick concepts.

The point is that some virtual absolutes are thinly based and others more thickly based. Now we need to apply this claim to God. The first thing to note is that God can be considered in a thin manner as well as in thicker manners. The thin nature of God, however, will nevertheless be fairly thick. God might be thought of thinly, for example, as omnipotent, omniscient, omnibenevolent, free, conscious, creative, and triune. Yet the relative thickness of the thin notion of God does not remove the possibility of the thin concepts being thickened in alternative ways in various world.

So, a Christian irrealist who understands God's core as independent of human noetic contribution might want to say that the thin concepts relevant to God are thicker than some other basic concepts. They are not so thick, however, as to be completely fixed or definitive across all the worlds (like abstract entities such as numbers), that is, such that God has all and only the same properties in all the worlds. That would demand a kind of radical essentialism for God where not only does God have certain essential properties but those properties are already so thick that no room is left for further thickening. That would close off any possibility of pluralism. Instead, I suggest some variation in how God is in various worlds without giving up (thin) essential properties of God. The thin concept of God is a minimal concept in which God has certain properties (the omni-properties or

God's triune nature). Those concepts must be filled out according to our various theoretical constructions and thus how God is omnipotent in one world may not be the same as how God is omnipotent in another. The fact of God's existence holds across worlds, and the thin concept of God is the same across worlds. In this way God is virtually absolute both from a human and a divine point of view.

I've suggested that the thin concept of God will be thicker than many other thin concepts, but not, perhaps, typically as thick as some others. Some very thin concepts are tree or grass and thicker concepts are abstract objects such as numbers or possible worlds. Trees need not show up in every world or ontology and hence can have very thin concepts, whereas numbers have very thick concepts so as to not be different at all from one world to the next. Here it is important to note that my use of the thin/thick distinction varies from Lynch's in some respects. Would Lynch allow for a world in which trees simply don't exist or would it be just that their natures vary world to world? Be that as it may, I think my appeal to the thin/thick distinction on these perhaps extended terms is in line with Goodman-like comments such as "we make the stars in the same way as we make constellations."[1]

Having said that, we can return to the main point, viz., God and humans (because conscious, free, and creative) are attached to concepts falling somewhere between the concepts attached to non-divine necessities and those attached to non-human contingencies. So in worlds in which trees do show up, they can be quite variously described and fleshed out, perhaps in more ways than humans or God can be, since even the thin concepts of God and humans are thicker than the thin concepts of trees.

The contrast between absolutes and virtual absolutes is the contrast between facts independent of any and all conceptual schemes or worlds and facts in each and every conceptual scheme or world but independent of none. God is a divine virtual absolute whereby there is no God independent of God's World. But God, because God is social, gives us the ability to interact with Godself, revealing the divine being in such a way that we can grasp a great deal about God. However, it is important to note that God is a contributor to the worlds (along with us) and shows up in each world not simply because we can't do without God but rather because the worlds themselves cannot do without God. Here the Christian irrealist theory preserves the traditional Christian claim that God makes the World. The claim goes along with this notion that wherever there is a thinker, there is also a world. This is not less true with God than with human thinkers. So, while it is clearly true that wherever there is a world, there is God, it is equally true that wherever God is, there is a world.

I am not suggesting that God is dependent upon any world as we construe it or on a world as a contingent entity as Whiteheadian panentheists have it. While that is a possible way of taking God within a world, it would need an independent argument.[2] As we've seen, by "world" here I simply mean a way things are vis-à-vis humans. But there is also a way things are independent of God's creating humans. The divine world was no more than the divine – perhaps just God alone, the Trinity at play, along with God's thoughts – but it was no less a world for that. God's thoughts and the interactions among the persons of the Trinity were world-producing, even when no humans contributed. I'm simply suggesting that when God made humans, we were included in the world-making process. There need to be thinkers for any world or ontology to obtain. While God is the premier thinker, God makes us creative and invites us to join in the making of the worlds.

In sum, it is important to recognize that there are clear limits on how God can be in various worlds, along with limits on how humans can be. A world in which humans are not free would be a world that construes humans in a way contrary to God's creative will for us. God, thus, in creating human essences, creates limits on the worlds. A world in which God is evil is not a world that humans can create either, for that would be contrary to God's presence in the worlds. In each case, there are limits on what humans can do and those limits ultimately rest in God. God, rather than truth, provides the objectivity and hence the limits on world-making. Objectivity is taken up in the next chapter. Now I want to say something about metaphor and truth.

2 GOD, METAPHOR, AND THE WORLDS

God is a virtual reality who exists in each and every world, each and every rightly rendered ontology, whether the worlds or ontologies are human or divine. As such, the thin concept of God is relative to each and every world or ontology. God exists in both W_1 and W_2, and because the same thin concept applies to God in each, it can truly be said in each world that God is omnipotent or omniscient or love.

So far, what I've said of God's being-in-the-worlds has assumed that our descriptions of the divine are literal descriptions. I've worked largely within the confines of a narrow sense of concepts in which concepts are solely understood as the constituents of propositions. Further, the account of truth I've relied on deals only with the literal, since only literal claims can be literally true. Metaphorical claims, in contrast, are strictly false. On the face of it, the claims found in the last paragraph – God is love, God is omnipotent, and God is omniscient – are literal. As such, they are literally true, if true at all. But many things we say of God – including a good deal of what we say in the Nicene Creed – are not literal but metaphorical. Such claims about God are metaphorically true, if true at all.[3]

Earlier I described traditional Christianity as holding four things. First, a traditional Christian is orthodox, and by "orthodox" I meant that one holds to the Nicene Creed, with or without the filioque clause. Second, a traditional Christian is one who takes the credal claims to be true claims, which is tied to the third requirement, that the traditional Christian holds that Christian claims are alethically real. The fourth requirement is that God's core being is not constituted by human noetic feats.

I also noted that the historic creeds are rife with metaphor and as such, alethic realism strictly speaking doesn't apply to those aspects of the creeds. The traditional Christian faces this issue whether she is an irrealistic pluralist or not. Nevertheless, it is worth reflecting on the nature of metaphorical truth, especially since I've proposed, following Goodman, that some worlds are metaphorical rather than strictly literal.

If the traditional Christian holds the Nicene Creed true in a realistic sense, then how does it fit into the various worlds the irrealistic pluralist makes? Does it hold across all worlds? The short answer is "yes," otherwise traditional Christianity won't hold in all worlds. How does this work? If the creed were to contain only thin literal descriptions, then what I've said about God being "thickened" in various worlds by human theorizing would work fairly smoothly. God as almighty (which I'll take to mean "omnipotent") can be thickened in various ways. The apparent problem is that terms such as "the Father" seem already to be too thick to function this way. The term "Father" seems already to have built in a patriarchal structure for God. This, along with other implications, makes the overly thick notion of God found in the metaphors of the creed unacceptable as an ontologically thin account of God.

A typical response to questions such as the one about patriarchy is that when we say "God is Father" we are speaking metaphorically. God isn't literally a father or literally male. But then from the point of view of irrealistic pluralism, the notion "behind" the Father language is more properly understood as the thin notion of God and hence the creed can't really function as an appropriately thin account of God holding across many worlds. Again, the metaphors are already too thick. Indeed, the challenge seems to be that all metaphorical accounts of God are too thick because they already suggest too much theory about God.

Another way to think about this problem is to suggest that metaphors belong within specific worlds and cannot hold across worlds. The term "Father" in the creed is extraordinarily complex, implying not just that God is personal but that God is Trinitarian. Such complexity, it may be thought, can only be the result of a thickening, in a given world, of a thinner concept. Just how secure is the concept "father" as a way of thinking about God? That depends, but in one world it could be suggested that the maleness of fatherhood has implications for the procession of the Son (and the Holy Spirit, and this last point is controversial because of the filioque clause) from the Father. So what are we to "reduce" the metaphor of the Father? It can't be simply that God is personal; God is a Trinity of whom the Father is, in some sense, primary, and that understanding may have come about simply in virtue of the fact that "father" is a male term understood in a patriarchal setting. The metaphor of fatherhood may express a certain relationship between the members of the Trinity with which not all may or can agree.

The underlying issue seems to be that metaphors rely in important ways on literalisms and literalisms are in some senses thinner than metaphors. My account of irrealist pluralism is primarily explained in terms of concepts that lend themselves to literal descriptive accounts of things. How do metaphors fit? Do they? Alethic realism accounts for literal but not metaphorical truth and because of traditional Christianity's commitment to alethic realism, one of the strictures on traditional Christianity is that some claims about God must be literal. So far so good. God is literally almighty qua omnipotent. Let's say too that Jesus is literally incarnate of the Virgin Mary; it is God's own self who becomes human. But is Jesus literally God's Son?

For the purpose here, I don't have to identify where the literal ends and the metaphorical takes up. If one pushed hard on the notion of the creed being strictly alethically real, then we'd have to strip the creed of metaphor to arrive at clear truth claims. I suppose some traditional Christians are inclined to attempt just that. But not all would be so inclined and I certainly am not. I think the noetic irrealist *cum* alethic realist can handle the metaphorical aspects of the creed and yet treat it as providing a thin concept of God.

Let's look first at some basic explanations of metaphor. Probably the most traditional is what Max Black calls the substitution view. Here the metaphorical term simply replaces a literal term. "According to the substitution view, the focus of a metaphor, the word or expression having a distinctively metaphorical use within a literal frame, is used to communicate a meaning that might have been expressed literally."[4] As one encounters a metaphor, one is to exchange the metaphor for the literal to grasp the metaphor's meaning. However, sometimes an author invents a metaphor because there is no term in the literal language that captures what she or he is after and thus the metaphor can quickly become part of the literal language. "Orange" is a good example. Such catechresis (the use of a word in a new sense to fill a gap in the literal language) tends to disappear when it works well. When the use of a metaphor is not due to catechresis, it is typically thought to be merely stylistic – a "prettying" up of language.

Black calls a second understanding of metaphor the comparison view. Here metaphor is one type of various figurative uses of language all of which result in a different trope where a literal meaning is transformed into a different meaning. In irony one uses a term in a sense opposite its literal meaning; in hyperbole the term's meaning is exaggerated. Following this pattern, we see that metaphors are used analogously or similarly to their literal meaning. Metaphors are, on this account, slightly more sophisticated similes. In the end, we can see that the comparison view is really a version of the substitution view where the metaphorical statement can be replaced by an equivalent comparison.

A third, and for our purposes the most promising, account of metaphor is Black's interaction view. The best way to access quickly what Black has in mind is to quote his discussion of a particular example.

Let us try, for instance, to think of a metaphor as a *filter*. Consider the statement, "Man is a wolf." Here, we may say, are *two* subjects

– the *principle subject*, Man (or: men) and the *subsidiary subject*, Wolf (or: wolves). Now the metaphorical sentence in question will not convey its intended meaning to a reader sufficiently ignorant about wolves. What is needed is not so much that the reader shall know the standard dictionary meaning of "wolf" – or be able to use that word in literal senses – as that he shall know what I will call the *system of associated commonplaces*.[5]

We need to know that wolves are understood as vicious or stand-offish or pack hunters. Such commonplaces need not be true but they need to be readily and freely evoked. Such a metaphorical use of terms organizes our view of Man (or men), raising up certain details, suppressing others.

This third account of metaphor admits that not all metaphors are reducible to the literal. Black writes:

substitution-metaphors and comparison-metaphors can be replaced by literal translations ... by sacrificing some of the charm, vivacity, or wit of the original, but with no loss of *cognitive* content. But "interaction-metaphors" are not expendable.
Their mode of operation requires the reader to use a system of implications (a system of "commonplaces" – or a special system established for the purpose in hand) as a means for selecting, emphasizing, and organizing relations in a different field. This use of a "subsidiary subject" to foster insight into a "principle subject" is a distinctive of *intellectual* operation ... demanding simultaneous awareness of both subjects but not reducible to any *comparison* between the two.[6]

Thus one cannot do without the metaphor; cannot reduce it to a literalism.

Black discusses metaphor, in part, in order to explore its usefulness in philosophy and science. One of the challenges to his view is that because such interaction-metaphors resist paraphrase, they tend toward catechresis. That is, they tend to become so stable in language that they no longer function as metaphors. If this is correct, then metaphors in some sense cease to be metaphors and become literal. The "leg" of a triangle, for example, is no longer really a metaphor. Furthermore, as Joseph Margolis points out, "it is simply not true [as Black has it] that non-paraphrasable metaphors always involve a new intellectual discovery; nor is it true that the assimilation of whatever might be supposed to have been the cognitive achievement associated with a metaphor entails the decline of that metaphor or its para-phrasability."[7] Margolis argues that we need to push further into un-derstanding the relationship between metaphor and the World (or in the case of the pluralist, worlds).

Goodman has pushed through to such an understanding, and I believe what he says, with some modification, can help us under-stand the role of metaphor in theology. In regard to the issue of cat-echresis of metaphors qua cognitive, Goodman notes,

> The usual (and metaphorical) answer is that a term like "cold color" or "high note" is a frozen metaphor – though it differs from a fresh one in age rather than temperature. A frozen meta-phor has lost the vigour of its youth, but remains a metaphor. Strangely, though, with progressive loss of its virility as a figure of speech, a metaphor becomes not less but more like literal truth. What vanishes is not its veracity but its vivacity. Meta-phors, like new styles in representation, become more literal as their novelty wears off. Is a metaphor then simply a juvenile fact, and a fact simply a senile metaphor? That needs some modifica-tion but does argue against excluding the metaphorical from the actual. Metaphorical possession is indeed not *literal* possession; but possession is actual whether metaphorical or literal. The met-aphorical and the literal have to be distinguished with the actual. Calling a picture sad and calling it gray are simply different ways of classifying it.[8]

Metaphors, although frozen, do not ever become literal, although they become more literal. The important point is that metaphors are actual, and not merely possible, ways the world is. Thus meta-phorical truth is not so far removed from literal truth as one might suggest on first reflection. Goodman continues later:

> Standards of truth are much the same whether the schema used is transferred or not. In either case, application of a term is fallible and thus subject to correction. We may make mistakes in apply-ing either "red" or "sad" to coloured objects; and we may bring tests of all sorts to bear upon our initial judgments: we may look again, compare, examine attendant circumstances, watch for

corroborating and conflicting judgments. Neither the status of initial credibility nor the process of verification by maximizing total credibility over all our judgments is different in the two cases. Of course, metaphorical sorting, under a given scheme is, since more novel, often less sharp and stable than the correlated literal sorting; but this is only a difference of degree ... Difficulties in determining truth are by no means peculiar to metaphor.[9]

Goodman here is describing tests for truth rather than the nature of truth, but it seems clear enough that if metaphorical claims are claims about the way a world is, then they are claims about the actual world. Furthermore, if the processes through which we judge the truthfulness of a metaphorical predication are nearly the same as the processes for literal truths, then one might suspect that an account of metaphorical truth might be very close to the account of literal truth.

So I propose that the irrealist can take a very close relative of alethic realism (if we want a name for this, call it alethic metaphorical realism) to apply to the metaphorical as alethic realism does to the literal. Metaphorical truth claims are rightness of rendering claims. This particular variety of rightness of rendering is very close to literal truth. In some straightforward sense, what makes it true that p is p, and this is the case even with metaphor. Metaphor is not just pretty language but rooted in a way a world is, a way that is actual but not reducible to the literal. What makes it true that a particular human male is (metaphorically) a cactus is that that particular human male is (metaphorically) a cactus. What makes it true that God is (metaphorically) the Father is that God is (metaphorically) the Father.

It is important to note a difference between literal worlds and metaphorical worlds. In a literal world, God's being described as both omnipotent and not omnipotent is contradictory. Within metaphorical worlds, the notion of contradiction is less firm and perhaps not the right notion at all even though metaphors can be incompatible with one another. While it is right to say that God can't be both Father and Mother literally, it is not right to say that God can't be both Father and Mother metaphorically, and that in the same world. But what kind of world? Here is the modification of Goodman's position I flagged earlier. Goodman seems to suggest that metaphorical worlds are worlds unto themselves. Here he seems to have in mind, perhaps, the world of a novel.[10] Nevertheless, it seems somewhat odd to take metaphorical statements as worlds unto themselves, for metaphors rely on literalisms even when they can't be reduced to them. I suggest that metaphorical worlds are built within larger literal worlds and thus are more radically context dependent. They are, more or less, worlds-within-worlds.

Metaphorical worlds that appeal to what are literally conflicting literalisms are more obviously compatible with one another than the literalisms themselves. We often think of our metaphors, although truly applied to an object, as not exclusively applied. So one thing can be both mother and father metaphorically and we can say this in the same breath because we note the competing contexts in the same instant. All this can be done within the same literal world, so metaphorical claims are often vying for centre stage within a larger conceptual context. The upshot is that metaphorical descriptions need not be as strictly kept apart as literal descriptions. We use metaphors to get at certain literal features that are, frankly, often ambiguous. Our use nonetheless captures something metaphorically true even when two metaphors apparently conflict.

While some realist traditional Christians may be inclined to explain the metaphorical in literal terms, the Christian irrealist can say that even as we decide which credal statements are literal and which are metaphorical, we can admit the richness and value and truthfulness of the metaphorical understood simply as metaphorical. Literal descriptions of God, using thin concepts, can be filled out in many ways, and remain, perhaps, on the level of the literal. But there is no requirement that the worlds created by human noetic work should be strictly literal when it comes to God. The irrealist simply doesn't need to worry about what makes the metaphors literally true. The metaphors are literally false. But taken as metaphorical truths, the concepts themselves will be truthfully, but metaphorically, applied to God. Nevertheless, the metaphors cannot be reduced to literalisms.

Here is the important point for the Nicene Creed serving as a thin framework across all worlds. The thin concepts of God (with which the more robust accounts of God within various worlds work) need not be literal to begin with. A metaphorical world can begin with the existence of God, just as the literal world will, but because the mode of communication is different, there is no worry about getting God literally right. Just as a fiction writer need only worry about getting her metaphors to be actual in the world of the novel, the theologian need only worry about getting God metaphorically actual in the world she is building. It helps if we start with thin understandings of metaphor in the first place. That the creeds propose God as Father is only a problem if we take "father" literally. If it is metaphorically thin to begin with, the irrealist theologian can easily move to other metaphors that will make God richer in various worlds as she theorizes about God. Of course, that job is no less difficult than that of the person giving a literal account of God in theoretical terms. However, to speak in this context of literal rather than metaphorical truth about God is a mistake. It is not as if God shows up in the metaphorical world with only literal descriptions attached to God's being. Rather, God shows up with metaphorical concepts attached and God does so from the initial thin but metaphorical description. Some things about God we simply cannot say literally.

But we can say them as descriptions of the way God actually is, within a world. As with the literal parts of the creed, where the concepts are thin ones that turn up in each and every world, so metaphorical concepts in the creed are thin (metaphorical ones) that turn up in each and every world. Of course, in both the literal case and the metaphorical case, it is God who actually turns up in the various worlds and is either literally or metaphorically described truthfully. The creed, in short, presents God as God minimally is at the divine core and this holds across all the worlds. It doesn't follow that God is only that way or even that that way is the most interesting.

There is much to explore about God's actual being-within-a-world as it is built and considered. This cannot be done apart from the actual work of theorizing and conceptual thickening. But in recognizing that the creed itself does not always provide literal statements about God, the irrealist celebrates the metaphorical presentation of God as part of the divine fullness as God seeks to help us understand. We do not have to worry about "reducing" the metaphor to something else that is literally true. Each line of the Nicene Creed (Jesus Christ is begotten not made, he was incarnate from the Virgin Mary, he suffered death and was buried, the holy catholic and apostolic Church, the resurrection from the dead, and so on) needs to be analyzed in terms of its metaphorical vs literal content. As we sort this out, we will find some of the creed that is literally descriptive of God's interactions with the World. Although not a hard and fast rule, I'm inclined to think the literal descriptions tend to line up with the historical events and the role of human beings in interaction with God. Those things, God and humans and their historical interactions, turn out to be divine furniture rather than worldly and some can be literally described. But as we get closer to God as God is "outside" of history, the language is more metaphorical. It is no less appropriate for that.

Thus, the Nicene Creed is true (either literally or metaphorically) in each and every world because God is (and humans are) present in each and every world. But where the creed metaphorically presents God to us, God is no less independent of human noetic feats for that. At some point, our language may simply not capture God literally. But that is no more true for the traditional Christian who holds to Christian irrealism than for the traditional Christian who holds to a realism leaning toward the global. Some statements about God are true, if thinly so, no matter what world one is in. God is love, God is powerful, God is omniscient, and so forth can all be true of God and literally so and these statements are true no matter what world one is in. As such, contradictory statements about God, uttered within a singular world, can't both be true. With the metaphors, however, this won't be so obvious. That God is Father is metaphorically true, and thinly so, so it turns out that God is Father in every world. But this does not entail that God is not also Mother, and arguably so in every world as well. As God is more fully revealed in dialogue and interaction with humans in particular worlds, we will discover, I hope, that the earlier thin accounts of God can be filled out very richly. God is not only Father but Mother too. The creed is a historical document and orthodoxy is not static. Perhaps as we explore God's being more deeply, we will realize that the creed needs additions. In building worlds, we may, indeed, discover, if painfully, that the historic creeds are not complete.[11]

16

God and Objectivity

It is common to think that objectivity rests in truth. I take it to be obvious by now that truth, while important, is not the only important rightness. All kinds of rightness, however, depend on some sort of objectivity. My goal in this chapter is to make some observations to help place the notion of truth in its proper context for Christian irrealism.

1 OBJECTIVITY AND SUBJECTIVITY

One of the main concerns in the realism debate is objectivity. Even irrealists are worried about losing objectivity and making the whole World nothing more than a subjective extension of ourselves. The word "objectivity" has the same roots as the term "object." An object is a kind of abstraction distinct from ourselves. Perhaps our striving for objectivity has roots in the notion that an object is an abstraction. To understand an object we must somehow stand "outside" our experience and our conceptual schemes and give an account of the object *sans* human influence. Much of what I've argued here calls into question the notion that we can stand outside ourselves either ontologically or epistemically. This sort of objectivity is beyond our reach. Subjectivity, however, has its own problems. While it gives one immediate access and a kind of certainty, it is access and certainty to which no one other than oneself has access. We – perhaps I should say I – verge on solipsism. We want more publicity than that.

One result of my proposed irrealism is that the division between the objective and the subjective can be overcome. Irrealism puts objects, including God and other human persons, within our reach because how they are is to some degree shaped by us. The reason is, ultimately, that the ontological basis for the World rests in the Trinitarian nature of the Christian God. The notion of the Trinity indicates that God's Oneness is fundamentally a personal (and hence subjective) rather than an abstract (and hence objective) relationship with God's Threeness. Of course we don't understand how this works in any detail. But God is what God is relative to divine thought, something God creatively makes as God lives. God's subjective life, so to speak, provides for the way the World is and God's own being from eternity and this, in turn, provides for the objectivity of God's being. The subjective is the objective and the objective the subjective in God.

The overcoming of the division of objective and subjective flows out of God's sociality, the intersubjective interactions of the Persons of the Trinity. This way of being extends to us by analogy as we are made in God's image. But it is also extended to us personally by a God who loves us and invites us into personal interaction with the ongoing personal intersubjective interaction of God. In God's overcoming the subjective/objective divide,[1] we understand ourselves as united in and with God through personal relationship. On the Christian notion of God, in the end, we will all have the same experiences of God, or better yet, the same experience in God. In coming into God we will see, as Meister Eckhart puts it, that to know God is to know ourselves and all others the way God does.[2] The intersociality of the Trinity is ultimately cross-personal intimacy. As I see it, the plurality of God is at the core of the plurality of the worlds. And we are invited into that inter-sociality. Our world-making is part of that process. This is not to say that the worlds we make will all finally collapse into one or be accountable in terms of one "absolute World." This won't and can't happen any more than the members of the Trinity can collapse into one person.

Related to the claim that God is not distinct from God's social being is that goodness, beauty, and truth are connected to one another as the ancients believed they were, viz., they are one. Just as God is One in Three, so truth, beauty, and goodness are three but one. I want to tease out the thought that God is not distinct from God's social being, following it up with the suggestion that God provides what we can continue to call "objectivity" even as it rests in God's, and by extension, our subjectivity.

One last observation before we move on to details. I noted above that objectivity is rooted in the notion of "object": something "out there" independent of humans and/or God. "Object" is rooted in the Latin *objectus*, something thrown before or presented to (the mind); it is from the past participle of *obicere,* to throw before or against. "Object," "objection," and "objective" all come from the same root terms. So "to object" is to throw against, an "object" is something thrown before or against, to be objective is what is thrown before, in the sense of a thing. We also talk about having objectives in our lives. This too seems rooted in the same linguistic history. I suggest that the object is also thrown before as a goal. What is the object of your life? What is the object of your search? Of course, having something thrown before us could happen via someone else or by us: the ambiguity runs deep in these words. So we have the terms "object" and "objective" both used as "goal" and as "thing." In effect, what I'm doing in the rest of the chapter explores this dual sense of the words object and objective, as a marker to teach us how the bifurcation between objectivity and subjectivity can be overcome.[3]

2 TRUTH AND OBJECTIVITY

The notion of truth does double duty. It is, on the one hand, a property attaching to some (linguistically rooted) truth-value bearer in virtue of the way things are and it is also, simply, the way things are and therefore not attached, per se, to a (linguistic) truth-value bearer. Of course, the ways things are can often be given account (with enough hard work) by linguistic truth-value bearers and that is the end to which we often put our language.

Which of these two emphases (the truth of statements or the way things are) one focuses on depends on one's needs and purposes at the time. Our cultural worries about truth, from the point of view of noetic realism, often seem confused. In the realist's drive to avoid ontological pluralism (at best) and radical relativism (at worst), some important connections between things and truth are often overlooked. Unveiling these matters is part of the burden of the first several parts of this work, including shifting from truth alone to other rightnesses of rendering.

Nevertheless, truth, when it comes to many things – traditional Christianity not the least – is very important. The truth of a truth-value bearer reveals the world, for the truth of a truth-value bearer just is the result of the limits of the world. That is to emphasize the derivative nature of truth from the world, i.e., to emphasize alethic realism. Confusion often occurs in discussing pluralism because worlds are often made by linguistically based concepts. It therefore seems odd to use concepts (put together into linguistic truth-value bearers) to describe the world. Which is it, the critic might say, making or describing? That oddity, however, rests in confusing noetic with alethic realism. On pluralism, no less than on monism, the truth of a truth-value bearer should be understood simply as the way things are. The way things are, if pluralism is right, can be different according to various conceptual systems. Still, in giving a realist account of truth, a truth-value bearer is true when things are as the truth-value bearer says they are. The concern for truth is often a concern, fundamentally, about words, statements, and other linguistic constructions.

But we also know, if my argument has been right, that how things are is the result of a variety of influences, including our creative noetic input, the nature of humankind, and the nature of God. As such, the ontologies available to us are richer and more open than a noetic realism allows and these ontologies are not just epistemological options but alternative realities. Truth is thus relative to the worlds in which the truth-value bearers are uttered and to some degree, what world we are in is dependent upon the humans constructing it. But to say that what is true is relative to the world is not to say that truth is entirely relative. There are some fixed things, including humans (as fixed by God) and God (as fixed in God's conceptual scheme). As humans join with God to make worlds, worlds are made according to the limits God, finally, has in place.

The importance of truth as a property of truth-value bearers in expressing these limits ought not to be downplayed. We communicate in language, among other symbol systems, and yet we need not see linguistic truth as reducible to a total relativism. Once truth is understood as getting things right rather than a "bare" matching of words to the world, then we see that there is much more flexibility in regard to the world and less flexibility in regard to true statements than one might usually suspect as attending radical relativism. Pluralism is not as wild as it is often cast. Having said all that, and knowing that truth is one important kind of rightness of rendering, we must also see that the many other rightnesses of rendering available are important too. What each of these has in common, in the final analysis, is not truth as if it were some sort of abstract entity but objectivity.

What objectivity captures is what we typically try to capture by truth. To say something is true is often to report that something is objectively the case. "Objectivity rests on truth" might be an appropriate slogan. But I suggest that instead of objectivity resting on truth, truth rests on objectivity, as do all kinds of rightness of rendering. We don't find rightness of rendering (including truth) and hence find objectivity. We find objectivity and hence find rightness of rendering (including truth).

Whence the objectivity that attends to the rightness of rendering of all things, including the nonhuman natural things around us, rocks and trees, oceans and bumble bees? The objectivity can't rest in truth as the noetic irrealist understands it, a truth restricted to worlds. While the irrealist can admit that truth should be understood in alethic terms, this is certainly a very minimal account of truth. This minimalist account allows two reasons why alethic realism won't succeed in providing objectivity. First, even if it were up to the job in some cases, it covers only part of the territory, specifically, it covers only worlds constructed as descriptive, linguistic worlds. Other worlds, artistic worlds, are not concerned with truth per se. Furthermore, and more importantly, truth simply isn't up to the job, as the pluralist irrealist construes truth. Truth itself is world-relative, as illustrated by the variety of different scientific and metaphysical theories about physical objects. What makes it true in an Aristotelian world that there is a chair here in front of me may be quite different from what makes it so in a Whiteheadian world. But alethic realism holds for both incompatible worlds. The objectivity would thus be limited to each world on its own terms and as such, nothing external constrains them and therefore nothing unifies them either.

Truth is world-relative for the pluralist irrealist and therefore can't provide objectivity for the limits of "what will go" in any and all worlds. But neither are the other kinds of rightness of rendering – metaphorical truth, perception, pictorial representation – up to the job. Which worlds are rightly rendered and which ones are not? Aren't all rightness of rendering questions internal to the worlds? Given this kind of world, X renders things better than Y but given another kind of world, Y renders things better than X. The answer to the rightness of rendering question seems to depend upon the frames of reference themselves. Truth is contextual, but so are all kinds of rightness of rendering. Other kinds of rightness of rendering can't help us with objectivity any more than truth can. Just as truth rests in objectivity and not the reverse, so rightness of rendering rests in objectivity and not the reverse.

What we long for is objectivity and objectivity, we think, rests in truth or rightness of rendering, that is, in getting the description correctly stated or matched to reality, or the painting "realistic." We think that objectivity rests in truth or accuracy, that in reaching the truth (of description) or an accurate portrayal (via a painting or sketch) we reach objectivity. But a better account is that in reaching objectivity (God) we reach truth and rightness of rendering. But rightness of rendering, no matter what kind, is not a matching of proposition (or picture or what have you) to reality but of making a world in which God is revealed.

3 A CHRISTIAN OBJECTIVITY

At this point, we begin to move explicitly toward a Christian position on objectivity. I propose that makings – all kinds of makings – are worshipful. In worship, we let God be God. In making worship beautiful, we reveal God and hence worship God. In making worship truthful, we reveal God and hence worship God. In making worship good (inviting the other in), we reveal God and hence worship. Worship involves all three: goodness, beauty, and truth. Truth, goodness, and beauty are revelations of God, an unveiling in the midst of world-making. The richer the story we tell of God – the richer the world in which we live– the more heavenly it is.

Worlds are created for purposes. We create subatomic worlds to understand supernovas. We create sculptures to understand various 3-D problems. We create paintings to decorate but also to exemplify certain themes or express emotions. We create theological accounts of salvation to understand how God relates to and sustains human life and well-being. Are the purposes outside the worlds? No. However, the differences between, say, Goodman's view and that of a Christian irrealist are important on just this issue. While no point of view outside a world exists, there is a point of view within a world. That point of view, no matter the world, is God's point of view and, to a lesser extent, the image-bearing human point of view. All worlds contain God and humankind. It is a virtual fact that God is present and has certain purposes. That God and divine purpose are present in each world are the features of the worlds providing for the objectivity we need to avoid radical relativism and providing, in turn, the internal purposes that hold the world together. All things are present to glorify God.

Certain notions are used within a given world because they make sense in light of our broader valuing of things in that world. We may value some of those things a certain way because of the world itself. Yet in the final analysis, doesn't each world itself have a purpose? One is tempted to say that the purpose of each world is "outside" the world itself, that God is completely external to the World or worlds. But the objectivity of the worlds need not depend on something external to the world, if the thing providing objectivity is God. God, if transcendent alone, is not accessible to us. God, as immanent, is. The Christian doctrine of incarnation is essential to making sense of our existence and the worlds in which we live. God reveals the divine to us in the context of the worlds we help to create. This is why the second nature naturalism of McDowell won't, in the end, provide us with meaning. Evolutionary naturalism, even when it extends to the making of a *Bildung* in which we find meanings, seems to create meaning out of nothing. God, who on the Christian story enchants the world, is a requirement we cannot do without.

God, thus, is the purpose of each and every world. Of course, there are multiple intermediate purposes in world-making, and those purposes can and do certainly relate to humankind or even to individual humans. There is, however, no one way of rendering the worlds *in toto* that "gets it right," the single way it is. Even if God's purposes were reducible to only one, it would not follow that that one purpose could only be fulfilled in a singular way. But even admitting that there are multiple ways the worlds are, we can recognize a unity among all these worlds in a final sense, for all our human purposes can be seen as united in God's purpose or purposes, at least when we render the worlds rightly. God made us in God's image, and God's purposes will not be thwarted in the end. Even if there are many right ways of rendering the worlds, limits remain and those limits rest in God, the ground of being.

So objectivity rests not in truth or in rightness of rendering but in God's way of being, which in turn is an intersubjective set of personal relationships formed in God's very thought life. While there are constraints within worlds (honesty of metaphor for the character described, appropriateness of colour to portray the sea at night, befitting lines for a graceful drawing, suitable canvas for a landscape painting, etc.), there are some constraints "outside" the humanly contributed aspects of the worlds too, for God is independent of human noetic schemes in God's core being. That is to say, God is an "exterior" limit on the worldly, the final objectivity, in that God is "outside" each and every worldly aspect of the worlds by being present "in" all the worlds as the independent basis for all the worlds. Humans, no matter that we contribute to God's being-in-a-world, do not make God. God transcends all worlds yet God is not completely absolute and independent of all worlds. God's transcendence to the worlds is God's human noetic reality in each and every world. God, in the final sense, allows things to be made the way they are in each world that is rightly rendered. So it is entirely plausible to think that some worlds humans attempt to create will be, in the eschaton, rejected by God. What criteria does (or will) God use to sort out which worlds are rightly rendered and which are not? The criteria rest in God's (final) purposes.

God shows up as thin in all worlds. A thin notion of God might begin with the omni-properties, or perhaps with the Nicene Creed itself. Or perhaps the thin notion of God might simply be "necessarily exists." Necessary existence is a property of God and as such, God shows up not only in the actual world but in each and every human world. But perhaps "necessary existence" is too abstract. Perhaps we'd do better with the thin notion of God being "necessarily loves." That, of course, is where the greater specificity of the creed comes in.

God is not beyond all our descriptions. This does not mean we can describe God accurately at every turn, if by accurate we mean "the way God is, independent of all worlds." We can describe God accurately within any given world but these worlds do not overlap, logically. God joins us in holding the law of noncontradiction as a principle of thought. If one goes this way, one can't also go that way, within a given world. What about outside a world? To go outside a world, logically, is simply to enter another world. In each case thinkers leaving one world gain another. We could not make worlds without ourselves and God and the law of noncontradiction.

The law of noncontradiction is part of God's core being, and part of ours as well. It is constitutive of us as thinkers and part of or one aspect of God's core being. Since we are in God's image, it is in us too. I've argued that the epistemic status of the law just is its ontological status. Since much of the World turns out to be constructed via noetic feats, this shouldn't be surprising. The most basic and framing thoughts must, it seems, find their home in God's very nature, and then by extension in ours. We intuitively know we can't hold the law in place ourselves. The law of noncontradiction is a virtual fact, divine and human, uniting all the worlds, for it is a permanent structure of God, who is also a virtual fact.

Christian irrealism is eschatological in nature. The worlds are changing as we create and live in them. God lets us live in worlds that are not complete, that are not rightly rendered in the full. God even lets us live in worlds that are deceptive, in which we have denied God and God's love. These semi-false worlds may have enough reality to them to let us live, but not enough reality to make us, finally, happy and fulfilled. God's purpose, in giving us freedom, includes the possibility, in our human arrogance, of denying even God. In the eschaton, however, such worlds will be revealed as less than well rendered. God is still in such worlds, but the human contributions to them wallpapers over God's presence.

Theologically, Christian irrealism has implications for worlds beyond our worlds, namely, heaven. Heaven is a world, or series thereof, yet to be made by us. Heaven, however, unlike worlds made by us now, will always recognize God and give God a proper place. Heaven (along with purgatory) could be a continuous series of new world-makings, each more fully expressing, representing, and exemplifying God in our individual and corporate lives. Any description, scientific or otherwise, is secondary in heaven, yet no less creative, and the process of creation no less enjoyable than the making of worlds in our present state. Yet each new world more fully reveals God and relationship. God is more and more pleased with successive worlds because each reveals God more richly, more creatively, more fully.

In each new earthly world, as in each new heavenly world, the thin notion of God remains constant but God remains open to human contributions, human understandings, human being. Our descriptions of God participate, in some platonic-like sense, in God, and God participates in our worlds. God is, if you will, incarnate in each world. God, of course, can do whatever is appropriate to bring about God's ends. God can encourage us in one direction rather than another in order to shape us toward a richer account of the Divine Person and, indeed, toward a richer account of our selves. As those in the Orthodox Church might say, our human process with

God (post-Fall) is a process of recreation and not simply a restoration. Our descriptions must always seek to move us out of the limited box of our concepts as we think of God (or represent, or exemplify, etc., God) and as we think of ourselves. Here we strive not simply for literal descriptions based on literal, linguistic concepts but rather for the grand breadth of concepts, linguistic, pictorial, emotional, and so forth.

Our worlds now, and our worlds in heaven, are always worlds. As Putnam might put it (using my language), "How is God outside all the worlds?" is a nonsense question not even God can answer. God's way of being is a revealed way of being and God's revelation occurs always within a world.

I may appear to be collapsing the revelation of God into a making of God by humans. At this point we must remember that we are not alone. God is in the mix, guiding and helping each human person in making worlds. The particularity of Christianity is a particularity of history. God is not to be thought of as some abstract generality. God is, within God's own being, three Persons in eternal loving relationship – *perichoresis*, the divine dance of hospitality, one trying to "outdo" the other in inclusiveness without coerciveness. It is this God who self-reveals into the World and, by extension, the worlds, by creating human persons with whom to interact. God is concrete and not merely abstract.

Outside history, what would we know of God? We are bound in space and time, our knowledge rooted in history. When we think of God, we think of God as conceived of by us. Is God outside time and space? Well, space and time are our creations too, and since we can typically think only in those terms, then, no, God is not outside space and time. Yet insofar as we can grasp an atemporal, aspatial reality, God fits there also. That, too, would be irreal, and yet God is no less present for being timeless. But the border between God's independent reality and core nature, on the one hand, and God's irreality as contributed by us, on the other, is not always clear. The debate is open both theologically and philosophically. Yet there is a line, for God cannot be just anything without everything collapsing into relativism.

The mystical experience – to which I'll return in the last chapter – may come into play here, for it is often reported as nonspatial, nontemporal, and completely extra-worldly. However, the reports as we have them are, for the most part, not literally descriptive but metaphorically so. But the mystic still is in a world and God, therefore, is in a world with her. That world, however, may contain only God and the mystic, and her focus is thus most strongly on God. That fact might explain why she is overwhelmed by the experience and finds it difficult to put into words. But no matter how we theorize about God and no matter how we make the worlds, God brings to those worlds the Divine Person, for God is divinely virtually absolute. There is no such thing as a true absolute – an absolute free of conceptual scheme – about God. To say God is a true absolute – something beyond all worlds – is to report something we can neither create nor experience.

But surely, the critic will say, God exists independently of our experience! The irrealist can affirm this, but can't know what it comes to, what it means, so far as our earthly life is concerned. We are up against the boundaries of reason. But fundamentally, why should a Christian think that God would not be present in each and every world, experience, and thought? From the Christian point of view, to say that God exists as an absolute, independent of the worlds, is to say that we would be "out of touch" with God. But to be out of touch with God is simply not to be. God is relational and this relationality makes us what we are. God is the very being of beings, the being who makes all being possible. We are talking about rightly made worlds and true world-versions. No such world can be made without God as the ultimate source.

4 GOD AND MYSTERY

Can we say anything univocally of God? As we saw in the discussion of the creed, within any given descriptive world, there will be statements literally true of God. Yet there will also be language metaphorically true of God. When we leave one world and go to the next, God might be described quite differently, both literally and metaphorically, but still accurately within that world. In all these worlds, some of the same things will be literally said of God, especially as God incarnates and thus reveals Godself in the world. As such, God's (human) noetic reality is fixed across the worlds. God is one way rather than another and that way remains true across the worlds. Perhaps here it would be better to say "genuine" than "true." Thus, there are limits to how a rightly made world can treat of God. God cannot be evil, no matter how much we construe God to be that way. Neither

can contradictory things be said of God within the same world. One
account of omnipotence, for example, true in world W_1, can be contradictory to another account of omnipotence true in another world,
W_2, if both were taken to be true within one world. Both cannot be
true within a singular world. But can God be anything less than omnipotent, even in one world? If omnipotence is a thin concept, then,
no, God will be omnipotent in all worlds. But what omnipotence
comes to may be fleshed out in a variety of ways in different worlds.
Our theories and thought contribute, in a variety of ways, to how
God is understood – that is, to how God is – within a given world.
But a world in which God's omnipotence is simply denied is not possible, for such a view would not be pleasing to God. Such a view falls
short not only of the way God is, but also falls short of the fullest
ways in which God can be thought to be by humans. God, being the
true ground of all being, doesn't expect us to provide the absolute
true description of what God is – there is no such thing. But God
does expect us to give a right description of God in terms of the highest ways we humans can conceive of God.

But none of that entails that we speak univocally of God. Literal
and metaphorical truths can still be analogical truths. We in the end
never speak univocally of God. This is consonant with the entire
tradition of Christianity. As Elizabeth Johnson writes,

> The doctrine of divine incomprehensibility or hiddeness is a corol-
> lary of this divine transcendence. In essence, God's unlikeness to the
> corporal and spiritual finite world is total. Hence human beings sim-
> ply cannot understand God. No human concept, word, or image, all
> of which originate in experience of created reality, can circumscribe
> divine reality, nor can any human construct express with any mea-
> sure of adequacy the mystery of God who is ineffable.
>
> This situation is not due to some reluctance on the part of God
> to self-reveal in a full way, nor to the sinful condition of the hu-
> man race, which makes reception of such revelation weak and
> limited, nor even to the contemporary mentality of skepticism
> about religious matters. Rather, it is proper to God as God to
> transcend all similarity to creatures, and thus never to be
> known comprehensively or essentially as God.[4]

I propose that the God Johnson speaks of here is God as God
is outside of human conceptual schemes. This God is ineffable,

incomprehensible, and hidden. But for all that, Johnson affirms that God does reveal Godself into the World. I'm suggesting that when God does so, God opens Godself to being-in-a-world of human creation and it is then that we can describe God. But we can do so only analogically, in the grand ongoing and developing tradition of Christian theology. Johnson notes that Augustine and Aquinas both recognize God's hiddenness and yet provide means by which humans can access God. But it is best reported by Johnson when she refers to Rahner. Rahner, she writes, "argues that the incomprehensibility of God belongs not at the margins or the end of the road in theology but at its very heart, insofar as God's inexhaustibility is the very condition for the possibility of the human spirit's self-transcendence in knowledge and love."[5]

All this matches well with the idea of a progressive revelation, viz., more and more is understood about God over time.[6] As our conceptual schemes develop, we are able to describe God more fully and rightly (but not more truly in the "matching" sense of the word, namely, outside any and all worlds.) Some other implications follow from these considerations. Truth, as noted, isn't up to the job of providing objectivity, for truth is found within the worlds themselves as we construct those worlds out of words and concepts. God, as holding the law of noncontradiction, must keep the worlds (at least those in which certain descriptions conflict with each other) separate from one another. God is the protector of truth, so to speak. It would follow that God has no beliefs, in the sense that (true) beliefs must "match up" to the way (or even the ways) things are. If God were to have truth-value bearers in God's mind, they would have to be the *source* of the way things are rather than true *because* of the way things are. I'd prefer to say that there are no truth-value bearers in God's mind. Instead, God is the truth-value bearer.[7] I would add that God is the Good-bearer and the Beauty-bearer. God simply is, and in the worlds where truth is important and hence emphasized, God's presence blesses the truths as rightly emerging from those worlds. God is not constrained by world-relative truths. They are constrained by God. World-relative truths are creations within a world but in rightly rendered worlds, God is always recognized, for God is always present. God allows and even encourages humans to create different kinds of worlds and God holds the worlds together in unity by the divine presence in them. God's presence in them is part of what makes the worlds individually coherent and therefore rightly rendered and corporately united in reflecting God's purposes.

Thus truth, in final terms, is not something that "binds" God, in the sense that truth is external to God and God therefore must accept it. Rather the world-relative truths are rooted in God's being and purposes. Here we must introduce the role of human being again. Insofar as human purposes fall in line with God's, the worlds created will have coherence among themselves and unity with God. Instead of God choosing among various possible worlds and being "forced" into one rather than another by something separate from God – a "matching" of beliefs to the "way things are" – there are many actual ways the World is. God is present in each world, and God's job, so to speak, is to keep them separate from one another (to avoid conflict according to the laws of logic and the central role they are given by God and humankind) but also to unify them by the divine presence in them. If God didn't keep the worlds separate there would be massive contradictions and no worlds at all. If God didn't keep them unified, there would be radical relativism and no truth. God is the unifier of all the rightly rendered but separate worlds, and hence God is in all those worlds. A world without God is, in the final sense, no world at all. Humans can persist in making worlds without God, or at least attempting to do so. Such worlds are not worlds rightly rendered, not being coherent and hence, finally, not real.

Here we may raise once again questions about the nature of necessity. Does the fact that virtual absolutes hold, but true absolutes don't, entail that God might not exist in some world? We've seen that the answer is negative. Nevertheless some ways the World might be haven't been thought of yet and hence not actualized. Some merely possible ways the World might be don't exist – yet. They don't exist simply because they haven't been worked out. What are the limits here? There might be many ways for worlds to be, but logical inconsistency isn't one of them, nor is a world without God or other necessary beings. I've already discussed various sorts of non-divine necessities but it is worth noting again that while humans are not necessary beings they are nevertheless conceptually necessary for there to be worldly worlds. Humans are virtually absolute (in terms of human irrealism) and so have being in any world humans can make.

It turns out, on irrealism, that not all truths about God's very being are necessary truths. Some are constructed as we construct the worlds and as we develop relationship with God. But God's existence is necessary. God's existence includes God's internal relationships, one person to another. Any property needed for these eternal relationships will be true of God across worlds – God's love, for example. There appears to be no upper limit. To say God is maximally good means more than just that whenever God can do something good God does it. Perhaps all the omniproperties are similar. Again a world-making that pleases God is one that magnifies God and, within the range of human powers, conceives of God as greater and greater. Self-surpassing greatness, as Charles Hartshorne suggests, is central to God. Hence, none of our theories will finally be complete but will always have before them the greatness of God that exceeds our theories and conceptualizations. But in relationship we will be drawn into the very being of God in love, on the eternal journey toward fellowship with God. We are drawn to the mystery of divine love knowing only the beginnings of the reality of God.

History thus is being drawn by God into relationship with God. We will always be particulars, individuals. But we are individuals in community and communion. That is our nature. It is a nature we can mould and shape toward God or away from God. But God should always be in front of us. Does all this imply contradictions within God himself? No. And yet God is one way in one world and another way in another world. But we should not confuse mere truth with Truth, or mere goodness with Goodness or mere beauty with Beauty, which I turn now to explore.

5 TRUTH VS TRUTH, GOODNESS VS GOODNESS, AND BEAUTY VS BEAUTY

We are familiar with the issues that arise when we make statements such as "God is good." Do we mean to say that there is some standard of goodness, exterior to God, by which we judge God and find God good, in a manner parallel to the way in which we judge some human person or action good against the universal standard of goodness? The answer is no. By "God is good" we mean, at least in part, that God is Goodness itself. Likewise when we claim that God is Truth. It is not that there is some standard (some singular way things are) against which we judge whether God has gotten it right epistemically and hence holds true beliefs. We mean something more. Somehow, God's Truth is God's Being. God's Truth is not a matching of God to Reality in an appropriate way. God simply is Reality. Everything else is derivative.

God as Truth is present in all the actual worlds – present in Being and in fullness of purpose and relationship. So as not to forget the human aspects of the world, we must note that just as worlds are not rightly rendered without a proper understanding of God, worlds are not rightly rendered without a proper understanding of human nature. The addition of this other component, the human, implies that the objectivity needed for rightness of rendering is rooted not just in God's being itself but in that of humanity too. Human and Divine being work together in purposive unity and harmony, at least when creativity works well. So God's being (and by extension human being) is fundamentally relational rather than some sort of abstract set of "truths." Although God has no beliefs understood as mental objects that match the world, God does have unlimited capacity for creativity, for purpose, for pleasure, and for relationship. God is a Trinity of Persons, and as the Greek fathers and mothers of the Church recognized, God should be understood as fundamentally relational rather than abstract.[8]

In the creation of the "original" universe, we have a glimpse of God taking sheer delight in being and creating being. It is not simply being as being in the abstract that is important but the act of creating being (including other creative forces in the world(s), viz., humans). So in God's fundamental creation, God makes human beings. We, too, are creative. Since God makes us in God's image, nothing pleases God more, we might say, then when humans rightly render a world. Our theorizing, novel writing, and artistic endeavours greatly please God, but only when we rightly render the world we are creating. One feature of such worlds is the presence of God as Truth, Goodness, and Beauty. These are manifest, however, only through social relationship: human to human, human to God, God to human, and God to God.

God is primarily relational. The Trinity is essentially personal and to be personal is to be in social relation. God, independent of the contingent creation, is social. Hence the Christian notion of God is, I think, superior to many other notions, for God is not simply personal but social in God's very nature. We are better able to see the centrality of God's sociality if we start with God as relational in essence rather than God as describable by (true) statements. God as Being is related Father to Son, Son to Spirit, Spirit to Father, etc. Or in less typical, but no less true language, God as Being is related Mother to Sophia, Sophia to Spirit, Spirit to Mother. In both these descriptions we have metaphor attempting to express the fundamentally social nature of God. The point is, the persons of the Trinity do not simply think true thoughts of one another but experience joy and love in the presence of each other, the mutual embrace of God's dance of union. Thus, the starting place for knowing God is knowing God as a person, not knowing a set of true (and abstract) propositions.

I didn't marry my wife simply because I believed a set of abstract propositions about her including that she loved me or because the abstract proposition "Susan loves me" is true. I married Susan because she loves me concretely. It was a revelation of her love that drew me, not an abstraction about it. Beliefs, construed as "being true," are an afterthought. Something's being true is, in the end, something's being real. Here the worldly content theory of truth comes into play, along with the identity theory of truth. True propositions just are facts, and true believings just are bits of the world. Something's being real is something's being made, and believing a proposition is believing a thing is such and so. But some things, God and people, are not fundamentally made by us. God makes humans but also reveals Godself to us. Under these circumstances, a proposition's being true just is a bit of reality revealed. When it comes to the concrete personal relationship, there is more to revelation than the abstract truths.

Believing in Susan is believing that she is able to fulfill her promises as well as trusting her that she does fulfill her promises. Unlike human social relationship in which my trusting Susan, along with countless other people – her mother or her friends – trusting her, helps bring Susan to the place where she can do what I trust her to, God's revelation to us is the final and complete promise since God is our source. God, in God's own nature, is social. God is love. God's sociality, however, is aimed completely "outward," first to the Persons of the Trinity and then toward us and all creation. While we can contribute to God on one level – the level of bringing our concepts of God to fullness and fruition in understanding God – God participates in world-making too, bringing God's own self to us. As we interact with God, we make God a certain way – a thick way – in a world lived out. But we do not make God simply any old way. We make God in relationship with God.

A true world-version is a genuine world-version, one that is pure and whole and therefore makes a world. When we say God is Truth, what do we say? Not that there are propositions about God that happen to be true or even are necessarily true but rather that God is True. To say that someone is true is to say that she has veracity, honesty, fullness of character, she acts well in the world, she can be trusted to do what she says, she will be constant. We err when we reduce all these to truth expressed in statements. Truth in statements is derivative from truth of character. Thus, true character and good character are the same thing. But it is because of the goodness of God's character that God is said to be true. Of course, goodness is a social, relational reality, not merely an abstract one.

Believing "in" vs believing "that" is an important distinction. We are prone to reduce the former to the latter when, indeed, we should be thinking of the latter in terms of the former. To say that I believe in God is, of course, to say that I believe certain things of God. However, to believe that God is love is not the same as believing in God's love. Another example is this. "I believe in the one true God" does not say just that the universe can only be truly described by admitting only one God. It also says that God is in Godself true. God's being true is many things, including God's being pure, like pure gold. The Truth of God has more fundamentally to do with God's purity, righteousness, and holiness than with abstract statements being true of God.

We cannot make up God any way we want. New worlds are made from old ones. With God with us, however, as a partner in the dialogue and exchange that is the creation of new worlds, as a social reality who responds to us as we respond to God, we can see that our beliefs are shaped and formed in the crucible of social exchange with God and with other humans. The core being of God is not to be understood in terms of abstractions such as propositions but rather in terms of relational concreteness. To truly believe in my wife is for her to be within my emotional range. To be in love is a purpose, a range of hoping, a supportive act of hospitality. God is that sort of love. God thus is not simply Truth, but Goodness and Beauty as well.

But caution is required to avoid misunderstanding my claims regarding truth. I am rejecting the view that truth is the only and most fundamental value in God. This is not to reject objectivity or, finally, to reject truth itself. Rather it is to place truth in its proper context among the values we should have in a culture and to elevate Truth as God's way of being. I believe this reflects more fully the nature of God. Truth (with a capital "T") should be thought of not as a matching of God's "thoughts" to "the way things are" but rather as God in Godself, in all God's Goodness and Beauty. God is fundamentally and essentially relational.

Colin Gunton says some intriguing things about how humans relate to God and to nature.

> Human being in the image of God is to be understood relationally rather than in terms of the possession of fixed characteristics such as reason or will, as has been the almost universal tendency of the [Western, Christian] tradition. By this I mean that the reality of the human creature must be understood in terms of the human relation to God, in the first instance, and to the rest of creation in the second. The relation to the remainder of creation falls into two. In the first place, to be in the image of God is to subsist in relations of mutual constitutiveness with other human beings. In the second place, it is to be in a set of relations with the non-personal creation. The human imaging of God is a dynamic way of being before God and with the fellow creature. [italics his]9

Just as the tendency in Western Christianity is to think of the image of God in humans as a fixed characteristic such as will or reason, so there is a tendency to think of truth as having primacy over goodness, beauty, or relationship. But, I submit, God can't be reduced to a set of truths. God is Truth. As Truth, God is also Goodness and Beauty. Within God, these are expressed among the members of the Trinity as hospitality.

Cornelius Plantinga Jr. writes:

> At the center of the universe, self-giving love is the dynamic currency of the trinitarian life of God. The persons within God exalt each other, commune with each other, defer to one another. Each person, so to speak, makes room for the other two ... we might almost say that the persons within God show each other divine *hospitality*. After all, John's Gospel tells us that the Father is "in" the Son and that the Son is "in" the Father (17:21), and that each loves and glorifies the other. The fathers of the Greek church called this interchange the mystery of *perichoresis* ... and added

in the Holy Spirit – the Spirit of both the Father and the Son. When the early Greek Christians spoke of *perichoresis* in God, they meant that each divine person harbors the others at the center of his being. In a constant movement of overture and acceptance, each person envelops and encircles the others.[10]

God is defined, thus, not in terms of static properties such as knowledge of true propositions. Rather God is defined in relationship with the personal members of the Godhead in terms of love, goodness, and the beauty that emerges in that love and goodness.

The worlds in which we live are largely human constructs, but constructs guided and forged in the kiln of God's Truth. Human construction of worlds has some comprehensive boundaries, however, including the presence and reality of God as Truth, Beauty, and Goodness. Thus, viewed from one position, I am not denying a universal set of truths, truths that will be true in all the actual (and rightly rendered) worlds, at least those worlds built with language and beliefs. In these rightly rendered worlds, "God exists" will be true. But the importance of the truth "God exists" in those worlds cannot be reduced to abstract fact (even the devils believe in God, and they tremble); God's reality shapes and influences every human construction within a rightly rendered world. World-making cannot go on without God and the objective limits God's reality brings with it.

What of worlds that are not descriptive but representational or exemplificatory? How does God play into these? For the former, the problem is no more complicated on this theory than on a more "realist" or traditional theory of art. How is God represented pictorially? But God is there, in any rightly rendered painting, just as God is there in any rightly rendered descriptive world. What about exemplificatory worlds? Similarly, God is there in any rightly rendered one.

Here we might enter into the nature of beauty and glory. Not that every abstract painting needs to be beautiful in the "traditional" sense. Nor do paintings in general have to be beautiful. Beauty does not require a lack of reality, and sometimes the reality in a given world is not attractive. As Bishop Richard Harries notes,

One of the disturbing features of art is the way it can beautify what is terrible, can render aesthetically pleasing what should shock us. This is seen most frequently in the case of the Crucifixion of Christ. Crucifixion was an excruciatingly painful means of

torture: the person died in agony. This anguish, like the anguish
of those who suffer in any way, should never be glossed over,
softened up or in any way made acceptable. Such pain is a horror,
crying out to be stopped; totally contrary to the absolute will of a
loving God, whatever may be allowed as an inescapable aspect of
a created world. Yet art cannot help but beautify ... I believe that
the beautifying effect of art has its justification in the Resurrection of Christ and only there ... This means that the beautifying
power of art, far from being a harmful illusion, is a pointer to the
redemptive work of God in Christ.[11]

God's presence in painting and the other arts may very well be the
source of the beauty we find in the arts, even those presenting ugly
or horrible realities.

The presence of God is a fact, even if not noticed. Meister Eckhart
wrote: "God is nearer to me than I am to myself; my existence depends on the nearness and presence of God. He is also near things of
wood and stone, but they know it not. If a piece of wood became as
aware of the nearness of God as an archangel is, the piece of wood
would be as happy as an archangel." He continues, "Our happiness
does not arise from this, that God is near us, and in us, and that he
possesses God; but from this, that we know the nearness of God, and
love Him, and are aware that the 'Kingdom of God is near.'" Further,
"God is equally near all creatures."[12]

An atheist's attempts to create a world in which God does not exist
won't succeed because God is a virtual absolute in the divine scheme of
things and thus shows up in every world. An atheistic world will be, at
some level, incoherent or otherwise not rightly rendered. God will be
wallpapered over, but God doesn't go away. If an atheist creates a
world without God, God may allow the person to live in that world,
but it is not (fully) actual until God allows it to be. But then, such a
world, by becoming actualized, becomes nonexistent and perhaps the
person goes with it, should she insist on doing so. Finally, the creative
power given to a human being is, by her choice, her undoing. Here
there may be some things to explore in regard to the doctrine of hell.

What about the final state of the many worlds that we can create?
So long as they make God dance, and there are a variety of ways of
doing that, God will bless them all. If they don't, finally, please God,
the humans creating them will be drawn into a fuller, more rich
world, or perhaps left to their own devices and hence perhaps end in
nonexistence (something akin to C.S. Lewis's version of hell).

For those worlds in which words are not important (artistic worlds) the unification is based less on truths per se and more on certain features or "presences" which are common. God is present (in a grand variety of ways) in all the worlds. In short, in the unification of all the (rightly rendered) worlds, certain presences will be constant (and hence in descriptive worlds, statements true). In linguistic worlds, one of these truths is about God. In artistic, nonlinguistic worlds truth is not relevant but being is. Thus God's presence will turn up in all rightly rendered nonlinguistic worlds.

Thus truth is, in the end, saved. But we shouldn't confuse truth with Truth. God is Truth. Where God is, Truth is. God's presence just is Truth. When Jesus says "I am the way, the truth, and the life" he identifies himself in some way other than what either Tarski or Pilate had in mind. Jesus is not some sort of matching between a linguistic construction and the world. The Truth is God. Goodness and Beauty are God as well. Truth (lower case), goodness, and beauty are contextually relevant to humanly constructed worlds. It will be true, in those worlds that are both rightly rendered and linguistically based, that "God exists." It will be the case that in all rightly rendered nonlinguistic, non-belief based worlds, God is present. But the presence of God or true claims about God do not make all the worlds reducible to a singular way the world is. As Goodman puts it, "how do you go about reducing Constable's or James Joyce's worldview to physics?"[13] So Truth (that is God) is present in all rightly rendered worlds, the worlds in which God is pleased, but there may be many actual worlds which are, indeed, incompatible with each other, in one feature or another. In short, there is objectivity without singularity, creativity within limits, and worlds with God.

As I've already noted, another feature of all rightly rendered worlds is the presence of human persons. God has made us and we are fixed in nature. If God were to destroy us all, the worlds we create would cease with us. Furthermore, since the worlds are what they are relative to human noetic feats, humanity's relationship to God and God's relationship to humanity are central in understanding the various worlds. One of the things we are told in the Christian story, of course, is that humans, from the beginning, attempted to recreate the world in a manner not pleasing to God. We live, in short, with the Fall. Humans thus stand in need of redemption, and redemption occurs in history with God becoming human. It is to these aspects of the rightly rendered worlds that I turn in the next chapter.

History, Humans, and God: Toward a Christian Irrealist View of God's Redemptive Work

If relativism is a general challenge in our culture, it is nowhere assumed to be more challenging than in religion, morals, and history. Among noetic realists, realism is often taken as extending only to the physical realm. Moral and religious claims are then accounted for in emotivist terms. Emotivism is understood as a sort of relativism or at least a relativist tolerance for the variety of moral and religious beliefs. History, although somewhat of a hybrid between the sciences and the humanities, is often grouped, somewhat reluctantly, with the other relativistic humanities. This tendency is reflected in the division among history departments over the question, does history belong in the division of humanities or the division of social sciences? This chapter's goal is to explain how God's role in history can be understood as part of the divine furniture whose ultimate source is in God rather than humans, even when there are many historical worlds. This issue emerges directly out of my earlier discussions of the creed.

1 SORTING OUT SUBJECTIVITY

In much of twentieth-century philosophy, many looked to the empirically verifiable (along with the definitional) as the only cognitive (and hence objective) claims. Religious, aesthetic, and moral claims were thought to be noncognitive and hence subjective. Truth or facts, at least in more popular culture, came to be thought of as primarily or ultimately resting in science. Scientific methodology gives us access to objective facts and truth whereas religion and morality, being subjective, cannot give us truth. If the latter do give us truth, it is a different kind of truth than that provided by scientific meth-odology, for it is a kind of relativized truth. History is often thought to fall somewhere between the two extremes of the scale. History is not, strictly speaking, science. Nor, on the other hand, is it as sub-jective as morality or religion.

Nowhere are the challenges of history more clearly paraded down main street then when historical and religious claims are combined as, for example, when we consider the historicity of the resurrection or the more general role of God's actions in history. At worst we find Christian theologians stating that God cannot act in history – what have the accidental truths of history to do with the universal truths of metaphysics? At best, if God does act in history, our objective historical methodology can explain only that the early Christians believed that Jesus rose from the dead and not that he did, indeed, rise. Historians qua historians can never make a deci-sion as to whether Jesus actually rose from the dead. If anyone forms a belief that Jesus came back from the dead on the basis of historical research, it is a decision she makes acting on faith rather than reason or historical evidence. In other words, such a belief is subjective and therefore relativized to the person believing it. The historian, qua historian, can't enter that territory.

Traditional Christianity, however, requires something beyond a subjectivized account of divine events in history. The creed should be taken as literally true, where it is, and metaphorically true other-wise. Where it is most clearly making literal statements, I believe the creed is describing historical events rather than God apart from his-tory. As such it seems that traditional Christianity cannot be happy with relativied accounts of history. Such accounts, it is thought, at best reduce the acts of God in history to subjective beliefs held pri-vately by Christians and at worst simply explain the resurrection away as not having happened in the empirical past at all.

Irrealism doesn't seem to help here and, in fact, seems to open the door to a more radical subjectivity. If irrealism holds, what is to stop the historian from making a historical world in which God never acted at all or a world where Jesus did not die and rise for all humanity? So far forth, the irrealist seems to be quite at home with the relativist his-toriographer's claims, and thus is in line with the general attitude in our intellectual culture, where it has become standard to hold that the sciences give us objectivity, the human sciences less, history less, and then the humanities, the arts, and perhaps theology least of all.

So far as our cultural attitude goes, the question of what history is is a problem, even for those inclined to noetic realism about the sciences. Unlike the natural sciences, where we can "repeat" experiments, history is neither repeatable nor testable. So we tend to subjectivize history, especially, I believe, as it opens up the possibility of generating meaning for humans. I've argued that objectivity does not entail a single story about the world. I now add that subjectivity does not entail relativism.[1]

I want to extend the view that the bifurcation between objectivity and subjectivity is overcome in Christian irrealism by arguing that history is not relative in any way that affects the objective presence of God in history. This does not entail that there is a "singular" history of the world. There can be many histories. However, none of the rightly rendered historical worlds fail to include God's presence and, in particular, the presence of Jesus Christ as the provider of redemption for humankind.

2 THE PROBLEM OF SALVATION

Human beings are ontologically linked. As a Christian, I believe this link is rooted in God and, in fact, that God is linked to us ontologically in rich and manifold ways. There is little new in these claims. What is perhaps somewhat novel is the following. The link among humans and between humans and God is fundamentally historical. God, humans and history must, therefore, all be included in a general theory.

How are humans linked to God and to one another? Traditionally, this question is given a somewhat abstract, metaphysical answer. Humans have a shared human nature – traditionally a noetically realist nature – given by God. Often this nature is explained in terms of human rationality, will, or some otherwise fixed characteristic. Human nature is thus linked to God's nature via our being made in the image of God. For a Christian irrealist, the question cannot be answered this way, or at least not without some alternate details to the typical explanation. The question about how humans are linked to God and to one another raises the further question, how are humans united in such a way that God saves them in a single, historical act? In traditional Christianity, humans share a common human nature, one created by God and made in God's image. But when *adam* (the human) sins, we all sin and fall short of the glory of God, with death at our heels. When Jesus dies and comes back from the dead, salvation is provided for all. Jesus, both divine and human, dies in history, so the questions of human nature, divine nature, and the nature of history are bound together.

For the noetic realist Christian, history is not relative. As such, history is less problematic. Through history God is revealed and, ultimately, through history salvation for humankind is provided. The Incarnation of God into the ebb and flow of human events is the fixed point by which God finally and completely identifies with humanity and provides salvation. For the noetic realist Christian, there is a singular story about history. Although the noetic realist Christian may not be sure of the details, she is sure that, because Jesus shares our humanity with us, his sacrifice on the cross universally covers our sins. The Christian irrealist, however, appears to be committed to historical relativism, for if humans make the worlds, then surely we make up history. If humans can write and rewrite history, each time coming up with a true, but relative, account of the past, then perhaps we can write God completely out of history. It is one thing, from a Christian point of view, to claim that matter is really a phenomenon in the human mind (à la Berkeley) or to challenge the typical Aristotelian account of metaphysical entities as things enduring through time and space and replace it with a Whiteheadian view of things as events. It is quite another to say that the work of Jesus Christ on the cross was not actually located in history. Christianity "demythologized" to that extent is no longer Christianity. Christianity reinterpreted as simply one among many religious stories, all of which are true, is no longer traditional Christianity. For traditional Christianity, we need a real divine-human person named Jesus, who died on a cross and was resurrected on the third day, ascending some forty days later into the presence of God. Some events in history, in other words, are central to the Christian account and we cannot remain traditional Christians without affirming them as the means by which salvation is offered to all humanity.

To move Christian irrealism toward a solution to this challenge, I propose that the order on the "objectivity scale" is nearly the reverse of what is typically thought. However, in order to reserve the term "objective" for the role God plays in world-making, I'll shift my term of choice to "fixedness" to capture what we are after in describing the subject matter of the various disciplines. The fixedness list accepted among intellectuals generally, as I noted earlier, is that the sciences give us (more or less) complete fixedness, the human sciences less, history less, and then the humanities, the arts, and theology the least. In contrast, if God is the most real thing, the most objective, with humans a close second, then theology, history, and the other human sciences, linked as they are in Christianity, will turn out to be the most fixed, with the sciences bringing up the rear with the least amount of fixedness. Somewhere in between, we find the arts and the humanities. Where they are placed may depend on their subject matter, for the fixedness of the subject matter of these disciplines has less to do with objectivity per se (there is, as we learn from Goodman, no lessening of rigour in rightness or rendering, only differences) and more to do with the "closeness" of the objects to human and ultimately to divine nature. The question is: What is the relationship between creative human noetic feats and fixedness? My main concern here is history and its subject matter, so I concentrate primarily on it.

3 THE NATURE OF HISTORY

I cannot hope to give a complete philosophy of history here. Rather my aim is to provide some basic ideas by which to clarify the relationship of humans and God in history. To begin, we should distinguish between events, facts, data, and history. Events, according to irrealism, are never "raw." Events, such as a rock falling from a cliff to the level ground below, are shaped and influenced by human noetic feats. Events need not attain the level of description. Facts are what humans work with in their theorizing and talking about things and events, based on the broad making of a world. So I can make an event (by conceptualizing) but I report the facts (in sentences and other linguistic occurrences). That is, a fact is a kind of report or description of events. Data are the (physical) source of such reports, such as orally told stories or second-hand observations, writings, videography, archaeological work, etc.

History is none of these. Instead, history is the story, the recounting, or the telling of the human past. It is important to note that prehistory, if there is such a thing, ended when humans came to be. Here I do not intend to imply that humans were created directly by an act of God such as that described in the Genesis accounts. Perhaps humans evolved from ancestors on their way to being human. At some point, they became capable of telling stories about the past. History began when humans began to speak it in their earliest stories and, eventually, came to write it. Before there were humans, there could only have been mere events, if anything at all. Of course, on irrealism, there were not even events, unless God or the angels made them. Let's for now ignore that possibility. We can say, however, that mere events are shaped by human conceptualizing without holding that the earliest humans were necessarily capable of reporting those conceptualizations in language in some complete way.

We can say, then, that history is constrained by empirical facts and the data. History is bordered or hemmed in by the events of the past. But while history is constrained by facts, to be history it must create a story, a recounting or a telling of events past and, in particular, events that are human. The human past is rooted in event, but told by story. So, when there were no humans, there could be no history. Prior to words, and eventually writing, there was no history, only prehistory.

History has its events and its story, but that is not all. The story, the recounting, the telling must come with meaning. History is the story, the recounting, the telling of past human events with meaning. Meaning cannot ultimately be separated from reference but the question is, reference to what? I submit that events alone do not have meaning. A rock falling from a cliff is an event but it need not have in itself any meaning. For meaning there must be context. For context, there must be words or other symbol systems. To put this point about symbols symbolically, when *adam* (the human) names the animals, a very basic level of meaning comes to be. We humans affirm the animals not simply as "what they are." We contribute to their being, laying alongside them symbols through which a world is created. This naming (in other words, this application of concepts in creativity) creates the animals, and all the other things in the world too, in such a way that we can speak of them. Science is begun in this very minimal but active use of names. Thus we initially create the events and things and then we report them in data as facts.

Historical storytelling is like the naming of the animals and things, at least in some respects. The important difference is that in naming the animals we are doing science and not necessarily bringing human aspects of culture into play. Science works with meaning at a lower level than do the humanities or the arts or theology. The similarities between the naming of the animals and history include the fact that in using language we humans are not completely free to create any world. There are constraints, both internal and external – rightness of rendering constraints rooted in God's being and purposes. And we are connected to other humans via our naming of things – we share conceptual schemes, language, culture, social relationships: we share a *Bildung*, if you will. In science, however, we do not find anything that will ultimately tell us who we humans are. At best science is an aspect of our *Bildung* but it cannot create human meaning or explain human purpose. But history, the telling of the story of the human past with meaning, connects us in our age to all those who have gone before. History is relational, the great communion of all persons, living and dead. It is the recognition of our relationship to all those of other ages. Again to speak symbolically, Sarah and Abraham carried the seed of the people of Israel in their bodies, indicating that all the people of Israel, and analogously, all humans, are related biologically. This is science. But when God renamed Jacob ("grabs the heel") Israel ("struggles with God"), the importance of historical naming beyond the biological is symbolically shouted. By this naming, a people were made, a nation created, and the story of salvation shaped. We are metaphysically, morally, and spiritually connected. Historical naming – the pressing into use of various conceptual schemes, and the telling, the writing, and the making of history that go with it – is thus to be contrasted to other human activities, such as the telling, the writing, and the making of fiction and its worlds, or the telling, writing, and making of scientific worlds.

Fictional naming – the making of a world out of whole cloth – is derivative upon historical naming and its use of concepts. So is scientific concept use. We create fictional worlds and scientific worlds by the use of language and concepts, epistemizing this over that, taking one thing to be more central than another, by categorizing, by composing, and by supplementing. But in both the fictional and the scientific, our thinking of a world potentially loses something. The former tends, sometimes, to subjectivize too much, while the later tends, sometimes, to overobjectivize. Tragedy goes awry, says Aristotle, when a good person is portrayed as becoming evil. Science goes awry, we might say, when scientists tell us that science explains human nature. But each has its own limits. Fiction, for example, arguably cannot bring us to the place where we actually accept a nonmoral framework.[2] Science faces limits when it leaps from description to prescription. Hence, history, and not fiction or science, is primary for world-making and rightness of rendering when it comes to telling us who we are as humans.

An important ambiguity lurks in this neighbourhood, for the term "history" is itself used in two ways. History can be understood as written and spoken on the one hand, and as lived and made on the other. What relationship holds between history as lived and made and history as written or spoken? What we do, what we say (short of telling stories about history), what we make, what we accomplish, these are the things of historical fact. These and these alone are the facts of history. The stories we tell of real people, of their triumphs, their failures, and their mediocrities, these are the things of written and spoken history. A difficulty arises here, for the facts upon which written history rests are recorded; otherwise there could be no written history. But in recording, whether that be in written, spoken, or other form, we interpret. When we interpret, we thereby give meaning to the facts. What are the facts? The facts are lived, in the first instance. But the facts are also recorded. So, facts can be said to be doubly "lived." The recording of the facts occurs simply as a person writes them. This is a reliving of the facts. They are lived and then relived in the recording. Written history entails that the twice-lived facts are interpreted again and therefore lived a third time. The lines cannot always be sharply drawn in sorting out facts and recorded *cum* lived facts, singly or doubly lived. Indeed, one cannot sort them out in some general way but must look case by case. For example, once a history text is written, it too becomes part of lived history.

Let's look first at being lived. What is it to live history, to make history? It is to act. We can distinguish an act from an event. In one sense, events are purely unhuman. It is tempting to say, then, that events can occur without us, to say that prehistory occurred in objective space and time, with no human watching, thinking, or commenting. But if irrealism is correct, there is no prehistory in this sense. Just as there are no stars if there are no humans, so there is no prehistory if there are no humans. To have events, we must have humans (or God or angels). Prehistory is like the World without humans. It is God's doing. For history, there must be humans. So enters our cognizing and epistemizing. Events are what they are via human noetic feats. Left on the level of "pure event," these things do not mean anything. Science, of course, tries to explain things. And philosophers provide accounts of material objects as well. There is meaning of various sorts, thus, in scientific or philosophical statements about events.

But that kind of meaning is distinct from the kind of meaning to which I want to call attention. In the realm of scientific and philosophical analysis of events, there are many worlds that we can create. I want to suggest that on this level of human endeavour, we cannot find meaning for ourselves as humans. Philosophical or scientific accounts of events are more or less left to work with the physical world. This is the realm of the "merely" natural, a realm that is inexplicable without another level of human interpretation. The human sciences cannot be reduced to the physical sciences. Naturalistic philosophy will not, in the end, provide human purposiveness. Neither can arts and theology be reduced to physics or chemistry. In the hierarchy of fixedness, the least fixed, the worlds to which humans can contribute the most noetically, are the scientific worlds. The more fixed are the social sciences, and then the arts, history, and theology. The reason is that the further toward humans we move, the further toward God's influence we move. We can and do impose a structure on our noetically created worlds at the scientific level, but there are many ways of doing so. As we go further up the ladder, closer to God, there is less variety of worlds. Humans are noetically real, from the point of view of human conceptual schemes. We do not make ourselves. The data is more firm, more fixed.

The meaning of events (beyond "what they are") can only be understood when there are meaning makers, that is, conscious, free persons. We are meaning makers, for we have purpose and intention, like God. Events become new and newly formed and shaped when humans are present, because humans have intentionality. Let's consider, for a moment, one implication of this. What are prehuman events for? What are they about? Do they mean anything? Such events, if we can even truly speak of them, can be about nothing, except in regard to our creative ability to invent them. Indeed, on Christian irrealism, prehuman events don't have being when there are no humans to experience them (except insofar as God or angels provide it). However, with humans comes the making of events about something – a meaning, a truth, a story. So we can look back at the realm and time of dinosaurs and create a prehuman world. But were there really events before humans? The only answer we can give, on Christian irrealism, is that had we been there, in the prehuman world, there would have been events. Our presence there now is only a presence through human construction (but not reconstruction) of the events. So what we refer to as prehuman prehistory could not, as such, possibly be on its own. Its reality depends on us and we weren't there. With the presence of the human, events come to mean something. Our affirming this or that event to talk about, to interpret, to make a story about, gives that event a meaning, a point, that it otherwise would not have.

Any event cognized is an event lifted out of one kind of being (that of the world we receive, so to speak, from other world-makers, whether God or humans) into another kind of world. And we do this by the lever of words and other symbol systems. We cannot know (read: come to discover the truth about) "plain" or "mere" events independent of our own conceptual schemes. Instead, we create the events and then know them, for such events are noetically irreal.

Human events, in contrast, we can know in a slightly different, although overlapping, way. Humans are both noetically real and also made by human noetic work. We are both received from God (and hence discoverable) and shaped by our own noetic feats (and hence discoverable as we create). Humans and our events arise out of our freedom and consciousness. However, there is a sort of sliding scale here, from the barest observation of human bodily movement (closer to the physical) to human intention (free and therefore made directly by the human who has the intention). Human events, as such, are the facts of history. Such events are lived events. Mere events are those with whom human noetic interaction is left on the level of science. These events, although interesting in their own right, are not going to explain human being in the end. We might say such events are not really lived at all but merely constructed for the purpose of science. Once-lived events, in contrast, are those that humans took note of, but of which there is no written, oral, or otherwise recorded account. No history can be written of these events. Twice-lived events are the facts of history, for they are recorded for posterity. Historical facts, then, are events – human events, twice-lived (experienced, named, and recorded). In so shaping and then recording events, we act. So there are actions. But actions also come in two kinds, actions dealing with events and pure actions.

Actions are in no sense mere events, for mere events come about by sheer force of nature. Our typical noetic realist way of talking about such things is to say events are what they are and we have no control over them. An irrealist can continue to talk this way, and should talk this way, for although human cognizing and epistemizing shape nature, we are still constrained by nature. Nature, no matter how we construct it, is still out of our control. There are limits to rightness of rendering.

Actions, in contrast, are in our control. They are made to come about by us. Actions are peculiar, nonnatural occurrences.[3] What is it to act? To act is to be human. To be human is to be free. Actions are free and not the result of blind nature. Herein lies the difference between mere events and actions. Mere events are "given" in a world. As such, mere events are not touched by the human even though we construct the way they are in a given world. In other words, we don't take the events of nature per se (even though they are theory-laden) to be events that have human meaning. Herein lies the difference between mere events and human events, for human events require free interpretation, the naming and shaping of events within conceptual schemes. This shaping and naming of events changes the ontology of mere events into human events and therefore into historical facts. Historical facts, then, are one and all interpreted, either named events or actions. The explosion of Mount Saint Helens is a named event, and therefore is historical fact. Named events occur at the intersection of "raw" nature and human interest. One acts when one names the explosion of Mount Saint Helens but one does not cause, pure and simple, the historical fact. But some things historical are simply human action: the decision to stay on the mountain, as some people did, even after being warned of its explosive potential. So we have historical facts rooted in event and historical facts rooted only in action. But all are named. Here we find the difficulty in talking about history as facts, as if the facts exist "out there," independent of human noetic contribution.

Now we face more directly the challenge of history. For on the one hand we know history to be a story bordered by and beholden to historical data, the written and spoken events and actions. On the other hand, human conceptualizing already touches these data, affirming them as important and meaningful. History seems to hold itself up by its own proverbial bootstraps. Yet history is unlike fiction, for fiction completely holds itself up by its bootstraps, whereas history does not. The fiction author can make up her facts. Historians cannot. The historian's facts are concocted out of "event-stuff," stuff that influences and therefore causes the historical facts to be the way they are. But historical facts also are influenced and therefore caused by the human, the other stuff of history. The human influence of conceptual schemes also contributes to the being of historical facts. Historical facts are left mysterious, neither simply determined nor simply free. History is not, thus, suspended above the earth by its own laces, but enigmatically suspended above and yet built upon the events that we cannot access without influencing. This mystery makes history distinctive. History is a spider's web so large that although it is suspended somewhat, we can't see where the anchors attach. We can only see the middle where we live and continue to give meaning to the web. We do this both by making parts of it and also by trusting that it all connects to parts made by others and, ultimately, that it is rooted in the "way things are." But the "way things are," the part we cannot see, remains shadowy.

The extreme relativist of antirealism or postmodernism is a subjectivist fiction writer on a cosmic scale, and therein lies the problem. We long to occupy the space of the Real, the Solid, the Impassable. Yet we don't want our lives drained of meaning and left cold and "objective" as the modernist physicalist image of nature would do. I suggest that the Truth lies in the mean between the "objective" world of modernist things and the "fictional" world of radical, rootless, postmodernism. Truth is manifest in the space we call history. History occupies the space between what is typically thought of as noetic realist facts – the supposed uninterpreted and thus "objective" events and stuff of the "way things are" – and the pure invention of radically subjectivized and fictionalized antirealism.

The key to why history lies between "objectivity" and "subjectivity" is that we humans are at its centre. Humans, unlike the nonhuman natural, are richly free, and that makes all the difference. Our freedom sets us apart from nature. Freedom is the central gift given to us. For in being free, we are made capable of using our conceptual creativity. And in using that creativity, we are capable of making worlds by affirming some things and denying others, of cutting, shaping, and moulding the World the way it seems best to us.

Our freedom enables our making history, both in the writing and in the acting. When we write history, we tell a story with meaning, for history is the story, the recounting, the telling of past human events with meaning. Yet when we act, we make history. Events alone do not a history make, for history is human and requires humans for its making. History is a garden, requiring order. Ultimately only free actions are the stuff of history, for mere events cannot play a part in that history. Only interpreted events can play a part. In interpretation, events cease to be mere events and become the events of historical data. As such, they have interacted with the freedom of the human and thus become something other than they were.

Our making of history is, then, dual. Our interpreting, our shaping of things, writes the history. Historian Perry Miller's *Errand into the Wilderness* is history written. It is based on historical facts, facts recorded. The recording is an action. Indeed, taking note of some event to record it involves an action. Our acting gives us something to write about. Our acting, then, is prior to writing history. Our acting makes history a thing with meaning. The meaning of history is not discovered but made by our actions. We act when we initially name historical facts either by interacting with events or by doing actions and later by recording them. Later we name, using our conceptual schemes, as we write history. The extreme antirealist claims there is nothing there to name. In raising up conceptual creativity to the status of what is most important, the extreme postmodern denies the very thing that gives naming its value, its rootedness in the facts of freedom. Extreme antirealism is freedom run amuck; it is freedom without limitations, without facts, without that mysterious objectivity in which the historian rests.

History thrives in the middle ground between "objectivity" – what the moderns wanted – and "subjectivity" – what the extreme antirealists sometimes revel in. Objectivity does not force the historian to leave the facts as "bare" facts. Facts are interpreted, they are "felt" facts – facts doubly and triply lived. Each historian tells a different story, makes a different world, by evaluating, emphasizing, sorting, weighing, and deciding which facts are to be presented and in what order, and with what importance. History is never fixed. The historian tells our past with both our actions and events important to those actions, and she tells this story with meaning. The historian makes our past. In this making, we are free. In this freedom we have our being. Our being, in turn, is rooted in God.

History, unlike radicalized subjectivism, is open to the future because of freedom. Indeed, history is never fixed because the future is never fixed. We are free to tell and, in fact, free to retell the story of the past. Yet mysteriously, freedom is bound by the fixedness of the past, to the facts of freedom. The stumbling block becomes the cornerstone. What is this objectivity? Whence this freedom?

Of course, our freedom as humans is part of our core being. It is present in each and every one of us as we live in history. This thin concept of the human is an important and central feature of humankind.

Freedom, of course, comes from God and it is in God that we find the final objectivity of the worlds. But in God, we find the intersociality of the Trinity. As such, although we come to view the worlds we make through our own eyes, our eyes are not finally separable from the eyes of God. Salvation is possible through the freedom God gives humans in creating us in God's image. The reason we are connected in and through history is that the objectivity qua subjectivity of God is extended into humankind. As we live into God's will, we live into the salvation that God provides for us as God incarnates the divine being into history to dwell among us as a human. What Jesus was by nature, we can become by grace. Grace is a publicly shared expression of God's love that God gives to us as the divine takes on human nature in the person of Jesus.

4 CHRISTIAN HISTORY: THE CREED

I return now to the very brief history recorded in the creed and the questions surrounding how the actions of God in history are fixed across the various historical worlds we can and do create in writing and telling history.

I've given an account of history as lived and history as spoken or written. History, in the latter sense, is the telling of past events with meaning. Let me illustrate with a simply example. Consider, again, the historical event. Historical events, I've suggested, have several aspects. The first is the empirical. The empirical, of course, is up for grabs on irrealistic terms. That a certain event – let's say that a rock fell on State Highway 101 in 1977 blocking the road and hence stopping traffic – occurred is something that is the way it is because of our noetic feats on the level of conceptualization, observations, and so forth. But we can report those events now because of human memory or written record (or video or related human record). Written or oral history is built on these records. Thus, written or oral history – the telling of these events with some sort of meaning – involves human noetic construction not only of events but of the past facts. We noted the event, singling it out, and thereby giving it human meaning, something beyond our basic linguistic meaning. There are two levels of fact, if you will, the event-fact, and the human-fact.

As a first order of clarity, then, I've distinguished between events (which are nonhuman – the rock falling) and actions (which are human

– the car stopping because of the rock – or better, the decision to stop the car). We might say that the fact that the rock fell is noetically constructed (that is, it is contextually embedded in some conceptual and epistemic scheme), while the human action (the decision itself) is more fixed. We can tell a lot of different stories about the nature of rocks and why they fall (scientific theories can abound), but fewer stories about the historical facts. Lest this seem an odd result, let me clarify.

If anything is noetically constructed, the decision itself is. But such decisions are entirely internal to the actor, who is among the divinely constructed entities of the World. The rock falling, however, is a publicly constructed event (via, let's say, an Aristotelian model of macro-size physical objects along with a certain account of chemicals interacting and/or subatomic features of physical objects). Others, however, might take it to be entirely different (via, let's say, a Whiteheadian account of "objects" with an alternative chemistry). But since there are humans involved, and humans are themselves given by the divinely created order, the presence of humans can't be explained away by some other human noetic activity. We are, so to speak, "stuck" with humans, but not with rocks.

So, when Jesus does his historical work on the cross, he does it by decision and hence we are all "stuck with" the actions he performed (the decision to follow the will of God, for example), as well as the actions others performed (Pilate, let's say, turning Jesus over to the guards for torture and death). While we can try to theorize the actions away, we cannot, at least if a world is rightly rendered. The actions of God and humans cannot be explained away or conceptualized out of being.

But what about the cross on which Jesus died? Is it fixed, so to speak? I think the answer is that the nature of the cross as a physical object is a whole lot less fixed than what the cross has come to symbolize in human culture. We all epistemize and cognize the religious nature of the cross the way we do (speaking English, knowing other things about the history of Roman torture and capital punishment, knowing the theology of the New Testament, etc.) but we could have cognized-epistemized the physicalness of the cross other ways than we do. So human action is more fixed than merely physical events. Science and other theoretical accounts of the world's facts are less firm than history and historical facts. History is less firm than divine facts. The reason for this is simple. God and God's decisions are involved in divine situations, that is, situations needful for God's interaction with humans, culminating in human salvation. Indeed, in the divine realm, we have left facts created simply by humans and moved into facts created increasingly directly by God's work. This does not mean there will not be competing ways the World is in regard to facts such as the death and resurrection of Jesus. However, God is a revelatory God and God reaches into history and shares the divine conceptual framework with us (albeit in our terms) and through the history of the Church continues to reveal the divine self to us. Theologically we call this the work of the Holy Spirit.

Of course, actions are interpretable in many ways, and we have many competing versions of historical actions. We can say that Jesus' death was an unfortunate event in the course of violent human history, and nothing more. Or perhaps we can say that Jesus was a fool, and his death was a worthless attempt to get us all to love one another. Or we can say it was God, in Christ, reconciling the world to God's own self. Which is it? Won't the historical fact of the matter be the result of world-making on our part? Won't there, in short, be different "worlds," one in which Jesus is accomplishing a cosmic good vis-à-vis humanity's relationship to God, one in which a mere human is trying to motivate his peers to act better, and one in which Jesus is simply caught in the machine-like, crushing movement of human violence?

At this point, I return to my earlier observations that some worlds are not worlds we can legitimately construct, that is, that some worlds do not please God. To create historical accounts of the work of God in history that deny God's work in history is just to wallpaper over the presences of God. Of course, sorting out which worlds please God and which don't is part of the challenge of human theorizing. But admitting this does not entail that just anything can go theologically. That God created human beings, that humans fell, that God provided a means of salvation so humans can enter the full fellowship of the love of God and the intimacy of the Trinity: these are the great truths of the Gospel. But our theories about how this works, of course, are creative attempts to understand the deep and profound mysteries of our creation and purpose and, indeed, the mysteries of the God who is both hidden and revealed.

Take, for example, the doctrine of the atonement and the several theories that attend it. Each one is a human construct, a way of creating a world, in which God's salvific activity makes sense. But let us say, without exploring the theories, that they are, strictly speaking, incompatible with one another. Does just one of them have to be true? No, not on Christian irrealism. Those who hold to an Anselmian model live in quite a different world from those who hold the *Christus victor* model or an Abelardian view. And each can be true, in its own world. The important point is not which is "finally right" – there is no one that is finally right. The point is, rather, is God pleased with our models and efforts at rightly rendering a theological world? I propose, in fact, that we will be living through all eternity exploring various models, creatively and with passion. But there is no one model that is true, outside the world in which the model itself is proposed. While God is interested in us having true beliefs, God is equally interested in us fulfilling our human potential for creativity, love, and beauty.

History, thus, is central among the sciences and arts, for in many ways, it overlaps the two. Furthermore, it is in the actions of history that new worlds are created and developed. We live and move in history, just as God acts and moves in history. Indeed, we live because God acts. Jesus' coming in history fixes certain things. But is there only one way to understand the work of Christ on the cross or is the theory of atonement that we attach to the historic events on the cross determined by history itself? No, these accounts and theories were developed as Christians saw the need to understand God's acts more fully, just as we have various new accounts of history, new stories we tell, based on new research, new pictures, and new theories of what has happened in other areas of human life. In a sense, history as we make it – that is, history as we live it – is the making of new worlds. But Jesus participates in our worlds too, for Jesus qua human and qua God participated in making a new aspect of the World, an aspect of the World we cannot deny, since Jesus is God. So, to answer the question, did Jesus have to die the way he did to provide salvation? Maybe not. The incarnation seems necessary but does his death on the cross? Perhaps there were alternatives, but they would have been alternative ways history would have gone, not alternatives from God's point of view theologically. God, too "makes it up" as God goes along in response to human choices, human insights, as well as human stupidities. But once things are fixed in the World, they are fixed. How we explain and understand them, however, is what the various histories and theologies are about, what the created human worlds are about. Yet the closer we get to God, the more fixedness there is in how we can make a world.

5 THEOLOGY, HISTORY, AND FICTION

Returning now to objectivity and subjectivity, I suggested that on Christian irrealism, religion and history are tied together at the more fixed end, with the social sciences next, followed by the arts and humanities and, finally, the sciences the least fixed. God is objective in that God is fundamentally independent of human conceptual schemes at God's core being. Humans are objective as well because of God's creative work. After that, the things made – the worldly – are increasingly "up to us." The things made by humans, whether in the arts or the sciences, are therefore less fixed than humans and certainly than God. But their makings are objectively based in the subjectivity of God and human makers. Thus the objective and the subjective come together in the Trinitarian God who exists at the core in the tri-unity of Three Persons in loving relationship and creativity with one another.

But if things become more fixed as we move from science to the arts, and then through history to religion, and if religion (and its theology) is loaded with metaphor, doesn't theology come close to the arts, and in particular poetry or fiction? Is theology all poetry or fiction, or at least all metaphor? No, not anymore than any science is. Theology can't be done independently of history and history is where God is. What kinds of stories we tell will of course involve metaphor. But metaphor is not without its own truth, as we have seen. Some metaphors fit God, some don't, just as is true with humans. But humans have a core nature created by God and thus there are limits to what can be said metaphorically of humans. To reduce humans to machines, for example, is a metaphor that doesn't fit. A world-version generating a world in which "humans are just physical" comes out true is a badly formed world-version and won't be a true one. Some metaphors don't fit. So it is with God. Some metaphors don't fit God and thus worlds in which they are used to describe God are poorly formed and finally to be rejected. However, the metaphors we find in the creed, such as that God is Father, Son, and Holy Spirit, are themselves historically rooted and as such, are not the only metaphors that we can and should use. We must hold to them, but we can describe God otherwise and still have a fit. Matriarchal language in which

God is Mother or Julian of Norwich's saying that we can "suckle at the breasts of Jesus"[4] are equally valuable and useful metaphors, also rooted in history. Such metaphors present God in profoundly helpful ways and we as theologians and Christians seeking to practice the life "after God's own heart" should strive to have as many appropriate metaphors as possible.

But still, the critic is likely to say, isn't there, in irrealism, a blurring of the lines between fiction and metaphor in contrast with literal, descriptive theology? But the irrealist can reply: What kinds of reality do we want to get at? Relational realities are communicated better by fiction than science. Theology, as rooted in history, is connected to fiction because we tell stories rooted in human experience. History overlaps, in its storytelling aspects, with fiction but is not identical to fiction. History is also rooted in the empirical and human facts. The facts, however, are world-rooted. But, then, which humans show up in the various worlds is world-rooted in the sense that decisions made by humans bring new humans into the World (via birth). How a given human turns out in a world is dependent on the decisions of people in the World. That is why the virgin birth is so important. This decision by Mary, in conjunction with the Holy Spirit, brought a new human into the World, a human who was God's own self. A new life was about to be lived and a new life about to be given for all humanity. Jesus, as an actor in the human drama, is not dependent on the noetic contributions of (other) humans at Jesus' core. At his core is his freedom and freedom, no matter how we might modify it theoretically, still is powerful for action in the World. In this way Jesus is like all other humans. Just as I do not create my wife Susan noetically at her core, so I do not create Jesus. However, Jesus, in virtue of his free choices, can decide how he is going to be, within the normal bounds of human constraint. But Jesus is also deity, God among us. As such, his actions and doings are those of God. As such, some of his actions, in particular the miracles, have a different status from the actions of the typical human person.

Now of course we can tell different stories about Jesus. But with Jesus, and other human persons, we begin to see the limits of history. Since God is revealed in this history, much of the truth told in the creed is literal, historical truth and, if we take the creed to be delivered via the Church councils under the work of the Holy Spirit, then we get a description of fact that will hold in each and every world made by human noetic contribution.

But what we say about those historical facts, how we bring meaning out of them, is open to considerable human noetic sway. Theology can be literal and it can be metaphorical and it can be both, just as the creed is. The traditional Christian can be irrealist about many ways of taking the creed, but the limits are set by the social and spiritual interaction between humans and God.

I close this chapter with a lengthy quote from C.S. Lewis. In an address, in which he was asked to answer the question, "Is Theology Poetry?" Lewis said,

> the differences between the Pagan Christs (Balder, Osiris, etc.) and the Christ Himself is much what we should expect to find. The Pagan stories are all about someone dying and rising, either every year, or else nobody knows where and nobody knows when. The Christian story is about a historical personage, whose execution can be dated pretty accurately, under a named Roman magistrate, and with whom the society that He founded is in a continuous relation down to the present day. It is not the difference between falsehood and truth. It is the difference between a real event on the one hand and dim dreams or premonitions of that same event on the other. It is like watching something come gradually into focus; first it hangs in the clouds of myth and ritual, vast and vague, then it condenses, grows hard and in a sense small, as a historical event in first century Palestine. This gradual focussing goes on even inside the Christian tradition itself. The earliest stratum of the Old Testament contains many truths in a form which I take to be legendary, or even mythical – hanging in the clouds, but gradually the truth condenses, becomes more and more historical. From things like Noah's Ark or the sun standing still upon Ajalon, you come down to the court memoirs of King David. Finally you reach the New Testament and history reigns supreme, and the Truth is incarnate. And "incarnate" is here more than a metaphor. It is not an accidental resemblance that what, from the point of view of being, is stated in the form "God became Man" should involve, from the point of view of human knowledge, the statement "Myth became Fact." The essential meaning of all things came down from the "heaven" of myth to the "earth" of history. In so doing, it partly emptied itself of its glory, as Christ emptied Himself of His glory to be Man. That is the real explanation of the fact that Theology, far from defeating

its rivals by a superior poetry, is, in a superficial but quite real sense, less poetical than they. That is why the New Testament is, in the same sense, less poetical than the Old. Have you not often felt in Church, if the first lesson is some great passage, that the second lesson is somehow small by comparison – almost, if one might say so, humdrum? So it is and so it must be. That is the humiliation of myth into fact, of God into Man; what is everywhere and always, imageless and ineffable, only to be glimpsed in dream and symbol and acted poetry of ritual becomes small, solid – no bigger than a man who can lie asleep in a rowing boat on the Lake of Galilee. You may say that this, after all, is a still deeper poetry. I will not contradict you. The humiliation leads to a greater glory. But the humiliation of God and the shrinking or condensation of the myth as it becomes a fact are also quite real.[5]

Apart from the description of Christ as becoming Man rather than human, in many ways, this sense of Lewis's about the presentation of truth and reality from the mythical to the historical captures what I want to say about the question, is theology poetry or metaphor or fiction. The objective and the subjective come together in irrealism and we should celebrate the historical, for in history God is revealed, but we have only begun to understand God.

Irrealism, the Worlds, and Mystical Experience: God as the Final Framework

In Genesis 2 we are told that God creates the world and places *adam* in it. God, finding no helper for *adam*, creates the animals out of the dust of the ground. God then brings all the beasts of the fields and the birds of the air to *adam* to name. After the naming is complete, the list includes beasts of the field, birds of the air, and livestock. Did *adam* name a new kind of category, did he create a world here? Perhaps. I wouldn't want to build an entire theological thesis on this point alone, but it is interesting. Suppose then that God, as the ultimate source of the first irreal world, and as the ultimate unity of the worlds, universes, and domains, is the key to understanding the many worlds that we can and do make. Why does God let so many worlds and their contents exist?

God made humans free, creative, and powerful. Why not expect there to be many worlds, although limited by concerns about rightness of rendering? Why not propose that the ultimate rightness of rendering concern is God? What feature or features of God are important for our right rendering of the worlds we make? I suggest two. One is the intersocial nature of the intimacy of the Persons of God in the unity of the Godhead. Second is God's pleasure in social relationship. God made us. God made us in God's own image. God made us creative, free, social, and capable of intimacy. God made us both to please God's Three Persons and to please each other.

Some worlds we create bring God pleasure. Some worlds, on the other hand, do not please God. Worlds of anger, racism, sexism, hatred, war, are all worlds with which God is not pleased. Worlds of love, kindness, and fairness are worlds with which God is pleased. But there are other worlds, too, with which God might be pleased, worlds incompatible with one another but quite whole and healthy within themselves. I've mentioned on a number of occasions one pair of these worlds, viz., the Aristotelian world of enduring substances and the Whiteheadian world of temporary moments. Each seems coherent and fruitful and interesting in its own description. Each seems true on the grounds laid out by the world described. Is there a singular account these worlds could be reduced to? Is one more right than the other? It is certainly hard for us to tell. On the basis of noetic irrealism, both can be equally good, equally beautiful, equally real and true, so long as both please God.

Another pair of worlds might be the Calvinian and the Arminian world. Full descriptions of these worlds seem incompatible with one another, yet both are interesting, powerful accounts of humanity's relationship to God. Which one is right? Is there some reduction of one to another or of both to a third that is plausible? Is one more right than another? Surely the world that a Calvinist lives in is not the world the Arminian lives in. One need only spend some time at Calvin College and then some time at my home institution, George Fox University, to see that the worlds are quite different. And rightly so, I believe. These two worlds should be celebrated, not deflated. God will, I think, bless both ways of creating worlds, even Christian worlds.

Throughout this book, but especially the last several chapters, there is a theme of creativity on the part of humans. This, I believe, is to be celebrated but not foolishly. Such creativity is both open and limited. It is open to God and all God's riches, and limited by God. God, in the divine social nature, creates us for community and opens the divine being to us. The theoretical side of this position has dominated the discussion. But there is also a practical, emotional, or spiritual side, if you will. I want to turn in this final chapter to consider that practical, spiritual side.

I THE UNITY OF FAITH AND THEORY: GOD AS THE UNITY OF THE WORLDS

Many Christian liberal arts colleges and universities strive toward an understanding of the integration of faith and learning. On the theory developed here, such integration will be deeply spiritual and reality-making. Reality has an eschatological nature. Beauty, Goodness, and Truth come together. The sciences and arts are two sides of the same coin because each can be spent in order to understand. Ultimately, all understanding is aimed toward God. As one's soul develops in relation to God, one's world-making – whether theory design, art making, or house building – does as well. But in the end, as we approach God the line between our human frailty and God's salvific work in developing relationship with us will blur. In the end, theory will drop off, as one step removed from the Real, and we shall be with God forever. Faith, hope, and love, we are told, but the greatest is love. Love is relational, not propositional or symbolic. Love, finally, is reality. If we try to live reflecting this way now, then the integration of faith and learning is not simply something done in one's head. It is something one lives out among people and with God.

The view of heaven as a total submersion of the human soul into the divine fellowship of God and the communion of the saints in the mystery of love is a model for the Christian university. Yes, we learn our theory. But reading books about sexuality is not sexuality itself. While analogies and metaphors can convey a little, they cannot convey the full reality. Parallel to our sexual relations, studying about the world and people is not living the life of love itself. The integration of faith and learning must finally end in a life well lived in solidarity with others.

The Christian understanding of the value of human life is not only a cognitive enterprise, it is a social reality. It is, finally, to understand the identification of ourselves with the other by living with the other. In the Christian story, our identification is to be, in particular, with the poor, the needy, the outcast. This is a life lived in the presence of God as God is present in other people. Christian solidarity is not just solidarity in the sense of all having the same goal but solidarity in the sense of the communion of the saints where all the goods of Jesus Christ are the goods of the members of the communion. Further development of this implication has to await another study. Note, however, that the goal of Christianity in love is a goal that helps us all overcome the bifurcation of the objective and subjective. The union of the two, the overcoming of the distinction, results in complete solidarity. In contrast to Rorty's extreme relativism, we don't have to choose between solidarity and objectivity.

In C.S. Lewis's *Narnia Chronicles,* Lucy always wants to know about Edmund's soul but Aslan repeatedly tells her to keep to her own life and business. So do we want to know about others and can't. Gossip is rooted in this kind of wanting to know. But true knowledge of the other is to assume that the other is more important than one's self. All my ethical actions have to have my name attached, but in attaching my name, I attach the name of Jesus, for in the Christian story I have the life of Jesus. Furthermore, in attaching Jesus' name, I attach the others, too, for then I hear their voices and we learn to speak as one. In the Kingdom, we will all know one another in knowing God, not seeking to know others in judgment but in self-same uniqueness, just as the Trinity knows and is known.

I've been speaking of goodness, but what of truth and beauty and the relationship among the three? Each of these is a revelatory act of God, an exemplification of God in and of Godself. Truth understood as a copy of something else, or beauty or goodness as representations of something else, fall short of the pure unity of these three. They don't copy the way things are, they exemplify it. The book *He Is There and He Is Not Silent*[1] is about the revelation of God in Scripture. I am suggesting not only that God is there and is not silent, but that God is there and is not abstract.[2] To reveal, we think, is to have something "there" that we can then show to others, like revealing what's behind the curtain. To reveal is to show what's hidden. But what's hidden on the view developed here is God and God will always be hidden in the sense that no matter how wide and broad and deep our creative means of expression, God is greater. Yet the Christian God is also the revealed God. In revelation, we know God intimately insofar as we can live in that world. But there is always more. Just as people are never psychologically "freeze framed" in their development, neither is God. Just as we achieve some truth, we see God being revealed elsewhere and in a different story.

Isn't this as frustrating as the view that God is fixed and we can never get God right? No, that is to misunderstand the very nature of the Trinity. The Persons of the Trinity are constantly self-surpassing themselves in goodness, beauty, and truth, yet fully living in the other. The difference, we might say, between humans and the persons of the Trinity is that we will never be infinite and our living in God has much catching up to do. But we have eternity.

2 MYSTICISM AND THE PRESENCE OF GOD

We don't always have to wait to glimpse that eternity. Let me say something about objectivity, mystical experience, and world-making.

Those who work on the subject of mystical experiences know that many reports of "high" mystical experiences are given in terms of an absolute sense of certainty. Often lifelong doubts disappear, a new sense of direction is given, and the recipient knows in some sense stronger than any other that he or she has experienced God. Yet often the recipient is also given a sense of the simplicity of reality. Mother Teresa is a good example. The gospel, she said, is simply love. Along with simplicity comes a deep commitment to God and yet an openness to alternative ways of understanding God that is very hard to explain in any clear and full sense. There is a knowledge that God is the only way of salvation, that there is only one ultimate way to God, and yet also a sense that people are on their own paths and that God will somehow take care of them.[3]

I think these results are best explained by a theory in which the actual content of beliefs formed in a mystical experience is God. This experience, then, is not to be taken as just some other belief-forming situation. The manner in which God is the content of one's theistic beliefs, given one of these powerful experiences, is different from the manner in which snow is white is the content of one's snow belief, even though there are some parallels. This difference in manner is explicable in terms of the difference in the kind of thing with which one is dealing. In the case of snow, the content is one of many alternative contents that might be the content of one's beliefs, depending on which world one lives in. In the case of God, there is no alternative content. There is only the finally and utterly Real, the one being who exists on its own and in no way relies in its core being on the creative activity of the human mind. One is here in contact with the objective God, the one who holds the universes and worlds together. But one becomes hesitant to say that the God of this experience is simply one way rather than another, that one theory about God is better than another. For all the worlds we create and all the ways in which we attempt to creatively respond to this objective God fall short of reaching the core of God in the divine totality. Now I see through a glass darkly, but then face to face. Knowledge will pass away – our sense, our need to "get things right" will pass away. And we shall not simply know God at a distance, but rather be in God's presence. Mystical experiences are glimpses of this place in which God is objectively present in our very souls. In that place all our attempts to "get God right" will be sorted out, blessed or cursed, and we shall stand not before the world, but before God, the Truth, the Good, and the Beautiful.

3 MYSTICISM AND CERTAINTY

Thus far, we've only the suggestion that the content of one's (mystical) beliefs is God's own being. In another place, I develop an epistemological framework showing how mystical experience could resolve what I call the existential problem of religious diversity.[4] There I interpret the story of the Garden of Eden in such a way that we (Adam and Eve) overstepped our ontological and epistemological bounds, thus letting sin enter the world. I also argue that what I call the Greek version of humility is a natural result of viewing the world with fallen eyes, whereas the Christian version corrects the mistakes in the Garden with regard to a kind of epistemic arrogance. For the mystics, humility is a prerequisite for, but not a guarantee of, experiencing God in authentic ways. In the Garden, we asserted ourselves in our will and detached ourselves from God's will. In the mystic experience – at least in its highest form, union without distinction – one's will becomes again united with God's by means of love. But in order to get there, in order for us to have such a direct contact with God, our selves must disappear – our sense, our imaginations, our understanding, and our wills. When God appears to the mystic, a certainty of God's presence replaces any doubt. But what is this certainty?

In *Repairing Eden*, I speculate about a less metaphorical account of what it means to have, as some of the mystics say, God burn or wound one's soul. Here's the speculation.[5] To be wounded or burned in one's soul is, I believe, to be epistemically transformed because one is ontically transformed. The first part of my suggestion is that in (some) mystical experiences, God simply rewires our epistemic faculties. I don't know how, of course. But I know that we don't have certainty about much, especially about things supernatural. Yet mystic after mystic claims to have a certainty about these experiences that he or she does not have about anything else. If this "rewiring" suggestion is correct, it may turn out that terms such as knowledge and belief (and perhaps even certainty itself) are just not applicable.

The second part of my suggestion is this. If the phenomenological reports of the mystics are accurate, then God really does enter the soul of the mystic in such a way that she or he is "metaphysically aware" (rather than simply epistemically aware) of God. Thus, one's epistemic mechanisms are changed because one's ontology is changed. I noted in chapter 1 that if Christian irrealism is correct, it will radically change our view of epistemology. Here I'm indicating one way in which such changes might go.

Certainty (and here I am not talking about psychological certitude but epistemic certainty) requires, in a special way, and unlike mere knowledge, that one cannot be mistaken. While it is true that if I know p, then p is true, it does not follow that I cannot be mistaken, for as we are aware from various versions of the Gettier problem, it is possible that p is true, that I be justified or warranted in believing p, and yet I not know p. There is a gap between the justification and the truth. With certainty, however, if I am certain that p, not only is p true, but I cannot be mistaken about p's truth. My justification (if it should be so called) guarantees the truth. I have certainty, then, if the justification cannot go awry without thereby making the belief held false.

But how can this be, that justification cannot go awry? We have learned from the history of epistemology that justification and all its cognates and near relatives never bring us to certainty, at least certainty about the way things are "out there." While we may have certainty, because of "privileged access," about our own mental states, such as that I'm in pain, or that I'm having a putative perception of redness, I can't have certainty that there is a tree outside my door or that there is a red ball in front of me. Indeed, our epistemic practices all standardly fall short not just of certainty, but even of what William Alston calls "full, reflective justification" – justification where one can, so to speak, step outside the practice and have justification for all one's justifiers. Epistemic circularity is involved in our doxastic practices in such a manner that at best we have a weaker kind of justification than we might prefer, and most surely than what would be required for certainty. While all this doesn't demand skepticism, it does tend to show that certainty about things "out there" isn't likely. So how is certainty possible for the mystics, if at all?

First let me say that when one has metaphysical awareness rather than epistemic awareness, one has moved from the realm of justified belief, or rationality, or knowledge to the realm of certainty. Certainty, thus, is not an epistemological notion, at least not in the sense of there being a (potentially) skeptical gap between what is known and how it is known. So long as we have justification (which is about having reasons or evidence or grounds, etc.) that is only truth-conducive, we cannot have certainty. To have certainty, the being true must somehow not be separable from the awareness of the truth, even in terms of justification. One's belief cannot be justified by something else.

Perhaps the solution lies in being clear about what one is certain about, if anything. It is often suggested that one cannot be certain about anything except what is "inside" one's mind. Since what is inside one's mind is subjective, and there are no completely reliable ways of moving from what is subjective to what is objective, certainty about external reality is not forthcoming. But this confuses a number of issues. The difficulty is not in moving from the so-called subjective to the objective, where the latter is some sort of synonym for the external world. It is just as much an objective fact about the world that Susan is in pain (when she is) as that there is a tree fifteen feet from the front of the house (when there is). One straightforward meaning of "objective" is simply "true." The difference between the Susan case and the tree case, then, is not their objectivity (their truth) but the situations that make the descriptions true. In the first case, "Susan is in pain" is true because of some mental state Susan is in, something which wouldn't and indeed couldn't be the case if Susan weren't aware of her mental states in general and, in this case, specifically the state of being in pain. In the tree case, no one's mental state need be involved in order for "there is a tree fifteen feet from the front of the house" to be true. Susan's being in pain is no less objective than the tree's being fifteen feet from the house, even though her pain is accessible only to her (directly).

Now of course there is some sense in which the former, but not the latter, is subjective. "Subjective" then means that what makes it true that Susan is in pain is that Susan is in a certain mental state, a state we recognize as obtaining internally to Susan. Because of that subjectivity, our means of accessing the truth about Susan's pain is different from our means of accessing the truth about external objects. The typical way in which we access the truth about the so-called external world is via some complicated set of doxastic practices in virtue of which our minds are put into some effective (causal) contact with things that are typically thought to be not in any way dependent upon our minds. In contrast, our means of accessing the truth about our inner states is immediate. There is no need for a causal chain from outside to inside, for the thing one is put into effective contact with is already inside. This privileged access is not, as I've already suggested, strictly epistemic. Rather, it is ontic.

Take the pain in my left leg. What is the difference between my seeming to have pain and my having a pain? The epistemic language of how things seem to me just is a description of the pain itself. Even if I am having a "phantom pain" in my now (let's say) amputated left leg, the pain is no less real, since it seems to me that I have it. The pain is objectively (truly) there, because it is subjectively (internally) felt. Another example. Suppose I'm thinking about my wife. What I am in effective contact with is not, of course, my wife, but my thought about her, at least on the typical analysis of these things. Simply to have the thought of my wife is what makes it true that I'm having the thought of her. I cannot be mistaken about having the thought. So here again, the thought is objectively (truly) there and I cannot be mistaken about it.

Whatever else one might think about Descartes' *cogito,* I believe his was an attempt to link the ontological structure of the world with a certain result. My mere thinking is enough, he argued, ontically to guarantee that I, in fact, am. I cannot think that I do not exist without thinking, and the thinking is enough to guarantee that I exist. The ontology guarantees the truth. One is tempted to say that "I am" is true because I think it is. But that isn't quite right, for that makes it sound as if there is some sort of causal relationship between my thinking p and p's being the case. The relationship isn't one of causality, at least in the direction from my thoughts to the world. And of course, one standard criticism of Descartes is that he can't move from mental events to a substantival ontology. At best, one gets direct access to one's thoughts, so certainty is limited to beliefs about my own mental events or perhaps reports of one's psychological states. The move from these "internal" events or states (one's thoughts) to some truth "external" to the mind (my being) is where skepticism slips in its invidious blade. But notice that in my examples above, I don't move from thought to "external" reality. I only claim that certainty is had about internal facts.

Nevertheless, skepticism does its filleting work where there is some metaphysical "gap" between the interiority of the knower and the exteriority of the thing known. To have certainty, there should be no gap, no place for doubt to enter. As Descartes himself wondered, one's knowledge of one's own body might be more than we can really know, let alone the rest of the so-called external world. And as the standard criticism of Descartes has it, one can't even get to the substantival notion of the self, for it, too, is external to thought. So perhaps all we are left with is thoughts. Enter a type of solipsism. Whereas solipsism as typically understood as a theory claiming that all that is are me and my thoughts, this more truncated brand of solipsism says that all there is are (my) thoughts.

Descartes can only take us so far, and he can't take us even to our own bodies. Here I want to emphasize not the existence of one's own body, but the experience of one's own body. It seems that Descartes is too much a rationalist and not enough an empiricist, resulting in his strong dualism. His radical separation of the soul from the body is more than is required metaphysically and, in fact, is just not part of our general experience. Aristotle is closer with his claim that we are ensouled bodies and to separate one from the other is, indeed, impossible, at least practically. I also suggest that we cannot think without thinking "through" a body. Kant is right when he begins with space and time. To be finite is to have a spatial/temporal location and framework. I might add that in certain ways, the Bible's account of human nature is closer to Aristotle's than it is to Descartes'. God takes earth and breathes into it and then *adam* becomes a "living soul." So humans are not soul plus body. Rather it is dirt plus God's breath that makes a living soul. But we needn't worry about the details of that issue here, for even if Descartes is right about his dualist ontology of humans, it remains that from an experiential point of view, it feels to us individually as if I am myself-in-my-body and it is the phenomenal "feeling" we are certain about. I cannot be mistaken about the fact that this is how my experience in the world is, whatever the world actually is. *Adam*'s experience of himself, as a being in his own (even if only phenomenal) body, was as certain for him as it is for us. Likewise for Descartes.

But thus far we have only solipsism – my thoughts. How is God to overcome this euhemeristic tendency in humans? How is God to make the divine "exterior" existence certain for us? We first must take a look at whether or not our wilful states belong in the category of objective (true), yet subjective (inner) certainties. I will to write this book. I will to pick up a pen. I will to do the right thing on this occasion, when I've so often done the wrong thing in the past. The willing state is a psychological state about which I am certain in the ontic sense I've described above. Just as being in pain and seeming to be in pain are ontically identical, so willing to do X and seeming to will X are ontically the same. Willing is a psychological state about which I can't be mistaken. Just as it makes little sense to say to a person who seems to herself to be in pain that she is not, so it makes little sense to say to a person who seems to herself to will to do X that she does not, actually, will X. So our wilful states are certainties.

But how is God to make the divine presence certain? Isn't God external to us, and rather more like the tree fifteen feet from the house than like the pain I feel? But the mystic doesn't understand God to be exterior in that sense. Rather, Godself enters into the soul of the human person, replacing the human will with God's own will. On the level of the will, there is no distinction between God and the mystic. Since God's will is infinite and infinitely greater than any human will, it thus seems to the mystic as if he or she were God. Just as I am in my body (where phenomenally, I cannot be mistaken), so the mystic is in God (or at least God's will). It is not only that God is present to the mystic; this leaves God as external only. Rather, the mystic is present in God, just as he or she is present in him- or herself (that is, in the phenomenal body, not just the body).

But the contrary is true as well. God is present in the mystic, just as the mystic's soul is present in the phenomenal body. This reflects the ontology of the "double inclusion" phenomena mentioned by Nelson Pike as he explains the mystic's claims. God is in the mystic and the mystic is in God. But both feel like "myself-in-my-(phenomenal)-body."[6]

But here we encounter a difficulty. The mystics often claim that their knowledge of God is more certain than anything else. How can anything be more certain than the certainty we have of our own being-in-my-body? My suggestion is that humans are a will plus a (finite) nature.[7] In our fallen state, our wills are united to our finite beings. In humility, we detach our wills from our finite beings, letting God's will replace our will. As such, God's will becomes alloyed with us. Because of this, our (relative) certainty about ourselves pales in comparison to the certainty of God's being, for our finitude is replaced by something of much greater, indeed, infinite magnitude.

So how is certainty possible? It's not, if one attempts to reach certainty about purely "exterior" things. But God is not purely exterior, if the mystics are right. God is interior in the same way that my own will is in the normal course of life. Since I can be certain about my own will, then when God's will replaces mine, I can be certain of God's will. Now of course there are some problems here. What does it mean to say that God's will replaces mine? Isn't this some sort of metaphor that needs further analysis? But why say that? If the phenomenal reports of the mystics can be taken at face value, as I think William Alston and Nelson Pike have shown, then their phenomenal reports must be accepted as certain for them, just as if they were reporting on their own psychological states or thoughts. This won't, obviously, have any bearing on whether I or you should accept the mystics' reports as certain for us. But that, surely, would be to expect too much of certainty, at least in this life.

But this life is not all there is, if the Christian account is right. And if Christian irrealism rightly renders the worlds, we can participate in making and thus understanding and thus knowing the very heaven that God wills for us. As we move toward willing what God wills, we will move toward willing the good, the beautiful and the true for everyone else. In the end, that is solidarity.

Notes

CHAPTER ONE

1 The basic distinction of "relative to" vs "in virtue of" is referred to by Michael Lynch. Lynch borrows it from Ernest Sosa. My way of unpacking the distinction, however, is my own. See Lynch, "Pluralism, Metaphysical Realism and Ultimate Reality," 72. See also Alston, *A Sensible Metaphysical Realism*, 11, 12, where he rejects the notion that humans causally make things via conceptual-theoretical schemes.

2 Taking the story seriously does not necessitate taking it literally.

3 But once again not necessarily as literal fact.

4 See Genesis 2 where before Adam named the animals, there is no mention of cattle or livestock but after Adam does his naming magic there is.

5 See Walton, *Mimesis as Make-Believe*.

6 Goodman, *Languages of Art*, 112.

7 Goodman, *Of Mind and Other Matters*, 42.

8 McDowell, *Mind and World*.

9 McDowell clearly attempts to reject idealism, at least of a certain sort. More on this below.

10 Putnam, "Foreword."

11 I admit, however, that a number of my uses of terms are reliant on William Alston and Michael Lynch.

12 There is more behind this suggestion than may first meet the eye. Michael Lynch develops an important distinction between thin and thick concepts that I press into use. Taking "world" to be elastic is a move analogical to Lynch's use of "object" as elastic. See Lynch, *Truth in Context*, 83–6.

13 This is the way I use the term. Unfortunately, there is little agreement on how to use it. So especially when I discuss Nelson Goodman's position, the reader needs to be on her guard so as not to read my understanding of the term into Goodman's, or vice versa.

14 This is unless you hold a position dealing with possible worlds such as David Lewis's where all possible worlds are also actual worlds. See Lewis, *On the Plurality of Worlds*.

15 Goodman and Elgin, *Reconceptions in Philosophy*, 51.

16 Lynch, *Truth in Context*, 94, 95.

17 Ibid., 1.

18 Ibid., 3.

19 Plantinga, "How to Be an Antirealist."

20 See Alston, *A Sensible Metaphysical Realism*, 15.

21 Of course, what it is to affirm or deny the existence of something or other is not quite as clear as one might suppose. For some comments on this matter, see Alston, *A Realist Conception of Truth*, 66.

22 Of course, language depends noetically on humans and, therefore, truth-value bearers, insofar as they are linguistic or linguistically related, are noetically dependent on humans.

23 See Alston, "Realism and the Christian Faith" for a discussion of why realism must apply to God, given traditional Christianity. See also chapter 13 of this volume.

24 One must be careful to distinguish between the "in virtue of" and the "relative to" sense of dependence here. There may be some ways in which my being is relative to my conceptual scheme but there is, I believe, no way in which my being exists in virtue of my conceptual scheme.

25 Rorty, *Philosophy and the Mirror of Nature*.

26 Putnam, *Realism with a Human Face*.

27 Goodman, *Ways of Worldmaking*.

28 McDowell, *Mind and World*, 4, 5.

29 Ibid., 9.

30 Ibid., 12, 13.

31 In this I follow Alston, *A Realist Conception of Truth*, 5.

32 Lynch, *Truth in Context*, 101.

33 For a classic statement of a deflationary account of truth, see Ramsey, "Facts and Propositions."

34 Lynch, *Truth in Context*, 3.

35 Alston, *A Realist Conception of Truth*, 22.

36 See for example Putnam, *Reason, Truth, and History*, 49.

CHAPTER TWO

1 Hales, *Relativism*, 184, 185 (hereafter cited in the text in this chapter as *Relativism*).
2 This suggestion comes from an anonymous reviewer for an essay based on this chapter: McLeod-Harrison, "Hales's Argument for Philosophical Relativism." See also Hales's response in "What to Do about Incommensurable Doxastic Practices" and my reply in McLeod-Harrison "Much 'to-do' about Nothing: Hales's Skeptical Relativism and Basic Doxastic Practices."
3 See Alston, *Perceiving God*.
4 Alston, "Religious Diversity and Perceptual Knowledge of God," 203, 204.
5 An anonymous reviewer (see note 2) proposed that one could simply reject the notion of doxastic practices altogether as incoherent or perhaps provide reasons why they could be bridged. But I'm a long-time supporter of Alston's doxastic practice approach and see no way to bridge the practices nor a good reason to reject them as incoherent.

CHAPTER THREE

1 Lynch, *Truth in Context*, 51 (hereafter cited in text in this chapter as *Truth*).
2 Goodman, *Of Mind and Other Matters*, 41, 42.
3 Lynch, *Truth in Context*, 56. See also Christopher Peacocke, *A Study of Concepts*.
4 Hales, "Lynch's Metaphysical Pluralism," 703.
5 On the commensurability of Hales's perspectives, see Hales, *Relativism*, 106–11, 115–18.
6 Hales, "Lynch's Metaphysical Pluralism," 701.
7 Ibid., 702.
8 Ibid., 705.
9 Ganssle, "On Pluralism and Truth," 488.
10 Ibid.
11 Ibid.
12 Ibid., 492.
13 Ibid., 494.
14 Lynch, "Pluralism and the Fluidity of Existence," 499.

CHAPTER FOUR

1 Goodman, *Ways of Worldmaking*, x (hereafter cited in the text in this chapter as *Ways*).

2 I am aware that Goodman, like Quine, likely rejects any notion of proposition that is overly metaphysically thick. I largely ignore this aspect of Goodman's philosophy.

3 Goodman and Elgin, *Reconceptions*, vii (hereafter cited in the text in this chapter as *Reconceptions*).

4 See Lynch, *Truth in Context*, 56.

5 Goodman, *Of Mind and Other Matters*, 29 (hereafter cited in the text in this chapter as *Of Mind*).

6 For the technical details of Goodman's argument for nominalism, see Goodman "A World of Individuals."

7 Here it simply is unclear whether I should capitalize "world" or leave it lower-case. Goodman's views on possibility and necessity and how they relate to noetically irreal worlds simply is more complicated or unclear than can be easily made out. We can say that the status of his worlds as actual is not the same as the status of worlds for someone like David Lewis, all of whose possible worlds are actual worlds. See Lewis, *On the Plurality of Worlds*.

8 Here we are in line with Goodman's usage of the term "world" except that he says nothing of such worlds being limited, as I have, and he might want to include the entire body of work from a painter.

9 My use of the term "just" may not be judicious. Sometimes getting the concept of a painting is very hard work.

10 Alston, *A Realist Conception*, 239.

CHAPTER FIVE

1 It's worth noting that while sometimes nominalism is taken as a reason for irrealistic pluralism, this is not so in Goodman's case since he argues that his nominalism is disconnected logically from his pluralism. However, if I am right in this chapter, nominalism in the end should never by itself be taken as a motivation for pluralism.

2 Goodman, *Ways of Worldmaking*, 95.

3 Ibid., 94–5.

4 Lynch, *Truth In Context*, 85.

5 Ibid., 88.

6 Ibid.

7 Ibid.

8 Plantinga, "Actualism and Possible Worlds," 261.

9 Rescher, "The Ontology of the Possible."

CHAPTER SIX

1 Hales, *Relativism*, 113.
2 Ibid., 114.
3 Ibid., 114.
4 Goodman, *Ways of Worldmaking*, 120.
5 Lewis, *On the Plurality of Worlds*.
6 See Lynch, *Truth in Context*, 72–4.
7 Lynch, "Pluralism, Metaphysical Realism, and Ultimate Reality," 76.
8 Ibid., 77.
9 I believe that Lynch, at least, *does* not and here's why. He seems to believe there is only one actual world (albeit a plural one) and as such, I believe he rejects, implicitly, Lewis's notion of all possible worlds being actualized. My evidence for this is not any comment he makes about Lewis's views but rather simply that he finds Goodman's notion of many actual worlds incredible. I see little reason to think he is more likely to be open to Lewis's notion.
10 See Rescher, "The Ontology of the Possible."
11 It is worth noting that Lynch elsewhere does not seem inclined to reject intensional items such as propositions or properties.
12 Lynch, "Pluralism, Metaphysical Realism, and Ultimate Reality," 77.
13 Loux, "Introduction: Modality and Metaphysics," 48.
14 This is certainly true of the "in virtue" sense of making. It is less clear in the "relative sense."
15 Lynch, *Truth in Context*, 95.
16 Lynch, "Pluralism, Metaphysical Realism, and Ultimate Reality," 75.

CHAPTER SEVEN

1 Hales, "Lynch's Metaphysical Pluralism," 702.
2 Lynch, *Truth in Context*, 16, 19.
3 Wolterstorff, "Are Concept-Users World-Makers?"
4 Later we'll consider further issues surrounding rightness of rendering which is supposed to provide some sort of limit to the ways a world can be (truly) described.
5 This argument was presented as an audience response to an ancestor of this chapter read at the Calvin College Conference on Realism and Antirealism, May 2000.
6 Williams, *Truth and Truthfulness*, 67, 68.
7 See Ganssle, "Real Problems with Irrealism."
8 See McLeod-Harrison "Epistemizing the Worlds."

9 Ganssle, "Real Problems with Irrealism," 455.
10 Ibid., 456.

CHAPTER EIGHT

1 See Lynch, "Ontological Pluralism, Metaphysical Realism, and Ultimate Reality."
2 Although I had read the early parts of McDowell, *Mind and World*, when I wrote the initial versions of this and the next chapter, it was only after reading (and rereading!) McDowell's work that I began to see how the position I'm taking here can be seen as a sort of response to McDowell. I've rewritten sections of the book with that in mind.
3 For an exploration of some important alternative readings of Descartes, see Clayton, *The Problem of God in Modern Thought*.
4 This summary is heavily reliant on Genova, "Review of *Reading McDowell on Mind and World*."
5 McDowell, *Mind and World*, 27.
6 Ibid., 28.
7 Ibid., 9.
8 Ibid., 12, 13.
9 Although their positions are different from the one I suggest above, there are some important arguments in Friedman, "Exorcising the Philosophical Tradition" and Pippin, "Leaving Nature Behind." Both Friedman and Pippin suggest, in different ways, that McDowell is more idealist – or should be more idealist – than he admits.

CHAPTER NINE

1 Kirkham, *Theories of Truth*, 59.
2 Ibid.
3 Plantinga, "How to Be an Anti-Realist," 66–7.
4 Williams, *Truth and Truthfulness*, 67.
5 Utterances and assertions seem also to be physical both as airwaves, in the first order, and as ink marks as well.
6 Sellars, *Sense, Perception and Reality*.
7 Andrew Cortens made this point in conversation.
8 Rorty's move here is rooted in a similar move made by Dewey. See a number of references to Dewey and Darwin in Rorty, *Objectivity, Relativism and Truth*, 10, 17, 63, 149 passim.
9 McDowell, *Mind and World*, 27.
10 See G.E. Moore "Truth and Falsity" and G. Frege "The Thought."

11　See Candlish, "The Identity Theory of Truth" and links to various articles found there.

12　David, "Truth as Identity and Truth as Correspondence," 684.

13　*Lynch, Truth in Context,* 127.

14　Ibid., 119.

15　Hornsby, "Truth: The Identity Theory," 663, 664.

16　Ibid., 670.

17　Ibid., 664.

18　Ibid.

19　Frege, "The Thought."

20　Hornsby, "Truth: The Identity Theory," 665–6.

21　Ibid., 675.

22　Lynch, *Truth in Context,* 120.

23　McDowell writes, "If content is dualistically opposed to what is conceptual, 'content' cannot mean what it often means in contemporary philosophy, namely, what is given by a 'that' clause in, for instance, an attribution of a belief: just to have a label, we can call content in this modern sense 'representational content.' Representational content cannot be dualistically set over against the conceptual. That is obviously so, however hospitable we are to the idea that some representational content is non-conceptual." McDowell, *Mind and World,* 3. That the world is best understood as presented (not represented) speaks of the fact that the experience is already conceptual when it is received.

24　Here one might consider some comments in David, "Truth as Identity and Truth as Correspondence," 684 on whether IT is a theory of truth or a theory of facts.

25　David, "Truth as Identity and Truth as Correspondence," 701–2.

26　McDowell, *Mind and World,* 28.

27　Williams, *Truth and Truthfulness,* 67.

28　Ibid.

29　Ibid., 67–8.

30　Ibid., 68.

31　Hornsby, "Truth: The Identity Theory," 664.

32　Here I will forestall entering a discussion of wishful thinking, pointing the readers toward a good discussion of this topic in Williams, *Truth and Truthfulness.*

CHAPTER TEN

1　McDowell, *Mind and World,* 12, 13.

2　Ibid., 12.

3 Lynch, *Truth in Context*, 74–5.

4 One anonymous reviewer asks whether these last two sentences don't form a circle. The answer is yes – but only partly so. What keeps it from being a tight and hence vicious circle is that one's act-beliefs are shaped through conceptual schemes – the reference to "in part" in the second sentence. Furthermore, falsity is a result of the world rather than a result (directly) of one's making a world.

5 An anonymous reviewer writes, noting my last sentence, "Does this mean the universe changed or my view of it changed? Did I come to believe what was already true about the universe or did I hold one true view and come to hold another incompatible view (which means there is no improvement for my epistemic catalogue)?" My answer is "both." The facts changed and my view changed, a world-view as well as a world. As to one's epistemic catalogue, I propose that the reviewer still sees epistemology through the eyes of a realist and one's catalogue is not glossy black and white but a wonderful and 3-D colour projection. How epistemology works on an irrealist view must be deeply rethought from the standard sorts of epistemology of the noetic realist. See some interesting essays on this in Goodman and Elgin, *Reconceptions*.

6 See Williams, *Truth and Truthfulness*, 191–8 for a fascinating discussion of this topic.

7 One anonymous reviewer writes, "How can an act-belief be true in one world and false in another? If it has no content in the second world, then it cannot be the same act-belief because in the first case you act-believe something and in the second you do not. Also, it might be that there cannot be the same act-belief in two worlds or situations. This depends on how they are individuated. It sounds like they are tokens and each is its own. There is no transworld or transconceptual scheme identity for act-beliefs."

I have three responses. First, one must remember that an act-belief is false when it has no genuine content. It is not the content (some sort of proposition) that is false but rather the psychological state. Thus an act-belief in one world could be true and yet that same psychological attitude be false in another world. This might occur, for example, when I change conceptual schemes and fail to notice that not all my psychological attitudes change with it. Second, as to individuating act-beliefs – the psychological states – one could do so in terms of purported content in connection with "locating" the psychological state in a given person – let's say Mary – who, as I note in the next chapter, exists in both worlds. So Mary's psychological attitude toward a purported content could be one and the same whether the act-belief is true or false. Finally, it's not clear to me that this problem is unique to my view, as we might have similar criticisms about individuating act-beliefs whose content (that is, in this case, a proposition) is thought to be true but later discovered false. Are the two act-beliefs distinct or the same?

8 Richard Rorty expresses concern that, on an absolutist understanding of the world, once we reached "the true description of everything" our lives would cease to be valuable or important. My model can alleviate some of this concern without giving up on the notion of truth.

9 In a rather disorienting novel, Huck is portrayed as the son of a white man and a black slave woman. See Clinch, *Finn*. Huck, in this alternative story, "passes" for white.

10 Goodman, *Languages of Art*, 32, 33.

11 Ibid., 36.

12 Ibid., 40–1.

13 Goodman and Elgin, *Reconceptions*, 158.

14 Ibid.

15 Ibid.

16 Ibid., 52.

17 Goodman, *Ways of Worldmaking*, 17–18.

18 Goodman, *Of Mind and Other Matters*, 34.

19 Ibid., 31.

20 See, *Ways of Worldmaking*, 57–70.

CHAPTER ELEVEN

1 Goodman, *Ways of Worldmaking*, 7.

2 In this chapter, although I continue to quote from various sources in Goodman, I assume that everything of value for irrealism can be captured by using my notion of the plural ways the World is – and hence the use of the lower-case "world" – without worrying about using Goodman's notion of pluralism I captured earlier by the term "G-world."

3 Goodman, *Ways of Worldmaking*, 4–5.

4 I am concurring with Goodman and Elgin on this. See Goodman and Elgin, *Reconceptions*.

5 Goodman, *Ways of Worldmaking*, 5.

6 Ibid.

7 I take it that this is true even in worlds that are not primarily to be thought of as rooted in conceptual schemes, that is, worlds created by painting, for

example. Here, however, the application of noncontradiction would not
be linguistic (that is, no contradictory statement can be true) but rather
simply that one can't do contradictory things.

8 Lynch, *Truth in Context*, 72.

9 Ibid., 163, note 11.

10 Ibid., 142.

11 Ibid.

12 Ibid., 144.

13 I won't take the time to argue the point, but it seems to me that insofar
as Hales makes philosophical truth relative to perspectives and also appeals to the notion that some truths might hold in all perspectives, he
will fall into the same infinite challenge as Lynch and Goodman.

14 This should be likened to the way pluralists often say that logical concepts and terms themselves are open to revision but rarely give interesting examples of what that might look like.

15 See Goodman, *Ways of Worldmaking*.

16 While some statements about God might be appropriately substituted
in for "p" and "-p," many will not be. More on this in the next section
of the book.

17 In this regard, it is instructive to consider some comments made in
Alston, *A Realist Conception of Truth*, 262–4, where Alston entertains
some speculation about why there is such a tendency toward irrealistic
conceptions of truth in our present philosophical culture.

18 Perhaps in this regard, at least, God's knowing just is "the ontology
of things."

CHAPTER TWELVE

1 Alston, "Realism and the Christian Faith."

2 Of course, so would Luther have repeated the creeds. His heresy, from
the point of view of the Roman church, was not so much a rejection of
the creeds but particular interpretations of what those creeds mean.
Fortunately, I don't need to go into detail on this matter here.

3 See Greer, *Mapping Postmodernism*, 7.

4 I started out by saying that the traditional Christian is one who holds the
Nicene Creed and I've now moved to the language of belief. Without getting bogged down here, let's just say that traditionally people were expected to believe the creed. However, there is a good case that can be
made, I think, that one might hold the creed without believing it.

5 I'm moving freely back and forth between "claims" and "beliefs"
knowing that these terms may require their own analysis.

6 I follow Alston, *A Realist Conception of Truth*, on this matter.

7 See an excellent discussion of these matters in Johnson, *She Who Is*.

8 Except perhaps trivial ones such as God knowing my thoughts, which don't change God's essence at all.

9 The one phrase in the Nicene Creed that needs to be clarified, from the point of view of this essay, is that God is the maker of all things, seen and unseen. More on this below.

10 See van Inwagen, *Metaphysics*.

11 The reasons for heresy are more complicated now. Once it was simply that one didn't hold the appropriate beliefs. Now it might be that you say you hold the right beliefs, but empty the beliefs of noetically real content.

12 See Rudolf Bultmann, *Theology of the New Testament*, 2nd ed. (Waco: Baylor University Press, 1997); R.M. Hare, "Theology and Falsification" in *New Essays in Philosophical* Theology, edited by Antony Flew and Alasdair MacIntyre (New York: Macmillan, 1955); Paul Tillich, *Systematic Theology*, volumes 1–3 (Chicago: University of Chicago Press, 1973).

CHAPTER THIRTEEN

1 Save, of course, for the obvious exceptions of thought, etc.

2 Plantinga, *Warranted Christian Belief*, 424, 425.

3 Plantinga, "How to be an Anti-Realist," 48.

4 Ibid., 49, 50.

5 Plantinga, *Warranted Christian Belief*, 425.

6 See the work of Arthur Danto, "The Artworld" and Nelson Goodman on works of art and the role in the former of the artworld and in the latter, the role of "worlds" in how to understand various of the arts.

7 Plantinga, *Warranted Christian Belief*, 425.

8 Ibid., 424, 425.

9 Alston, "Realism and the Christian Faith" (hereafter cited in the text in this chapter as "Realism").

10 Alston, *A Realist Conception of Truth*, 2.

11 Alston, *A Sensible Metaphysical Realism* (hereafter cited in the text in this chapter as *Metaphysical Realism*).

12 *Ibid.*, 17, 18. It is worth noting that the "relative to" and "in virtue of" language I use does not match Alston's.

CHAPTER FOURTEEN

1 Plantinga, "How to be an Anti-realist," 54.

2 Perhaps some version of panentheism is true, where everything has a type of consciousness (for example, Whitehead's notion of "prehension"). In that case the whole world would shape the rest of the world. I simply set the issue aside. For various accounts of panentheism, see Peacocke and Clayton, *In whom We Live and Move and Have Our Being*.

3 Two points. First, Plantinga calls this the more awkward "divine creative antirealism." Second, it is worthwhile noting the connections between what I've just suggested and the identity theory and the worldly content theory. Both would fit God as well as humans, with the following important caveat. With humans, the world, so to speak, is in the mind and therefore the propositions or beliefs we hold are true. With God, it is thinking the world a certain way that makes it so and therefore God's beliefs are true because God makes them so.

4 Johnson, *She Who Is*, 199–200. The interior quotation is from Karl Rahner, *The Trinity*, 21–4 82–103 passim.

5 Johnson, *She Who Is*, 200.

6 I do not mean to deny here that some worlds are purely divine, that is, made completely by God without human aid. I mean only to speak of worlds in which the human mind has a creative role.

7 The status of propositions, given the way I've proposed we think about truth, may need to be considered in different terms, but that is best taken up in a separate project. The main issue is simply stated, however. Given that true propositions just are bits of the world, how should true contingent propositions be thought of vis-à-vis abstract objects? Aren't they concrete instead?

8 See Matthew Davidson, "God and Other Necessary Beings."

9 I'm not confident that the other two don't or can't also play a role.

10 See Plantinga, *Does God Have a Nature?*, and "How to Be an Antirealist"; Christopher Menzel and Thomas Morris, "Absolute Creation."

11 They originated the term "theistic activism."

12 Menzel and Morris, "Absolute Creation," 355.

13 See Davidson, "God and Other Necessary Beings." Davidson goes on to press other matters against theistic activism, but I'll leave the reader to explore them.

14 Lynch, "Pluralism, Metaphysical Realism and Ultimate Reality," 75–6. The internal quotations are from Nagel, *The Last Word*, 61, 67.

15 Lynch "Pluralism, Metaphysical Realism and Ultimate Reality," 76. The internal quotation is from Bennett, "Descartes's Theory of Modality," 639–67.

CHAPTER FIFTEEN

1 An anonymous reviewer raised the following question about my use of the thin/thick distinction: "If the concept of tree is thin because there are not trees in every world, then the thin/thick distinction is not then what Lynch thought and what I thought. It tracks the contingent/necessary distinction." I'm not sure the reviewer's observation is right, as it sounds as if she or he runs possible worlds together with worlds. I'm not suggesting that thicker concepts are necessary in the traditional sense but rather just that they are virtually absolute.

2 Here one must consider the details of process thought and panentheistic thought more generally to see whether the world they are attempting to make is a generatively true one. For an excellent collection on panentheism, see Philip Clayton and Arthur Peacocke, *In Whom We Live and Move and Have Our Being*.

3 I recognize that in addition to metaphor, there are other issues that arise in speaking of God. What of analogical application of terms to God, as opposed to the equivocal or the univocal? However, in a book that is already quite lengthy, I can't consider all the details of these questions.

4 Black, "Metaphor," 540. What follows in the next few paragraphs is heavily indebted to Black's seminal essay.

5 Black, "Metaphor," 544.

6 Ibid., 548.

7 Margolis, "Metaphor," 532.

8 Goodman, *Languages of Art*, 68.

9 Ibid., 79.

10 Here one might consider the work of Paul Ricoeur on metaphor, but in particular Ricoeur, "Metaphor and the Central Problem of Hermeneutics."

11 We might turn to Arthur Danto's analysis of the role of the artworld in making something into a work of art for inspiration on how to think about the fact that orthodoxy is both fixed and changing. In short, as the artworld surrounds a new piece and does its theoretical work, new predicates are added to what counts as art. Perhaps something similar could be proposed for the theological world and new tenets of orthodoxy. See Arthur Danto, "The Artworld." Furthermore, it is arguable that the historic, ecumenical creeds would have shaped a better world if they had included more claims about orthopraxy as well as orthodoxy. For example, the Early Church was largely pacifist and inclusivist in terms of gender but this never worked its way into the creeds. I believe it should have.

CHAPTER SIXTEEN

1 God does not literally overcome the divide. It never existed in the first place.
2 Eckhart, "The Nearness of the Kingdom."
3 George Steiner argues that Heidegger's Being is close to, if not the same as, God. If we accept Steiner's analysis, Heidegger's talk of the "thrown-ness" of human being has deep resonances here. See Steiner, *Martin Heidegger.*
4 Johnson, *She Who Is,* 104–5.
5 Ibid., 111.
6 Of course this is not what the hard-core realist about God will say progressive revelation is, but at this point, I'm not overly worried about this difference. Progressive revelation itself may be thickly projected in different ways.
7 Some of Jeffrey Brower's suggestions on divine simplicity, aseity, and truth-makers are worth considering. See Brower, "Simplicity and Aseity."
8 See Gunton, *The One, the Three, and the Many* for an extended discussion of God as relational. See also the essays by the Eastern Orthodox theologians in Clayton and Peacocke, *In Whom We Live and Move and Have Our Being.*
9 Gunton, *The One, the Three, and the Many,* 3.
10 Plantinga, *Engaging God's World,* 20–1.
11 Harries, *Art and the Beauty of God,* 138–9.
12 Eckhart, "The Nearness of the Kingdom."
13 Goodman, *Ways of Worldmaking,* 5.

CHAPTER SEVENTEEN

1 The simplest example of this point is this: That I'm in pain is a subjective feature of the world and no one but me has access to it. Nevertheless, it is not clear that that makes my pain any less a feature of the world, even if the world is completely nonrelative with a single, true description as the noetic realist might suggest.
2 See the argument in Walton, "Morals in Fiction and Fictional Morality," 27–50.
3 These nonnatural occurrences are in part what McDowell tries to capture with his notion of second nature. It is, I think, a valiant but ultimately misguided attempt. Humans need God, in the end, to make sense of their world.

4 Julian of Norwich, *Revelations of Divine Love.*
5 Lewis, "Is Theology Poetry?" 83–5.

CHAPTER EIGHTEEN

1 Schaeffer, *He Is There and He Is Not Silent.*
2 I have Charlie Kamilos to thank for this line.
3 This is not to say that such mystics become wishy-washy on theological matters. But some of that is, I think, driven by the Church rather than by the experience.
4 See McLeod-Harrison, *Repairing Eden.*
5 The next several pages are taken more or less directly from McLeod-Harrison, *Repairing Eden.*
6 See Pike, *Mystic Union.*
7 See McLeod-Harrison, *Repairing Eden,* for details.

Bibliography

Alston, William. *Perceiving God: The Epistemology of Religious Experience*. Ithaca: Cornell University Press 1992
– "Realism and the Christian Faith" in *International Journal for Philosophy of Religion*, 38, (1995): 37–60
– *A Realist Conception of Truth*. Ithaca: Cornell University Press 1996
– "Religious Diversity and Perceptual Knowledge of God." Reprinted in *The Philosophical Challenge of Religious Diversity*. Edited by Philip Quinn and Kevin Meeker. Oxford: Oxford University Press 2000. Originally appeared in *Faith and Philosophy* 5, (1988): 433–48
– *A Sensible Metaphysical Realism*. Milwaukee: Marquette University Press 2001
Bennett, Jonathan. "Descartes's Theory of Modality." *Philosophical Review* 103, no. 4: 639–67
Black, Max. "Metaphor." Reprinted in *Philosophy Looks at the Arts*. Third Edition. Edited by Joseph Margolis. Philadelphia: Temple University Press 1987. Originally in *Proceedings of the Aristotlian Society* 45: 273–94
Brower, Jeffrey. "Simplicity and Aseity." http://web.ics.purdue.edu/-brewer/Research.htm (date accessed 7 July 2007)
Candlish, Stewart. "The Identity Theory of Truth." http://plato.stanford.edu/entries/truth-identity (date accessed 8 July 2005)
Clayton, Philip. *The Problem of God in Modern Thought*. Grand Rapids: Eerdmans 2001
Clayton, Philip and Arthur Peacocke eds. *In Whom We Live and Move and Have our Being: Panentheistic Reflections on God's Presence in a Scientific World*. Grand Rapids: Eerdman's 2004

Clinch, Jon. *Finn*. New York: Random House 2007

Danto, Arthur. "The Artworld." *The Journal of Philosophy* 61: 571–84.

David, Marian. "Truth as Identity and Truth as Correspondence." Reprinted in *The Nature of Truth: Classical and Contemporary Perspectives*, 638–704. Edited by Michael Lynch. Cambridge, MA: MIT Press 2001

Davidson, Matthew. "God and Other Necessary Beings." http://plato.stanford.edu/entries/god-necessary-being (date accessed: 3 July 2007)

Eckhart, Meister. "The Nearness of the Kingdom." www.ccel.org/e/eckhart/sermons/htm/v.htm (date accessed: 4 February 2003)

Frege, G. "The Thought." Reprinted in *Philosophical Logic*, 17–38. Edited by P. Strawson. Oxford: Oxford University Press 1967

Friedman, Michael. "Exorcising the Philosophical Tradition." In *Reading McDowell on Mind and World*, 25–57. Edited by Nicholas Smith. New York: Routledge 2002

Ganssle, Greg. "On Pluralism and Truth: A Critique of Michael P. Lynch's *Truth in Context*." *Philosophia Christi* 3, no. 2: 485–96

– "Real Problems with Irrealism: A Response to Mark McLeod-Harrison." *Philosophia Christi* 8: 433–58

Genova, A.C. "Review of *Reading McDowell on Mind and World*." *Notre Dame Philosophical Reviews*. http://ndpr.nd.edu/review.cfm?id=1207 (date accessed: 15 October 2005)

Goodman, Nelson. *Fact, Fiction, and Forecast*. Cambridge, MA: Harvard University Press 1979

– *The Languages of Art: An Approach to a Theory of Symbols*. Indianapolis: Hackett 1976.

– *Of Mind and Other Matters*. Cambridge, MA: Harvard University Press 1984

– *The Structure of Appearance*. 3rd ed. New York: Springer 1977

– *Ways of Worldmaking*. Indianapolis: Hackett 1978

– "A World of Individuals." Reprinted in *Problems and Projects*, 15–34. Indianapolis: Hackett 1972. Originally in I.M. Bochenski, *The Problem of Universals: A Symposium*. Notre Dame: University of Notre Dame Press 1956

Goodman, Nelson and Catherine Elgin. *Reconceptions in Philosophy and Other Arts and Sciences*. Indianapolis: 1988.

Greer, Robert. *Mapping Postmodernism: A Survey of Christian Options*. Downers Grove, IL: Intervarsity Press, 2003

Gunton, Colin. *The One, The Three, and the Many*. Cambridge: Cambridge University Press 1993

Hales, Steven. "Lynch's Metaphysical Pluralism." *Philosophy and Phenomenological Research* 63, no. 3: 699–709

– *Relativism and the Foundations of Philosophy.* Cambridge, MA: MIT Press 2006

– "What to Do about Incommensurable Doxastic Practices: Reply to Mark McLeod-Harrison." In *Philosophia Christi* 11: 201–6.

Harries, Richard. *Art and the Beauty of God: A Christian Understanding.* New York: Mowbray 1993

Hornsby, Jennifer. "Truth: The Identity Theory." Reprinted in *The Nature of Truth: Classical and Contemporary Perspectives.* Edited by Michael Lynch. Cambridge, MA: MIT Press, 2001. Originally in *Proceedings of the Aristotlelian Society* 97: 1–24

Johnson, Elizabeth. *She Who Is: The Mystery of God in Feminist Theological Discourse.* New York: Crossroad 1992

Julian of Norwich. *Revelations of Divine Love.* Translated by M.L. del Mastro. New York: Doubleday 1977

Kirkham, Richard. *Theories of Truth: A Critical Introduction.* Boston: MIT Press 1992

Lewis, C.S. *The Magician's Nephew.* New York: Harper Collins 1955

– "Is Theology Poetry?" in *The Weight of Glory and Other Addresses.* New York: Macmillan 1980

Lewis, David. *On the Plurality of Worlds.* Oxford: Blackwell 1986

Loux, Michael. "Introduction: Modality and Metaphysics." In *The Possible and the Actual: Readings in the Metaphysics of Modality*, 15–64. Edited by Michael Loux. Ithaca: Cornell University Press 1979

Lynch, Michael. "Pluralism and the Fluidity of Existence: A Response to Ganssle." *Philosophia Christi* 3, no. 2: 497–503.

– "Ontological Pluralism, Metaphysical Realism, and Ultimate Reality." In *Realism and Antirealism*, 57–78. Edited by William Alston. Ithaca: Cornell 2002

– *Truth in Context: An Essay on Pluralism and Objectivity.* Cambridge, MA: MIT Press 1998

Margolis, Joseph. "Metaphor." In *Philosophy Looks at the Arts*, 529–54. Edited by Joseph Margolis. Philadelphia: Temple University Press 1987

McDowell, John. *Mind and* World. Cambridge, MA: Harvard University Press 1994

McLeod-Harrison, Mark. "Epistemizing the Worlds." In *Philosophia Christi* 8: 439–51

– "Hales's Argument for Philosophical Relativism." In *Philosophia Christi* 10: 411–26

- "Much 'to-do' about Nothing: Hales's Skeptical Relativism and Basic Doxastic Practices." In *Philosophia Christi*: 11: 207–14
- *Repairing Eden: Humility, Mysticism, and the Existential Problem of Religious Diversity.* Montreal & Kingston: McGill-Queen's University Press 2005

Menzel, Christopher and Thomas Morris. "Absolute Creation." *Philosophical Quarterly* 23: 353–62

Moore, G.E. "Truth and Falsity." In *Dictionary of Philosophy and Psychology.* 190 1–1902. Reprinted in *Selected Writings*, 20–2. London: Routledge, 1993.

Nagel, Thomas. *The Last Word.* Oxford: Oxford University Press 1997

Peacocke, Christopher. *A Study of Concepts.* Cambridge: MIT Press 1992

Pippin, Robert. "Leaving Nature Behind: Or Two Cheers for 'Subjectivism.'" In *Reading McDowell on Mind and World*, 58–75. Edited by Nicholas Smith. New York: Routledge 2002

Pike, Nelson. *Mystic Union: An Essay in the Phenomenology of Mysticism.* Ithaca: Cornell University Press 1992

Plantinga, Alvin. "Actualism and Possible Worlds." Reprinted in *The Possible and the Actual: Readings in the Metaphysics of Modality*, 253–73. Edited by Michael Loux. Ithaca: Cornell University Press 1979. Originally in *Theoria* 42: 139–60
- *Does God Have a Nature?* Milwaukee: Marquette University Press 1980.
- "How to Be an Anti-realist." In *Proceedings and Addresses of the American Philosophical Association* 56, no. 1 (1982): 47–70
- *Warranted Christian Belief.* Oxford: Oxford University Press 2001

Plantinga, Cornelius. *Engaging the World: A Reformed Vision of Faith, Learning and Living.* Grand Rapids: Eerdmans 2002

Putnam, Hilary. "Foreword." In Nelson Goodman. *Fact, Fiction, and Forecast*: Cambridge, MA: Harvard University Press 1979
- *Realism with a Human Face.* Cambridge: Harvard University Press 1900
- *Reason, Truth and History.* Cambridge: Cambridge University Press 1981

Rahner, Karl. *The Trinity. Theological Investigations*, vol. 2. New York: Crossroad 1980–1992

Ramsey, F.P. "Facts and Propositions" reprinted in *F.P. Ramsey: Philosophical Papers*, 34–51. Edited by D.H. Mellor. Cambridge, MA: Harvard University Press 1990

Rescher, Nicholas. "The Ontology of the Possible." Reprinted in *The Possible and the Actual: Readings in the Metaphysics of Modality*, 166–81. Edited by Michael Loux. Ithaca: Cornell University Press 1979. Originally in *Logic and Ontology.* Edited by Milton Munitz. New York: New York University Press 1973

Ricoeur, Paul. "Metaphor and the Central Problem of Hermeneutics." In *Hermeneutics and the Human Sciences: Essays on Language, Action and Interpretation*, 165–81. Edited and translated by John B. Thompson. Cambridge: Cambridge University Press 1981

Rorty, Richard. *Objectivity, Relativism and Truth*. Cambridge: Cambridge University Press 1990

– *Philosophy and the Mirror of Nature*. Princeton: Princeton University Press 1979

Schaeffer, Francis. *He is There and He Is Not Silent*. Carol Stream, IL: Tyndale 1972

Sellars, Wilfred. *Sense, Perception and Reality*. New York: Humanities 1963

Steiner, George. *Martin Heidegger*. Chicago: University of Chicago Press 1978

Strawson, Peter. *Analysis and Metaphysics*. Oxford: Oxford University Press 1992

Van Inwagen, Peter. *Metaphysics*. Boulder: Westview 1990

Walton, Kendall. *Memesis as Make-Believe: On the Foundations of the Representational Arts*. Cambridge, MA: Harvard University Press 1990

– "Morals in Fiction and Fictionality." *Proceedings of the Aristotlian Society* 68: 27–66

Williams, Bernard. *Truth and Truthfulness*. Princeton: Princeton University Press 2002

Wolterstorff, Nicholas. "Are Concept-Users World-Makers?" *Nous Supplement: Philosophical Perspectives* 1: 233–67

Index

absolute idealism, 27

absolutes, virtual. *See* virtual absolutes

absolutism, content version, 60; fact version, 60

abstract, vs concrete, 346

abstract entities, 272–4

act-beliefs, 171–7; and alethic realism, 175; and facts, 175; as truth-value bearers, 171

actions, vs events, 331; as free, 332

actualism, 116

actuality, 116; and existence, 116

actual world, 12, 274; and conceptual schemes, 12

adam, 17, 324, 327, 343

alethic irrealism, 26–8

alethic realism, 17, 26–8; consistent with noetic irrealism, 54; definition of, 27; and noetic irrealism, 131, and noetic realism, 131, 303

Alston, William, 242–57; and alethic realism, 28, 242–4; and alethic realism*, 242–4; and doxastic practices, 47; and revisionist Christianity, 224, 248; and sensible metaphysical realism, 15, 16; on sensible metaphysical realism, 251–7; on traditional Christianity and alethic realism, 244–8; and truth as property, 59, 102

analogy between God and humans, 258, 264–5

angels, 261

animals, nonhuman, 262

art, 87–8

artifact, 8, 9, 28

artifact, vs natural, 8, 9

atheism, 18, 320; totalizing, 19

atonement, theories of, 337–8

bald naturalism and noetic irrealism, 201

beauty, 305

Beauty, vs beauty, 314–21

beliefs, content of, 161–2; vs reality, 6; world as content of, 162–3

believing in, vs believing that, 317

believings, 6, 171–7; and alethic realism, 175; and facts, 175; as truth-value bearers, 171

Bennet, Jonathan, 275–6
Berkeley, George, 18, 325
Bildung, 149, 152–3, 167, 217,
    260, 306, 328
Black, Max, 293–4
Bradley, F.H., 27

causality and cognition, 28, 29;
    and *creatio ex nihilo*, 30
certainty, 349; and epistemology,
    349; and mystical experience,
    348
Christian history, 335
Christian irrealism, 223–354; as
    eschatological, 309–10; and
    heaven, 309–10
Christian liberal arts colleges and
    universities, 344
Christian objectivity, 305–10
cognition and causality, 28
cognizing, 21–6
common sense, 8
concepts, 6–7, 9, 72; and choice,
    183–7; crystalline, 54–5; and ex-
    perience, 25; as fluid, 55; as lin-
    guistic, 6; as minimal, 56; as
    nonlinguistic, 6; as robust, 56;
    role of, 25; and world view, 10
conceptual schemes, 53; and actual
    world, 12; and commensurabil-
    ity, 61; and God, 264; human
    and divine, 268–71
conceptualizing, 22; and epistemiz-
    ing, 137, 141; Goodman and hu-
    man, 120; as human, 120–3;
    Lynch and human, 120, 121
concrete, vs abstract, 346
consciousness, 287
consistency dilemma, 61–4, 95,
    102; content version of, 62; fact
version of, 62; and Ganssle, 144;
    and intensionalism, 102; and
    modality, 102, 112–23; and pos-
    sible worlds, 63, 112–23; solu-
    tion to, 63
core argument, 132–41
create, 10
creatio ex nihilo, 11, 274
creation, 5; and God, 289; necessi-
    ties vs freely chosen, 272; theo-
    logical vs actual world, 274
creativity, 344
creed, 225–31; and literal descrip-
    tion, 291; and metaphor, 287,
    290–9; as thin framework, 297;
    and thin metaphorical descrip-
    tion, 298

David, Marian, 164
decisions, 136; and epistemologiz-
    ing, 137; and God, 336; and
    Jesus, 336; as noetically con-
    structed, 336
deflationary theory of truth, 27;
    and minimal realism, 58
Descartes, René, 275, 276, 351–2
descriptive worlds, 86
Dewey, John, 27
the divine, 230, 258–62
divine irrealism, 265; and Plant-
    inga, 280
divine simplicity, 273
doctrine as developing, 225

economic Trinity, 266–7
education, 7
Elgin, Catherine, 72, 74, 78
emoting, 23
emotions, 7
emotivism, 18

entrenchment, 11
epistemic neutrality, 133–4
epistemic transformation, 348
epistemic warrant and metaphysics, 134
epistemizing, 22, 131, 172; and conceptualizing, 131, 137, 141
epistemological pull, 129
epistemology, 128; and certainty, 349; and ontology, 267; separate from metaphysics, 128, 133
events, vs action, 331; as facts, 335; as meaningful, 330
existence, 5, 56–60; and actuality, 116; as fluid, 56; and instantiation, 116–17; not a property, 57, 107, 116–17; as property, 102–7; as property and irrealism, 117
experience, and concepts, 25
experience, mystical. *See* mystical experience.
extensionalism, 96–102; and irrealism, 105, 118–21; and pluralism, 118–21

facts as events, 335; as human, 335; and propositions, 170
faith and theory, unity of, 344
false version, 187–8
falsity, 180–1; as nonepistemic, 189
family resemblance, 9
fictionality and history, 328
frames of reference, 74; as part of world version, 74
freedom, 10, 129, 130, 286, 334–5; and history, 333, 334; and radical antirealism, 334
Frege, G., 164, 166
F-schema, 59

Ganssle, Gregory, 141–4; criticism of Lynch, 66–9; Lynch's reply to, 69
generative truth, 85, 187–9
Genesis, 343
global antirealism, challenges to, 255–7
global irrealism, challenges to, 255–7
global noetic irrealism, 21
global noetic realism, 21
global relativism, self-refutation of, 36–7
God, 284–99; and abstract entities, 272–4; and abstraction, 11; analogy of being, 215; analogy with humans, 258, 264–5; as Aristotelian vs Whiteheadian, 285; as beauty, 314–21; as beauty bearer, 312; and beliefs, 312; and concepts, 273; and conceptual schemes, 264, 268–71; as conceptualizer, 281; and creation, 4, 289; and decisions, 336; epistemizing/cognizing of, 216; and exemplary worlds, 319–21; and external relations, 284–5; and Genesis, 4; and global ontological monism, 234–7; as good, 314–21; as good bearer, 312; and history, 322–42; and human conceptual schemes, 264; as humanly shaped, 263; as immanent, 270; independent of human schemes, 307; and interaction with worlds, 11; knowledge of, 282; as limit, 307; and limits, 7, 11; literal vs metaphorical description of, 298; many ways, 284–99; many ways, motivating

factors for, 264; and metaphor, 290–9; as minimal and robust, 284–90; and morality, 271; and mystery, 12, 266, 310–14; nature of, 284–99; as necessarily existing, 307; as necessarily loving, 307; and necessity, 313; and noetic realism, 240–1, 246–50, 282; non-representational worlds, 319–21; not bound by truth, 313; not a construct, 267; and objectivity, 11, 79, 300–21; and omniproperties, 307; and pleasure, 7; as present mystically, 353; and purpose, 306; as Reality, 315; as relational, 315–19; and relationality, 11, 318; relationality vs abstraction, 315–19; role in world-making, 214–15; as self-surpassing greatness, 314; and sociality, 270, 279; and space and time, 309; as thick and thin, 284–90; thoughts, 273, 274; as transcendent, 270; as truth, 314–21; as Truth, 315; as truth bearer, 312; truth bound by, 313; uncreated at divine core, 269; and understanding, 268; and well-formed conceptual schemes, 271; and the World, 31; and worlds, 31

God's: cognitive abilities, 265; conceptual scheme, 271–2; core, 5; in irrealism vs realism, 286; nature, 284–99; purposes, 307; World, 10, 280–3; worlds, 281

Goodman, Nelson, 13, 24, 70–94; and actuality, 82, 83; and art, 87–8; and common nonsense, 7; on concepts, 72; on conflicting pairs, 73; on construction of worlds, 52; on contradiction, 73, 75; and correspondence, 85; and dependence of world features, 90; and descriptive worlds, 86; and exemplification, 88; on extensionalism, 96–102, 119; on extensionalism as basis for nominalism, 98–9; and frames of reference, 73–8; on generative truth, 85; and human conceptualizing, 120–1; on individuals, 99–101; on induction, new problem of, 92–3; and intensionalism, 96–8, 110; as irrealist, 70–3; and Lewis, David, 110; and the linguistic, 71; and metaphor, 295; as meta-theorist, 80–1; and new world versions, 35; on nominalism, 78–80, 95–102; and nondescriptive worlds, 86–8; on the nonlinguistic, 72; on nonlinguistic systems, 76; on platonism, and Quine, 79, 95–6; on possible worlds, 110, 119; and radical antirealism, 101; and radical relativism under constraints, 71; and realism, 80–1; on realms, 74; and rightness, 71; on right world-versions, 85; on schemes, 74; on space and time, 83; and star making, 9; on symbol systems, 72, 76, 88–9; on system, 75; and truth, 71, 84–94; truth and acceptability, 93; truth, approaches to, 90–2; truth, importance of, 89–90; truth and minimalism, 92; on world-versions vs worlds, 77

goodness, 305

Goodness, vs goodness, 314–21
Gunton, Colin, 318
G-world, definition of, 12

Hales, Steven, 35–50; and alternative epistemic sources, 41; and
Christianity, 41; criticism of
Lynch, 64–5; and doxastic practices, 47; and epistemic accounts
of truth, 48–50; and foundationalism, 39–40; on God, 215; on
intensionality, 108–9; and the
Jívaro, 41; and naturalism, 40;
and nihilism, 42; perspectives
and possible worlds, 109; and
philosophical propositions, 38,
39; and philosophical relativism,
35; on possibility, 108–9; rejection of Hales's argument, 43–6;
and relativism, 42; and skepticism 42–3; and skepticism, definition of, 43
Harries, Richard, 319
Hartshorne, Charles, 314
heaven, 309–10, 345
historical facts, 332
history, 10–12, 314, 322–42; and
act, 329; ambiguities of, 329; between objectivity and subjectivity, 333–41 and bootstrapping,
332–3; as central among academic disciplines, 338; Christian,
335–9; constrained by empirical
facts, 327; and creed, 335–9;
definition of, 326; as divine furniture, 262; and events, 326; and
fictionality, 328; and freedom,
333; and God, 309, 322–42; and
human facts, 335; importance of,
340; and limits, 337; as lived,

329; and meaning, 327; nature
of, 326–35; as noetically irreal,
331; as noetically real, 331; as
story, 327; and traditional Christianity, 322–42; as twice-lived,
329
human conceptualizing, 120–3
human conceptual schemes and
God, 264
human facts, 335
human irrealism, 265
humans, analogy with God, 258,
264–5; and cognitive abilities,
277–8; and conceptual schemes,
269; consciousness, 262; core
being of, 260, 261; as divine furniture, 259–61; divinely created
at their core, 269; and God historically linked, 324; as in virtue
of creatures, 261; and knowledge
of God, 282; as self-shaped, 260;
and sociality, 279; uncreated by
humans at their core, 269

idealism, 10, 30, 145–54; and in virtue of, 146; vs metaphysical realism, 146: modest, 15; and noetic
irrealism, 146; and relative to,
146; spectre of, 145; strong, 15
identity theory of truth, 164–71;
abandonment of, 175; and David, Marian, 164; and Frege, G.,
164; and Hornsby, Jennifer, 165–
7; and Lynch, Michael, 165,
168–9; and McDowell, 165–7;
and Moore, G.E., 164; as realist
theory, 168–9
image of God, 278–9
immanent Trinity, 267
incomplete worlds, 187–8

individuals as minimal and robust, as thick and thin, 100–1

induction, new riddle of, 11, 92–3; and entrenchment, 11

infinite regress challenge, 203–10; and God, 215–20; and Lynch, 206–9; possible response to, 210–14; response to, 215–20

instantiation, 116–17; vs existence, 116–17

intensionalism, 96–8; and irrealism, 105

in virtue of, 30; and idealism, 146

irrealism, 4, 5; and antirealism, 17; argument for, 127–44; compartmentalization of, 21, 24; divine, 265; and existence, 17; and existence as a property, 117–18; human, 265; and modal actualism, 118; and nonrealism, 17; and subjectivity, 323

irrealist theory of truth, 27

James, William, 27

Johnson, Elizabeth, 266, 311–12

Kant, Immanuel, 13, 213; antinomies and McDowell, 150

knowability, 44

knowledge and irrealism, 201

law of noncontradiction, 129, 135, 210–18; and infinite regress challenge, 203–10

Lewis, C.S. ix, 320, 341, 345

Lewis, David, and consistency dilemma, 113–14; and Goodman, 110, 122; on modality, 112–14, and transworld identity and the consistency dilemma, 113

lived history, 329

Loux, Michael, 116

Lynch, Michael, 13, 51–69; on concepts, 54; on conceptual schemes, 53; on construction of concepts, 52; on construction of reality, 52; existence, property of, 102–7; Ganssle's criticism of, 66–9; Hales's criticism of, 64–5; and human conceptualizing, 120–3; on metaphysical realism, 114; on pluralism definition, 14; on possibility and necessity, 110–11, 276–7; on possible worlds, 119; and relativized Kantianism, 54; and Rescher, 114; on self-identity, 104; on truth, not a property, 102, 103; on truth, property of, 102–7; on voluntaristic necessities, 275–7; on world view, 51

make believe vs make/believe, 6

make/believing, 4, 6, 7; and choice, 183–7

making, 4; and equivocation, 10; and humans, 5; in virtue of, 4; relative to, 4; worlds and limits, 11

makings, active vs passive, 15; continuum of, 9

many-worlds pluralism, 14

Margolis, Joseph, 294

McDowell, John, 147–54; and bald naturalism, 10; and *Bildung*, 153; and coherentism, 148; and concepts, 24, 25, 26; and denial of idealism, 147; and idealism, 25; and independence of reality, 151; and Kantian antinomies, 150;

and logical space of reasons, 10; and Myth of the Given, 148; and noetic irrealism, 201; and relaxed naturalism, 148; and second nature, 148; and spontaneity, 10; and supernaturalism, 147, 149; and tempered platonism, 148; and theism, 149; and thought, 150

Meister Eckhart, 301, 320

Menzel, Christopher, 273

metaphor, 292–9; as comparison, 293; frozen, 295; as interaction, 293–4; and literalism, 292; and Max Black, 293–4; as substitution, 293; and truth, 296

metaphysical awareness, 348

metaphysical realism, definition of, 30; vs idealism, 146

metaphysics, 128; separate from epistemology, 128, 133

minimal realism and deflationary theories, 58; and truth, 60

modal actualism, 116; and irrealism, 118

modality, 108–23; and consistency dilemma, 112–23; Plantinga on, 116; Stalnaker on, 116

modal possibilism, 112

modal questions unanswerable, 115

monist, 13

Moore, G.E., 164

Morris, Thomas, 273

Mother Teresa, 347

mystery, 310–14

mystical experience, 310–11, 343–54; account of, 346–8; and certainty, 348; and orthodoxy, 347; and presence of God, 347

Myth of the Given, 25

Nagel, Thomas, 275, 276

naming and history, 328

natural objects, 8, 28

nature and enchantment, 10

necessities, voluntaristic, 275–80

noetic feats, 20

noetic irrealism, 20–1, 28; and alethic realism, 131; argument for, 127–44; compartmentalized, 24; core argument, 132–41; and demythologizing history, 325; final argument version for, 143; and idealism, 146; initial argument, 130; and physicalism, 200–1

noeticism, 13–16; noetic irrealism, 15; strong, 14, 15; and weak, 14

noetic realism, 18, 20–1, 28; and alethic realism, 131, 303; exceptions to, 20–1; global, 21; and history, 325

nominalism, 95–102; argument against, 99–101

noncontradiction, law of, 129, 135, 210–18; and infinite regress challenge, 203–10

nondescriptive worlds, 86

nonexistent objects, 108, 116

noumena, 4

noumenal material, 10, 31

noumenal world, 15

objectivity, and aesthetics, 262; and God, 11, 306; and morality, 262; and mystical experience, 350; and religion, 262; resting in God, 306; and subjectivity, 300–2, 339–42, 350–1; and truth, 302–5

objects as fluid, 56
ontological arguments, 19
ontological pluralistic irrealism, 6
ontological pluralism, 4, 5, 6, 13–16
ontology and epistemology, 267

Peacocke, Christopher, 54
perceiving, 23
perichoresis, 309, 318
philosophical relativism, 35–50;
    and logic of, 36–8
philosophy, 330
pictorial rightness, 87–8
Plantinga, Alvin, 237–42; on God's
    thoughts, 273; on modality, 116;
    on noetic realism and truth, 237–
    9; on postmodernism, 237–8;
    and self-identity, 104; and theistic
    creative antirealism vs theistic ir-
    realism, 15, 266; and truth, 104
Plantinga, Cornelius, 318
platonism, 95–102; tempered, 148,
    217
pluralism, 6, 13; content version,
    60; definition of, 14; and exten-
    sionalism, 118–21; fact version,
    60; and irrealism, 118; and lan-
    guage, 131; and limits, 202; and
    Lynch, 14; without unity, 202
poetry and theology, 339
possibilism, 112
postmodernism, 17
prehistory, 330
progressive revelation, 312
properties, as intensional, 105–6;
    as nonintensional, 106
property, fluid concept of, 105
propositions, 29, 158–60, 169–72;
    as bits of the world, 170; and
    facts, 170; as thin, 58

purpose, 306
Putnam, Hilary, 11, 24

quarks, 18
Quine, W.V.O., 79, 95, 97–101,
    109, 159, 195

radical antirealism, 16
radical postmodernism, 16
Rahner, Karl, 266
realism and existence, 17
realist theory of truth, 27
reality, vs belief, 6
relative to, 14, 30; and idealism,
    146
relativism, extreme, 10, 11
relativism, radical, 10, 11
relativized Kantianism, 54
religion, as objective, 262
representations, 156–7
Rescher, Nicholas, 105, and Lynch,
    114; on modality, 114
revelation, 309; progressive, 312
revisionist Christianity, 231; and
    modernity, 224–5
rightness of rendering, 71, 190–4;
    and art, 191–2; and artistic real-
    ism, 191–2; and entrenchment,
    192; and fitting, 193–4; and
    habit, 192; nondescriptive, 194–
    9; and presentation, 190–1
right world version, 85; limits on,
    93
Rorty, Richard, 23, 161–2

salvation, problem of, 324–6; and
    irrealism, 324–6
science, 330; and meaning, 328;
    modern, 25
second nature, 148

self-surpassing greatness, 314
sensible metaphysical realism, 15,
    16, 251–7; and theistic irrealism,
    252–3
simple existence realism/nonreal-
    ism, 18–20
singular world pluralism, 14
skepticism, and certainty, 351; and
    Hales, 42–3
social reality, value of, 345
solidarity, 354
solipsism, 21; and certainty, 352
spirituality, 344
Stalnaker, Robert, 116
star making, 9
stars *sans* humans, 15
statement truth, 187–9
strong noeticism, definition of, 15;
    and noetic irrealism, 16
subjective idealism, 18
subjectivity, 322–6; and academic
    disciplines, 322–6; and history,
    322–6; and irrealism, 323; and
    mystical experience, 350; and
    objectivity, 300–2, 339–42, 350–
    1; and religion, 322–6
symbol system, 9, 72

Tarski, Alfred, 91, 321
theistic irrealism, 6; and idealism,
    147; and skepticism, 218; vs the-
    istic creative antirealism, 15; and
    weak idealism, 15
theories, 7
theories of truth, 155–81; and
    alethic metaphor theory, 296;
    and metaphor, 297. *See also*
    truth, theories of
thinkables, 165–6
thought, 22

traditional Christianity, 5, 11,
    223–33; and alethic realism,
    226; and beauty, 235; global on-
    tological monism, 234–7; and
    God as maker of heaven and
    earth, 236; and history, 322–42;
    and metaphysics, 227–8; and
    morality, 235; and noetic real-
    ism, 228–9; and noetic realism's
    range, 240–1; and orthodoxy,
    223, 226; and Plantinga, 237–
    42; and truth, 226, 302–3
transworld identity, 122
truth, 305; alethic metaphorical
    theory of, 296; concept vs prop-
    erty, 59; and conceptualiz-
    ing,132; as fluid, 56; and God,
    11; identity theory of, 164–71;
    and metaphor, 296; minimalist,
    92; and minimal realism, 60; and
    objectivity, 11, 302–5; not a
    property, 102–3; as property, 59,
    102–7, 303; as purity, 317; rela-
    tivized, 132; and self-identity,
    104; and statements, 187; theo-
    ries of, 27, 155–81; as veracity,
    317; worldly content theory of,
    177–9; as world relative, 304
Truth vs truth, 314–21
truth-value bearer, 26, 151–61;
    and alethic realism, 29; as asser-
    tion, 159; as belief, 159; as
    proposition, 158, 160; as sen-
    tence, 160
T-schema, 58; and minimal real-
    ism, 58

understanding in irrealism, 201
unity of worlds, 202
unknowability, 44

valuing, 306
van Inwagen, Peter, 133
virtual absolutes, 61, 122; and God, 263; and necessary truth, 122; and necessities, 288; thin and thick, 287
voluntaristic necessities, 275–80

Williams, Bernard, 136, 159, 176–7, 186
Wolterstorff, Nicholas, 128–30, 134–5
"World," 6, 13; and realism, 13
World, definition of, 12; *sans* humans, 15; and worlds, 12

world, definition of, 12; as elastic term, 12; other uses of term, 13; as quasi-literal term, 12
the worldly, 230
worldly content theory of truth, 177–9; and falsity, 180–1; and irrealism, 179–80
world-making and choice, 183–7
worlds, and cognitive dealings, 28; God's interaction with, 11; in transition, 187–8; *sans* humans, 15, 30; and unity, 202
world-versions vs worlds, 77
world view, 51
worship, 305; making as, 305